Public Reason Confucianism

"Public reason Confucianism" is a particular style of Confucian democratic perfectionism that calls on an active role for the democratic state in promoting a Confucian conception of the good life; at the heart of which are such values as filial piety and ritual propriety. It is also fully compatible with core values of democracy such as popular sovereignty, political equality, and the right to political participation.

Sungmoon Kim presents "public reason Confucianism" as the most attractive option for contemporary East Asian societies that are historically and culturally Confucian.

SUNGMOON KIM is Professor of Political Theory at City University of Hong Kong.

Public Reason Confucianism

Democratic Perfectionism and Constitutionalism in East Asia

SUNGMOON KIM

City University of Hong Kong

CAMBRIDGE
UNIVERSITY PRESS

32 Avenue of the Americas, New York NY 10013

Cambridge University Press is part of the University of Cambridge.

It furthers the University's mission by disseminating knowledge in the pursuit of education, learning, and research at the highest international levels of excellence.

www.cambridge.org
Information on this title: www.cambridge.org/9781107106222

© Sungmoon Kim 2016

This publication is in copyright. Subject to statutory exception and to the provisions of relevant collective licensing agreements, no reproduction of any part may take place without the written permission of Cambridge University Press.

First published 2016

A catalog record for this publication is available from the British Library.

Library of Congress Cataloging in Publication Data
Names: Kim, Sungmoon, author.
Title: Public reason Confucianism : democratic perfectionism and constitutionalism in East Asia / Sungmoon Kim, City University of Hong Kong.
Description: New York : Cambridge University Press, 2016. | Includes bibliographical references and index.
Identifiers: LCCN 2015045745 | ISBN 9781107106222 (Hardback : alk. paper)
Subjects: LCSH: East Asia–Politics and government. | Confucianism–Political aspects–East Asia. | Democracy–East Asia. | Democracy–Religious aspects–Confucianism. | Political participation–East Asia.
Classification: LCC JQ1499.A91 K544 2016 | DDC 320.95–dc23 LC record available at http://lccn.loc.gov/2015045745

ISBN 978-1-107-10622-2 Hardback

Cambridge University Press has no responsibility for the persistence or accuracy of URLs for external or third-party Internet Web sites referred to in this publication and does not guarantee that any content on such Web sites is, or will remain, accurate or appropriate.

For Seoyoon

Contents

Acknowledgments		*page* ix
Introduction		1
	PART I: PERFECTIONISM	
1	Confucian democratic perfectionism	35
2	Public reason Confucianism: A construction	69
	PART II: CONSTITUTIONALISM	
3	Public reason Confucian constitutionalism	107
4	Public equality and democratic pluralism	138
	PART III: CIVIC VIRTUE	
5	Between moral virtue and civic virtue	171
6	The right to political participation	204
	Conclusion	241
Bibliography		247
Index		265

Acknowledgments

This book's motivation was to provide a philosophical foundation for my political vision that I presented in my earlier work *Confucian Democracy in East Asia: Theory and Practice* (Cambridge University Press, 2014). One of the most frequent questions I have received since the publication of *Confucian Democracy* has been how I can reconcile the apparently nonneutral promotion of Confucianism in my democratic theory and my embracement of public reason, a philosophical apparatus commonly associated with state neutrality. Relatedly, some Confucian critics have noted that my suggestion to differentiate between civic virtue and moral virtue has strong resonance with the Rawlsian strategy, aimed at state neutrality, and is difficult to harmonize with the old paradigm of Confucian virtue politics in which no distinction between moral virtue and civic virtue is posited. In this book I attempt to offer a principled rejoinder to this misgiving by articulating the perfectionist dimension of my democratic political theory and examining its constitutional implications.

At the heart of my project is to justify a particular mode of Confucian democratic perfectionism – what I call *public reason Confucianism* – in which perfectionism is intertwined with partial comprehensive Confucianism in mediation of public reason, understood as the reason of democratic citizens. I argue that if the idea of Confucian democracy is reformulated in terms of public reason Confucianism and Confucian democratic perfectionism is reconceived from the broader perspective of democratic constitutionalism, the practical distinction between moral virtue and civic virtue becomes an unavoidable feature of the modern democratic and constitutional Confucian polity. I hope that readers can not only see clearly how some of the most challenging philosophical questions arising from *Confucian Democracy* have been attended (and resolved) in the course of my exploration of public reason Confucianism but further understand its contributions to democratic constitutionalism that is most attractive in East Asia's Confucian societal context.

In writing this book, I have incurred numerous debts. My colleagues at the Center for East Asian and Comparative Philosophy (CEACOP) and the Department of Public Policy at City University of Hong Kong have been my most vigorous conversation partners and they offered many useful comments throughout the manuscript-writing process. I would like to thank Youngsun Back, Ruiping Fan, Eirik Harris, Richard Kim, and Hsin-wen Lee for their friendship. I am particularly grateful to P. J. Ivanhoe for extensive written and verbal comments on the earlier versions of the manuscript. I am also grateful to Jong-cheol Kim at Yonsei Law School and his Social Science Korea (SSK) project team who visited CEACOP to discuss my idea of Confucian democracy; to Albert Chen, Chaihark Hahm, and Marie Seong Hak Kim, who participated in the "Confucianism and Constitutionalism" workshop held at City University of Hong Kong in 2015 and offered valuable suggestions on my formulation of public reason Confucianism; and to participants in the "Political Theory and Theorizing East and West" workshop held at City University of Hong Kong in 2015 who critically discussed the early version of Chapter 6, including Elton Chan, Joseph Chan, Yvonne Chiu, Jane Mansbridge, Al Martinich, Rahul Sagar, and Justin Tiwald. A debt of gratitude is owed to many others who have read or simply discussed various parts of my argument and offered helpful suggestions and criticisms. They include: Tongdong Bai, Benjamin Barber, Daniel Bell, Thomas Christiano, John Dryzek, David Elstein, Sandra Field, Owen Flanagan, Jeff Flynn, Baogang He, Jung In Kang, Bihwan Kim, Chandran Kukathas, George Letsas, Chenyang Li, Michael Slote, Rogers Smith, Sor-hoon Tan, Christina Tarnopolsky, David Wong, and Bernard Yack. Last, I would like to thank Robert Dreesen, my editor at Cambridge University Press, for believing in this project and the three anonymous reviewers for their critical suggestions.

Earlier versions of various portions of this book were presented at the Center for Comparative Philosophy at Duke University, the Asan Institute for Policy Studies, the Global Academy for Future Civilizations at Kyung Hee University, Sogang University's Department of Political Science, Sungkyunkwan University's Department of Political Science, the "Rationality in Politics & Its Limits" conference held at the Department of Political Science at National University of Singapore, the "Human Rights, International Relations, and Global Governance" conference held at

NUS's Lee Kuan Yew School of Public Policy, and the annual meetings of American Political Science Association and Midwest Political Science Association, in addition to the aforementioned CEACOP events. Feedbacks from these venues were immensely helpful in refining and strengthening my argument.

A slightly different and shortened version of Chapter 2 was previously published under the same title at *American Political Science Review*, 109:1 (2015), pp. 187–200 and I am grateful to Cambridge University Press for permission to reprint the essay here. A substantive portion of Chapter 4 was published under the title of "Civil Confucianism in South Korea: Liberal Rights, Confucian Reasoning, and Gender Equality," in Sungmoon Kim (ed.), *Confucianism, Law, and Democracy in Contemporary Korea* (London: Rowman and Littlefield International, 2015), pp. 105–124, and my thanks are due to Sarah Campell, the editor at Rowman and Littlefield International, for permission to reprint parts of the essay here. Finally, a portion of Chapter 6 is based on my article entitled "Confucianism, Moral Equality, and Human Rights: A Mencian Perspective," published in *American Journal of Economics and Sociology*, 74:1 (2015), pp. 149–185. The relevant portion has been reprinted with permission from John Wiley & Sons.

The research of this book was supported by a research grant from the Research Grants Council of the Hong Kong Special Administrative Region, China [Project No. 11403814].

Introduction

TWO KINDS OF CONFUCIAN PERFECTIONISM

Over the past two decades, political theorists of East Asia and beyond have been struggling with nonliberal political regimes and practices pertinent in East Asia's Confucian philosophical and societal contexts, resulting in the emergence of Confucian political theory as an important subfield in political theory. Earlier in this development, the major concern was constructing Confucian democracy as an alternative to the dominant Western-style democracy by critiquing its underlying liberal premises, then dialectically reconnecting the ideals and institutions of democracy, decoupled from liberalism (particularly liberal rights-based individualism), to Confucian ethics and practices.[1] Overall, in its developing stage, Confucian political theory was primarily a democratic project, even though the robustness of its democratic character was sometimes questioned, especially against the societal backdrop of pluralism.

What is distinctive about the more recent developments of Confucian political theory, often formulated in terms of *political meritocracy*, is its deep skepticism of, even objection to, democratic ideals (such as popular sovereignty and political equality) and democratic practices (such as competitive election based on "one person one vote" and universal

---

[1] Most representative studies in this endeavor are David L. Hall and Roger T. Ames, *The Democracy of the Dead: Dewey, Confucius, and the Hope for Democracy in China* (Chicago: Open Court, 1999); Sor-hoon Tan, *Confucian Democracy: A Deweyan Reconstruction* (Albany: State University of New York Press, 2004); Brooke A. Ackerly, "Is Liberalism the Only Way toward Democracy? Confucianism and Democracy," *Political Theory* 33:4 (2005), pp. 547–576.

political participation).[2] Daniel Bell, an ardent advocate of political meritocracy, defines the term as "the idea that a political system should aim to select and promote leaders with superior ability and virtue."[3] Most often, in efforts to justify their normative position, advocates of Confucian political meritocracy draw attention to various social and political problems of Western liberal democracies – problems that they argue are directly correlated with popular sovereignty and political equality. Some even point to the recent economic success of China or Singapore to make a case for political meritocracy. Bell is most vocal in this regard when he asserts, "the world is watching China's experiment with meritocracy. China, unlike Singapore, can 'shake the world.' In the early 1990s, nobody predicted that China's economy would rise so fast to become the world's second largest economy. In twenty years' time, perhaps we will be debating how Chinese-style political meritocracy set an alternative model – and perhaps – challenge to Western-style democracy."[4]

Justification for Confucian meritocracy as a normative theory goes even further than these practical concerns. Though varied in their individual proposals, advocates of Confucian meritocracy largely share some *perfectionist* assumptions: (1) Confucian ethics is a kind of perfectionist ethics that assumes the existence of an objectively good life and thus aims for moral perfection of the people; (2) given the inseparability between Confucian ethics and politics, the supreme goal of Confucian politics lies in promoting the objectively good life (as stipulated in Confucian ethics) as well as securing socioeconomic conditions that enable such a life; and therefore (3) the state in a Confucian polity is morally authorized to promote a particular (Confucian) conception of the good life in a non-coercive way. There are two underlying arguments here: first, democracy

---

[2] Tongdong Bai, *China: The Political Philosophy of the Middle Kingdom* (New York: Zed Book, 2012); Daniel A. Bell, *Beyond Liberal Democracy: Political Thinking for an East Asian Context* (Princeton: Princeton University Press, 2006); idem., *The China Model: Political Meritocracy and the Limits of Democracy* (Princeton: Princeton University Press, 2015); Joseph Chan, *Confucian Perfectionism: A Political Philosophy for Modern Times* (Princeton: Princeton University Press, 2014); Ruiping Fan, *Reconstructionist Confucianism: Rethinking Morality after the West* (Dordrecht: Springer, 2010); Jiang Qing, *A Confucian Constitutional Order: How China's Ancient Past Can Shape Its Political Future*, eds. Daniel A. Bell and Ruiping Fan and trans. Edmund Ryden (Princeton: Princeton University Press, 2013).

[3] Daniel A. Bell, "Introduction: The Theory, History, and Practice of Political Meritocracy," in *The East Asian Challenge for Democracy: Political Meritocracy in Comparative Perspective*, eds. Daniel A. Bell and Chenyang Li (New York: Cambridge University Press, 2013), p. 7.

[4] Ibid., p. 5.

is largely instrumentally valuable or altogether unimportant as long as the perfectionist ends are promoted by the state without the use of violence or illegitimate coercion, and second, the key agents of state perfectionism are "leaders with superior ability and virtue."

When philosophically justified in terms of perfectionism, Confucian meritocracy poses a formidable challenge to Confucian democrats wrestling with democratic citizenship and participation in the Confucian societal context. Simply put, it is difficult for Confucian democrats to deny the heavy perfectionist elements in early Confucianism, by which both they and the champions of Confucian meritocracy are equally inspired,[5] and therefore it is also difficult for them to reject the attempt to rejuvenate and enact Confucian perfectionism and by implication Confucian meritocracy – or, put together, *Confucian meritocratic perfectionism* – in modern East Asian societies with a Confucian heritage. Thus, it is not surprising that David Hall and Roger Ames, advocates of Deweyan Confucian democracy, condone, if not actively support, political meritocracy, notwithstanding their strong commitment to universal political participation.[6] The dilemma for them and many other "Confucian" democrats, including myself, is therefore as follows: on the one hand, Confucian democrats are also perfectionist as long as they wish to make East Asian polities a *Confucian* (democratic) polity, and hence nonneutral to other competing ideas of the good life including liberalism;[7] on the other hand, Confucian democrats embrace democracy (and the ideals and values integral to it such as popular sovereignty and political equality) as noninstrumentally valuable under the modern circumstances of social diversity, value pluralism, and moral disagreement, and reject (or wish to reject) political elitism implicated in traditional Confucian ethics and

---

[5] Deweyan Confucian democrats such as David Hall and Roger Ames (and arguably Sorhoon Tan) offer an interesting case because while they do not believe that Confucian ethics is premised on the existence of the objective good and instead understand Confucianism mainly as an aesthetic ideal of human creativity in which each person is author of her or his own life, their communitarian political vision is clearly perfectionist, aimed at moral growth of the people.

[6] For criticisms on the elitist components in Hall and Ames's vision of Deweyan Confucian democracy, see Shaun O'Dwyer, "Democracy and Confucian Values," *Philosophy East and West* 53 (2003), pp. 39–63, esp. pp. 53–57, and Sungmoon Kim, "John Dewey and Confucian Democracy: Towards Common Citizenship," *Constellations* 22:1 (2015), pp. 31–43.

[7] Liberalism is often regarded as a universal moral system, neutral to other comprehensive moral values. I contest this conventional wisdom, particularly in Chapter 2, by critically engaging with Rawls's political liberalism, arguably the most neutral form of contemporary liberalism.

political philosophy.[8] We can call this dilemma faced by Confucian democrats the *perfectionism dilemma*.

The aim of this book is twofold. First, it attempts to relieve Confucian democrats from the perfectionist dilemma by defending *Confucian democratic perfectionism*, a mode of comprehensive Confucian perfectionism that not only can accommodate the plurality of values in civil society but also is fully compatible with constitutive values of democracy such as popular sovereignty, political equality, and the right to political participation. After defending Confucian democratic perfectionism against the recent challenge of Confucian meritocratic perfectionism, it then explores what I call *public reason Confucianism*, a particular style of Confucian democratic perfectionism that is, as will be argued, the most attractive option in contemporary East Asian societies that are historically and (public) culturally Confucian.

DIFFICULTIES OF CONFUCIAN MERITOCRATIC PERFECTIONISM

One of the major problems in recent proposals of Confucian meritocratic perfectionism is their shifting attitudes toward democracy. For instance, while arguing for the perfectionist promotion of Confucian values (such as filial piety) and family-oriented public policies (such as family ownership of property) in East Asian countries,[9] Daniel Bell finds it "tempting to conceive of the possibility of reconciling the Confucian emphasis on rule by wise and virtuous elites [required due to the sheer complexity of public affairs] with the democratic values of popular participation,

---

[8] Note that even the strongest Confucian critics of Confucian political meritocracy have yet to advance a coherent normative stance toward perfectionism on which Confucian meritocracy is justified, leaving their critique incomplete from a philosophical standpoint. For instance, see Sor-hoon Tan, "Beyond Elitism: A Community Ideal for a Modern East Asia," *Philosophy East and West* 59 (2009), pp. 537–553. I admit that the same criticism is equally applicable to my earlier work *Confucian Democracy in East Asia: Theory and Practice* (New York: Cambridge University Press, 2014) in which I did not show in a philosophically lucid and systematic way how the nonneutral promotion of Confucian public reason can be compatible with intrinsic values of democracy in the societal context of value pluralism. In this current work, I attempt to provide a more robust philosophical foundation for my normative idea of Confucian democracy from a perfectionist standpoint.

[9] Bell, *Beyond Liberal Democracy*, pp. 243–251; Daniel A. Bell, "Confucian Constraints on Property Rights," in *Confucianism for the Modern World*, eds. Daniel A. Bell and Chaibong Hahm (Cambridge: Cambridge University Press, 2003), pp. 218–235.

accountability, and transparency."[10] Famously, Bell's solution is to create a bicameral legislature, with a democratically elected lower house and a "Confucian" upper house composed of representatives selected on the basis of competitive examinations in the Confucian classics, among other things. What imparts to this arrangement a distinctively "Confucian" mark is the constitutional formula providing supermajorities in the upper house with the right to override majorities in the lower house.[11] Bell's institutional proposal, which resonates strongly with the Chinese Confucian scholar Jiang Qing's tricameralism (consisting of the house of Confucian scholars, the house of the nation, and the house of the people),[12] has influenced many contemporary Confucians, though these scholars – whom I call throughout this book advocates of Confucian meritocracy or simply Confucian meritocrats – disagree on what should be the proper method of nondemocratic selection of members of the upper house: while Tongdong Bai and Ruiping Fan embrace Bell's exam model,[13] Joseph Chan and Chenyang Li prefer recommendation over examination.[14]

It is important whether or not Confucian meritocrats' institutional proposals are politically plausible in contemporary East Asian societies, but this practical question goes beyond the scope of this book. My prominent concern here is rather with a theoretical difficulty underlying such proposals, that is, whether or not these scholars can have both (bits of) meritocracy and (bits of) democracy in their proposed way(s), which they understand as grounded in completely different, even opposing, sources of legitimacy, without compromising the theory's internal coherence. If we prefer "Confucian democracy" over liberal democracy solely

---

[10] Bell, *Beyond Liberal Democracy*, p. 152.   [11] Ibid., pp. 165–172.
[12] Jiang Qing, *Zhengzhi Ruxue: Dangdai Rujia de zhuanxiang, tezhi yu fazhan* [Political Confucianism: Contemporary Confucianism's Challenge, Special Quality, and Development] (Beijing: San lian shu dian, 2003). For a helpful English summary of Jiang's tricameralism, see Albert H. Y. Chen, "Three Political Confucianism and Half a Century," in *The Renaissance of Confucianism in Contemporary China*, ed. Ruiping Fan (Dordrecht: Springer, 2011), pp. 205–223. Also see Jiang, *Confucian Constitutional Order*.
[13] Tongdong Bai, "A Confucian Version of Hybrid Regime: How Does It Work, and Why Is It Superior?" in *East Asian Challenge for Democracy*, pp. 55–87; Fan, *Reconstructionist Confucianism*, pp. 62–63. In his recent essay, though, Fan finds Jiang's original tricameralism more convincing, at the pinnacle of which lies the transcendental authority of Heaven, and deliberately distances himself from other Confucianists, who are, in his view, "secular liberal." See his "Confucian Meritocracy for Contemporary China," in *East Asian Challenge for Democracy*, pp. 88–115.
[14] Chan, *Confucian Perfectionism*, pp. 100–109; Chenyang Li, "Equality and Inequality in Confucianism," *Dao* 11 (2012), pp. 295–313.

because of the substantive, putatively Confucian goods it can bring about,[15] in other words, if our perfectionist justification of Confucian democracy is entirely consequentialist, why do we care about democratic procedures such as popular election operating on the principle of "one person one vote (OPOV)," even in the lower house or in local public affairs? What good (Confucian) consequences can we reasonably expect from such democratic institutional mechanisms?[16] Why not simply advocate a traditional Confucian one-man monarchy, operating on the idea of a benevolent government (*renzheng* 仁政) or Platonic philosopher-kingship, if what matters is good consequences *and* if good consequences are correlated in a non-question begging way with the ruling elites' epistemic competence and moral virtue?[17] Or, if we reject (for the most part) democratic ideals of popular sovereignty, political equality, and the right to political participation in our meritocratic understanding of Confucian democracy, on what normative grounds can we justify democratic practices of popular election and political participation, and how can they be justified in ways that can simultaneously and coherently endorse the value of meritocracy, again understood as rule by the elite, and its attendant political institutions? Moreover, if we need to introduce democratic mechanisms into our preferred meritocratic institutional settings in order to check the meritorious upper house, why do we not simply opt for equally nondemocratic or less democratic measures, such as a nondemocratically selected judiciary or bureaucracy, as the counterbalancing force of our otherwise "knowledgeable and virtuous" leaders? But if members of the meritorious upper house also need be checked by and held accountable to ordinary citizens, what is the point of pitting meritocracy against democracy in the first place? Why do we not instead reconceptualize democratic representation (e.g., with emphasis on the co-subject dimension of our citizenship as much as its co-author dimension) and/or devise new institutional mechanisms of democracy that can make political

---

[15] Bell's strong emphasis on good economic performance in some East Asian countries as a justification for *Confucian* meritocratic perfectionism is puzzling in this regard.

[16] Joseph Chan seems to be the only Confucian meritocrat who offers an answer to this question and he does so in terms of democracy's institutional expression of the mutual commitment of the ruler and the ruled (*Confucian Perfectionism*, p. 86).

[17] Among recent Confucian perfectionists, Kang Xiaoguang appeals directly to the Confucian ideal of benevolent government for his antidemocratic political paternalism. See his *Renzheng: Zhongguo zhengzhi fazhan de disantiao daolu* [Benevolent Government: A Third Road for the Development of Chinese Politics] (Singapore: Global Publishing, 2005).

decisions epistemically superior as well as politically accountable?[18] In short, why should we care about democracy (even the Schumpeterian minimal democracy) if we are strongly convinced of the disvalue of democracy?

We can approach the same issue from a related yet somewhat different angle. Political scientists working in the field of democratic transition and consolidation have long struggled with the problem of what Giovanni Sartori aptly called "conceptual stretching."[19] According to Sartori, a qualitative (i.e., value-ridden or normative) concept such as democracy travels and ought to travel to different cultural contexts, and because of this conceptual traveling we can have an interesting category of comparative political analysis. The problem is that when traveling across cultures, the concept in question is often stretched and this poses a critical obstacle to reliable measurement and rigorous comparison. This is not to say that conceptual traveling always presents a liability in social science research – quite to the contrary, it can occasionally contribute to conceptual innovation. For instance, if we understand democracy minimally in terms of periodic competitive election, the proliferation of various conceptual forms of democracy, or "democracy with adjectives," is the most likely consequence. In fact, contemporary political science is saturated with alternative conceptual forms such as "authoritarian democracy," "neo-patrimonial democracy," "military-dominated democracy," and "proto-democracy."[20] The challenge for political scientists, then, is how to achieve conceptual innovation without abandoning the precision of the concept.

"Confucian democracy" is a powerful instance of conceptual traveling and an interesting case of democracy with adjectives. We can celebrate Confucian democracy as a concept only if it illuminates a form of democracy, distinct not only from various sorts of liberal democracies but also from other forms of non-Western democracies. Though Confucian

---

[18] On recent democratic theory in this direction, see Hélène Landemore, *Democratic Reason: Politics, Collective Intelligence, and the Rule of the Many* (Princeton: Princeton University Press, 2013); David Estlund, *Democratic Authority: A Philosophical Framework* (Princeton: Princeton University Press, 2008).

[19] Giovanni Sartori, "Conceptual Misformation in Comparative Politics," *American Political Science Review* 64:4 (1970), pp. 1033–1053. Also see David Collier and James E. Mahon, JR., "Conceptual 'Stretching' Revisited: Adapting Categories in Comparative Analysis," *American Political Science Review* 87:4 (1993), pp. 845–855.

[20] David Collier and Steven Levitsky, "Democracy with Adjectives: Conceptual Innovation in Comparative Research," *World Politics* 49:3 (1997), pp. 430–451, at p. 431.

democracy, by definition, does not have to be modeled after a Western-style liberal democracy, it must meet certain minimum requirements to be called a "democracy" at all. For political scientists such minimums include, among other things, regular competitive election both for selection of political representatives and for peaceful handover of political power, as well as an autonomous civil society that can offer citizens a space for public contestation.[21] What should not be forgotten here are the things implicated with these institutional minimums (and other additional institutional arrangements) – namely the foundational democratic ideals of popular sovereignty, political equality, and the right to participation.[22]

As a subject of comparative political analysis, Confucian democracy may be characterized by its own unique modes of electoral system, election mechanism, civil society, political authority, and the relationship between state and civil society, qualitatively (or culturally) different from those we are familiar with in Western liberal democracies. In addition, the way democratic ideals of popular sovereignty, political equality, and the right to political participation are manifested in Confucian democracy might also be distinguished from the way they are understood and practiced in Western liberal democracies. And of course, Confucian democracy can have additional cultural institutions, practices, and values that may reinforce, supplement, or, if necessary, constrain democratic institutions and practices of Western provenance, as long as they do not undermine democratic ideals or principles that citizens have constitutionally affirmed. In no event, however, can our refusal to model blindly Western-style liberal democracy and explore instead a Confucian democracy lead us to support a polity that demands serious compromises of democratic ideals themselves, which make democracy morally valuable. What we deal with then is not so much an innovated concept of democracy but a democracy whose concept has been stretched, a regime that goes beyond not only liberal democracy but democracy in toto.[23]

It is true that there is meaningful difference between normative political theory, aimed at a philosophical articulation of the normatively attractive mode of democracy, and empirical political science, the main interest of which lies in producing a reliable category of scientific measurement and

---

[21] Robert A. Dahl, *Polyarchy: Participation and Opposition* (New Haven: Yale University Press, 1971).
[22] See Robert A. Dahl, *On Democracy* (New Haven: Yale University Press, 1998).
[23] This is the criticism raised by Fred Dallmayr to Daniel Bell's *Beyond Liberal Democracy*. See his "Exiting Liberal Democracy: Bell and Confucian Thought," *Philosophy East and West* 59 (2009), pp. 524–530.

comparison.[24] That said, the lesson from the problem of conceptual stretching for a normative theory of Confucian democracy is rather obvious: it is implausible to adopt the institutions of democracy (mainly election), without its underlying principles and values, by arbitrarily decoupling the concept of democracy from its related philosophical postulates.[25] From a philosophical standpoint, however, democracy is a constellation of interrelated postulates such as popular sovereignty, political equality, and the right to political participation. As I said earlier, what kind of a constellation Confucian democracy is and how distinct it is from other democracies are valid questions, philosophically as well as empirically. It seems arbitrary, for instance, to espouse democratic election based on the principle of OPOV without acknowledging the underlying moral principle of political equality.[26] And as I show in Chapter 6, when we embrace popular sovereignty and political equality as related postulates of democracy, it is difficult not to acknowledge the right to political participation as another postulate of democracy, given the moral demand to respect every citizen's dignity and his or her material and moral interests.

That being said, there are seemingly three ways to address these difficulties of Confucian meritocratic perfectionism. One way to forestall the charge of conceptual overstretching is to rename what has been called Confucian democracy with, for example, "Confucian aristocracy" (Ruiping Fan), "Confucian constitutionalism" (Jiang Qing), "Confucian perfectionism" (Joseph Chan), "Confu-China" (Tongdong Bai), or simply "(Confucian) political meritocracy" (Daniel Bell). That is, we can simply shift our conceptual focus away from Confucian democracy to something else that contains some democratic components. However, this move does not fully relieve the theoretical difficulties we have discussed thus far. Our earlier questions – *why should we bother with democracy if its disvalue is*

---

[24] I regret though that sometimes this difference becomes too significant for empirical political scientists in democracy studies and normative democratic political theorists to have an intelligent and productive conversation.

[25] For a crucial importance of the coherent relation among postulates for theory-building, see Michael Oakeshott, *On Human Conduct* (Oxford: Clarendon, 1975).

[26] My judgment is supported by works such as Jeremy Waldron, *Law and Disagreement* (Cambridge: Cambridge University Press, 1999); Henry S. Richardson, *Democratic Autonomy: Public Reasoning about the Ends of Policy* (New York: Oxford University Press, 2002); Corey Brettschneider, *Democratic Rights: The Substance of Self-Government* (Princeton: Princeton University Press, 2007); Thomas Christiano, *The Constitution of Equality: Democratic Authority and Its Limits* (Oxford: Oxford University Press, 2008).

so obvious and practically unbearable? and *what is the normative basis for election given the rejection of political equality?* – still remain unanswered.

Another, more plausible, way to avoid these sorts of theoretical difficulties is to call the polity in which meritocratic and democratic institutions are mixed a "mixed regime" in the sense that Western republican theorists, most notably Aristotle and Montesquieu, understood the term.[27] This, however, raises a different theoretical difficulty. In the republican tradition a mixed regime is pursued not merely to attain political order and stability, but, far more importantly, to secure political liberty and public freedom – hence Montesquieu's fascination with the constitution of England. Ironically, the best modern example of a mixed regime is found in the United States of America, the most frequent target of criticism by Confucian meritocrats as the epitome of all negative things that liberal democracy stands for. Daniel Deudney famously dubbed the American constitutional system (i.e., the Philadelphian system) as "negarchy," a mixed regime that structurally resists both one-man tyranny and the tyranny of majority, thereby creating a space for political liberty and public freedom.[28] Deudney shows not only that a mixed regime, whose polar opposite is despotism, aims at a particular set of political goods, all revolving around political liberty, which most Confucian meritocrats either reject outright (by associating them with liberalism) or simply bypass, but also that there is no inherent tension between a mixed regime and (constitutional) democracy with all its conceptual postulates.[29] This is essentially a matter of institutional design.

Though there is no prima facie reason that a Confucian mixed regime must be modeled after either the Roman-republican or American-democratic mixed regime, we cannot brush away the overarching political purpose of instituting a mixed regime and the regime's coherent operative

---

[27] For instance, see Bai, "Confucian Version of Hybrid Regime."

[28] Daniel H. Deudney, "The Philadelphian System: Sovereignty, Arms Control, and Balance of Power in the American States-Union, circa 1787–1861," *American Political Science Review* 49:2 (1995), pp. 191–228.

[29] This does not mean that an American-style democratic negarchy, focused on resistance, is most effective in "getting things done" but this practical difficulty, characteristic of American democracy, does not directly vindicate the disvalue of democracy. For statements addressing this issue from the perspective of democratic theory, see Jane Mansbridge, "On the Importance of Getting Things Done," *PS: Political Science and Politics* 45:1 (2012), pp. 1–8; Mark E. Warren and Jane Mansbridge et al., "Deliberative Negotiation," in *Negotiating Agreement in Politics*, eds. Jane Mansbridge and Cathie J. Martin (Washington, DC: American Political Science Association, 2013), pp. 86–120.

mechanism serving that purpose. In any event, we cannot rationalize any undisciplined (philosophically as well as politically) mixing of a bit of aristocracy and a bit of democracy in the name of mixed regime, as understood in political theory, without laying out the supreme purpose of the regime and articulating how the regime coherently buttresses its constitutional goal, especially when we reject or only selectively embrace democratic principles of popular sovereignty, political equality, and the right to political participation. As they stand, proposals for a "Confucian mixed regime," singularly concentrated on the tyranny of the many and which wrongly identifies it as the natural outcome of popular sovereignty, do not clearly articulate which moral and political goods the regime stands for and how to guard the guardians. They offer neither convincing empirical evidence to demonstrate nor a compelling philosophical reason for why political meritocracy, as they define the term, is normatively superior to representative democracy, which is just another good example of the mixed regime.[30]

Finally, one can avoid the theoretical difficulties of Confucian meritocratic perfectionism by embracing democracy largely for instrumental reasons, and this is the strategy many liberal perfectionists employ. Steven Wall, for one, vindicates the idea that perfectionism is a kind of consequentialism with his notion of *complex instrumentalist monism* in justifying political authority and the legitimacy of political procedures. In his critique of Thomas Christiano's dualistic account of justified democratic authority,[31] Wall expounds upon instrumentalist monism, according to which the legitimacy of political procedures (democratic or otherwise) is evaluated solely in terms of their results.[32] In his argument

---

[30] For meritocratic elements of Western liberal representative democracy, see Philip Pettit, "Meritocratic Representation," and Stephen Macedo, "Meritocratic Democracy: Learning from the American Constitution," both in *East Asian Challenge for Democracy*, pp. 138–157 and pp. 232–256, respectively. Also see Jane Mansbridge, "A 'Selection Model' of Political Representation," *Journal of Political Philosophy* 17:4 (2009), pp. 369–398; Jane Mansbridge, "Clarifying Political Representation," *American Political Science Review* 105:3 (2011), pp. 621–630.

[31] To note briefly, the dualistic account of democratic authority establishes two evaluative stances in the assessment of democracy, both procedural and substantive. According to this view, "[a] conception of democratic authority must show that while decisions can be evaluated from an independent standpoint, the fact that the democratic assembly has made the decisions gives each person a pre-emptive and content-independent reason for complying." See Thomas Christiano, "The Authority of Democracy," *Journal of Political Philosophy* 12:3 (2004), pp. 266–290, at p. 268.

[32] Steven Wall, "Democracy, Authority, and Publicity," *Journal of Political Philosophy* 14:1 (2006), pp. 85–100.

Wall distinguishes complex instrumentalist monism, his preferred view, from simple instrumentalist monism. The distinctive feature of complex instrumentalist monism is that it focuses not only on the "tasks of government," the problems that citizens need government to solve, but also on the "effects of governing," that is, the full range of consequences of governing.[33] Simply put, complex instrumentalist monism promotes the good tasks of government, the direct target of its consequentialism, as well as the good effects of governing without developing an internal contradiction. In this view, democratic values, such as public equality, common citizenship, and political participation, are not so much the tasks of government but the effects of governing. Wall asserts that "the complex view ... rejects the claim that democratic procedures are intrinsically just. That is, it rejects the claim that the method by which political decisions are made should be intrinsically fair, irrespective of its contribution to good outcomes."[34]

Wall's view has strong resonance with Joseph Chan's moderate perfectionism, by which several Confucian meritocrats are inspired.[35] Since I thoroughly examine in Chapter 1 whether Chan's instrumental justification of democracy (and his notion of moderate perfectionism) offers a philosophically robust justification for Confucian meritocratic perfectionism in contemporary East Asia, let us point out just two difficulties here, those that in my view pose a general, more critical challenge for Confucian meritocratic perfectionists than for liberal perfectionists. The first difficulty arises from the elitism that Confucian meritocratic perfectionists tend to endorse but to which liberal perfectionists explicitly object.[36] As noted, Confucian meritocratic perfectionists tend to tie their perfectionism too tightly to political elitism by integrating meritocratic institutions into their overall normative vision, such as the nondemocratically selected upper house, justified independently of core democratic ideals. Once integrated into a perfectionist theory, elitism, working through the coercive power of the state, slowly corrodes the normative force of democratic institutions and practices from within that are only instrumentally justified, then transforms the ostensibly democratic regime into something qualitatively different. This sort of normative corrosion does not

---

[33] Ibid., pp. 95–96   [34] Ibid., p. 96.
[35] See Joseph Chan, "Democracy and Meritocracy: Toward a Confucian Perspective," *Journal of Chinese Philosophy* 34:2 (2007), pp. 179–193.
[36] Steven Wall, *Liberalism, Perfectionism and Restraint* (Cambridge: Cambridge University Press, 1998), pp. 15–17; George Sher, *Beyond Neutrality: Perfectionism and Politics* (Cambridge: Cambridge University Press, 1997), pp. 5–6.

necessarily happen in liberal perfectionism (though it is possible) because valuing democracy for instrumental reasons is not directly tantamount to taking it lightly, nor does it necessitate a search for an alternative nondemocratic or partially democratic regime. In short, while the *why democracy?* question does not necessarily arise for liberal perfectionists, it constantly hunts down Confucian meritocratic perfectionists because of their political elitism.

The second difficulty of Confucian meritocrats' instrumental adaptation of democracy is related to what Jeremy Waldron calls *circumstances of (modern) politics*, which are marked by value pluralism and moral disagreement, and which increasingly characterize East Asian societies. The gist of this difficulty lies in how Confucian perfectionism as a comprehensive moral doctrine (a la Rawls) can come to terms with the plurality of values in civil society and the moral disagreement resulting from it when it is undergirded on nondemocratic political meritocracy. Once again, liberal perfectionists are less vulnerable to this difficulty, if not completely insulated from it, first, due to their outright rejection of any form of elitism, second, due to their perfectionist valorization of personal autonomy, and third, due to their comprehensive commitment to liberalism, which *together* work favorably to make room for and support pluralism.[37] Given the coerciveness of political power and law, how can Confucian perfectionism, operating on nondemocratic meritocracy, effectively accommodate and further avoid unjust suppression of citizens' diverse moral interests? Under the fact of pluralism, on what basis can we determine the *merit* of the members of the meritocratic upper house or the "constitutional academy," the highest constitutional authority of the putative Confucian polity, without being embroiled in moral controversy and political contestation?[38] If the merit in question is solely based on (fully comprehensive) Confucianism or, more problematically, it is what the (Confucian) elites declare it to be, how can we promote the *differentiated* moral well-being of citizens in a pluralist society?[39]

The theoretical difficulties that Confucian meritocratic perfectionism is chronically exposed to and the unsatisfactory responses to them give rise to a need for an alternative normative political theory that is both

---

[37] Joseph Raz, *The Morality of Freedom* (Oxford: Clarendon, 1986); Sher, *Beyond Neutrality*, pp. 45–105; Wall, *Liberalism, Perfectionism and Restraint*, pp. 127–182.

[38] For the proposal of the Confucian-style constitutional academy, see Ngoc Son Bui, "Beyond Judicial Review: The Proposal of the Constitutional Assembly," *Chinese Journal of Comparative Law* 2:1 (2013), pp. 43–77.

[39] I raised the same question in *Confucian Democracy*, pp. 87–92.

Confucian-perfectionist and robustly democratic, as well as more responsive to the fact of pluralism. I present Confucian democratic perfectionism as such an alternative and articulate public reason Confucianism as the most attractive version of Confucian democratic perfectionism practicable in contemporary East Asia.

CONFUCIAN DEMOCRATIC PERFECTIONISM

Two conditions

As a form of Confucian perfectionism, Confucian democratic perfectionism embraces the perfectionist element of Confucian meritocratic perfectionism, but as a democratic perfectionism it objects to the elitist aspect of Confucian meritocratic perfectionism by making integral to it core democratic values of popular sovereignty, political equality, and the right to political participation, thereby shaping Confucian perfectionism in ways compatible with the plurality of values.

First, like Confucian meritocratic perfectionism, Confucian democratic perfectionism is based on the conviction that in a modern East Asian, historically Confucian, society, the state is permitted to publicly promote a (characteristically) Confucian way of life, at the heart of which lies a constellation of values such as, but not limited to, filial piety, ritual propriety, respect for elders, ancestor worship, harmony within the (extended) family, and social harmony. More specifically, the state can implement public policies aimed to promote Confucian values such as a reduced tax rate for "filial sons and daughters" who live with and/or economically support their aged parents, or make laws that, for example, prohibit filing criminal complaint against one's family members and enhance punishment for crimes committed against family members.[40]

---

[40] For instance, South Korea's Criminal Code prohibits filing of criminal complaint against one's (and the spouse's) lineal ascendants (Articles 224 and 235) and imposes enhanced punishment for crimes committed against one's lineal ascendants (Articles 250[2] and 259[2]) and recently the Korean Constitutional Court reaffirmed the provisions' constitutionality, proclaiming the Korean polity's perfectionist commitment to traditional Confucian values, especially filial piety. For a detailed analysis of the Court's decisions, see Marie S. H. Kim, "Confucianism that Confounds: Constitutional Jurisprudence on Filial Piety in Korea," in *Confucianism, Law, and Democracy in Contemporary Korea*, ed. Sungmoon Kim (London: Rowman & Littlefield International, 2015), pp. 57–80. Note that while celebrating filiality-enhancing criminal provisions such as those mentioned, Confucian democratic perfectionism, committed to public equality as shall be discussed shortly, rejects the traditional Confucian priority to lineal ascendants in

Furthermore, citizens (especially young citizens) are encouraged, at least in public schools, to cultivate Confucian values mentioned earlier as *civic virtues*, along with other typical civic virtues such as patriotism, public-spiritedness, tolerance, and reciprocity.

However, unlike Confucian meritocratic perfectionism (at least its most common variations), Confucian democratic perfectionism neither upholds a perfect or monistic congruence between Confucian ethics and Confucian politics nor aims at moral perfection of the people. Its perfectionist dimension is much more moderate, in the sense of permitting the state's nonneutral commitment to a constellation of Confucian values that citizens in East Asia still broadly share and practice despite their diverse private moral values and/or religious faiths. Here two conditions are worth close attention, conditions that combine to contribute to the moderateness of Confucian perfectionism. First, the values to be promoted publicly are ones affirmed in the Confucian tradition as *Confucian* (with all its intracultural variations), either culturally or philosophically, and continue to be practiced by East Asian citizens who otherwise subscribe to diverse comprehensive doctrines as private individuals, even though the actual practice of such values might have changed rather dramatically in modern times. Put differently, these publicly promoted values must have a meaningful historical connection with traditional Confucianism but do not have to manifest themselves in the modern context the way they did traditionally where Confucianism entertained moral, religious, and political orthodoxy, as what John Rawls calls a (fully) comprehensive doctrine. Let us call this the *continuity condition*.

Second, these Confucian values do not merely refer to discrete values or certain "items" of values without cultural or philosophical connections among themselves. They exist as a constellation of internally related values that together express their cultural intelligibility. Suppose that the Confucian state promotes filial piety (*xiao* 孝) as a public value. Given the inextricable cultural and philosophical intertwinement between filial piety and other Confucian values such as respect for elders, fraternal love, ritual propriety, ancestor worship, and harmony within the family, it is not only practically difficult but unreasonable to allow the state to promote this value alone, but not other related values, as if they can be separated from one another conveniently. For instance, if the putative

---

criminal protection. Also see Lusina Ho, "Traditional Confucian Values and Western Legal Frameworks," in *Confucianism for the Modern World*, pp. 288–311, for the Confucian influence on the law of succession in East Asian countries.

Confucian state is no longer interested in ancestor worship publicly and dissociates it by law from filial piety and harmony within the family, values with which it has been traditionally affiliated, this implies that the corresponding public meanings of filial piety and harmony within the family have also significantly altered. Likewise, if filial piety is no longer practiced in a ritually appropriate way, however socially contestable the meaning of appropriateness can be in the modern society, it would be extremely difficult to call it *xiao* as the Confucian cultural tradition has understood the term. The value or virtue in question can be called filial piety but obviously filial piety per se is not an exclusively Confucian asset. The value's Confucian credential can reasonably be put into doubt unless it is shown that it is an inseparable part of a constellation of internally entwined values or virtues that is intelligibly Confucian as a whole. Let us call this Confucian democratic perfectionism's *intelligibility condition*.

Though each of these conditions speaks for a different dimension of Confucian democratic perfectionism (i.e., contemporary social relevance and internal coherence), they are intimately related and together make Confucian democratic perfectionism a moderate perfectionism. Briefly put, they enable Confucian democratic perfectionism to be compatible with the plurality of values, without forsaking the comprehensive moral character of Confucianism as a way of life. In other words, these two conditions combine to render Confucian democratic perfectionism a comprehensive philosophical doctrine that is only *partially* comprehensive.[41] As will be discussed shortly, the partial comprehensiveness of Confucian democratic perfectionism is further reinforced by its democratic dimension, which morally requires comprehensive Confucianism to adapt to democratic-constitutional principles (such as gender equality) and institutions, especially those undergirding democratic rights.

Thus far, we have examined how Confucian democratic perfectionism is inspired by but distinct from Confucian meritocratic perfectionism. What distinguishes Confucian democratic perfectionism from Confucian meritocratic perfectionism more decisively, however, is its outright rejection of political elitism; its embrace of democratic principles of popular sovereignty, political equality, and the right to political participation as noninstrumentally valuable; and its institutional dependence on democratic

---

[41] For a distinction between *full* and *partial* comprehensive doctrine, see John Rawls, *Political Liberalism* (New York: Columbia University Press, 1993), p. 13. I fully engage with this distinction in Chapter 4 where I reconstruct public reason Confucianism as a partially comprehensive Confucianism and distinguish it from traditional Confucianism.

constitutionalism. Simply put, Confucian democratic perfectionism stipulates that Confucian perfectionism that meets both the continuity condition and the intelligibility condition must be carried out only by a democratic state. Then, what is *democratic perfectionism*, of which Confucian democratic perfectionism is a culturally specialized subset?

Democratic perfectionism

Democratic perfectionism is one of the most underdeveloped concepts (and theories) in contemporary political theory. In some sense, the lack of philosophical interest in this concept is surprising because many democratic political theorists who either oppose state neutrality or are wary of unreasonable pluralism support the (democratic) state's nonneutral commitment to certain democratic goods or purposes (most importantly, democratic citizenship) and the "secondary" goods that would be instrumental to the promotion of democratic goods. For instance, Benjamin Barber argues that

> [t]o insist on [the democratic good of] inclusion for democratic forms of community is, ironically, to define civil society non-inclusively! Not every community meets the standard. ... Biting the bullet, advocates of strong democratic civil society acknowledge that they are less than neutral: their conception of civil society is a rather restricted subset of all possible forms of association, and they limit it to forms that are at least nominally or potentially democratic and open.[42]

This view presented by Barber is widely shared by civic liberals and democrats who, most tellingly, contest the majority decision of the *Wisconsin v. Yoder* litigation in 1972 in which the court upheld Amish parents' right to free religious exercise over common democratic citizenship, including their right to not send their teenage children to public school where they could be "contaminated" by secular liberal values of the mainstream American society.[43]

In addition, while Amy Gutmann was the first political theorist to introduce the term "democratic perfectionism" to democratic theory,

---

[42] Benjamin R. Barber, *A Place for Us: How to Make Society Civil and Democracy Strong* (New York: Hill and Wang, 1998), pp. 52–53.

[43] *Wisconsin v. Yoder*, 406 U.S. 205 (1972). See the views that give priority to common democratic citizenship over cultural or religious membership, Amy Gutmann, *Democratic Education* (Princeton: Princeton University Press, 1987), p. 294; Ian Shapiro, *Democratic Justice* (New Haven: Yale University Press, 1999), pp. 101–102; Stephen Macedo, *Diversity and Distrust: Civic Education in a Multicultural Democracy* (Cambridge: Harvard University Press, 2000), pp. 207–209.

she showed no interest in the philosophical development of its political theory, mainly intending it to be a practical concept to come to terms with the democratic state's nonneutral subsidy of culture.[44] Gutmann's purpose with this concept was to justify the instrumental value of state subsidy of culture for democratic citizenship and public welfare. For her, "[d]emocratic perfectionism sanctions state subsidy of culture only if it is publicly approved, and then only if it satisfies the standards of nonrepression and nondiscrimination."[45] Among liberal perfectionists, George Sher presents his normative position explicitly in terms of democratic perfectionism but he does not articulate the concept, leaving unexplained both his understanding of democracy and whether he accepts democracy as instrumentally or noninstrumentally valuable.[46]

In this book I understand democracy as *collective self-government of free and equal citizens* and democratic perfectionism as a normative political theory that justifies *public promotion of particular cultural values in the service of democratic citizenship under the normative constraints of core democratic principles*.[47] Confucian democratic perfectionism refers to a particular kind of democratic perfectionism, focused on a constellation of Confucian cultural values and aimed at Confucian democratic citizenship. Institutionally, it is largely predicated on democratic constitutionalism. Nested in democratic constitutional institutions but committed to a (modern) Confucian way of life, therefore, Confucian democratic perfectionism sees Confucian democratic citizenship not so much as a static constitutional goal or philosophical norm but as a legal and political product of ceaseless dialectic cultural negotiations between Confucian cultural values and democratic-constitutional principles such as individual dignity and gender equality.

Thus understood, my understanding of democratic perfectionism is far more expansive than Gutmann's. The overall liberal outlook of Gutmann's

---

[44] That said, some of her philosophical insights into democratic perfectionism can be gleaned from Amy Gutmann, "Rawls on the Relationship between Liberalism and Democracy," in *The Cambridge Companion to Rawls*, ed. Samuel Freeman (Cambridge: Cambridge University Press, 2003), pp. 168–199.

[45] Gutmann, *Democratic Education*, pp. 258–259 (emphasis in original).

[46] Sher, *Beyond Neutrality*, p. 15.

[47] My understanding of democracy is indebted to, among others, Benjamin R. Barber, *Strong Democracy: Participatory Politics for a New Age* (Berkeley: University of California Press, 1984); Amy Gutmann and Dennis Thompson, *Democracy and Disagreement* (Cambridge: Belknap Press, 1996); Joshua Cohen, *Philosophy, Politics, Democracy: Selected Essays* (Cambridge: Harvard University Press, 2009); Christiano, *The Constitution of Equality*; and Brettschneider, *Democratic Rights*.

democratic theory renders her idea of democratic perfectionism singularly focused on cultural assets that are conducive to the good of democratic citizenship. For Gutmann, democratic citizenship is a liberal democratic citizenship and cultural assets worth perfectionist protection do not make a political impact on the liberal public character of citizenship. They are valuable mainly because of their incidental contribution to liberal democratic citizenship. In my idea of democratic perfectionism, however, cultural values are understood not merely as cultural assets that require state protection but as goods or ends that can reshape the overall character of democratic citizenship itself and with which ostensibly "liberal" democratic values and rights have to be negotiated. In short, in my understanding of democratic perfectionism, there is an indirect congruence between cultural values, the target of perfectionist promotion, and democratic citizenship, the supreme purpose of democratic constitutionalism.

PUBLIC REASON CONFUCIANISM

While Confucian democratic perfectionism is a particular kind of democratic perfectionism, public reason Confucianism is a specific mode of Confucian democratic perfectionism that best articulates the complex relationship between Confucian cultural values and Confucian democratic citizenship under the institutional constraints of democratic constitutionalism and within the normative parameters of democratic principles. It also provides a robust democratic theory of Confucian democratic perfectionism that is socially practicable in contemporary East Asia's increasingly pluralist and multicultural societal context. As a political theory, what is distinct about public reason Confucianism is that it mediates between public reason, commonly affiliated with liberal neutrality, and perfectionism, which endorses the state's nonneutral promotion or prohibition of particular goods or values. Seen in this way, public reason Confucianism is an important subset of what can be called *public reason perfectionism.*

Public reason perfectionism is a normative position that stipulates that (1) public reason, understood as the reason of democratic citizens, is not independent of but is deeply influenced by the most dominant comprehensive moral or religious doctrine of the background culture in civil society, which generally but not fully defines the polity's public character; and (2) the state, democratically controlled by its citizens, should operate on public reason, which not only gives citizenship a distinctive public character (as liberal, Muslim, or Confucian) but also induces social pluralism to be reasonable in light of the overarching public purpose of democratic citizenship. Though universally applicable as a normative theory, public reason perfectionism is of special relevance in non-Western, culturally nonliberal societies where a particular cultural or religious system has long enjoyed salient social, cultural, and political hegemony until the "Western impact" in the late nineteenth and early twentieth centuries, and still remains influential, especially in forms of mores, habits, and moral sentiments, even while at times massively modified by liberal values. What makes public reason perfectionism (which can potentially be nonliberal) robustly democratic nonetheless is that the content of public reason, tethered with a particular comprehensive doctrine to which citizens partially subscribe, is open to democratic contestation both in formal public forums and in civil society.

There are two important democratic advantages of this unusual nexus between public reason and comprehensive perfectionism (i.e., perfectionism based on a particular comprehensive doctrine). First, by connecting comprehensive perfectionism with public reason, the quintessential political question of whether political authority of our otherwise perfectionist polity is democratic or nondemocratic is firmly settled. A comparison might be helpful here. Joseph Raz's service conception of authority is centered on what he calls the normal justification thesis (NJT), which derives the right to command from a practical reason for better compliance.[48] Political liberals find the political reasoning implicated with NJT deeply illiberal because it violates personal autonomy, despite Raz's declared commitment to this liberal value.[49] From a democratic standpoint, however, the problem with the service conception of authority undergirded on NJT lies in the fact that it does not necessarily require the political authority to be democratic, making it vulnerable to the

---

[48] NJT claims that "[t]he normal way to establish that a person has authority over another person involves showing that the alleged subject is likely better to comply with reasons which apply to him (other than the alleged authoritative directives) if he accepts the directives of the alleged authority as authoritatively binding and tries to follow them, rather than by trying to follow the reasons which apply to him directly" (Raz, *The Morality of Freedom*, p. 53). Note that some Confucian meritocratic perfectionists such as Joseph Chan are strongly inspired by Raz's service conception of authority. See Joseph Chan, *Confucian Perfectionism*, pp. 27–45; "Political Authority and Perfectionism: A Response to Quong," *Philosophy and Public Issues* 2:1 (2012), pp. 31–41.

[49] Jonathan Quong argues that practical reason accounts of legitimacy such as NJT fail to explain "why the brute fact that *I* have reason to do something should affect what rights *you* have with regard to me" (Jonathan Quong, *Liberalism without Perfection* [Oxford: Oxford University Press, 2011], p. 115).

charge of (undemocratic) paternalism.[50] That is, in Raz's liberal perfectionism, it is a matter of political contingency whether or not the perfectionist political authority in question is formed by citizens' collective self-determination.[51] Public reason perfectionism redresses this democratic deficit in the dominant theories of (liberal) perfectionism by making democratic citizens' shared reason the single source of political authority, while not using it purely in the service of (neutralist) procedural justice and public justification. Inextricably intertwined with a comprehensive doctrine, public reason perfectionism refuses the normative severance between the right and the good, the hallmark of public reason liberalism.[52]

The second democratic advantage of public reason perfectionism is that it takes seriously the coerciveness of political power. Some political theorists tend to believe that political coercion is diametrically opposed to individual freedom and rights, or in the case of Confucian political theorists, to benevolent government. But this is a serious misunderstanding. When the state makes laws and implements public policies, citizens are bound to comply with them and failure in compliance entails legal liability. Political power is coercive precisely in this sense. Though political power is by nature coercive, coercion can be either legitimate or illegitimate (or more or less legitimate or illegitimate) depending on who exercises it and for what purposes it is exercised.[53] In addition, coercion

---

[50] Ibid., pp. 73–107. Note though that Quong's criticism is focused on the illiberal aspect of paternalism in (liberal) perfectionism, but not on its undemocratic dimension.

[51] In his later publication, though, Raz seems to acknowledge an important connection between participatory democracy (or representation) and the political philosophy of authority. Here Raz says that the aim of political philosophy is "to develop a doctrine of political authority which makes its legitimacy conditional on the existence of a population which regards the government as its representation, and in which people identify with the common interest, so that they regard its pursuit as their business and the law as their law. Here too, consent by itself, actual consent to a social contract, cannot solve the problem. But a theory of participatory government in a society in which conditions exist that enable each to see his own well-being as tied up with the prosperity of others can do so. The development of such a theory has been the aim of political philosophy since Rousseau. Its achievement is eagerly awaited" ("Introduction," in *Authority*, ed. Joseph Raz [Oxford: Basil Blackwell, 1990], pp. 1–19, p. 17). Nevertheless, it is still dubious whether Raz self-consciously integrates this democratic faith into his overall political philosophy of authority – especially in NJT – in a principled manner.

[52] See Gerald F. Gaus, *Justificatory Liberalism: An Essay on Epistemology and Political Theory* (New York: Oxford University Press, 1996); Charles Larmore, *The Autonomy of Morality* (New York: Cambridge University Press, 2008); Quong, *Liberalism without Perfection*.

[53] According to Philip Pettit, coercion can be either dominational or nondominational and only the latter type of coercion, which protects and enhances freedom, is legitimate. See

can be more or less agreeable to those for whom it is exercised, depending on how it is exercised. The problem with the Razian service conception of authority is that it does not fully engage with the fundamentally coercive nature of political authority. It has powerful explanations for the purpose of political authority and the mode of its exercise, with its emphasis on practical reason and perfectionist ends, but it does not clarify who should have political power – citizens, the elite, the law, or the state? – and how power should be distributed and/or organized – one/monarchy, few/aristocracy, or many/democracy?[54] But if it is acknowledged that political power is coercive and that modern people's moral interests are diverse and sometimes incommensurable, these fundamental political questions cannot just be brushed away, as if good practical reason alone matters regardless of who has political power and how it is organized. By making public reason integral to it, public reason perfectionism stipulates that given its coercive nature, political power is legitimate and authoritative only if it is wielded by all citizens, its co-subjects, either directly or, more preferably in our modern society, by means of electoral representation.

Public reason Confucianism is a particular mode of public reason perfectionism, specifically tailored for contemporary East Asian societies in which Confucianism has historically prevailed but now remains largely in forms of mores, habits, moral sentiments, and rituals, with which

---

his *Republicanism: A Theory of Freedom and Government* (Oxford: Oxford University Press, 1997) and *On the People's Terms: A Republican Theory and Model of Democracy* (Cambridge: Cambridge University Press, 2012). For an argument for "legitimate coercion" in democracy theory, see Jane Mansbridge, "Taking Coercion Seriously," *Constellations* 3:3 (1997), pp. 407–416, and Jane Mansbridge, "What is Political Science For?" *Perspectives on Politics* 12:1 (2012), pp. 8–17.

[54] Pointing out the difference between coercive and noncoercive forms of perfectionism, Joseph Chan argues that while on the former the state may use legal coercion to require people to adopt and lead valuable ways of life or to relinquish worthless ones, on the latter, the aim of the state is to create a social environment which is more conducive to the promotion of goods and worthwhile ways of life and it can achieve this goal by noncoercive means, such as subsidies, tax exemptions, and education. See his "Legitimacy, Unanimity, and Perfectionism," *Philosophy and Public Affairs* 29:1 (2000), pp. 5–42, at pp. 14–15. This distinction may be heuristically useful in understanding why perfectionism is an attractive normative position. However, in my view, Chan's account of noncoercive perfectionism, focused singularly on the agreeable mode of perfectionist policies, largely bypasses the coerciveness of political power itself in the nonideal situation. I am not sure how even policies such as subsidies, tax exemptions, and education can be noncoercive, when implemented by the state in terms of law and public policy, especially from the perspective of those who are excluded from, thus cannot claim to, such nonneutral state benefits but whose tax money, which is compulsory, is to be used to support them.

people today are still deeply saturated.[55] In terms of content, it is these uniquely Confucian mores, habits, moral sentiments, and rituals that make public reason Confucianism distinct from other forms of public reason perfectionism, including public reason liberalism (or political liberalism), because they are the sources of a nonrationalist mode of public reasoning that defines Confucian public reasoning.[56] As a political theory, though, public reason Confucianism is marked by all of the central features of public reason perfectionism discussed so far. I construct the theoretical outline of public reason Confucianism in Chapter 2 and offer its detailed philosophical substance with an explanation about how it can operate in practice in subsequent chapters. Here let me briefly introduce some core premises of public reason Confucianism, both normative and sociological.

First, as a species of Confucian democratic perfectionism, public reason Confucianism has two normative premises: (1) there is a valuable Confucian way of life that is distinct from (if not starkly opposed to) a liberal way of life and (2) it is permissible for a state, one that is democratically controlled by its citizens, to promote or discourage some activities, ideas, or ways of life, based on the grounds of a constellation of Confucian values such as, but not limited to, filial piety, respect for elders, ancestor worship, ritual propriety, harmony within the family, and social harmony. These normative premises are internally related to Confucian democratic perfectionism's two guiding conditions: the continuity condition and the intelligibility condition. Underlying these premises is the normative conviction that democratization of East Asian countries such as South Korea and Taiwan (and a strong moral demand for China to democratize) is not tantamount to Western-liberal democratization because democracy in these countries of Confucian heritage can be realized differently than in Western liberal societies, through dialectical interactions between Confucian values and democratic-constitutional rights and institutions, and with the aim of Confucian democratic citizenship.

While public reason Confucianism's normative premises speak for the theory's motivational dimension, the following three sociological premises of public reason Confucianism inspire the theory's philosophical

---

[55] See Anna Sun, *Confucianism as a World Religion: Contested Histories and Contemporary Realities* (Princeton: Princeton University Press, 2013); Philip J. Ivanhoe and Sungmoon Kim (eds.), *Confucianism, A Habit of the Heart: Bellah, Civil Religion, and East Asia* (Albany: State University of New York Press, forthcoming).

[56] I discuss the nonrationalist dimension of Confucian public reason(ing) in Kim, *Confucian Democracy*, chap. 5.

substances, thereby making it a unique kind of public reason perfectionism: (1) a one-man monarchy that has undergirded the political institution of traditional Confucianism is completely obsolete in contemporary East Asia (the republican premise); (2) with the advent of the republican era, traditional Confucianism's political ritualism, which divided people into different social classes and prescribed a set of proper social conduct for each class, has become equally obsolete, rendering everyone as equal as citizens (the political equality premise); (3) with the collapse of traditional Confucian monarchy and therewith the sage-king paradigm, there is no *Confucian* political ground on which political leaders, however selected, can justify the monistic value system and the lexical ordering of values, which subsequently enables people to subscribe to a diverse range of values (the value pluralism premise).

Public reason Confucianism's normative and sociological premises combine to establish several key propositions, but from the philosophical standpoint, the most important is what I call *the public equality proposition*, which consists of three internally related postulates of popular sovereignty, political equality, and the right to political participation. They together distinguish public reason Confucianism not only from traditional Confucianism, to which these values are foreign, but also from Confucian meritocratic perfectionism. The public equality proposition has a series of stipulations: (a) every human being has moral dignity; (b) every human being has both material and moral interests and the best way to respect one's moral dignity is to protect his or her basic material and moral interests; (c) interests (especially moral interests) are plural and the plurality of interests gives rise to moral disagreement; (d) each citizen has moral (and material) interests and the foundational ideal of human dignity requires the state to protect the diverse moral interests of its citizens; (e) each citizen's moral (and material) interests deserve equal public protection; (f) the state that can resolve moral disagreement authoritatively and make laws and policies without violating citizens' (basic) moral and material interests is one that is democratically controlled by citizens themselves; and finally (g) citizens can control the state democratically and express their moral and material interests publicly without fear, only if they have the right to political participation. Whether or not these stipulations that undergird the three postulates of the public equality proposition can be justified from the perspective of Confucianism is perhaps the most daunting challenge in philosophical construction of public reason Confucianism. I turn to this issue in Chapter 6.

The importance of the public equality proposition does not lie solely in its innovative philosophical implications. In a sense, its cultural and political implications are more far-reaching because it proffers a strong moral correction to traditional Confucian sex discrimination and gender inequality, among the greatest obstacles to modernizing Confucianism. In reinventing traditional Confucianism into modern Confucianism, political theorists tend to focus too much on classical Confucianism's philosophical potentials that would make it safe in the modern world, even when they consider the moral value and political utility of rituals (*li* 禮), but pay surprisingly little attention to how Confucianism was actually manifested in East Asia historically, especially in seriously oppressing women, by institutionalizing, among other things, the heavily patriarchal, patrilineal, and androcentric family structure,[57] and how some relics of such oppression and discrimination still remain in the laws and social practices of contemporary East Asian societies.[58]

By integrating public equality, public reason Confucianism actively rectifies the gender discriminating elements in traditional Confucianism and upholds public equality between men and women as one of the core democratic-constitutional principles with which Confucian values, worth perfectionist protection and promotion, ought to be negotiated. The product of such complex processes of legal, political, and civic negotiations may look like liberalism because it is nested in the discourse of rights and other modern constitutional values, but the mode of public reasoning that enables the modern constitutional reinvention of Confucianism is characteristically Confucian – hence Confucian public reasoning. For instance, public reason Confucianism stipulates that the best way to attain public equality between men and women is not by top-down imposition of substantive liberal notions of gender equality but through the expansion of filial piety beyond gender barriers and the redefinition of ritual propriety to be suitable for democratic relationships in civil society.

---

[57] See Kai-Wing Chow, *The Rise of Confucian Ritualism in Late Imperial China: Ethics, Classics, and Lineage Discourse* (Stanford: Stanford University Press, 1996); Dorothy Ko, Jahyun K. Haboush, and Joan R. Piggott, (eds.), *Women and Confucian Cultures in Premodern China, Korea, and Japan* (Berkeley: University of California Press, 2003); Martina Deuchler, *The Confucian Transformation of Korea: A Study of Society and Ideology* (Cambridge: Council on East Asian Studies, Harvard University, 1992).

[58] For a powerful discussion on Confucianism-influenced gender inequalities in contemporary Korean civil codes, see Hyunah Yang, *Han'guk kajokbŏp ilkki: Chŏntong, shingminjisŏng, chendōŭi kyoch'aroesŏ* [*Reading Korean Family Law: At the Crossroads of Tradition, Coloniality, and Gender*] (Seoul: Ch'angbi, 2011).

Thus understood, the public equality proposition not only vindicates public reason Confucianism's paramount interest in procedural justice and public justification, the aspect it shares with public reason liberalism, but it also shows its deepest moral commitment to the comprehensive democratic good of gender equality, justified with reference to Confucian public reason(ing). One of the central features of the constitutionalism that public reason Confucian gives rise to, what I call *public reason Confucian constitutionalism*, is its dual perfectionist commitments to, on the one hand, liberal constitutional principles, which most East Asian countries formally uphold, though in varying degrees, and Confucian values on the other. Public reason Confucian constitutionalism produces and sustains a coherent public identity of Confucian democratic citizenship by substantiating the moral content of formal, otherwise liberal, constitutional principles and rights with Confucian values on which citizens and public officials draw for their public reasoning, while taking full advantage of core institutional merits of liberal-democratic constitutionalism such as checks and balances and accountability-enhancing mechanisms.

OUTLINE OF THE BOOK

This book consists of three parts, each comprised of two chapters. In Part I, I engage in the philosophical construction of public reason Confucianism, first by defending Confucian democratic perfectionism as a mode of normative Confucianism that is most plausible in East Asia's increasingly pluralist societal context, then by laying out the philosophical outline of public reason Confucianism as a specific kind of Confucian democratic perfectionism that weaves (partial) comprehensive Confucianism and perfectionism in mediation of public reason.

In Chapter 1, I construct and defend Confucian democratic perfectionism by critically engaging with Joseph Chan's moderate political Confucian perfectionism. It should be recalled that Confucian meritocratic perfectionism, to which I present Confucian democratic perfectionism as a normative alternative, has two components – Confucian perfectionism and political meritocracy – and, roughly speaking, Confucian democratic perfectionism embraces the first component, in which Confucianism is generally understood as a comprehensive doctrine, while rejecting the second component because political meritocracy here, more like meritocratic elitism, is justified independently of democratic principles and procedures. Joseph Chan's idea of moderate political Confucian perfectionism is thought-provoking, because it provides an important twist to the first component by decoupling the Confucianism in question from any version of comprehensive Confucianism. Convinced that no comprehensive doctrine is compatible with value pluralism while taking value pluralism seriously, Chan argues that only if Confucian perfectionism is political (i.e., noncomprehensive) can it be *moderate*, that is, compatible with value pluralism. I challenge Chan's core assumption on the incompatibility between moderate perfectionism and comprehensive Confucianism and argue for moderate comprehensive Confucian perfectionism with special focus on the intelligibility condition. My central claim is that in order for (comprehensive) Confucian perfectionism to be moderate, it must embrace as noninstrumentally valuable core values of democracy such as popular sovereignty and political equality.

After articulating my overarching normative vision of Confucian perfectionism, in Chapter 2 I turn to a specific mode of Confucian democratic perfectionism that is most plausible in contemporary pluralist East Asia. I argue that the predicament Confucian perfectionism ineluctably faces with regard to value pluralism can be avoided by making a constellation of Confucian values and goods (i.e., partially comprehensive Confucian perfectionism) constitutive of public reason. First, I explore the political theory of public reason perfectionism as the most proper philosophical mode of democratic perfectionism by critically revisiting John Rawls's political liberalism, one of the most dominant versions of public reason liberalism. Here I take full advantage of Rawls's "inclusive view" of public reason and what he calls *the proviso* stipulated in "The Idea of Public Reason Revisited" and derive public reason perfectionism from Rawls's own insights. In this endeavor, I show that public reason perfectionism shares with public reason liberalism its grave concern with the coerciveness of political power and its strong emphasis on the duty of civility under the fact of pluralism, with the significant difference that public reason perfectionism permits the (democratic) state to promote a set of particular values generally cherished by self-governing citizens or prohibiting values unpalatable to the citizenry's cultural–moral sentiments. Public reason Confucianism, then, is presented as a specific mode of public reason perfectionism most plausible in East Asian societies where citizens are still deeply soaked in Confucian mores, habits, rituals, and moral sentiments, which continue to influence their public reasoning. In addition to public reason Confucianism's two normative premises, this chapter further offers its six propositions: the valuable Confucian way of life (P1), the Confucian habits of the heart in a pluralist society (P2), public equality (P3), democratic pluralism (P4), Confucian public reason (P5), and Confucian legitimacy (P6).

In Part II, I discuss the constitutional implications of public reason Confucianism (especially P3 and P4) with special focus on gender equality, the value that I argue tracks best the most important features of both public equality and democratic citizenship in a Confucian society. Though this part of the work continues to engage in philosophical construction of public reason Confucianism, it differs importantly from Part I in terms of mode of engagement, as the two chapters here aim to illuminate what public reason Confucian constitutionalism (or the constituted dimension of Confucian democratic citizenship) looks like in practice, by examining some landmark court decisions in postdemocratic South Korea.

In Chapter 3, I explore public reason Confucian constitutionalism by critically engaging with the Korean Constitutional Court's decision to scrap the family-head (*hoju*) provision (and other related provisions) from the Korean Civil Code, which has publicly undergirded inequality between men and women, more accurately, between sons and daughters and between husbands and wives. The reason I pay attention to this case is twofold: first, the intense public debate surrounding the constitutionality of the family-head system was precisely about what it means to be a democratic citizen in contemporary Korea's culturally Confucian and politically democratic societal context, and second, the long public reasoning process involved in this case (the Court's jurisprudence in particular), in which traditional Confucian values and practices were ceaselessly negotiated with democratic-constitutional values of gender equality and human dignity, tracks remarkably well the course that public reason Confucianism should take. My central claim in this chapter is that unlike liberal constitutionalism, whose perfectionist aim is to achieve *direct* congruence between the principles of the constitution and the character of citizenship, public reason Confucian constitutionalism realizes the congruence *indirectly* by allowing various sorts of legal, political, and social negotiations between democratic-constitutional democratic principles, rights, and values that the polity formally upholds on the one hand, and Confucian values and goods, to which it is publicly, but not direct-constitutionally, committed, on the other. It is undoubtedly a daunting task to balance dual perfectionist ambitions in a principled way and thereby produce a coherent public identity of Confucian *and* democratic citizenship. I argue nevertheless that public reason Confucianism not only can provide an explanatory framework to make sense of ongoing social, legal, and political practices in East Asia that are neither

Western-style liberal democratic nor traditionalist Confucian, but also can function as what Kant calls a "regulative ideal," to which East Asian societies can normatively aspire and by which their current practices can be evaluated, justified, or criticized.

Chapter 3 demonstrates empirically the critical difference between public reason Confucianism and traditional Confucianism. Simply put, traditional Confucian institutions and practices that critically violate core democratic principles such as gender equality and individual dignity have no place in public reason Confucianism. However, this does not mean that public reason Confucianism is completely decoupled from traditional Confucianism or from the comprehensive moral dimension of Confucianism as a way of life. Chapter 4 illuminates this complex relationship between public reason Confucianism and traditional Confucianism from a philosophical perspective by drawing on Rawls's important but often neglected distinction between *full* and *partial* comprehensive doctrines and attributing full and partial comprehensiveness to traditional and public reason Confucianism respectively. After establishing this important philosophical and conceptual distinction, the chapter then continues to articulate the essential features of public reason Confucianism by engaging with another Korean court case regarding unequal membership between men (sons) and women (daughters) within traditional Confucian clan organizations. This case not only vindicates partial comprehensiveness of public reason Confucianism, attained through discursive negotiations between two – direct-liberal and indirect-Confucian – perfectionist ambitions of a single constitutionalism (i.e., public reason Confucian constitutionalism as a form of democratic constitutionalism), but also articulates how public reason Confucianism at the same time protects the interests of those who persist in various forms of nondemocratic and/or nonliberal associational life (including the traditional Confucian way of life) through the constitutional right to freedom of association, as long as they do not critically encroach upon the constitutional principles and values endorsed by public reason Confucianism. Like the argument of the previous chapter, the argument of this chapter unfolds with special focus on gender equality.

In Part III, I revisit Chan's moderate political Confucian perfectionism from the standpoint of public reason Confucian constitutionalism with special attention to civic virtue. In Chapter 5 I turn to the implications of public reason Confucianism's perfectionist interest in democratic pluralism (P4) for civic virtue and challenge Chan's virtue monism, according to which moral virtue is more effective than civic virtue in making democracy function well and therefore there should be a monistic overlap between moral and civic virtues, allowing no moral value to the latter independent of the former. At the heart of Chan's virtue monism, which stipulates that a good person is naturally a good citizen, are the assumptions that there is a universal moral standard by which to determine the goodness of a person and that there is an equally universal (and simultaneously Confucian) ethical system of moral self-cultivation. The difficulty is how Chan's Confucian virtue monism, which closely tracks traditional Confucian virtue monism, can be compatible with his outright rejection of comprehensive Confucianism. A deeper challenge is how plausible this monistic view of virtue is in a modern constitutional democracy whose society is increasingly pluralist and where citizens have different ideas of a good person. In this chapter, I argue that civic virtue as a set of traits and/ or dispositions that people possess qua citizens is qualitatively, but not conceptually, different from moral virtue that concerns a person qua human being, and it is this sort of virtue that is required in sustaining the Confucian constitutional order as well as developing a Confucian democratic citizenship. Central to my argument is that in a Confucian constitutional polity envisioned from the perspective of public reason Confucianism, there is an important practical distinction between the Confucian virtues (X, Y, Z) that are cherished within traditionalist Confucian associations and moral communities and the conceptually same set of Confucian virtues (x, y, z) that are widely shared and practiced by citizens in general regardless of their associational membership, the virtues that are publicly valuable in the Confucian constitutional polity. Though hardly distinguishable conceptually, the former set of virtues (i.e., moral virtues) is concerned directly with the moral well-being of the members of a particular association and thus subject to differing sectarian conceptualizations, whereas the latter set of virtues (i.e., civic virtues) functions as bridging capital among those who otherwise belong to different moral communities or associations as private individuals and thus is open for public contestation and discursive negotiations. This practical distinction in virtue corresponds with both the philosophical distinction between the traditional fully comprehensive Confucianism and public reason Confucianism that is only partially comprehensive, as well as the institutional distinction between associational membership and Confucian democratic citizenship.

Chapter 6, then, draws attention to one particular civic virtue, namely political participation, and establishes the right to political participation as an indispensable component of public reason Confucianism. I begin with the public equality proposition (P3), the normative foundation of public reason Confucianism, and discuss how its two postulates – political equality and popular sovereignty – combine to justify the right to political participation, making this another crucial postulate of the proposition, without which the constituting dimension of Confucian democratic citizenship can hardly be satisfied. One of the central tasks of this chapter is to justify this right, along with the two other postulates of P3, from a Confucian perspective and my justification proceeds in steps: first by reinterpreting Mencian Confucianism with special focus on Mencius's philosophical commitment to moral equality and human dignity and second by reconstructing Mencian political theory in such a way to be unencumbered by the historical Mencius's lingering allegiance to old aristocratic political ritualism, and thus directly corresponds to his moral philosophy. After deriving the seminal right to political participation from this reconstructed, thus only partially comprehensive, Mencian Confucianism, I then argue that under the circumstances of modern Confucian politics marked by public reason Confucianism's three sociological premises (the republican premise, the political equality premise, and, especially, the value pluralism premise), this right, which has only partial moral justification even in our reconstructed Mencian Confucianism, is fully justified as the best institutional means by which to protect one's moral (and material) interests and address the moral conflict in the process of citizens' collective exercise of coercive political power over themselves. Finally, I highlight the pivotal importance of the right to political participation in carrying out the democratic aspiration of public reason Confucianism, namely the simultaneous satisfaction of the democratic trinity of rule of, by, and for the people.

I conclude this book by anticipating and responding to two critical questions – first, whether public reason Confucianism is too diluted or deracinated a version of Confucianism to be recognizable to self-identified Confucians, and second, whether public reason Confucianism can remain socially relevant even if the public moral consensus, on which it is premised, has become more Western liberal.

PART I

PERFECTIONISM

I

Confucian democratic perfectionism

Roughly speaking, my main concern in this book revolves around the following practical question: how can we justify *in a pluralist democratic society* such public policies or laws as public recognition of and award for "filial (*xiao* 孝) sons and daughters" and "benevolent (*ren* 仁) parents or grandparents," a reduced tax rate for filial adult children who live with and/or economically support their aged parents or grandparents, government subsidies for or priority to such virtuous people in public housing sale/rent, prohibition of filing criminal complaint against one's family members and enhanced punishment for crimes committed against family members, and a court-ordered public apology in the case of defamation or insult – in other words, policies and laws that are morally palatable to Confucian public sentiments? Put differently, how can citizens in pluralist East Asia promote such nonneutral policies and laws while fully embracing democratic values of popular sovereignty, political equality, and the right to political participation; democratic-constitutional principles of individual dignity and gender equality; and core democratic rights such as freedom of expression, freedom of speech, religious freedom, freedom of movement, and freedom of association? In this book, I argue that there is a normative insight that can justify this nonliberal nexus between Confucianism and democracy and capture this insight in terms of Confucian democratic perfectionism.

Having said that, there can be multiple ways to flesh out Confucian democratic perfectionism into a coherent normative political theory and, as noted in the Introduction, my choice is public reason Confucianism in which (partially) comprehensive Confucianism and perfectionism are intertwined by means of public reason. Then, our philosophical challenge lies in (1) clarifying the mode of normative Confucianism, on the one hand, and the type of perfectionism, on the other, that are to be connected and (2) connecting the two in a philosophically convincing and politically attractive way. This is the primary task this and next chapters take up. In the present chapter, I defend my normative idea of Confucian democratic perfectionism by clarifying the appropriate mode of normative Confucianism that is worth perfectionist promotion.

The chapter consists of five main parts. In the following section, I examine the possible modes of normative Confucianism (comprehensive Confucian perfectionism, comprehensive Confucian antiperfectionism, political Confucian perfectionism, and political Confucian antiperfectionism) that are available in Confucian political theory and show that comprehensive Confucian perfectionism alone is the philosophically and politically viable normative position in East Asia's pluralist societies. I then argue that Joseph Chan's recent proposal of moderate political Confucian perfectionism is implausible, despite his important attempt to make Confucian perfectionism *moderate*, that is, compatible with and further accommodating value pluralism. Then, after revisiting Chan's dyadic philosophical framework of "moderate versus extreme" perfectionism and proposing "moderate versus immoderate" comprehensive perfectionism as its alternative, I show why in order for (comprehensive) Confucian perfectionism to be moderate, it must embrace democracy and its underlying principles such as popular sovereignty and political equality as noninstrumentally valuable, thereby justifying Confucian democratic perfectionism. I conclude by laying out my basic idea of Confucian democratic perfectionism as a normative position.

MAPPING NORMATIVE CONFUCIANISM

Though perfectionism commonly refers to a particular normative position in contemporary liberal political theory, as an ethical and political theory positing the objective conception of the human good as well as concerned with the development (or "perfection") of human nature, its long history traces back to Aquinas and Aristotle.[1] In this broad understanding, perfectionism considerably overlaps with virtue ethics, and given that Confucian ethics is generally understood as a sort of virtue ethics (akin

---

[1] Steven Wall, "Perfectionism in Moral and Political Philosophy," *The Stanford Encyclopedia of Philosophy* (Winter 2012 Edition), Edward N. Zalta (ed.), available at http://plato.stanford.edu/archives/win2012/entries/perfectionism-moral/.

to Aristotelian ethics),[2] the identification of Confucianism as perfectionist is hardly surprising.[3] But the fact that perfectionism is associated with various kinds of virtue ethical and political traditions is distinct from the claim that a perfectionist political theory is relevant in modern society. We cannot simply apply ancient perfectionist thought, be it Aristotelian or Confucian, to modern society without considering its drastically altered societal conditions, most notably value pluralism.[4] And of course what we are interested in here is *Confucian perfectionism* as a modern normative theory best suited for contemporary East Asian societies. But before discussing various conceptualizations of Confucian perfectionism of late, let us examine, albeit briefly, how perfectionism is conceptualized in contemporary political theory.[5]

---

[2] Bryan W. Van Norden, *Virtue Ethics and Consequentialism in Early Chinese Philosophy* (New York: Cambridge University Press, 2007); Philip J. Ivanhoe, *Confucian Moral Self Cultivation* (Indianapolis: Hackett, 2000); Jiyuan Yu, *The Ethics of Confucius and Aristotle: Mirrors of Virtue* (London: Routledge, 2007). It is important, however, to note that Confucian virtue ethicists acknowledge important differences between Confucian and Aristotelian forms of virtue ethics in substance. Also worth nothing is that not all modern Confucian scholars understand Confucian ethics as a virtue ethics. For instance, scholars such as Roger Ames and Henry Rosemont Jr. argue that Confucian ethics can be better understood in terms of "role ethics," which posits neither the teleological conception of human nature nor the objective conception of the good. See Roger T. Ames, *Confucian Role Ethics: A Vocabulary* (Honolulu: University of Hawaii Press, 2011); Henry Rosemont Jr., "Rights-Bearing Individuals and Role-Bearing Persons," in *Rules, Rituals, and Responsibility*, ed. Mary I. Bockover (Chicago: Open Court, 1991), pp. 71–101.

[3] In a sense, Confucian perfectionism as a normative political idea and theory is a contemporary reappropriation of Confucian virtue politics (*dezhi* 德治), the core stipulation of which states: a good government founded on the Way (*dao* 道) is predicated on the political actor's personal moral virtue and there is no qualitative difference between the ruler's virtue and the virtue(s) at which the people, equally capable of becoming a sage, the highest Confucian moral ideal, are to ultimately arrive. Of course, whether Confucian meritocracy, the political manifestation of Confucian perfectionism, is faithful to the spirit of original Confucian virtue politics is another matter. On Confucian virtue politics, see Eric L. Hutton, "Character, Situationism, and Early Confucian Thought," *Philosophical Studies* 127 (2006), pp. 37–58.

[4] This is not the only problem. We no longer adhere to the narrow teleological views about human nature that underwrite these theories nor can we tolerate their views about gender. It is not *just* the plurality of values that stands in the way of more perfectionist accounts, though I argue this is one of the most salient *political* challenges. For a powerful argument that draws attention to our modern pluralist societal condition, see Jack Knight and James Johnson, *The Priority of Democracy: Political Consequences of Pragmatism* (Princeton: Princeton University Press, 2011).

[5] It should be noted that though perfectionism is associated with both Western and non-Western ethical traditions, contemporary normative political theory of perfectionism is developed against the liberal philosophical backdrop.

Even in liberal political theory, perfectionism means different things to different people. For instance, some are focused on the perfection of human nature while others are more interested in the promotion of the objective good without associating it with the development of human nature. Still, scholars such as Joseph Chan define perfectionism as "the view that the state should promote valuable conceptions of the good life,"[6] while self-conscious liberal political theorists such as Steven Wall refer to (liberal) perfectionism as "a perfectionist account of political morality that holds that personal autonomy is a central component of human flourishing."[7] Recently, Jonathan Quong has offered the following questions as the litmus test to identify the various normative positions in liberal political theory:

1. Must liberal political philosophy be based in some particular ideal of what constitutes a valuable or worthwhile human life, or other metaphysical belief?
2. Is it permissible for a liberal state to promote or discourage some activities, ideals, or ways of life on grounds relating to their inherent or intrinsic value, or on the basis of other metaphysical claims?[8]

According to Quong, those who answer "yes" to Question 1 are *comprehensive liberals* who believe that there is a particular liberal conception of the good life in which personal autonomy is given a central place. J. S. Mill and Joseph Raz are most representative of this position. On the other hand, those who answer "no" to Question 1 are committed to *political liberalism*. Comprehensive liberals can be either perfectionists or antiperfectionists depending on whether they answer "yes" or "no" to Question 2: *comprehensive perfectionists* answer in the affirmative, believing the state may permissibly aim to promote the good life and discourage harmful ideals, values, or ways of living, while *comprehensive antiperfectionists* answer in the negative, believing that the liberal state must remain neutral between competing conceptions of the good life, though they are also committed to a particular view of human flourishing that gives personal

---

[6] Joseph Chan, "Legitimacy, Unanimity, and Perfectionism," *Philosophy and Public Affairs* 29 (2000), pp. 5–42, p. 5.
[7] Steven Wall, *Liberalism, Perfectionism and Restraint* (Cambridge: Cambridge University Press, 1998), p. 2n3.
[8] Jonathan Quong, *Liberalism without Perfection* (Oxford: Oxford University Press, 2011), p. 15.

autonomy a central place.⁹ Finally, political liberals can also answer "yes" or "no" to Question 2. If the answer is affirmative, then it yields *political perfectionism*, the thesis that "liberalism is not grounded in any particular conception of the good, but that the liberal state can nevertheless justify laws and policies by reference to beliefs about the good life,"[10] while on the other hand the negative answer yields *political antiperfectionism*, which is commonly identified with political liberalism advocated by John Rawls and Charles Larmore.

Quong admits that this matrix does not necessarily cover all the positions available in liberal political theory (e.g., libertarianism and republicanism) and does not discuss how democracy is tied with each liberal normative position, though democracy is obviously compatible with all four liberal positions. Now, let us create a similar type of matrix with reference to Confucianism by substituting "liberal" with "Confucian" in the questions. (We will refer to whether the resulting positions make sense in the Confucian context shortly.) We can then likewise generate four types of normative Confucianism: *comprehensive Confucian perfectionism* ("yes" to both questions), *comprehensive Confucian antiperfectionism* ("yes" to Q1 and "no" to Q2), *political Confucian perfectionism* ("no" to Q1 and "yes" to Q2), and *political Confucian antiperfectionism* ("no" to both). Table 1.1 presents the four types of normative Confuicanism that can be derived from Quong's test. In my view, of these four, only comprehensive Confucian perfectionism can be a plausible normative position. I will first explain why the other three positions cannot be viable options in Confucian political theory.

Comprehensive Confucian antiperfectionism answers "yes" to Q1 but "no" to Q2. Since Confucianism, unlike (though arguably) liberalism, is *already* a self-contained ethical system and a comprehensive doctrine,[11] the answer for Q1 is unavoidably "yes." Otherwise, there would be no

---

[9] Ibid., pp. 15–19. I also consulted Jonathan Quong, "*Liberalism without Perfection*: Replies to Gaus, Colburn, Chan, and Bocchiola," *Philosophy and Public Issues* 2 (2012), pp. 51–79, pp. 58–59.

[10] Quong, *Liberalism without Perfection*, p. 20.

[11] Although scholars such as William A. Galston believe liberalism is ineluctably a comprehensive doctrine and hence perfectionist, however moderate it may be (*Liberal Purposes: Goods, Virtues, and Diversity in the Liberal State* [Cambridge: Cambridge University Press, 1991]), many liberal political theorists (especially neutralist liberals) posit normative liberalism as heavily abstract and theoretical. To my knowledge, there is no Confucian equivalent to the normative *idea* of liberalism that can be either comprehensive or noncomprehensive (i.e., political) and I am not sure whether it is possible (and desirable even if possible) to conceive of Confucianism in a similar way.

TABLE 1.1. *Conceptual Space of Normative Confucianism*

	Comprehensive Confucianism	Political/Noncomprehensive Confucianism
Perfectionism (State Nonneutrality)	Comprehensive Confucian Perfectionism	Political Confucian Perfectionism or Moderate Confucian Perfectionism (Chan)
Antiperfectionism (State Neutrality)	Comprehensive Confucian Antiperfectionism	Political Confucian Antiperfectionism

compelling reason to struggle with Confucian political theory in the East Asian context; East Asians can simply transform themselves into liberal democrats upon regime transition – attitudinally, cognitively, and conatively, as some political scientists assert[12] – and submit themselves to a liberal normative standard. All that comprehensive Confucians claim is that the Confucian ideal constitutes a valuable human life (in East Asia).[13] Then the remaining question is whether comprehensive Confucians can answer "no" to Q2. I do not think they can, because unlike liberals, the perfectionist value (say, filial piety) to which they are *primarily* committed cannot be personal autonomy, the commitment to which is compatible with state neutrality (recall liberal comprehensive antiperfectionism earlier). This does not mean that Confucians are ex ante prevented from making personal autonomy their perfectionist value. My point is that when personal autonomy is given a *central* place in a given, putatively Confucian, normative position, it is difficult to see how it can be called "Confucian" perfectionism.

Political Confucianism (whether perfectionst or antiperfectionist), which answers "no" to Q1, is difficult to maintain for the same reason. Again, when East Asians decided to remain Confucian (whatever this means in practice) in the face of the globalizing force of liberalism, they reaffirmed that *their* Confucian way of life is nonneutrally good or valuable, even when they embrace liberal democratic institutions for political reasons. In other words, their decision to remain Confucian is already a perfectionist

---

[12] See, for example, Doh Chull Shin, *Confucianism and Democratization in East Asia* (New York: Cambridge University Press, 2012).

[13] "East Asia" is in brackets because *from the comprehensive Confucians' standpoint* Confucian values are universally good beyond East Asia, though quite often their otherwise universal horizon is limited to a particular Confucian society of their interest.

decision.[14] As long as they identify themselves as Confucian, it is impossible to be perfectly neutral in regard to other competing values, hence the implausibility of antiperfectionism. As a candidate normative position, therefore, political Confucianism has no substantive meaning.

Thus understood, it is no coincidence that most proposals for Confucian meritocracy are predicated on comprehensive Confucian perfectionism. Let me reproduce the three core perfectionist stipulations in the existing studies on Confucian meritocracy introduced at the beginning of this book:

1. Confucian ethics is a kind of perfectionist ethics that assumes the existence of the objectively good life and thus aims for moral perfection of the people.
2. Given the inseparability between Confucian ethics and politics, the supreme goal of Confucian politics lies in promoting the objectively good life (as stipulated in Confucian ethics) as well as securing socioeconomic conditions that enable such a life.
3. Therefore the state in a Confucian polity is morally authorized to promote a particular (Confucian) conception of the good life in a noncoercive way.

Let us call these stipulations S1, S2, and S3, respectively. S1 shows that advocates of Confucian meritocracy answer "yes" to Q1, which makes them *comprehensive* Confucians. S2 justifies the promotion of the Confucian way of life which is nonneutrally good and supplements S1 by stressing the importance of socioeconomic conditions that enable a good life.[15] Finally, S3 reveals that Confucian meritocrats answer "yes" to Q2,

---

[14] For a similar reason, William Galston criticizes Rawls's political liberalism. According to Galston, political liberalism's core stipulations make us unable to form evaluative judgments about different regime types (or ways of life) because public reason is parasitic on liberal democracy, and thus cannot be used by those who question the very regime. See William A. Galston, *Liberal Pluralism: The Implications of Value Pluralism for Political Theory and Practice* (Cambridge: Cambridge University Press, 2002), p. 44.

[15] It is not clear whether S2 is integral to perfectionist political theory in general, although some liberal perfectionists show a deep concern for the socioeconomic conditions enabling a good life. See, for example, Chris Mills, "Can Liberal Perfectionism Generate Distinctive Distributive Principles?" *Philosophy and Public Issues* 2 (2012), pp. 123–152. It is worth noting that Confucian political theorists (mostly perfectionists, I believe) have long struggled with S2. See Daniel A. Bell, "Confucian Constraints on Property Rights," and Joseph Chan, "Giving Priority on the Worst Off: A Confucian Perspective on Social Welfare," both in *Confucianism for the Modern World*, eds. Daniel A. Bell and Chaibong Hahm (Cambridge: Cambridge University Press, 2003), pp. 218–235 and 236–253, respectively. Also see Joseph Chan, "Is There a Confucian Perspective on Social Justice?" in *Western Political Thought in Dialogue with Asia*, eds. Takashi Shogimen and Cary J. Nederman (Lanham: Lexington Books, 2008), pp. 261–277; Ruiping Fan, *Reconstructionist Confucianism: Rethinking Morality after the West* (Dordrecht:

making them comprehensive Confucian *perfectionists*. Among Confucian meritocrats, Ruiping Fan advances the most coherently comprehensive Confucian perfectionist argument. Consider the following statement:

> Confucian moral and political thought ... emphasizes that every individual learn the virtues (such as *xiao, ren, yi, zhi, xin, zhong*, and *he*) by observing ritual (*li*) (i.e., a series of familial and social norms, ceremonies and patterns) affirmed by the tradition. ... A good Confucian polity inevitably involves substantive Confucian moral and political norms that provide specific guidance as to how rulers should rule. Without engaging such norms, it is impossible to offer an adequate account of Confucian meritocracy, because they are at least needed to inform what "merit" is precisely for a Confucian meritocracy.[16]

The perfectionist value in which Fan is particularly interested is filial piety (*xiao*) and the good life that he claims the state (i.e., the Confucian state) should promote is a family-oriented way of life:

> [A]n essential component of human well-being consists in developing and maintaining an appropriate family-based and family-oriented way of life, which has been sustained by Confucian virtues and rituals. This way of life is not only family-based in the sense that Confucian society is composed of the family as the primary and permanent human community; it is also family-oriented in the sense that the telos of Confucian society is to promote the integrity, continuity, and prosperity of the family.[17]

Though it is certainly an exaggeration to say that all existing proposals for Confucian meritocracy perfectly conform to the three core stipulations of Confucian perfectionism, and though there is no consensus among Confucian political theorists as to precisely which Confucian values constitute the essence of the good life and thus should be promoted in the Confucian polity, it is not far-fetched to say that comprehensive Confucian perfectionism is the most salient normative position undergirding the recent proposals for Confucian meritocracy.[18]

Springer, 2010), chap. 6. Among Confucian political theorists, Chan is only one who self-consciously presents S2 from the Confucian perfectionist perspective. See his *Confucian Perfectionism*, pp. 160–190.

[16] Ruiping Fan, "Confucian Meritocracy for Contemporary China," in *East Asian Challenge for Democracy*, pp. 88–115, p. 88.

[17] Ibid., p. 100. Also see Fan, *Reconstructionist Confucianism*, pp. 95–98.

[18] Though scholars such as Jiang Qing and Tongdong Bai consciously pursue more directly "political" Confucianism not implicated with metaphysical elements in early Confucianism (e.g., the right account of human nature) as a proper mode of Confucian political theory in contemporary China, they do not deny the core Confucian ethical idea that humans ought to be good and that the quintessential role of the state is to promote the good life. See Jiang Qing, *Zhengzhi Ruxue: Dangdai Rujia de zhuanxiang, tezhi yu*

JOSEPH CHAN'S MODERATE POLITICAL CONFUCIAN PERFECTIONISM

Seen in this way, Joseph Chan's idea of moderate political Confucian perfectionism is surprising as well as counterintuitive – surprising because as the only Confucian political theorist who frames his normative position explicitly in terms of Confucian perfectionism,[19] he prefers political Confucian perfectionism to comprehensive Confucian perfectionism; counterintuitive because, as noted earlier, political Confucian perfectionism is an implausible position (for East Asian citizens) to take. How, then, does Chan justify his normative position? To make full sense of Chan's political theory of Confucian perfectionism, we should revisit his earlier work on *moderate perfectionism*.

Chan's preferred mode of perfectionism, defined as the view that "the state should promote valuable conceptions of the good life," is *political perfectionism*. Recall that, according to Quong's litmus test, political perfectionism is a normative position that answers "no" to Q1 and "yes" to Q2. However, Chan's position is quite ambiguous in light of this test. Clearly, Chan answers in the affirmative to Q2, and this is how he defines the very concept of perfectionism. But his attitude toward Q1 is not clear. Chan seems to say that (political) perfectionists do not have to posit the existence of an objective good and that the good life promoted by the state does not have to be metaphysically or comprehensively good. Put differently, the good in question does not have to be understood in terms of what Rawls calls a comprehensive doctrine.

According to Chan, conceptions of the good life not only involve judgments about *ways of life* or comprehensive doctrines but also judgments about *agency goods* (virtues or dispositions that constitute the good life) and/or *prudential goods* (goods or values that contribute to a person's good life). Chan argues that while judgments about ways of life

---

fazhan [*Political Confucianism: Contemporary Confucianism's Challenge, Special Quality, and Development*] (Beijing: San lian shu dian, 2003); Tongdong Bai, *Jiubang Xinming: Gujin zhongxi canzhaoxia de gudian Rujia zhengzhizhexue* [*A New Mission of an Old State: The Contemporary and Comparative Relevance of Classical Confucian Political Philosophy*] (Beijing: Beijing daxue chbanshe, 2009).

[19] Recall that the title of Chan's recent book is *Confucian Perfectionism: A Political Philosophy for Modern Times*. Without calling himself a Confucian perfectionist, Stephen Angle, too, embraces the version of state perfectionism advanced by Chan. See Stephen C. Angle, *Contemporary Confucian Political Philosophy: Toward Progressive Confucianism* (Cambridge: Polity, 2012), pp. 140–141; *Sagehood: The Contemporary Significance of Neo-Confucian Philosophy* (New York: Oxford University Press, 2009), pp. 204–209.

(a person's overall pattern of living, which involves the two other goods) are controversial and susceptible to moral debate and political contestation, judgments about the other goods are not incommensurable across different moral communities, hence less controversial.[20] What this implies is that Rawls's celebrated phrase "political, not metaphysical" fatally glosses over a middle ground that is neither purely political, concerned solely with the public conception of justice, nor comprehensive, which "covers all basic aspects of human life, organiz[ing], rank[ing], and balanc[ing] values in a more or less coherent manner,"[21] and in which noncomprehensive goods can be viable resources for the state's nonneutral engagement with individuals as well as associations in civil society. Thus understood, Chan's response to Q1 is a qualified "no" – or rather, "no" if what is meant by "a valuable or worthwhile human life" are comprehensive ways of life, but "yes" if it means noncomprehensive goods (i.e., agency goods or prudential goods). Chan calls this particular mode of (political) perfectionism *moderate perfectionism*, distinguishing it from *extreme perfectionism* that is nothing other than comprehensive perfectionism in Quong's typology.[22]

It is important to note that when Chan introduced the notion of moderate perfectionism in his 2000 essay, he did not discuss how it can be manifested in the Confucian context, which is his main concern in his recent book *Confucian Perfectionism*, as well as most of his philosophical writings of the past decade.[23] Like most philosophical literature in liberal political theory, Chan's earlier essay is highly abstract and contextless, making others (certainly Quong) believe he was contributing to liberal perfectionist theory.[24] This issue is worth noting because political perfectionism makes good sense in the liberal philosophical context precisely because the state can permissibly promote some activities, traits, and types of relationships that are inherently valuable without positing metaphysical essentialism with regard to either human nature or the

---

[20] Chan, "Legitimacy, Unanimity, and Perfectionism," pp. 11–12.   [21] Ibid., p. 13.

[22] Other constitutive elements of moderate perfectionism include (1) objection to political liberalism's asymmetric treatments of disagreements about the good life and disagreements about the principles of justice and (2) rejection of the dichotomy of state and civil society.

[23] Note that at least four essays published in the 2000s are incorporated as chapters into Chan's recent book.

[24] Quong, *Liberalism without Perfection*, p. 21; "Replies," p. 66 (calling him "an innovative and leading proponent of liberal perfectionism"). Also see Franz F. L. Mang, "Liberal Neutrality and Moderate Perfectionism," *Res Publica* 19:4 (2013), pp. 297–315.

conception of the good.[25] And since political liberal perfectionism's answer to Q1 is always a qualified "no" (embracing valuable traits, activities, or relationships while rejecting the comprehensive ideal of the good life), the result is necessarily moderate perfectionism.

Perfectionism cannot be moderate in Chan's intended sense, however, when it is associated with a particular comprehensive ideal or philosophical doctrine such as Confucianism. Though Chan sees no dilemma here (hence his advocacy of moderate political Confucian perfectionism), there is one and its two horns are:

1. Moderate perfectionism as a sort of political perfectionism is only plausible when it is not tied to any comprehensive conception of the good life – thus plausible only in the context of political liberalism. ("No" to Q1.)
2. Confucianism, *for it to be identified intelligibly as such*, cannot but be a sort of comprehensive doctrine. (The intelligibility condition.)

The idea that in order for moderate political Confucian perfectionism (or any Confucian perfectionism, for that matter) to have a normative standing Confucianism must be *identified intelligibly as such* is an important proviso – what I called in the Introduction "the intelligibility condition." Otherwise, a highly idiosyncratic notion of Confucianism might be problematically affiliated with moderate political perfectionism, preconceived independently of the real Confucianism (however we make sense of it philosophically) affirmed in tradition, and endorsed and practiced by East Asians. Does Chan neglect this problem? Does he have a robust case for moderate political Confucian perfectionism? Or can Confucianism be reconstructed as noncomprehensive without forfeiting its philosophical and public intelligibility? Consider the following passage in which Chan summarizes his philosophical project succinctly and empathetically.

The Confucian perfectionism in political philosophy and politics that I espouse thus takes the form of moderate perfectionism. As a moral philosophy Confucianism may develop its conception of the good life comprehensively and rigorously. However, as a political or public philosophy for modern times, this conception should not be derived from a comprehensive doctrine of the good. It should offer a list of items that constitute the good life and good social order – such as valuable social relationships, practical wisdom and learning, sincerity, harmony, social and

---

[25] This is George Sher's view, another political perfectionist according to Quong. See his *Beyond Neutrality: Perfectionism and Politics* (Cambridge: Cambridge University Press, 1997), pp. 18–19.

political trust and care, moral and personal autonomy, and economic sufficiency and self-responsibility – and explore the implications of these items for social and political arrangements. ... Moderate perfectionism requires us to justify Confucian values in terms that do not require prior acceptance of Confucianism, and that can be shared by others who do not necessarily accept other elements within Confucianism.[26]

The last sentence explains why Chan prefers moderate political perfectionism over comprehensive Confucian perfectionism and what he means by *moderate*. Given the unique modern societal conditions characterized most notably by value pluralism, Chan believes comprehensive Confucian perfectionism cannot offer a viable normative framework under which non-Confucian values can flourish. This preference, if political Confucian perfectionism were possible, is perhaps a reasonable position to take, but whether it is the only option for a modern Confucian political theorist is questionable and a topic I will revisit later. The question here is whether the Confucianism Chan has in mind can meet the intelligibility proviso.

Chan's Confucianism consists of a list of *items* that constitute the good life and good social order, including "valuable social relationships, practical wisdom and learning, sincerity, harmony, social and political trust and care, moral and personal autonomy, and economic sufficiency and self-responsibility." Following Edward Shils,[27] Chan calls these items *civility* and attaches this concept exclusively to moderate political Confucian perfectionism: "Promoting Confucianism as a comprehensive doctrine is, I believe, undesirable because it damages civility. ... Confucianism as a comprehensive doctrine constitutes a form of ideological politics that must be rejected if we regard civility as an important virtue."[28] But on what grounds are these items *Confucian* values? Chan may respond that all of those traits, virtues, and relationships are amply found in Confucian classics, and that there is no reason to believe they are not Confucian. Certainly, if we understand the items of civility or good traits, characters, and/or relationships in generic terms, they do seem harmonious with Confucianism. And as Shils acknowledges, Confucianism is a civil tradition by any standard.[29]

---

[26] Chan, *Confucian Perfectionism*, pp. 203–204.
[27] Edward Shils, *The Virtue of Civility: Selected Essays on Liberalism, Tradition, and Civil Society*, ed. Steven Grosby (Indianapolis: Liberty Fund, 1997).
[28] Chan, *Confucian Perfectionism*, p. 201.
[29] Edward Shils, "Reflections on Civil Society and Civility in the Chinese Intellectual Tradition," in *Confucian Traditions in East Asian Modernity: Moral Education and Economic Culture in Japan and Four Mini-Dragons*, ed. Tu Wei-ming (Cambridge: Harvard University Press, 1996), pp. 38–71. Notice, however, that the Confucian tradition Shils has in mind is undeniably a *comprehensive* philosophical, cultural, and intellectual system.

However, this line of reasoning has two major problems. First, the fact that a particular set of civilities (generally understood with reference to [liberal] civility literature) is found in Confucian classics does not make them *Confucian civilities*, in the absence of a compelling philosophical justification of what renders civil traits, activities, or relationships intelligibly Confucian. For example, what valuable social relationships consist of can be understood vastly differently across different cultural traditions. There is no reason to believe, for example, that Kantian deontology and Confucian virtue ethics stand for the same values and principles of moral autonomy. What appears to be a trivial difference at first glance can lead to a world of difference when considering the whole cluster of one's personal and social life. In fact, the recent fascination among students of comparative philosophy is in large part studying how values (such as love and friendship) whose generic meanings are widely shared hold different meanings across cultures. It might be possible to identify intrinsically valuable traits, activities, or relationships and make a case for political perfectionism *against the broader liberal societal backdrop*, as George Sher and Chan (in his earlier essay) do, even though it remains controversial whether such perfectionist goods can be completely severed from the comprehensive idea of the good life.[30] However, it is not at all clear why or in what sense one can call such a normative position focused on good traits and civilities Confucian-perfectionist. Chan makes the controversial claim that "as a political or public philosophy for modern times, [the Confucian] conception [of the good life] should not be derived from a comprehensive doctrine of the good," but he fails to construct a philosophically intelligible notion of *political Confucianism*. While discussing some items that can contribute to a good life, his theory of Confucian perfectionism renders the very idea of the good life too ambiguous. One of the consequences of this ambiguity is the massive blurring of the meaningful difference between Confucian and liberal perfectionism.[31]

---

[30] To the extent that political liberal perfectionism and comprehensive liberal perfectionism self-consciously contribute to distinctively liberal political theory, it is always ambiguous whether political liberal perfectionism can be completely insulated from comprehensive liberalism – hence Quong's qualified attribution of political (liberal) perfectionism to Sher and Chan (Quong, *Liberalism without Perfection*, p. 21). In contrast, its distinction from political liberal antiperfectionism (viz., Rawls's political liberalism) is very clear.

[31] Apparently, Chan is aware of the potential caveats of his idea of moderate political Confucian perfectionism when he says, "One may wonder to what extent a society can be called 'Confucian' if the legislative and policy-making process is guided by moderate perfectionism. The answer is that the actual extent of Confucian influence in a society will and always should be determined by the continuous process of democratic discussion and policy making over time. Just as human society is always changing, so should

The second problem is that irrespective of whether a set of items contributing to a putatively good life can be selectively pulled from Confucianism, Chan's attempt to put civility at the center of his moderate political Confucian perfectionism is likely to reintroduce the state neutrality that he set out to overcome in the first place. Again, Chan is attracted to the normative force of civility given the increasing challenge of value pluralism.

> In modern pluralistic societies, citizens live according to various ways of life and beliefs, including different religions. Civility is of crucial importance for this kind of society. Civility is the attitude of fellow citizens toward each other that shows a concern for the *common bond* despite differing opinions or conflicts of interest. Civility tries to diminish conflict by seeking *common ground* underlying opposing opinions and a *common good* transcending partisan interests. To seek a common ground and a common good, civility requires citizens to be open-minded, to justify opinions with reasons that others can share, to attempt to limit the extent and depth of moral disagreement, and to be willing to make compromises if full agreement cannot be achieved.[32]

There is no objection to the statement itself. However, recall that perfectionism occupies a unique position in contemporary (particularly liberal) political theory because it gives a justification to a normative position that permits the (liberal) state to promote valuable conceptions of the good life without inhibiting the exercise of personal autonomy and encroaching value pluralism, which, for some liberal thinkers, is an impossibility given the compulsive nature of the state.[33] Furthermore, John Rawls too objects to liberal perfectionism ("ethical liberalism" as he calls it), a la Joseph Raz and Ronald Dworkin, precisely because it holds that there is "but one conception of the good to be recognized by all citizens who are fully reasonable and rational." In this view, political philosophy is "always viewed as part of moral philosophy, together with theology and metaphysics," and its aim is merely to "determine [the] nature and content" of that conception.[34] Implicit here is the judgment that no comprehensive doctrine, including liberal perfectionism, is genuinely compatible with value pluralism. Interestingly, though critical of Rawls and political

---

Confucianism" (Chan, *Confucian Perfectionism*, p. 204). However, it is difficult to understand how this statement *answers* the question raised earlier.

[32] Ibid., p. 201 (emphases in original).

[33] See Michael Oakeshott, *On Human Conduct* (Oxford: Clarendon 1975), pp. 314–316.

[34] Rawls, *Political Liberalism* (New York: Columbia University Press, 1993), pp. 134–135. Of course, whether or not Rawls's understanding of Raz's and Dworkin's views on value pluralism is correct is another matter.

liberalism in general, this is the view that Chan also subscribes to, although he never clearly distinguishes his perfectionist position from that of Raz.[35] All the more interesting and ironic is that by making civility the centerpiece of his perfectionist theory, understood as aiming for a *common bond, common good, common ground*, and *shared reason* to which all citizens must subscribe, Chan turns out to have much more in common with public reason liberals such as Rawls than perfectionists such as Raz, and especially Steven Wall. Let me explain.

The reason Rawls finds perfectionism implausible in the post-Reformation world is what he calls "the burdens of judgment" faced by all reasonable citizens in a free society. According to Rawls, moral disagreement is neither a regrettable result of social conflict nor mere irrationality, but rather a pervasive feature of modern pluralist society in which there is no privileged epistemic standard or a prepolitical consensus, or an independent ground on which we may arbitrate our differences.[36] The disagreement is reasonable in the sense that its sources are "the many hazards involved in the correct (and conscientious) exercise of our powers of reason and judgment in the ordinary course of political life."[37] In short, reasonable disagreement is the disagreement among reasonable people who are conscious of the epistemic limits and fallibility of one's judgment, and acknowledge that others can reasonably disagree with them regarding moral, religious, and philosophical questions – namely, comprehensive doctrines. For Rawls, under the fact of reasonable pluralism, enduring free institutions are only possible if the same political conception of justice, concerning the constitutional essentials and basic structure, is agreed upon among citizens through an overlapping consensus and by use of public reason.

From this short recapitulation of Rawls's idea of reasonable pluralism (or reasonable disagreement), two points can be gleaned that present

---

[35] In fact, Chan occasionally draws on Raz, a notable champion of comprehensive liberal perfectionism, when critiquing neutralist liberals including Rawls. See Chan, "Legitimacy, Unanimity, and Perfectionism," pp. 6n3 and 18n25.

[36] Jeremy Waldron aptly calls plurality in opinions and the resulting moral disagreement "the elementary circumstance of modern politics" (*Law and Disagreement* [Oxford: Oxford University Press, 1999], p. 144). Also see Benjamin R. Barber, *Strong Democracy: Participatory Politics for a New Age* (Berkeley: University of California Press, 1984); Amy Gutmann and Dennis Thompson, *Democracy and Disagreement* (Cambridge: Belknap Press, 1996); and Knight and Johnson, *The Priority of Democracy*, for similar descriptions of the *condition* of democratic politics.

[37] Rawls, *Political Liberalism*, p. 56. On this page and next Rawls provides a list (albeit incomplete) of the sources of reasonable disagreement.

Rawls's political liberalism as antiperfectionist: (1) consensus on public good can be attained through a deliberative process in which citizens give each other reasons that they can mutually agree upon; (2) on matters of constitutional essentials and basic justice, the basic structure and its public policies are to be justifiable to all citizens and thus the state can exercise its public authority (especially when it interferes with an individual citizen's private life or the internal affairs of a particular association joined by individuals as members who enjoy the constitutional right to freedom of association) by giving reasonable citizens a justifiable reason in light of public reason. Let us call these the *reciprocity condition* and the *justification condition*, respectively.

Chan takes issue with the core stipulations implicated in political liberalism's justification condition, according to which the state is not authorized to promote a particular conception of the good life (that can be deemed by reasonable citizens as an imposition or at least paternalistic, if not outright coercive) and its public action must be morally justified to reasonable citizens who hold different comprehensive doctrines,[38] while embracing its reciprocity condition, according to which citizens must be epistemically charitable (given the burdens of judgment) and seek principles that others could accept.[39] Indeed, Chan's idea of reciprocity in terms of shared reasons justifiable to citizens who have moral disagreements, which he believes is indispensable to achieving a common bond and common ground in a pluralist society, has a striking resemblance to what Rawls calls the *duty of civility*: "[S]ince the exercise of political power itself must be legitimate, the ideal of citizenship imposes a moral, not a legal duty – the duty of civility – to be able to explain to one another on those fundamental questions how the principles and policies they advocate and vote for can be supported by the political values of public reason. This duty also involves a willingness to listen to others and a fair-mindedness in deciding when accommodations to their views should reasonably be made."[40]

The problem is that, as Steven Wall convincingly notes, the duty of civility is independent of moral content. Often, Confucian perfectionists (in this case comprehensive Confucian perfectionists) have a particular set of *Confucian* traits, virtues, or relationships in mind, such as filial piety – again, not any

---

[38] Chan, "Legitimacy, Unanimity, and Perfectionism," pp. 16–22.
[39] For these two components of the reciprocity condition see Wall, *Liberalism, Perfectionism and Restraint*, p. 73.
[40] Rawls, *Political Liberalism*, p. 217.

generic notion of filial piety but the filial piety (*xiao*) that is intelligibly Confucian – when they espouse Confucian perfectionism as their normative theory, which has direct implications for numerous other political questions.[41] Given the valorization of filial piety as the perfectionist good: is family welfarism preferable to state welfarism? Should abortion be legally protected? Should same-sex marriage be prohibited? Suppose the same Confucian state also promotes harmony (*he*) as a valuable social relationship (as the state of China currently does). Again, the following political questions inevitably arise: to what extent should freedom of expression be tolerated? What kinds of associations are prohibited or protected? What constitutes defamation or libel? Following Wall, we can call these considerations *content considerations*.[42] While the normative attraction of perfectionism lies in its capacity to offer a principled answer to these otherwise controversial moral and political questions, surprisingly, Chan's *civility consideration*, focused on common bond, common ground, common good, and shared reasons, has almost nothing to say about them.

This is not to argue that the civility consideration cannot accommodate perfectionism. The point I want to make is that if, as Chan argues, the civility consideration has priority over content considerations, not only does the normative theory in question lose its perfectionist quality, but more problematically (insomuch as the theory declares itself to be perfectionist), it ends up being more akin to liberal neutrality. Wall criticizes Rawls's political liberalism precisely on this ground: "[I]f the civility consideration has priority over all other considerations, then it is not possible for us to ask the question we want to ask: Is it permissible for the Reds to impose sound principles on the Greens even though the Greens could reasonably reject them? ... But notice that this is just another way of saying that the correct principles of justice simply are the principles that no one could reasonably reject; and it is precisely this claim that we are seeking to evaluate."[43]

Seen in this way, Chan's idea of moderate political Confucian perfectionism has difficulty in standing as a robust normative political theory. Not only can it not be completely severed from comprehensive Confucianism (as long as it wants to be intelligently Confucian both philosophically

---

[41] Interestingly, Chan includes "filial piety and familial relationships" as items that the (Confucian) state should promote as they "constitute the good life and the good social order" but he never struggles with the political implications of the perfectionist promotion of such *Confucian* values. See Joseph Chan, "On the Legitimacy of Confucian Constitutionalism," in Jiang, *Confucian Constitutional Order*, pp. 99–112, p. 102.
[42] Wall, *Liberalism, Perfectionism and Restraint*, p. 79.   [43] Ibid., p. 80.

and culturally), but it also cannot make civility its core because it then verges on neutralist liberalism, to which it objects. Within the normative framework of Confucian perfectionism, the civility considerations can have priority over others *only if* they are Confucian considerations in the substantive sense, that is, *only if* they are simultaneously content considerations. Therefore, I conclude that comprehensive Confucian perfectionism is the only plausible mode of normative Confucianism.

"MODERATE VERSUS EXTREME" REVISITED

Let me recapitulate the core theses of Joseph Chan's moderate political Confucian perfectionism: (1) as a political philosophy for modern times, Confucian perfectionism should not be predicated on the comprehensive Confucian doctrine of the good but must be a kind of moderate political perfectionism; (2) as a moderate political perfectionism, Confucian perfectionism should offer a list of items that constitute the good life and good social order and allow the state to promote them in a piecemeal way; and (3) given the fact of pluralism, the items that the (Confucian) state is permitted to promote are a set of civilities composed of good traits, virtues, and relationships (i.e., agency or prudential goods). What underlie these core claims are the problematic assumptions that *any* comprehensive doctrine, including Confucianism, is incompatible with the fact of pluralism and that the virtue of civility is possible only if the comprehensiveness of the given moral, religious, or philosophical doctrine is reconstructed into a moderate political perfectionism.[44] These assumptions enable Chan to subscribe to an equally problematic presumption that comprehensive perfectionism, which in his view is none other than ideological politics in the sense that Edward Shils understands it, is ineluctably committed to what he calls *extreme perfectionism*. Consider Chan's definition of extreme perfectionism with reference to Confucianism:

Extreme perfectionism says that the state should adopt a comprehensive doctrine of the good life as the basis of state constitution, legislation, and policy. Following John Rawls, by "comprehensive doctrine" I mean those conceptions of the good life that involve systematic theorization about human life: they explain why certain things are good to human life, rank those goods into a certain hierarchy,

---

[44] Chan says, "Confucianism as a comprehensive doctrine constitutes a form of ideological politics that must be rejected if we regard civility as an important virtue" (*Confucian Perfectionism*, p. 201).

specify concrete ways to realize those goods, and tie them to a tradition of thought that is distinct from, and in conflict with, other traditions. Traditional Confucianism did contain a comprehensive conception of the good life understood in this sense.[45]

Chan's notion of extreme perfectionism is best suited for critiquing Christian or Islamic theocracy or any religious fundamentalism, or (the extreme version of) what Michael Oakeshott calls "the politics of faith."[46] In addition, Chan criticizes Jiang Qing's recent proposal of political Confucianism in which Confucianism is presented as a state-established religion, representing the entirety of Chinese civilization,[47] precisely because it attempts something akin to Christian or Islamic constitutionalism.[48] But is it fair to say that Ruiping Fan's Confucian perfectionism, which according to Chan's taxonomy is a form of extreme perfectionism, is as extreme as Jiang's Confucian fundamentalism, even though Fan's major concern is with the public promotion of family virtues and familial relationships? Chan's sweeping criticism of the whole category of comprehensive Confucianism notwithstanding, comprehensive Confucianism is internally diverse and some versions of it – especially what I call *public reason Confucianism* in this book – can be more hospitable to pluralism than others.

The problem with defining extreme perfectionism in terms of its association with *any* comprehensive doctrine is even clearer once we apply the notion to comprehensive liberal perfectionism of the kind advanced by Joseph Raz and Steven Wall, a perfectionism associated with the comprehensive value of autonomy.[49] Comprehensive liberal perfectionism is compatible with value pluralism but it in no way promotes something

---

[45] Chan, "On the Legitimacy," p. 101.
[46] Michael Oakeshott, *The Politics of Faith and the Politics of Scepticism*, ed. Timothy Fuller (New Haven: Yale University Press, 1996).
[47] Jiang says that "in past, present and future, Confucianism is destined to be practiced; it has to establish its principles, justify its order, materialize its ideal, and finally build a ritual-political system that manifests the nature and principles of the way of heaven" (Jiang, *Zhengzhi Ruxue*, p. 37; reprinted from Chan, "On the Legitimacy," p. 103).
[48] Jiang says, "Confucian constitutionalism is the only thing that can respond to Christian or Islamic constitutionalism because in both these cases 'Christian' and 'Islamic' refer to civilizations formed in history and culture and not to mere schools of thought alone" (Jiang, *Confucian Constitutional Order*, p. 217n5). For a similar criticism of Jiang's Confucian constitutionalism, see Angle, *Contemporary Confucian Political Philosophy*, pp. 31–33.
[49] Joseph Raz, *The Morality of Freedom* (Oxford: Clarendon Press, 1986).

TABLE 1.2. *Chan's Dyadic Framework*

	Comprehensive	Political/Noncomprehensive
Perfectionism (State Nonneutrality)	Extreme Perfectionism → Is comprehensive liberal perfectionism a la Raz or comprehensive liberal antiperfectionism a la Dworkin extreme?	Moderate Perfectionism

like "liberal fundamentalism" if such a thing is even possible.[50] While moderate political perfectionism is intelligible only in the form of normative liberalism, extreme perfectionism, its dyadic counterpart, is completely irrelevant in liberal perfectionist theory from which illiberal perfectionist ends that are potentially in tension with the value of autonomy are precluded in the first place.[51]

As such, Chan's dyadic framework of "moderate versus extreme perfectionism," as shown in Table 1.2, cannot, in a philosophically meaningful way, come to terms with comprehensive liberal perfectionism with an equal force, and this leads us to conclude that there is something truly odd about this framework. At the minimum, it is inherently biased against all kinds of *nonliberal* forms of perfectionism, which are ineluctably comprehensive, however "moderate" they are in a nontechnical sense. In noting this problem in Chan's theory, my point is simply that there is no prima facie reason to suppose that comprehensive Confucian perfectionism is inherently at odds with value pluralism and personal autonomy, or incompatible with civility. Just as civility is an integral element of normative liberalism, comprehensive or otherwise, it also constitutes the backbone of normative Confucianism, which is comprehensive, both philosophically and culturally. It is true that by virtue of civility a comprehensive philosophical doctrine or culture becomes moderate, but there

---

[50] The same is true of comprehensive liberal antiperfectionism as well. See Ben Colburn, *Autonomy and Liberalism* (New York: Routledge, 2010).

[51] In this regard, consider Eamonn Callan's following statement: "[A]lthough it might make sense to talk of a comprehensive Islam or Christian politics, on some but not all interpretations of Islam and Christianity, the centrality of individual freedom to any recognizably liberal polity is incompatible with a comprehensibly enforced ordering of values" (*Creating Citizens: Political Education and Liberal Democracy* [Oxford: Oxford University Press, 1997], p. 18).

is no monolithic idea of civility. There are only many different *conceptions* of civility.

In the remainder of this chapter, I explore a mode of moderate comprehensive Confucian perfectionism, what I call *Confucian democratic perfectionism*, that is most attractive as a normative ideal in pluralist East Asian societies of Confucian heritage, by critically engaging with some of the existing proposals for Confucian meritocratic perfectionism that in my view fail in their attempts to accommodate value pluralism.

MODERATE CONFUCIAN PERFECTIONISM: TOWARD DEMOCRATIC PERFECTIONISM

Though the dyadic framework of "moderate versus extreme" perfectionism is not so meaningful in the context of normative liberalism, it is still relevant when it comes to (comprehensive) Confucian perfectionism.[52] That said, since extreme Confucian perfectionism a la Jiang Qing is normatively unattractive for obvious reasons,[53] I argue that a more relevant criterion to evaluate the normative attractiveness of a particular mode of Confucian perfectionism is whether it is moderate or immoderate in the sense employed by Joseph Chan – that is, how well it can accommodate value pluralism and the resulting moral disagreement. I find most proposals for Confucian perfectionism advanced thus far "immoderate" because of the two arguments underlying the three core perfectionist stipulations (S1, S2, and S3) of Confucian meritocracy, which I introduced earlier. They were

(1) Democracy is either (largely) instrumentally valuable or altogether unimportant as long as the perfectionist ends are promoted by the state without the use of violence or illegitimate coercion.
(2) The key agents of state perfectionism are "leaders with superior ability and virtue."

Let us call them A1 and A2, respectively. Most proponents of Confucian meritocratic perfectionism subscribe to these, explicitly or not. Consider

---

[52] Unless noted otherwise, by "Confucian perfectionism" I generally mean comprehensive Confucian perfectionism.
[53] See Sungmoon Kim, "Oakeshott and Confucian Constitutionalism," in *Michael Oakeshott's Cold War Liberalism*, ed. Terry Nardin (New York: Palgrave Macmillan, 2015), pp. 133–150.

the following statement by Chenyang Li, which I believe sums up most clearly what these scholars have in common, albeit in varying degrees.

Confucian proportional equality in politics on the basis of talents and virtue comes with political inequalities. Confucians are not in favor of extending political inequality for the sake of inequality. Some inequalities are appropriate, however, because they are not only inevitable in achieving proportional equality, but they are also grounded on the reality of human limitations and justified on the overall good of society.... In the Confucian view, political inequalities that allow the educated, virtuous, and talented to make governmental decisions, and consequently make wise decisions for the common good, are justified. Otherwise, they are unjustified. In the meantime, Confucianism can accommodate limited universal political participation (see the following). The Confucian pursuit of equality in political arenas is to be realized mainly in creating opportunities for people to get educated, to become virtuous, and to develop talents, so they come to be equipped to serve in government and to participate in government decision-making in meaningful ways.[54]

According to Li, in Confucianism, political inequalities (A2) are morally justified *to the extent* that they contribute to "the overall good of society," which includes people becoming educated, becoming virtuous, and developing talents (A1). In the Confucian perfectionist regime envisioned by Li, democratic values (such as universal political participation) are not outright dismissed. In fact, unlike some "strong" Confucian meritocrats such as Daniel Bell and Tongdong Bai, who have a principled objection to political equality and the one-person-one-vote system,[55] Li upholds the so-called *general participation principle* on the basis of Confucianism's

---

[54] Chenyang Li, "Equality and Inequality in Confucianism," *Dao* 11 (2012), pp. 295–313, p. 308. In stressing the wise decisions for the common good, both Li and Chan tend to downplay the complex meaning of the common good in the societal context of value pluralism. The following statement by David Wong gives an important corrective to this sort of tendency generally found among Confucian meritocrats: "Because the common good is a complex whole including a plurality of goods and within which these different goods may come into conflict, there always will be some disagreement over which goods are included and the most reasonable way to deal with conflicts between the goods that are included. The vision of a society united around a shared and unambiguous vision of a common good is dangerously simplistic and, moreover, ignores bases for community other than such a shared conception of the common good" (David B. Wong, "Rights and Community in Confucianism," in *Confucian Ethics: A Comparative Study of Self, Autonomy, and Community*, eds. Kwong-loi Shun and David B. Wong [Cambridge: Cambridge University Press, 2004], pp. 31–48, at p. 44).

[55] Daniel A. Bell, *The China Model: Political Meritocracy and the Limits of Democracy* (Princeton: Princeton University Press, 2015); Tongdong Bai, "A Mencian Version of Limited Democracy," *Res Publica* 14 (2008), pp. 19–34 and "A Confucian Version of Hybrid Regime: How Does It Work, and Why Is It Superior?" in *East Asian Challenge for Democracy*, pp. 55–87.

basic respect for humanity and submits that "all citizens should have the opportunity to participate in general elections" and "state leaders and legislators at all levels should be elected through general election."[56] However, this democratic principle is conditioned upon what Li calls the *qualification principle*, which says, "All candidates for public offices must meet respective qualifications before they can be elected. Unlike the first principle, this principle is an exclusion principle. It sets standards to prevent people without adequate qualifications to occupy public offices. By this principle, candidates must pass screening for their qualifications with regard to knowledge, skills, and moral characters."[57]

Li's proposal is reasonable but ambiguous as a normative idea. Furthermore, it is immoderate, for several reasons. First, the normative rationale for the general participation principle is so obscure that it is puzzling why Li upholds this principle at all. Li says that this principle "cannot be found in classic Confucianism" and Confucianism's basic respect for humanity as a justification for the principle "is not grounded in logical necessity." Rather, Li continues, "such a principle coheres with the concept of basic respect for humanity, and thus it can be grounded on such a Confucian concept."[58] If the general participation principle does not directly contribute to the overall good of society, which for Li can be attained through certain political inequalities on which political meritocracy is predicated, and it further has no strong moral justification in Confucianism,[59] then why this principle in the first place? Li enlists the help of Joseph Chan, who acknowledges the instrumental role democratic institutions can play in achieving the perfectionist good, to which I turn shortly, but he offers no clear explanation for the grounds on which, even instrumentally, the general participation principle can be justified in his Confucian perfectionist regime.

This leads to the second problem: the general participation principle does not cohere with Li's complete rejection of the principles of popular sovereignty and political equality.[60] If political inequalities are justified by consequentialist reasons (i.e., to the extent that they contribute to the overall good of society) and no intrinsic value of political equality and

---

[56] Li, "Equality and Inequality," p. 310.   [57] Ibid.   [58] Ibid.
[59] For a completely contrary judgment on the same premise, see Ranjoo S. Herr, "Confucian Democracy and Equality," *Asian Philosophy* 20 (2010), pp. 261–282.
[60] Though like Li some Confucian meritocrats (such as Daniel Bell, Tongdong Bai, Joseph Chan, Ruiping Fan, and Jiang Qing, to name a few) acknowledge the limited value of democratic elections, they all reject the democratic values of popular sovereignty and political equality.

popular sovereignty is acknowledged (and as noted for Li there is no necessary Confucian ground for this principle), then on what grounds can the general participation principle be justified? It is precisely because of this logical incoherence that Joseph Chan, who equally rejects popular sovereignty and political equality,[61] understands democracy strictly in institutional terms and embraces it largely instrumentally while downplaying the value of political participation and civic education.[62] In other words, unlike Chan, who has a reason to embrace democracy understood as a political system but to reject political participation,[63] Li offers no morally justifiable reason to uphold the general participation principle.

Chan, though differentiating himself from comprehensive Confucian perfectionists, has a more sophisticated view of perfectionist Confucianism and democracy, and in a sense it is precisely because he is "mixing" Confucianism and democracy that his Confucian perfectionism becomes more moderate than that of others.[64] Since Li and many other Confucian meritocrats agree with the way Chan understands democracy in the Confucian polity, let us examine his argument before turning to why the existing proposals for Confucian meritocratic perfectionism are immoderate relative to value pluralism and moral disagreement.

Chan makes a vivid distinction between democratic values and democratic institutions, and claims that the latter can be pursued independently of the former for instrumental reasons, in terms of the good effects they bring to society. Therefore, in Chan's view, democracy is justified *because* it "has a reasonably strong ability to produce right outcomes, in the sense of meeting people's demands or needs and solving social problems, offers a better protection against tyranny or abuse of power than other political systems, [and more indirectly] promotes self-respect, civic responsibility, governing ability, a sense of belonging to society, and so forth."[65] And as noted earlier, since Chan believes these desirable effects are all verified in

---

[61] Chan says, "No doubt democracy as a political system gives power to the people and distributes votes equally. But such a system need not be justified by, or be seen to express, popular sovereignty or political equality as a moral principle or ideal" (Chan, *Confucian Perfectionism*, p. 85).

[62] Ibid., pp. 94–100.

[63] Of course, whether Chan's reason is *good* is a different matter. See Chapter 6 for my critical engagement with Chan's argument.

[64] Chapter 4 of Chan's *Confucian Perfectionism* is titled "Mixing Confucianism and Democracy."

[65] Joseph Chan, "Democracy and Meritocracy: Toward a Confucian Perspective," *Journal of Chinese Philosophy* 34 (2007), pp. 179–193, p. 180. For a similar view, see Steven Wall, "Democracy, Authority, and Publicity," *Journal of Political Philosophy* 14 (2006),

the view of Confucian thought, democratic institutions, now disconnected from its guiding moral principles, such as popular sovereignty, political equality, and the right to political participation, can be mixed with perfectionist Confucianism. The democratic institutions in which Chan is particularly interested and which he finds instrumentally valuable are elections because they can be "both a means of selecting good rulers and a way of expressing the mutual commitment of the ruler and the people."[66] Following Jane Mansbridge, Chan claims that the selection model of representation can be instrumental in selecting leaders of virtue and ability.[67]

I find Chan's more directly political proposal (e.g., the selection model) reasonable, but I note it too has some serious problems. For instance, even if Chan's appropriation of the selection model of representation in the Confucian context is reasonable, its democratic quality is questionable. The main concern of the liberal advocates of the selection model such as Mansbridge is how to enhance democratic accountability, thus focusing on a particular mode of representation, namely *gyroscopic representation*, that the selection model enables.[68] Chan, however, downplays the importance of democratic accountability, associating it with the sanctions model,[69] and concentrates largely on how to place qualified people in leadership positions amid the generally myopic, self-interested, and ignorant masses, and how to maintain trust and harmony between the leaders and the people. Chan denies that his view is "elitist" by claiming that Mansbridge's view, on which his idea is built, is not elitist, but it is

---

pp. 85–100, where he distinguishes "the tasks of government" and "the effects of governing" from the perfectionist standpoint.

[66] Chan, *Confucian Perfectionism*, p. 86. Revising his earlier purely instrumentalist view of democracy (in "Democracy and Meritocracy"), Chan here acknowledges the expressive value of democracy because he now believes democratic institutions such as elections can express some normative ideal or value (e.g., mutual commitment of the ruler and the people) endorsed by Confucianism. However, it is unclear whether Chan thereby claims that moral commitment of the ruler and the people is an intrinsic value *of* democracy (which seems to me a highly idiosyncratic view of democracy). At any rate, what is important is that even in this revised view, Chan clearly rejects the values of popular sovereignty, political equality, and the right to political participation, namely the constitutive values *of* democracy.

[67] Ibid., pp. 69–79. On Mansbridge's idea of the selection model, see Jane Mansbridge, "A 'Selection Model' of Political Representation," *Journal of Political Philosophy* 17 (2009), pp. 369–389; "Clarifying the Concepts of Representation," *American Political Science Review* 105 (2011), pp. 621–630.

[68] Jane Mansbridge, "Rethinking Representation," *American Political Science Review* 97 (2003), p. 515–528, p. 521.

[69] Chan, *Confucian Perfectionism*, p. 74.

dubious how well this claim coheres with his active refutation of popular sovereignty, political equality, and the right to political participation, which is the foundational premise of Mansbridge's democratic theory. Moreover, when he, like strong Confucian meritocrats such as Jiang Qing and Daniel Bell,[70] introduces a nondemocratically elected second chamber filled with "virtuous politicians," not only for better political deliberation and public judgment but for the sake of moral education of the general public,[71] his earlier argument for the selection model undergirded by the one-person-one-vote mechanism loses its force. If the political system in question operates on bicameralism and there is an established nondemocratic selection mechanism to place the "virtuous" politicians in the upper house, what is the point of adopting the selection model in the first place?

Ultimately, my criticisms of Chenyang Li's and Joseph Chan's (and their company's) proposals for Confucian meritocratic perfectionism boil down to this final point – not only do these proposals suffer internal incoherence, but more importantly, they are immoderate.

Despite many differences in detail, Confucian meritocratic perfectionists generally hold the following proposition: that "[G]overnment should be staffed by virtuous, knowledgeable, and talented people, and that only people with such qualities are qualified to produce legislation. Therefore, political processes should be designed to enable the virtuous, knowledgeable, and talented to make legislation and to serve in governmental posts."[72] There could be a variety of questions regarding how to define "merit" given its elastic meaning and how to identify meritorious people.[73] Though these are important questions in political theory, my concern here is rather with the underlying assumption of this proposition.

What is implicit in this proposition is the vertical distance between the leaders and the people; whatever constitutes the core meaning of merit and by whatever method (examination, selection-model of election, or

---

[70] Jiang, *Confucian Constitutional Order*, pp. 41 (actually proposing tricameralism with two meritocratically selected upper houses); Bell, *Beyond Liberal Democracy*, pp. 165–179.
[71] Chan, *Confucian Perfectionism*, pp. 100–109; Joseph Chan, "Political Meritocracy and Meritorious Rule: A Confucian Perspective," in *East Asian Challenge for Democracy*, pp. 31–54, pp. 41–49.
[72] Li, "Equality and Inequality," pp. 309–310.
[73] For an illuminating discussion on these issues in Chinese history, see Yuri Pines, "Between Merit and Pedigree: Evolution of the Conception of 'Elevating of the Worthy' in Pre-imperial China," in *East Asian Challenge for Democracy*, pp. 161–202.

recommendation) the leaders are selected, the leaders are those who are *more* virtuous, *more* able, *more* talented, and know *better*. They might not be the "guardians" as idealized in traditional Confucianism[74] but they are deemed role models and they should be virtuous enough to care about as well as knowledgeable enough to know not only the long-term interest of the people but also the interest of nonvoters, including "future (and past) generations and foreigners."[75] They should know what constitutes the good life, namely, the perfectionist goods to be promoted by the state of which they are at the helm, and they must somehow embody such goods (i.e., traits, virtues, or characteristics) in themselves to govern, "serve," or transform the people who only vaguely understand what the intrinsically valuable goods are or what the true meaning of the good life is and are prevented from living such a(n) (objectively good) life because of their myopic self-interest or lack of formidable character, or sheer irrationality.[76]

In this view, the world is paradise ("Grand Union," as the Chinese people call it) lost but its shadow still lingers over our modern situation. The ideal world is impossible to restore because the sages (*shengren* 聖人) are long gone but our nonideal world may approximate the ideal, by means of either democratic or nondemocratic measures, *if only* we live a good life and *if only* we have the people who can lead us there.[77]

However, as nearly all proponents of Confucian perfectionist meritocracy admit, the societal fact that conditions the lives of the East Asian people is value pluralism and as Rawls rightly notes, every citizen in these pluralist societies is individually loaded with the burdens of judgment. Contra David Hall and Roger Ames, two vigorous advocates of Confucian democracy, moral disagreement in contemporary East Asia is not an

---

[74] Chan says that "the theory of guardianship, attractive though the ideal may be, is not *realistic*" ("Democracy and Meritocracy," p. 188).
[75] Bai, "Confucian Version of Hybrid Regime," p. 56.
[76] Following Raz, Chan calls his Confucian perfectionist conception of authority the *service conception* (Chan, *Confucian Perfectionism*, pp. 29–32), though Chan's idea of service is more literal in the sense of serving the people in addition to offering a better reason for compliance. For Raz's own service conception, see his *Morality of Freedom*, pp. 53–57.
[77] Among Confucian meritocrats, Joseph Chan, quite surprisingly, given his objection to comprehensive Confucianism, is most expressive of this sentiment when he recapitulates the challenge of theorizing moderate Confucian perfectionism as: "to demonstrate the attractiveness of the ideal even though it is unlikely to work in the real world, and to show that a feasible nonideal conception of order still tallies with the ideal conception, in the sense that people who live under the nonideal order are nonetheless aware of the ideal and regard it as an aspiration" (Chan, *Confucian Perfectionism*, p. 1).

anomaly but what characterizes everyday social and political life, even as the public culture there is still by character and intelligibly Confucian.[78] Not only do the people subscribe to different religious, moral, and philosophical doctrines but, even in cases where people share religious faith, they are often divided on political ideologies. In short, people in pluralist East Asia have different moral and material *interests*. No single conception of the good life can encompass holistically plural interests, moral interests in particular, that are often in conflict, nor can they be harmonized, without positing the sage's transcendental eye and in the absence of a preconceived and independent moral standard.[79] There might be such a standard (so we do not have to be moral skeptics) but it is hubristic for someone to claim that he or she knows what it is or how to harmonize the moral conflict, which in his or her view could be nothing more than the deplorable result of moral confusion.[80]

---

[78] See David Hall and Roger T. Ames, *Democracy of the Dead: Dewey, Confucius, and the Hope for Democracy in China* (Chicago: Open Court, 1999), p. 182. For some empirical evidence that attests to this claim, see Shin, *Confucianism and Democratization*.

[79] Chan is least susceptible to this charge and he indeed reveals an awareness of the unavoidable fact of disagreement when he anticipates a criticism against his proposal of the nondemocratically elected second chamber: "I should conclude with a common criticism of the idea of the second chamber. It argues that although people do want to select good leaders, they often differ in their evaluation of candidates. Because of this, we should not give power to individuals or groups the assessment of which others may disagree with. Instead, we should let every citizen vote, because democratic voting is fairer, hence more preferable, way of setting disagreements. I do not find this criticism unanswerable. From the fact of disagreement on the quality of candidates, it is wrong to infer we should put aside our concern for candidates' quality and simply adopt whatever content-independent voting principle as seems fair to everyone involved" ("Political Meritocracy and Meritorious Rule," p. 49). However, Chan's scope of "the fact of disagreement" is too narrow and says little about the more fundamental fact of moral disagreement arising from the plurality of moral interest which goes far beyond a mere difference in one's evaluation of candidates. It is difficult to see how Chan's statement here *answers* the theoretical challenge posed by value pluralism, for instance, Jeremy Waldron's, who forcefully argues for the moral legitimacy of the majoritarian principle (see Waldron, *Law and Disagreement*).

[80] And this *someone* includes us academic philosophers. Among the advocates of Confucian meritocracy, Chenyang Li is most fascinated by the Confucian ideal of harmony. See his *The Confucian Philosophy of Harmony* (New York: Routledge, 2013). Though I consider harmony as one of the crucial Confucian values, worth public promotion in contemporary East Asia, my interpretation (which understands harmonization as a consensus-building process under value pluralism and the resulting moral disagreement) is qualitatively different from Li's (see Sungmoon Kim, *Confucian Democracy in East Asia: Theory and Practice* [New York: Cambridge University Press, 2014], chap. 2). According to David Wong, "The problem with Confucianism ... has lain in its assumption that the different aspects of a person's social identity, which correspond to the different goods that go into the common good, can all somehow be subsumed and

One may object by saying that "with regard to their own interests, it is questionable whether voters alone can be the best judge of what those interests are and how to satisfy them,"[81] and it is on this very ground that Joseph Chan justifies the service conception of authority – to better satisfy the (long-term, more educated) interest of the people. However, it is not only presumptuous to deny that an individual citizen is the best judge of his/her interest in a pluralist society characterized by pervasive moral disagreement on virtually every moral question – abortion, same-sex marriage, euthanasia, freedom of expression, freedom of association, social welfare, and so on. It also leads to the heavily paternalistic notion of political authority.

The notion of authority in terms of better satisfaction of one's interest makes good sense in various private relationships, most notably between parents and their child. There is nothing morally wrong with parents authoritatively admitting their drug-addicted son into a rehabilitation center in order to help him become healthy and thereby live a flourishing life, which is in his long-term interest. But in this case, what justifies the parents' authority over their son is the nature of the relationship between any parents and *their* child. Parents have moral obligations to take care of their child and the parents in question did what they were obligated to do as caring parents. Can the state exercise such paternalism over juvenile (even adult) drug addicts to satisfy their long-term interests? The answer is debatable: unlike liberals, Confucians, whether meritocrats or democrats, have no prima facie reason to oppose state paternalism in this and related cases (i.e., cases that *vitally* concern the physical well-being of the citizenry). But in most other areas the state, a compulsory organization by nature, has no parental authority over adult citizens who have diverse, often conflicting and incommensurable, moral interests.[82] To distinguish

---

ordered under some grand harmonizing principle" ("Rights and Community," p. 46). For a similar worry about the danger of the Confucian valorization of harmony, see Randall Peerenboom, "Confucian Harmony and Freedom of Thought: The Right to Think Versus Right Thinking," in *Confucianism and Human Rights*, eds. Wm. Theodore de Bary and Tu Wei-ming (New York: Columbia University Press, 1998), pp. 234–260.

[81] Bai, "Confucian Version of Hybrid Regime," p. 56.

[82] Chan asserts that his Confucian perfectionism is not "paternalistic" because it does not rely on the use of coercion, which according to him is how the concept "paternalism" is commonly defined in contemporary political and legal philosophy (Chan, *Confucian Perfectionism*, p. 44n33). However, most contemporary political and legal theorists do not understand paternalism in terms of the use of coercion. See Quong, *Liberalism without Perfection*, chap. 3, for a criticism of the paternalistic nature of (liberal) perfectionism. Also see Thomas Christiano, "The Authority of Democracy," *Journal of Political Philosophy* 12 (2004), pp. 266–290, for a criticism of Raz's service conception of authority from a similar standpoint.

from the paternalism vitally involving the citizenry's physical well-being, we can call the latter type of state paternalism *value paternalism*, the state's paternalistic involvement in the moral interests of citizens and/or of their voluntary associations.

Some Confucian meritocratic perfectionists may say that in the Confucian context state paternalism does not matter too much because they deny one's moral status as free and equal, for the violation of which paternalism is found presumptively wrong in liberal political theory.[83] It is beyond the scope of this chapter to investigate whether Confucianism as a philosophical tradition indeed denies one's moral status as equal and (arguably) free.[84] However, insofar as they argue that Confucian meritocratic perfectionism is the most attractive normative vision in a pluralist East Asia, and to the extent that they believe that Confucian meritocracy can accommodate value pluralism, they must offer a principled philosophical explanation of how state paternalism, now redeemed as a positive integral element of Confucian meritocracy, can do the same and come to terms with the resulting moral disagreement. Such an explanation is hardly found in the existing proposals for Confucian meritocracy. In the end, the predicament faced by Confucian meritocrats can be recapitulated in the following way:

(1) There seems to be no philosophically viable way for Confucian meritocratic perfectionism (CMP) to not be paternalistic in terms of the people's material and moral well-being.
(2) Value paternalism cannot come to terms with moral disagreement in a pluralist society.
(3) From (1) and (2), we can conclude that CMP cannot come to terms with moral disagreement in the societal context of value pluralism.
(4) However, Confucian meritocrats believe that CMP can be the most attractive normative vision in East Asia's pluralist societies; they even argue that CMP can accommodate value pluralism.
(5) (3) and (4) are not compatible.
(6) From (5) we can conclude that CMP is *immoderate* (in the sense defined earlier).

---

[83] Quong, *Liberalism without Perfection*, p. 74.
[84] For a supportive view, see Irene T. Bloom, "Mengzian Arguments on Human Nature (*Ren Xing*)," in *Essays on the Moral Philosophy of Mengzi*, eds. Xiusheng Liu and Philip J. Ivanhoe (Indianapolis: Hackett, 2002), pp. 64–100; Chung-ying Cheng, "A Theory of Confucian Selfhood: Self-Cultivation and Free Will in Confucian Philosophy," in *Confucian Ethics*, pp. 124–147.

Earlier, we noted that among the various possibilities of normative Confucianism, only *comprehensive Confucian perfectionism* is plausible, and we also noted that to be a viable normative vision in contemporary East Asian societies, Confucian perfectionism must be moderate – it should be compatible with and accommodating to value pluralism and the moral disagreement that results from it. And now we have concluded that (comprehensive) Confucian meritocratic perfectionism is immoderate given the state paternalism associated with it (reminiscent of the sage's transcendental eye), which does not acknowledge plurality of moral interests, the very source of moral disagreement and the very meaning of value pluralism. Therefore, to make (comprehensive) Confucian perfectionism moderate, it is necessary to first remove value paternalism from it, and, second, to make it fully acknowledge and respect the plurality of moral interests among citizens. Given that individual citizens have different moral interests in a pluralist society, these two requirements – nonpaternalism[85] and respect of the plurality of moral interest – give rise to the third requirement, that each citizen's moral interest be given equal weight and that this equality among the citizens of diverse moral interests must be reciprocally and publicly acknowledged. Following Thomas Christiano, we can call this requirement the *public equality* requirement. Christiano explains forcefully why state paternalism of the kind associated with Confucian meritocratic perfectionism is critically at odds with the principle of public equality. Note that Christiano calls what I call the sage's eye "a god's eye" but their political implications are quite similar.

In a sense, from a god's eye point of view, public equality does not have intrinsic value. And by implication democracy and liberal rights do not have intrinsic value since they are public realizations of equality. The idea here is that a god can determine without error exactly what equal advancement of interests really requires in every instance. Perfect knowledge and power ... can sidestep the requirement of publicity in trying to implement equality. This is because none of the imperfections of fallibility, disagreement, and cognitive bias are attributable to such a god, by hypothesis. But we face the problem of what we must do once we acknowledge the fact that we do not occupy the divine standpoint. We must attempt to argue for and defend standards for social justice, which makes sense to us and in a way that treats each person as an equal.[86]

---

[85] Aimed at the removal of state value paternalism, nonpaternalism is distinct from antipaternalism, which is to oppose *all* kinds of state paternalism.
[86] Thomas Christiano, *The Constitution of Equality* (Oxford: Oxford University Press, 2008), pp. 71–72.

If we agree with Christiano that given the background conditions of value pluralism, namely, the facts of diversity, pervasive disagreement, cognitive bias, and fallibility, the public realization of equality is *intrinsically* just and democracy is one essential component of the public realization of equality,[87] we are finally led to conclude that in order to be moderate, comprehensive Confucian perfectionism must acknowledge the intrinsic value of democracy with its underlying principles, such as popular sovereignty, political equality, and the right to political participation, and be predicated on democratic institutions that operate on public deliberation and contestation. In other words, only when it is *Confucian democratic perfectionism* can comprehensive Confucian perfectionism be moderate.

CONCLUSION

It is now clear that the reason existing proposals for Confucian meritocratic perfectionism not only suffer internal incoherence but are also found to be immoderate, if not extreme, is that either they are insufficiently democratic or they embrace mainly the *instrumental* value of democracy to the extent that democracy, understood as a set of political institutions disconnected from its constitutive principles of popular sovereignty, political equality, and the right to political participation, can contribute to the Confucian conception of the good life. We also noted that Joseph Chan's moderate political Confucian perfectionism is either implausible given the impossibility of political Confucianism as the possible mode of normative Confucianism, or, if possible, because it verges on political liberalism a la Rawls, to which Chan objects. I argued that given the fact of pluralism in East Asian societies, as acknowledged even by the advocates of Confucian meritocracy who generally subscribe to comprehensive Confucian perfectionism, which I argued to be the only plausible mode of normative Confucianism, the Confucian perfectionism in question must embrace democracy as noninstrumentally valuable. I submitted that this is the only way that (comprehensive) Confucian perfectionism can be moderate.

One remaining question is: what does Confucian democratic perfectionism, thus understood, look like? In following chapters I try to answer this question. By way of conclusion of the present chapter, let me lay out the basic ideas I will appeal to in order to construct a proper answer.

---

[87] Ibid., p. 71.

Confucian democratic perfectionism refers to a normative position that stipulates that (1) there are valuable conceptions of the good life endorsed by Confucian philosophy and social practice and (2) the state can permissibly aim to promote such types of life (among many possible variations depending on the particular situation). By promoting *a* Confucian collective way of life, Confucian democratic perfectionism distinguishes itself from *a* distinctively liberal political theory, be it liberal perfectionism or political liberalism. These stipulations have important provisos, however. First, a valuable Confucian way of life refers to what is counted as such by *Confucian citizens*, who are still deeply and pervasively influenced by Confucian mores and habits, which are undoubtedly perfectionist goods and values, despite their subscriptions to various moral, religious, or philosophical doctrines.[88] Second, the state that is permitted to promote the Confucian way of the good life must be a democratic state (meeting the nonpaternalism requirement) by means of the one-person-one-vote mechanism (meeting both the respect of the plurality of moral interest requirement and the public equality requirement). These stipulations and provisos together lend support to *democratic perfectionism* in a sense similar to how George Sher understands the term, now with a distinctively Confucian characteristic: "[A] democratic polity may, through its representatives, induce or even compel its own members to live what it collectively judges to be good life. Although the idea of collective self-compulsion is, as always, faintly paradoxical, it is no more paradoxical when the aim is to promote the good than when it is (say) to maintain public order or protect the environment."[89] Seen in this way, Confucian democratic perfectionism can be understood as a normative theory that expresses Confucian citizens' collective self-determination (externally) and democratic self-government (internally). It justifies *public promotion*

---

[88] That is, what can be called the *Confucian habit of the heart* can coexist or overlap with one's comprehensive doctrine, enabling intriguing dual identities such as Confucian-Christian or Confucian-Buddhist. For sociological observations of this interesting phenomenon, see Fenggang Yang, *Chinese Christians in America: Conversion, Assimilation, and Adhesive Identities* (University Park: The Pennsylvania State University Press, 1999); Robert C. Neville, *Boston Confucianism: Portable Tradition in the Late-Modern World* (Albany: State University of New York Press, 2000); Byung-ik Koh, "Confucianism in Contemporary Korea," in *Confucian Traditions*, pp. 191–201.

[89] Sher, *Beyond Neutrality*, p. 6. Sher also says that admitting nonneutral arguments does not necessarily require a decision-making elite "for the question of which grounds for political decisions are legitimate is quite different from the question of who should *make* those decisions" (p. 5).

of *Confucian cultural values in the service of democratic citizenship under the normative constraints of core democratic principles.*

Accommodated to democratic institutions and constrained by democratic principles, the *Confucianism* in Confucian democratic perfectionism is qualitatively different from the traditional Confucianism that actually was practiced in pre-modern East Asia, which is androcentric, patriarchal, and undemocratic. In fact, as I construct in the following chapter, Confucian democratic perfectionism enables what I call *public reason Confucianism* – under which, like other voluntary associations, various Confucian organizations that operate on traditional Confucian ethical precepts (most notably clan organizations) entertain the political right to freedom of association, but this right is protected only within the constitutional limit which in turn is guided by Confucian democratic perfectionism. Unlike traditional Confucianism, this renewed Confucianism is *moderate* in the sense I have employed throughout this chapter. However, it is still a comprehensive doctrine not only because it is rooted in traditional comprehensive Confucianism, despite significant modification, but more importantly because it is still intelligibly Confucian, distinct from non-Confucian ethical systems such as liberalism.

This is only a brief sketch of Confucian democratic perfectionism as philosophical concept and political practice, and greater clarification is required with regard to content. I hope, though, that even from this abbreviated presentation we can identify the meaningful difference between Confucian democratic perfectionism and the existing proposals for Confucian meritocratic perfectionism. In the next chapter, I construct public reason Confucianism as a distinctive normative political theory of Confucian democratic perfectionism.

2

Public reason Confucianism

A construction

The recent interest in Confucian political theory among East Asian scholars (as well as Western scholars deeply concerned with East Asian cultures) is closely tied with three propositions broadly shared by many liberal nationalists: (1) each nation (or people) has a right to national self-determination; (2) national self-determination can be exercised meaningfully only in the context of "societal culture";[1] and (3) global value monism of (Western-style) liberal democracy is critically at odds with the pluralist ways of life of self-governing peoples.[2] What motivates Confucian political theory as a *normative* theory is similar to the convictions underlying these propositions – that the Confucian way of life, in which East Asian citizens are still deeply entrenched, is qualitatively different from the liberal way of life (even when it has incorporated some liberal or democratic elements) and East Asian peoples' collective self-determination can be exercised meaningfully in the societal context of a Confucian culture.[3] In light of these related claims, contemporary normative Confucian political theory is inevitably *perfectionist*, if we understand

---

[1] Will Kymlicka defines societal culture as "a culture which provides its members with meaningful ways of life across the full range of human activities, including social, educational, religious, recreational, and economic life, encompassing both public and private spheres" (*Multicultural Citizenship* [Oxford: Oxford University Press, 1995], p. 76).
[2] David Miller, *On Nationality* (Oxford: Oxford University Press, 1995); Yael Tamir, *Liberal Nationalism* (Princeton: Princeton University Press, 1993). Also see John Rawls, *The Law of Peoples* (Cambridge: Harvard University Press, 1999).
[3] Daniel A. Bell, *East Meets West: Human Rights and Democracy* (Princeton: Princeton University Press, 2000); Stephen C. Angle, "Decent Democratic Centralism," *Political Theory* 33 (2005), pp. 518–546.

the term as the state's nonneutral promotion of a particular, valuable way of life.

At the heart of recent Confucian political theory is how to make intelligible and express publicly the persistent faith among East Asian citizens in core Confucian values such as filial piety and ritual propriety in the face of the global hegemony of rights-based individualism. Interestingly, even those East Asians (Koreans or Taiwanese, among others) who have successfully consolidated a liberal form of democracy, at least in terms of its institutional structures, harbor no illusion that history has ended with the victory of liberal democracy. For them, unless the liberal democracy that they have achieved is simultaneously a *Confucian democracy* in which liberalism (institutions as well as rights and values) is accommodated to Confucian ends and goods that they still cherish, despite their increasing subscriptions to different moral values and/or religious faiths as private individuals,[4] *their* democracy has yet to be realized.

Here arises a dilemma: if recent Confucian political theory (Confucian democratic theory in particular) has emerged as a pluralist correction to the global monism of liberal democracy in terms of Confucian people's collective self-determination, and if the theory is essentially perfectionist, how can it align with the societal fact of value pluralism *within* the putative Confucian polity? This is not to imply that there is an inherent tension between perfectionism and value pluralism. For instance, liberal perfectionism avoids this potential tension even as it is committed to comprehensive liberal values by making personal autonomy the most important perfectionist value[5] or by decoupling perfectionism (in this case *political perfectionism*) from comprehensive moral values, including autonomy.[6] However, can Confucian perfectionism, committed to particular comprehensive Confucian values such as filial piety and ritual propriety, avoid such a tension? How can the state promote particular

---

[4] Stephen C. Angle, *Contemporary Confucian Political Philosophy: Toward Progressive Confucianism* (Cambridge: Polity, 2012); Joseph Chan, *Confucian Perfectionism: A Political Philosophy for Modern Times* (Princeton: Princeton University Press, 2014); Sungmoon Kim, *Confucian Democracy in East Asia: Theory and Practice* (New York: Cambridge University Press, 2014).

[5] Joseph Raz, *The Morality of Freedom* (Oxford: Clarendon, 1986); Steven Wall, *Liberalism, Perfectionism and Restraint* (Cambridge: Cambridge University Press, 1998).

[6] George Sher, *Beyond Neutrality: Perfectionism and Politics* (Cambridge: Cambridge University Press, 1997); Joseph Chan, "Legitimacy, Unanimity, and Perfectionism," *Philosophy and Public Affairs* 29 (2000), pp. 5–42.

Confucian values, thereby imparting to it Confucian public character, without restricting the plurality of values in civil society?

In this chapter, I argue that the predicament Confucian perfectionism ineluctably faces with regard to value pluralism can be avoided by understanding (and reconstructing) Confucian perfectionist goods as the core constituents of public reason with which citizens can justify their public opinions and arguments to one another and by which the state (i.e., the democratic state) can justifiably exercise its public authority to reasonable citizens who otherwise subscribe to various moral, philosophical, and religious doctrines. When Confucian perfectionism works through Confucian public reason broadly shared by citizens – let us call this type of Confucian democratic perfectionism *public reason Confucianism* – not only can it avoid elitism, to which many advocates of Confucian perfectionist meritocracy are susceptible,[7] but it can also balance the Confucian polity's internal value pluralism and the people's collective self-determination (and by implication global pluralism). My central claim is that by providing citizens with shared reason through which they can render their constitutional democratic rights in such a way as to be culturally relevant to their moral sentimentality and negotiate the tensions between different rights, public reason Confucianism makes the Confucian polity *more* democratic as well as *more* just.

This chapter consists of four main parts. In the following section I examine how public reason is understood (especially in relation to perfectionist good and values) in contemporary political theory by closely examining John Rawls's political liberalism (which first introduced the idea of public reason into contemporary liberal political theory), and critique public reason liberalism from the perfectionist perspective. I then attempt to construct the theory of *public reason perfectionism* by revisiting Rawls's idea of public reason, a democratic perfectionism that is deeply concerned with the coerciveness of political power while permitting the state to promote particular values generally cherished by democratic citizens. After showing how Rawls's public reason liberalism verges on public reason perfectionism in the following section, I finally introduce and discuss the core stipulations of public reason Confucianism, which I present as a type of public reason perfectionism and as a distinctive normative political theory of Confucian democratic perfectionism that is most suitable to contemporary East Asian societies.

---

[7] See my critique of Confucian meritocratic perfectionism in Chapter 1.

LIBERALISM, PERFECTIONISM, AND PUBLIC REASON

In contemporary political theory, public reason is almost exclusively associated with the doctrine of liberal neutrality, especially John Rawls's political liberalism. Indeed, the idea of public reason is one of the most interesting (as well as controversial) aspects of political liberalism.[8] Central to political liberalism is the claim that the exercise of political power must be publicly justifiable to the citizens over whom the power is exercised and it is by relying on public reason that the exercise of the (democratic) state is publicly justified. Put differently, as the shared reason of democratic citizens, public reason enables "an equal share in the coercive political power that citizens exercise over one another."[9] While political liberalism notes the coercive nature of state action and is deeply concerned with the publicly justifiable exercise of political power, especially under the societal fact of pluralism in which reasonable citizens who are equally loaded with the "burdens of judgment"[10] subscribe to different comprehensive doctrines, it also upholds the *liberal principle of legitimacy*, according to which "our exercise of political power is proper and hence justifiable only when it is exercised in accordance with a constitution the essentials of which all citizens may reasonably be expected to endorse in the light of principles and ideals acceptable to them as reasonable and rational."[11] For Rawls, therefore, coerciveness of political power and reasonable pluralism conspire to make democratic citizens honor the "limits of public reason," which apply only to constitutional essentials and matters of basic structure, along with the "duty of civility," which

---

[8] John Rawls, *Political Liberalism* (New York: Columbia University Press, 1993), chap. 6; "The Idea of Public Reason Revisited," in *The Law of Peoples*, pp. 129–180. According to Charles Larmore, for Rawls, though the idea of public reason has emerged as an explicit theme in his later writings on political liberalism (culminating in *Political Liberalism*), "the concept itself has always been at the heart of his philosophy" ("Public Reason," in *The Cambridge Companion to Rawls*, ed. Samuel Freeman [Cambridge: Cambridge University Press, 2003], pp. 368–393, p. 368).

[9] Rawls, *Political Liberalism*, p. 217. On an insightful interpretation of Rawls's appeal to coercision, see Michael Blake, "Distributive Justice, State Coercion, and Autonomy," *Philosophy and Public Affairs* 30:3 (2001), pp. 257–296.

[10] Factors such as conflicting and complex evidence, disagreement about weighing shared considerations, different interpretations of moral and political concepts, different experiences all burden the free and equal citizens equally and force them to be epistemically charitable to each other (Rawls, *Political Liberalism*, pp. 54ff).

[11] Rawls, *Political Liberalism*, p. 217. Also see Jonathan Quong, *Liberalism without Perfection* (Oxford: Oxford University Press, 2011), pp. 108–136.

stipulates that citizens and public officials ought to offer one another arguments that others can also endorse.[12]

Understood as an essential component of political liberalism, then, public reason ensures state neutrality in a liberal society that is marked by the fact of pluralism. Thus Steven Wall, a liberal perfectionist, says, "[public reason] requires citizens to appeal only to 'political values,' 'presently accepted general beliefs,' 'the forms of reasoning found in common sense' and 'the methods and conclusions of science when these are not controversial.' Thus, the values of public reason exclude appeal to non-public modes of reasoning in political argument.... The content of a political conception of justice, then, is fixed by respecting the principles of restraint."[13]

Wall takes what Rawls calls "the limits of public reason" to be the restraint of unbridled pluralism, through which pluralism becomes *reasonable*. From a slightly different angle, Frank Michelman concurs with Wall's interpretation, that for Rawls "neutrality of aim is the only reasonable approach to adjusting the conflicting claims to liberty, all based on differing ethical convictions, and thus political legitimacy in a liberal democracy does not come without its price, namely, the constraint of public reason."[14] Interpreting Rawls's idea of public reason more expansively, Stephen Macedo asserts that "diversity needs to be kept in its place; diversity is not always a value and it should not, any more than other ideals, be accepted uncritically."[15] While not sharing Macedo's emphasis of the "the liberal educative project" of public reason that "shapes diversity for civic purposes,"[16] Jonathan Quong echoes Rawls-inspired civic liberals by arguing for a much broader scope of public

---

[12] Rawls, *Political Liberalism*, pp. 215–217.
[13] Wall, *Liberalism, Perfectionism and Restraint*, p. 49.
[14] Frank L. Michelman, "Rawls on Constitutionalism and Constitutional Law," in *Cambridge Companion to Rawls*, pp. 394–425, p. 414.
[15] Stephen Macedo, *Diversity and Distrust: Civic Education in a Multicultural Democracy* (Cambridge: Harvard University Press, 2000), p. 3. Also see his *Liberal Virtues: Citizenship, Virtue, and Community in Liberal Constitutionalism* (Oxford: Oxford University Press, 1990). It is precisely on this more expansive interpretation of public reason that William A. Galston, a liberal pluralist, criticizes Rawls for being half tempted to "civic totalism" (*The Practice of Liberal Pluralism* [Cambridge: Cambridge University Press, 2005], pp. 38–40).
[16] Macedo, *Diversity and Distrust*, p. 3. For a similar civic interpretation of public reason, see Amy Gutmann and Dennis Thompson, *Democracy and Disagreement: Why Moral Conflict Cannot Be Avoided in Politics, and What Should Be Done about It* (Cambridge: Belknap Press, 1996); Amy Gutmann, *Identity in Democracy* (Princeton: Princeton University Press, 2003).

reason so that it can regulate all political decisions in a liberal democratic society.[17]

Despite the many interpretations of Rawls's work, Rawls's own understanding of the "limits of public reason" seems to point in quite a different direction. He explicitly says that "the limits imposed by public reason do not apply to all political questions but only to those involving what we may call 'constitutional essentials' and questions of basic justice."[18] Although religious critics of Rawls often complain that he has thereby made religious discussions off limits in public forum, as if they are purely *private*,[19] for Rawls the scope of public reason ought to be limited only to constitutional essentials and matters of basic structure, leaving most other political questions as well as a vast number of issues in which citizens daily engage in civil society widely open for free deliberations relying on nonpublic reasons or comprehensive doctrines.[20] Most tellingly, Rawls says, "In a democratic society nonpublic power, as seen, for example, in the authority of churches over their members, is freely accepted. ... Whatever comprehensive religious, philosophical, or moral views we hold are also freely accepted, politically speaking; for given liberty of conscience and freedom of thought, we impose any such doctrine on ourselves."[21] In this regard, Rawls clearly departs from Habermas, who advocates uninhibited use of public reason in civil society, and Rawls's political liberalism is more moderate than other forms of public reason liberalism championed by some Rawlsian civic liberals.[22]

---

[17] Quong, *Liberalism without Perfection*, pp. 256–289.
[18] Rawls, *Political Liberalism*, p. 214.
[19] Most notably, Jeffrey Stout, *Democracy and Tradition* (Princeton: Princeton University Press, 2004); Nicholas Wolterstorff, *Understanding Liberal Democracy: Essays in Political Philosophy* (Oxford: Oxford University Press, 2012).
[20] In Larmore's view, Rawls's emphasis of self-discipline that brings to [the citizens'] deliberations about issues of justice only those convictions that can form part of a common point of view does not necessarily lead to a strong version of civic-educational liberalism as advocated by Macedo (Larmore, "Public Reason," p. 376).
[21] Rawls, *Political Liberalism*, pp. 221–222.
[22] See Rawls's "Reply to Habermas," in *Political Liberalism*, pp. 372–434. Thus, Charles Lamore says, "Political debate rightly shows a greater mix of voices in areas of society other than the circumscribed realm of public reason, and it would be wrong to suppose that Rawls's theory of public reason means to encompass the 'public sphere' in this broader sense, which was the topic, for example, of a widely influential study by Jürgen Habermas" (Larmore, "Public Reason," pp. 381–382). But note that Rawls does use the phrase "the wide, or educative, role of public reason" when he discusses the court's role as the exemplar of public reason (Rawls, *Political Liberalism*, p. 236).

Differing interpretations of the scope of Rawls's public reason notwithstanding, one thing that remains unchallenged is that for Rawls (and for other public reason liberals), public reason is categorically different from nonpublic reasons heavily informed by comprehensive doctrines, religious or nonreligious. It is only concerned with *political values* such as basic rights, liberties, and opportunities and "assigns a special priority to [political values] with respect to the claims of the general good and of perfectionist values."[23] Neither grounding his normative position on some particular idea of what constitutes a good life nor permitting the state to promote or prohibit a particular way of life, Rawls's political liberalism turns out to be a kind of political liberal antiperfectionism, different from both comprehensive liberal perfectionism a la Raz and comprehensive liberal antiperfectionism a la Dworkin.[24]

Here, what drives Rawls's antiperfectionist argument is the fact that the state is a compulsory organization and political power is by nature coercive. No comprehensive doctrine or perfectionist end or value should be promoted by the state because whatever it is, the exercise of political power or public policy aimed at it is unjustifiable to citizens who subscribe to different comprehensive doctrines. Not only can the perfectionist state suppress plurality in ways of life, the defining characteristic of a free society,[25] but more seriously, it can wield political power without legitimacy because the fact that it may have or actually has a (good perfectionist) reason to do something does not lead to the claim that it has the right to do so. Since in a democratic society the state expresses collective self-determination of equal citizens who exercise political and coercive power over one another, its right to do something in the name of the entire citizenry must be publicly justifiable to and endorsed by citizens themselves who share public reason. Thus understood, for political liberals who believe that the issue of justice is categorically different from that of the good and that legitimate authority is a question of distribution of rights and duties, it is wrong to derive the right to command from a practical reason for better compliance.[26]

---

[23] Rawls, *Political Liberalism*, p. 223.
[24] Rawls calls both positions "ethical liberalism" (*Political Liberalism*, pp. 134–135).
[25] Nancy L. Rosenblum, *Membership and Morals: The Personal Uses of Pluralism in America* (Princeton: Princeton University Press, 1998).
[26] Based on this judgment, Quong criticizes Joseph Raz's service conception of authority (*Liberalism without Perfection*, pp. 112–120). Also see Thomas Christiano, "The Authority of Democracy." *Journal of Political Philosophy* 12 (2004), pp. 266–290.

At the heart of political liberalism (or public reason liberalism) is what perfectionists call the *asymmetry thesis*, the asymmetric treatment of disagreements over the good life and disagreements over the principles of justice. As noted, political liberals assert that disagreements over the good life are mainly reasonable yet fundamental (or incommensurable) disagreements and that the reasonableness of disagreement over the good life makes it illegitimate for the state to play an active role in promoting a particular conception of the good life. In contrast, disagreements over the principles of justice are only justificatory in nature in that participants already share premises that serve as a mutually acceptable standard of justification and therefore it is legitimate for the state to act on reasons of justice.[27] Perfectionists find the asymmetry thesis unacceptable on two grounds.

First, perfectionists find the asymmetry thesis unfair because there are no grounds on which to believe that the issue of conceptions of the good life is the only public issue that arouses fundamental moral disagreements among citizens. In fact, even reasonable citizens in a liberal democracy disagree with one another, sometimes vehemently, about the conceptions (and principles) of justice under which they should live a common public life. If the conception of justice is as contestable as that of the good life, why is the action of the state based on an argument of the good life illegitimate? As we have seen, Rawls would respond to this objection by pointing to the supreme importance of political stability in a liberal democratic society, which he believes can be achieved by categorically distinguishing constitutional essentials and questions of basic justice, to which the principles of justice (and public reason) are directly applied, from other political questions involving laws and public policies.[28] However, perfectionists rightly criticize Rawls's argument, first for the arbitrariness in distinguishing between "constitutional essentials" and other lower-level political matters in the nonideal situation, and second, for the possibility of fundamental disagreement over constitutional essentials and questions of basic justice.[29]

The second reason that perfectionists (especially moderate perfectionists) object to the asymmetry thesis is closely related to the way political

---

[27] Quong, *Liberalism without Perfection*, pp. 192–193.
[28] On Rawls's supreme concern about the question of stability, see Brian Barry, "John Rawls and the Search for Stability," *Ethics* 105 (1995), pp. 874–915.
[29] Chan, "Legitimacy, Unanimity, and Perfectionism," p. 7n7. Also see Simon Caney, "Anti-Perfectionism and Rawlsian Liberalism," *Political Studies* 42 (1995), pp. 248–264; Wall, *Liberalism, Perfectionism and Restraint*, pp. 49–50.

liberals understand the good life and the citizenry's moral disagreement over it. As we have seen in Chapter 1, according to Joseph Chan, conceptions of the good life may involve judgments about (1) *agency goods* (virtues or dispositions that constitute the good life), and/or (2) *prudential goods* (goods or values that contribute to a person's good life), and/or (3) *ways of life* (a person's overall pattern of living involving the above two goods). Even though (3) might be readily susceptible to moral debate, since judgments on it usually involve comprehensive doctrines, (1) and (2) are less controversial (certainly not incommensurable) across different moral communities.[30] The problem is that political liberals fail to differentiate the good life conceptually in this complex way and tend to attribute all kinds of moral disagreement, including somewhat malleable ones resulting from judgments on (1) and/or (2), singularly to the fundamental disagreement involving judgment on (3). Moderate perfectionism, while authorizing the state to promote a particular conception of the good life, restrains itself from making a comprehensive doctrine the only legitimate moral and political end, according to which the state ought to govern its citizens. As such, it is compatible with diverse conceptions of the good life in civil society or value pluralism.

Two important points can be gleaned from the perfectionist critique of political liberalism: First, if public reasons are purely political values – whether strictly limited to constitutional essentials or expanded to general political debates in the political public forum – there is no meaningful connection between perfectionism, concerned with a particular conception of the good life, and public reason, focused on liberal legitimacy and public justification. Understandably, no perfectionist has yet to attempt to make public reason, so understood, an integral part of their normative political theory. Second, if the asymmetry thesis is indeed not sustainable (I believe perfectionists and democrats are right on this), that is, if there are as many serious disagreements over justice as there are over the good life,[31] we are down to one of the following possibilities.

---

[30] Chan, "Legitimacy, Unanimity, and Perfectionism," pp. 11–12. Also see Franz F. L. Mang, "Liberal Neutrality and Moderate Perfectionism," *Res Publica* 19 (2013), pp. 297–315. Note that in Chapter 1 I argued that Chan's distinction among perfectionist goods, which is highly useful in the current – that is liberal – philosophical (and societal) context, is difficult to sustain when it comes to *Confucian perfectionism* where Confucianism is inevitably a kind of comprehensive doctrine for it to be intelligible to East Asian people as such, as *their* cultural value.

[31] Strong democrats' long struggle with neutralist liberals revolves around the fundamental disagreement among citizens about the conception and principles of justice. See Benjamin

First, we should abandon the very idea of public reason (as a neutralist constraint) because it is impossible to posit such a thing in a free society where there can be no foundational consensus on matters of justice among citizens who are radically different from one another – the agonistic path.[32] Second, even when there is broad social agreement among the citizens on what constitutes the basic elements of public reason (i.e., rights, liberties, opportunities, and duties), there can be multiple, even competing, accounts of public reason – the plurality path. Or third, following perfectionists, we can reject state neutrality implicated with the asymmetry thesis and allow the state to promote a particular conception of the good life – the perfectionist path.

Later, I will explore a way to make public reason relevant to perfectionism in the Confucian societal context by reconstructing the idea of public reason with regard to the perfectionist ends to which Confucian East Asian citizens are generally committed. I do so without relying on differentiation of the perfectionist goods as moderate perfectionists suggest who decouple comprehensive doctrines from perfectionism, thus making it political, *hence* moderate.[33] That is, I explore *public reason Confucianism* by embracing and combining the perfectionist and plurality paths. But why is the pluralist path important for our Confucian constructive project? I now turn to this question by again engaging with Rawls's public reason liberalism. By doing so we will find a new mode of normative theory in which public reason is entwined with perfectionist concerns.

THE PLURALIST PATH AND PUBLIC REASON PERFECTIONISM

In a sense, the perfectionists' asymmetry objection to Rawls's political liberalism is misguided because Rawls does not deny the possibility of

---

R. Barber, *Strong Democracy: Participatory Politics for a New Age* (Berkeley: University of California Press, 1984); Jeremy Waldron, *Law and Disagreement* (Oxford: Oxford University Press, 1999). As Waldron notes, this very problem goes back to modern social contract theorists (especially Locke and Kant) who struggled with the idea of the state of nature. See his *The Dignity of Legislation* (Cambridge: Cambridge University Press, 1999).

[32] Stuart Hampshire, *Justice Is Conflict* (Princeton: Princeton University Press, 2000); Chantal Mouffe, *The Return of the Political* (London: Verso, 1993); Mark Wenman, *Agonistic Democracy: Constituent Power in the Era of Globalisation* (New York: Cambridge University Press, 2013).

[33] For moderate perfectionists, political perfectionism *is* a moderate perfectionism in that it is severed from comprehensive doctrines.

serious disagreement over justice. In fact, Rawls reminds us that political liberalism has many forms, "depending on the substantive principles used and how the guidelines of inquiry are set out." That is, for Rawls the idea of public reason is not affiliated with any particular conception of justice or any substantive moral content of public reason, not to mention any particular conception of a valuable life. Rawls says,

> Accepting the idea of public reason and its principle of legitimacy emphatically does not mean, then, accepting a particular liberal conception of justice down to the last details of the principles defining its content. We may differ about these principles and still agree in accepting a conception's more general features. We agree that citizens share in political power as free and equal, and that as reasonable and rational they have a duty of civility to appeal to public reason, yet we differ as to which principles are the most reasonable basis of public justification.[34]

Rawls's statement tracks the plurality path remarkably well. Citizens can have reasonable agreement on society's core political values as the shared premise of mutual justification and reciprocity, while at the same time reasonably disagreeing with one another on substantive moral content. Unlike agonistic liberals, Rawls does not believe that disagreements over justice in a well-ordered society go "all the way down" because practically that means the fragmentation of the basis of mutual cooperation among citizens, or, worse, the disintegration of a democratic-constitutional society, a situation that a social-contractrian such as Rawls cannot allow. Here disagreements are often deep but they are not fundamental in the way that disagreements over the good life are. The nature of disagreements over justice is in essence justificatory.[35]

I share Rawls's core premises regarding public reason that first, given the coerciveness of political power and the compulsory nature of the state, public reason as the shared premise of mutual cooperation is of supreme significance, and second, given the fact of pluralism, public reason is the only plausible way to stabilize political society without employing outright coercion. I also agree with Rawls that disagreements over justice are justificatory disagreements and that there can be multiple interpretations of what constitutes public reason. What I find unconvincing is Rawls's effort to affiliate his neutralist commitment with public reason understood in this pluralist way. First, we must distinguish between two claims that are often conflated – the claim that disagreements about justice *are* justificatory disagreements and the claim that such disagreements *ought*

---

[34] Rawls, *Political Liberalism*, p. 226.
[35] Quong, *Liberalism without Perfection*, pp. 192–220.

to be justificatory. Rawls is not always clear about this distinction. But considering that his political liberalism is predicated on the *idea* of public reason, it would not be too far-fetched to think that the second claim better describes Rawls's actual position. Furthermore, the second claim gives us a good explanation as to where the normative force of public reason comes from: it comes primarily from the coerciveness of political power.

However, the second claim I attribute to Rawls does not explain the grounds on which reasonable citizens disagree about the conception of justice. Why do citizens subscribe to different conceptions of justice even within the boundary of public reason, that is, even if they generally agree on the core political values of their society? The issues I am concerned with here are not merely how to rank shared political values – for example, how freedom of assembly compares with freedom of expression when the two are in conflict. The issues here are also not regarding choice among rights that are by definition mutually exclusive, such as the right to political participation and the right to be left alone. The problem goes much deeper. Even if democratic citizens may have general agreement about the political values of some core liberal rights, they can differ radically as to the substantive moral content of each right and liberty, the political value of which they all cherish. But what can be the source of this difference if not the comprehensive doctrine that guides a person's ethical (religious or nonreligious) life?

By acknowledging the possibility of plural interpretations of public reason, Rawls seems to open a backdoor allowing comprehensive doctrines to sneak into the domains of public reason. In a sense, this is an inevitable consequence of Rawls's conceptualization of public reason in a non-Hobbesian way, despite his profound concern with coerciveness of public power. Unlike Hobbes, for whom public reason's normativity as *restraint* derives solely from coerciveness of political power,[36] in *Political Liberalism*, Rawls aims to achieve simultaneously restraint of and respect for diversity. Though for Rawls public reason *ought* to be a ground of mutual reciprocity and foundational consensus (as will be discussed shortly), his commitment to democratic pluralism prevents him from taking the Hobbesian path and allows him to respect value pluralism in civil society. The result is acknowledgment of the possibility of competing interpretations of public reason. Rawls's un-Hobbesian path, therefore,

---

[36] See Michael Ridge, "Hobbesian Public Reason," *Ethics* 108 (1998), pp. 538–568.

renders the line between comprehensive doctrines and public reason far more porous than it is usually believed to be or even intended to be by Rawls himself.

Political liberals may find this unintended consequence of Rawls's respect of pluralism, namely, the intertwinement between public reason with some perfectionist concerns, regrettable or unacceptable because it undermines political liberalism's core commitment to state neutrality.[37] In my view, however, the overlap between public reason and comprehensive doctrines enables us to explore a new mode of normative theory, which can be called *public reason perfectionism*. Like political liberalism, and far more so than the existing theories of perfectionism (particularly ones subscribing to Raz's service conception of authority), public reason perfectionism takes the coerciveness of political power seriously and thus understands disagreements about justice primarily as justificatory disagreements. However, unlike political liberalism, which formally rejects interactions between public reason and comprehensive doctrine,[38] public reason perfectionism allows such interactions without denying the important distinction between the two, both conceptually and practically, in consideration of the indispensable connection between *public* reason and democratic citizenship. As will be discussed later, public reason Confucianism is one particular type of public reason perfectionism that enables as well as expresses the collective self-determination of the Confucian people, despite their internal diversity.

---

[37] Quong, *Liberalism without Perfection*, p. 200.

[38] It is worth noting that while "formally" rejecting an interaction between public reason and comprehensive doctrines, Rawls endorses what he calls the "inclusive view" of public reason, which "allow[s] citizens, in certain situations [where there is a serious dispute with regard to principles of justice], to present what they regard as the basis of political values rooted in their comprehensive doctrine, provided they do this in ways that strengthen the ideal of public reason itself" (*Political Liberalism*, p. 247). Also see what Rawls calls *the proviso* and the "wide view" in "The Idea of Public Reason Revisited," pp. 143–144, 152–156. Rawls's examples include the nonpublic reasons (particularly religious doctrines) presented by the abolitionists during American Civil War and Martin Luther King Jr. during the civil rights movement in the 1960s (*Political Liberalism*, pp. 249–250). However, what I call the unintended entwinement between public reason and comprehensive doctrine is qualitatively different from Rawls's inclusive/wide view in that while the former points to plural interpretations of public reason (and the source of disagreement among reasonable citizens with regard to what constitutes public reason), the latter is mainly concerned with contributions that comprehensive doctrines that are themselves not part of public reason can, nevertheless, strengthen public reason in the long run (see Larmore, "Public Reason," p. 385).

But before turning to public reason Confucianism, let us grapple a bit further with an important question: how public reason can be connected with perfectionist values in a pluralist society. Surprisingly (and perhaps disappointingly for many public reason liberals), Rawls's political liberalism reveals one way to think about public reason perfectionism. An investigation of Rawls's political liberalism once more with regard to its surprising connection with (liberal) perfectionism can provide us with an important comparative backdrop against which we can construct a theory of public reason Confucianism as the most plausible mode of Confucian democratic perfectionism.

BETWEEN PUBLIC REASON LIBERALISM AND PUBLIC REASON PERFECTIONISM

The central importance of public reason in Rawls's political liberalism is his supreme concern with stability in a free society marked by the plurality of various comprehensive doctrines. And, as is well known, Rawls's solution is overlapping consensus on a particular set of principles of justice which then ought to be endorsed by (reasonable) comprehensive doctrines as true or right. Rawls calls this type of stability "stability for the right reason."[39] For Rawls, however, overlapping consensus is not derived directly from comprehensive doctrines, because it must be a consensus on the principles of justice each person should have both sound and identical reasons to embrace. Rawls explicitly notes that in making public justifications, citizens are to "appeal only to presently accepted general beliefs and forms of reasoning found in common sense, and the methods and conclusions of science when these are not controversial."[40]

In one of the most controversial passages in *Political Liberalism*, Rawls even says that the content of the political conception of justice is "expressed in terms of certain fundamental ideas seen as implicit in the public political culture of a democratic society,"[41] implying the existence of a deep consensus (or "common sense") among reasonable citizens, who otherwise subscribe to different comprehensive doctrines, *prior to* an overlapping consensus. In short, for Rawls, overlapping consensus ought to be derived from shared perspectives or common sense – namely, public reason. Charles Larmore's following statement illuminates this important aspect of Rawls's political liberalism most clearly.

---

[39] Rawls, "The Idea of Public Reason Revisited," pp. 173, 176.
[40] Rawls, *Political Liberalism*, p. 224.   [41] Ibid., p. 13.

Yet an important question is whether this shared perspective, rooted as it must be in reasons which citizens can acknowledge only by abstracting from their divergent visions of the human good, nonetheless coheres with the comprehensive conceptions to which they are attached. Only if the consensus shaping their public reasoning about justice also forms an overlapping consensus, a common element in their otherwise different points of view, is the structure of their political life likely to endure. The notion of overlapping consensus serves therefore to connect a conception of justice already arrived at, and already marked by a more fundamental kind of consensus, to the question of its stability. ... [Therefore] we should not overlook the idea of consensus that does figure in the initial determination of these principles [of justice]. Publicity requires that they draw on reasons which all can acknowledge.[42]

Here, however, arises the thorny question: if public reason is a value that reasonable citizens (ought to) acknowledge prior to an overlapping consensus, how can it be justifiable to those who reject the *liberal* idea of public reason in the first place? It is important to note that for Rawls, being reasonable is not merely an epistemological idea, though he defines it largely in epistemological terms especially with regard to the burdens of judgment. "Rather," says Rawls, "[reasonableness] is a part of a political ideal of democratic citizenship that includes the idea of public reason. The content of this ideal includes what free and equal citizens as reasonable can require of each other with respect to their reasonable comprehensive views."[43] And it is on this foundational idea of reasonableness that Rawls adamantly declares that political liberalism does not engage with the critics of public reason, calling them "unreasonable."[44]

But if political liberalism applies only to those who accept the fundamentally *liberal* idea of free and equal "personhood," on which Rawls's entire notion of democratic citizenship is built,[45] and thus no one can reasonably disagree with fundamental political values of a liberal democratic society, then how can it be thoroughly political and thus neutral in relation to controversial moral values? Stephen Mulhall and Adam Swift are puzzled over this problem when they say that

---

[42] Larmore, "Public Reason," pp. 377–378.   [43] Rawls, *Political Liberalism*, p. 62.
[44] Rawls, "The Idea of Public Reason Revisited," pp. 132–133.
[45] Consider the following statement by Rawls: "In giving reasons to all citizens we don't view persons as socially situated or otherwise rooted, that is, as being in this or that social class, or in this or that property and income group, or as having this or that comprehensive doctrine. Nor are we appealing to each person's or each group's interests, though at some point we must take these interests into account. Rather, we think of persons as reasonable and rational, as free and equal citizens, with the two moral powers" (Ibid., p. 171).

it now appears that recognizing the burdens of judgment will only result in the right sort of respect for the values of political liberalism if one's comprehensive doctrine endorses a view of political society as just such a system of fair cooperation. In short, his response is entirely circular. By defining "the reasonable" as including a commitment to a politically liberal vision of society, Rawls defines anyone who queries or rejects that vision as "unreasonable," but he offers no independent reason for accepting that morally driven and question-begging definition.[46]

They then conclude, "This means that what, for Rawls at least, makes political liberalism so distinctive and attractive – its claim to have extended the principle of tolerance to philosophy itself, to have discovered a way of defending political anti-perfectionism without invoking controversial value-judgements [sic] about the relative worth of competing comprehensive doctrines – disappears."[47]

Noting this very problem latent in public reason liberalism, Jonathan Quong distinguishes the so-called internal conception of political liberalism from the external conception of political liberalism. Roughly, the external conception of political liberalism stipulates that public reason liberalism must be justifiable to persons who cannot be assumed to endorse any basic liberal norms and values, assuming that the fact of pluralism is a fact about the world to which liberalism must accommodate itself, while the internal conception understands pluralism not so much as a fact about the world but as a consequence of liberalism itself. What is interesting about this distinction is that Quong attributes the latter to Rawls's own position, while finding the former too ambitious, ultimately untenable.[48] Quong says,

> I do not believe liberal rights and principles can be consistently justified to persons who do not already embrace certain abstract liberal values (e.g., the moral ideal of persons as free and equal, and of society as a fair system of cooperation). The internal conception's more modest ambition – to work out a model of political justification for *liberals* – is not an attempt to do the impossible, and thus it avoids the difficulties that beset the external model.[49]

---

[46] Stephen Mulhall and Adam Swift, "Rawls and Communitarianism," in *The Cambridge Companion to Rawls*, pp. 460–487, p. 483.

[47] Ibid., p. 484.

[48] Quong, *Liberalism without Perfection*, pp. 137–160. Indeed, Rawls says, "Political liberalism assumes that, for political purposes, a plurality of reasonable yet incompatible comprehensive doctrines is the normal result of the exercise of human reason within the framework of the free institutions of a constitutional democratic regime" (*Political Liberalism*, p. xviii).

[49] Quong, *Liberalism without Perfection*, p. 140.

Quong's (and Larmore's) interpretation of Rawls's political liberalism as advocating the internal conception is widely shared by other scholars, though some clearly object to this line of interpretation.[50] However, if public reason liberalism is only relevant to "liberals" and "reasonableness" can be derived directly from the liberal conception of personhood as free and equal without going through the painstaking *political* process of overlapping consensus,[51] it is difficult to differentiate it meaningfully from the comprehensive liberalism that it criticizes. Certainly, Rawlsian public reason liberalism does not *actively* or *self-consciously* promote controversial notions of the good or flourishing, but as Gerald Gaus rightly notes, it is as sectarian as perfectionism in the sense that it promotes the values that nonliberals cannot endorse.[52] As long as public reason liberalism promotes a particular (if not fully comprehensive) understanding of a valuable life endorsed only by the liberal citizens *already* committed to liberal constitutional values, it is inevitably perfectionist. It is precisely for this reason that William Galston finds Rawls's political liberalism verging on "a kind of democratic perfectionism."[53]

Seen in this way, even though Rawls may allow multiple interpretations of public reason out of his non-Hobbesian respect for plurality, in the framework of his political liberalism, all such interpretations, however different they may be, must be *substantively* liberal in both their

---

[50] For instance see K. Roberts Skerrett, "Political Liberalism and the Idea of Public Reason: A Response to Jeffrey Stout's *Democracy and Tradition*," *Social Theory and Practice* 31 (2005), pp. 173–190; George Klosko, *Democratic Procedures and Liberal Consensus* (Oxford: Oxford University Press, 2000), p. 4.

[51] See T. M. Scanlon, "Rawls on Justification," in *The Cambridge Companion to Rawls*, pp. 139–167, pp. 164–165. Eamonn Callan thus says, "Rawlsian public reason is only freestanding relative to a much more restricted range of persons – namely, those who adhere to the strenuous ideal of the reasonable contained in his political conception of the person" (*Creating Citizens: Political Education and Liberal Democracy* [Oxford: Oxford University Press, 1997], p. 33).

[52] Gerald Gaus, "Sectarianism without Perfection? Quong's Political Liberalism," *Philosophy and Public Issues* 2 (2012), pp. 7–15.

[53] William A. Galston, *Liberal Purposes: Goods, Virtues, and Diversity in the Liberal State* (Cambridge: Cambridge University Press, 1991), p. 148. In his more recent work, Galston criticizes Rawls's political liberalism as a kind of democratic dogmatism: "Comprehensive doctrines are deemed 'unreasonable' to the extent that they stand in tension with constitutional democracy, inviting us to believe that the rejection of democracy is itself unreasonable. If this is what Rawls means, then he must offer reasons to show why there is no basis for accepting nondemocratic modes of governance. Because the idea of public reason is parasitic on democracy, it cannot be used against those who question democracy" (*Liberal Pluralism: The Implications of Value Pluralism for Political Theory and Practice* [Cambridge: Cambridge University Press, 2002], p. 44).

assumptions and form. We should not gloss over Rawls's repeated reminder that the political conception of justice he has in mind in *Political Liberalism* is "broadly liberal in character."[54] The substantively liberal character of Rawls's political liberalism becomes even more salient when Rawls revisits his political theory from an international perspective. In *The Law of Peoples*, Rawls acknowledges that each reasonable people has and can have its own internal government, liberal-democratic or nonliberal-but-decent,[55] and based on this judgment, which parallels his consistent respect of pluralism, he, unlike many "Rawlsian" scholars, does not apply the idea of the original position, which he admits is *a liberal idea*, to the domestic justice of decent nonliberal regimes.[56]

The finding that political liberalism as *a* kind of public reason liberalism – perhaps the most representative kind – is *morally* committed to substantively liberal values[57] and has the liberal conception of personhood as its foundational premise, thereby verging on liberal-democratic perfectionism, enables us to understand that public reason, insomuch as it is the reason of democratic citizens, cannot be completely severed from comprehensive doctrines and/or perfectionist concerns.[58] At the same time, perfectionists should learn from public reason liberalism that political power, which is by nature coercive, must be justified to citizens who despite their internal diversity must have common premises that can serve as the standard for mutual justification and reciprocity. Although for political liberals, public reason perfectionism may be a borderline oxymoron or an embarrassment, for those who are not morally committed to state neutrality it presents quite a coherent and attractive normative position.

---

[54] Rawls, *Political Liberalism*, p. 223.   [55] Rawls, *The Law of Peoples*, p. 3.
[56] Ibid., p. 70. In *Political Liberalism*, Rawls offers a clear account on how liberal public reason and (the liberal conception of) the original position have essentially the same grounds: "In justice as fairness, and I think in many other liberal views, the guidelines of inquiry of public reason, as well as its principles of legitimacy, have the same basis as the substantive principles of justice. This means in justice as fairness that the parties in the original position, in adopting principles of justice for the basic structure, must also adopt guidelines and criteria of public reason for applying those norms" (p. 225).
[57] Rawls emphatically says, "Political conceptions of justice are themselves intrinsically moral ideas [and a]s such they are a kind of normative value" ("The Idea of Public Reason Revisited," p. 174n91).
[58] Callan even says that "Rawls's political liberalism in particular is really a disguised instance of comprehensive liberalism" (*Creating Citizens*, p. 13). Also see Richard Dagger, *Civic Virtues: Rights, Citizenship, and Republican Liberalism* (New York: Oxford University Press, 1997), pp. 181–192.

Thus understood, from the perspective of public reason perfectionism, there is nothing wrong with involving controversial ideas about the good life in public deliberation and the political decision-making process if they can contribute to a more robust democratic citizenship and democratic justice. Public reason perfectionism is especially relevant for non-Western societies that aspire to become democratic (or more democratic) while struggling to balance new democratic institutions and practices with their nonliberal values and ways of life. Public reason perfectionism can provide nonliberal but democratic peoples with a powerful normative theory that allows them collective self-determination as well as democratic self-government undergirded on common (nonliberal) citizenship and mutual reciprocity without suppressing ever-increasing internal plurality in civil society and also without denying the democratic value of public equality.[59] Public reason Confucianism is one variation of public reason perfectionism that is best suited for East Asian societies.

PUBLIC REASON CONFUCIANISM

Public reason Confucianism has two core normative premises: (1) there is a valuable Confucian way of life that is distinct from (if not starkly opposed to) a liberal way of life and (2) it is permissible for a state, one that is democratically controlled by its citizens, to promote or discourage some activities, ideas, or ways of life based on the grounds of a constellation of Confucian values such as, but not limited to, filial piety, respect for elders, ancestor worship, ritual propriety, harmony within the family, and social harmony. These premises are supplemented by six propositions that together render public reason Confucianism a kind of democratic perfectionism.

P1: The valuable Confucian way of life refers to the collective way of living widely shared and cherished by citizens in a Confucian society.

---

[59] Thomas Christiano presents public equality as an intrinsic value of democracy by deriving its moral value from the foundational liberal conception of personhood and individual dignity, thereby rooting both democracy and liberal rights on the same moral ground. See his *The Constitution of Equality: Democratic Authority and Its Limits* (Oxford: Oxford University Press, 2008). This may be a plausible way to make a coherent sense of *liberal democracy*. I argue, however, that in a nonliberal democracy, public equality, though valuable intrinsically, does not have to be rooted in the liberal conception of personhood and its foundational moral value.

P2: Citizens in a Confucian society are still saturated with Confucian habits, mores, and moral sentiments, despite their subscriptions to various comprehensive doctrines, and even though they may not hold Confucianism as their self-consciously chosen personal value system.

P3: In a Confucian society, all citizens are equal to one another qua public citizens and together they exercise popular sovereignty.

P4: The Confucian (democratic) state respects constitutional rights held by its citizens, among others, the rights to religious freedom, freedom of conscience, freedom of expression, and freedom of association; thus the state has no desire either to suppress value plurality in civil society or to elevate Confucianism as the state religion.

P5: Confucian public reason refers to the reason of the democratic citizens in a Confucian society and it is rooted in Confucian mores, habits, and moral sentiments such as, but not limited to, filial piety and ritual propriety; it delineates the legitimate boundary of state action and provides moral content (which is open for public contestation) for basic rights, duties, and liberties.

P6: A subscription to Confucian public reason (as stipulated in P5) on the part of voluntary immigrants and cultural associations formed by them is the inevitable price for the fair terms of integration into the Confucian society (such as the equal right to freedom of association). While Confucian public reason must be justifiable to *all* citizens in a Confucian society, including immigrants, immigrated citizens should strive to negotiate their religious or nonreligious comprehensive doctrines with Confucian public reason in order to fully exercise their constitutional rights and liberties.

In the remainder of this chapter, I will expound on each of these key propositions of public reason Confucianism.

P1: The valuable Confucian way of life

P1 stipulates that a collective way of life among the citizens in East Asian societies of the Confucian heritage (*Confucian citizens* hereafter) is distinctly different from a characteristically liberal way of life, and Confucian citizens value their own way of living even when their formal political institutions are more or less liberal democratic. Consider the following statement made by a Korean political scientist a decade after South Korea's democratization.

[L]iberal democracy has been the ideal for the majority of South Koreans in name only. Very few Koreans understand either the theoretical assumptions or the normative standards which undergird liberal democracy and its institutions. Moreover, once they are explained to them, few would espouse liberal democracy with as much ardor and enthusiasm.[60]

When non-Western people are trying to transform authoritarian regimes into democratic ones, they rarely reflect on the *kind* of democracy that they would have after their painstaking struggles. In most cases, their future is unpredictable and almost everything depends on political contingency. In such circumstances, all they can hope for is that their struggles succeed, culminating in regime change. This is true not only of mass ascendant democratization of the kind South Koreans and Taiwanese experienced, in which citizens themselves were major agents to the regime change, but also of other forms of democratic transitions in which political elites play more substantial roles. The question of "what kind of democracy?" becomes important only *after* a successful regime change that political scientists call "democratization" and it is at this "consolidation" stage that scholars and citizens begin to wrestle with the new mode of collective life that they want to have under democratic institutions.[61]

Since democratic institutions that have been (fully) introduced are characteristically liberal and the liberal rights discourse is almost unfailingly affiliated with democratic institutions and practices that now ought to be "the only game in town,"[62] the question generally revolves around whether democratization should be a *liberal democratization* in which there should be a congruence between liberal democratic institutions and liberal public reasons and civilities,[63] or if it is possible (or even desirable) to develop an indigenous mode of democracy whose democratic institutional structures operate on public reason and civilities informed by local culture. The statement quoted earlier reveals that the latter path was the case with South Koreans, and I argue that it is the most desirable way

---

[60] Chaibong Hahm, "The Confucian Political Discourse and the Politics of Reform in Korea," *Korea Journal* 34:4 (1997), pp. 65–77, 66.
[61] Larry Diamond and Marc F. Plattner (eds.), *The Global Divergence of Democracies* (Baltimore: Johns Hopkins University Press, 2001).
[62] Juan J. Linz and Alfred Stepan, *Problems of Democratic Transition and Consolidation: Southern Europe, South America, and Post-Communist Europe* (Baltimore: Johns Hopkins University Press, 1996), p. 5.
[63] George Kateb, for instance, is strongly convinced of the liberal democratization thesis when he says, "The possibly nonindividualistic experience of democracy outside America must be treated circumspectly" (*The Inner Ocean: Individualism and Democratic Culture* [Ithaca: Cornell University Press, 1992], p. 77).

to conceive of democracy in a nonliberal context. For only then can there be congruence between the people's collective self-identity (as Confucian) and their democratic self-government so that people can be democratic without transforming themselves into (Western-style) *liberals*, which they never anticipated during their democratic struggles. As Chaibong Hahm observes, "[a]lthough the vocabulary used by all sides in Korean politics today are couched in liberal democratic concepts and theories, the logic which undergirds the actual practice of politics derives from the traditional Confucian political discourse."[64] I call this type of democracy a *Confucian democracy*.[65]

Now, if we revisit the philosophical debate between political liberals (particularly political liberal antiperfectionists such as Rawls) and comprehensive liberals (particularly comprehensive liberal perfectionists such as Raz) from the standpoint of the actual political experience of democratizing East Asia, it is clear that both forms of liberalism are *substantively* liberal and have little cultural resonance with ordinary East Asian citizens – Confucian citizens, as I call them. Even the efforts to implement political liberalism a la Rawls or Habermas (usually made by local political theorists trained in the West) are perceived as futile attempts to achieve congruence between democratic institutions and liberal culture. For Confucian citizens, the public reason that is emphasized is hardly neutral because it is always *liberal* public reason that they are encouraged to embrace and embody.

Thus understood, the perfectionist values of the Confucian way of life are most intelligible and self-consciously recognized when Confucian citizens are under staggering pressure to transform themselves into liberals. The normative vision of public reason Confucianism is enacted when citizens of East Asia reclaim, albeit with considerable modification under democratic institutions, *their* valued way of life, and try to be reasonable with one another, those with whom they share political power.

P2: The Confucian habits of the heart in a pluralist society

As noted, recent Confucian political theory has been sought as a pluralist correction to the global hegemony of Western-style liberal democracy.

---

[64] Hahm, "Confucian Political Discourse," p. 66. Also see Sungmoon Kim, "Confucianism in Contestation: The May Struggle of 1991 in South Korea and Its Lesson," *New Political Science* 31 (2009), pp. 49–68.
[65] See Kim, *Confucian Democracy*, pp. 4–11.

Yet, when Confucian political theorists construct their normative political theories, they tend to assume that the East Asian society of their interest is *the* Confucian society in a culturally monistic sense. Most notably, Jiang Qing presents a political theory of Confucian constitutionalism that can make sense only if the contemporary Chinese state has Confucianism as its state religion and its citizens are all comprehensively committed to religious Confucianism.[66] Even Joseph Chan, a moderate political Confucian perfectionist, presents his political theory in a way that can track the comprehensive Confucian ideal of the Grand Union under the assumption that this utopian ideal is widely shared by the Chinese people whose nonideal situations quite regrettably prevent them from realizing it.[67]

By terms such as "Confucian citizens" or "the Confucian way of life" I do not mean that contemporary East Asian societies are Confucian in an institutionally guided, culturally monolithic, or philosophically monistic sense. Contemporary East Asian societies, especially those that have been democratized, are characterized by vibrant civil societies that are internally diverse. People there are increasingly pluralist and multicultural, subscribing to different moral, philosophical, and religious doctrines. For instance, even among South Koreans, the most Confucian historically[68] as well as to this day,[69] albeit arguably, only a negligible number of people self-consciously identify Confucianism (i.e., religious Confucianism) as their personal value system.[70]

Given increasing value pluralization in East Asia's historically Confucian societies, what is truly remarkable is that they still remain deeply Confucian in terms of their ways of thinking and living, especially when others, particularly family members, are involved.[71] According to survey

---

[66] Jiang Qing, *A Confucian Constitutional Order: How China's Ancient Past Can Shape Its Political Future*, eds. Daniel A. Bell and Ruiping Fan and trans. Edmund Ryden (Princeton: Princeton University Press, 2012).

[67] Chan, *Confucian Perfectionism*, pp. 1–14.

[68] Martina Deuchler, *The Confucian Transformation of Korea: A Study of Society and Ideology* (Cambridge: Council on East Asian Studies, Harvard University, 1992).

[69] Tu Wei-ming, "The Search for Roots in Industrial East Asia: The Case of the Confucian Revival," in *Fundamentalisms Observed*, eds. Martin E. Marty and R. Scott Appleby (Chicago: University of Chicago Press, 1991), p. 761.

[70] According the statistical data culled in 2005, only 0.004% (104,575/24,970,766) of those who said that they have religion declared themselves Confucian. See Korean Ministry of Culture, Sports, and Tourism, "Religions in Korea" [Han'gugŭi Chonggyo hyŏnhwang], 2011 (publication number: 11-1371000-000391-01).

[71] Some useful statistical data can be found in Doh Chull Shin, *Confucianism and Democratization in East Asia* (New York: Cambridge University Press, 2012). According to

research on the value orientation of liberal-minded middle class, mostly Western-style educated, Korean citizens, approximately 80 percent responded that South Korea's rapid economic development, democratization, and liberal individualization notwithstanding, their value system has been helplessly impoverished. In addition, over 90 percent agreed that the reinvigoration of Confucian values such as filial piety (*hyo* 孝, c. *xiao*), respect for elders (*kyŏngno* 敬老, c. *jinglao*), the principle of the mean (*chungyong* 中庸, c. *zhongyong*), and people-centrism (*minbon* 民本, c. *minben*) is critical to restoring the Koreans' collective value system and social norms.[72] Varied statistical research conducted more recently consistently attests to the fact that Koreans (and other East Asians), despite their liberal individualization and diversification in terms of moral and/or religious value, are simultaneously committed to core Confucian values, most notably filial piety, respect for elders, and ritual propriety (*li* 禮).[73] All the more surprising, social scientists in the East Asian region and beyond are increasingly persuaded that the cultural locomotive underlying Korean and Taiwanese democratization is Confucian values, with which the democratic activists there rarely, if ever, self-consciously associate their political actions.[74]

Su-yeong Ryu's fascinating statistical research, the guiding (public or social) value system for the predominant majority of the contemporary Korean people are still heavily informed by Confucian values such as benevolence (*ren* 仁), ritual propriety (*li* 禮), and sense of appropriateness (*yi* 義) ("Han'guginŭi yugyojŏk kach'ich'ŭkchŏngmunhang kaebal yŏn'gu" [Item Development for Korean Confucian Values], *Korean Journal of Management* 15 [2007], pp. 171–205).

[72] Sangjin Han and Kisu Eun, "Kaehyŏkchiyangjŏk chungsanch'ŭngŭi kach'igwanchiyang'gwa ch'amyŏjŏk shillyoesahoe kuch'uk" [The Value Orientation of the Progressive-Minded Middle Class and the Construction of a Participatory Fiduciary Society], The Ministry of Education Research Report, South Korea, 1999.

[73] Mun-jo Bae and Se-jeong Park, "Taehaksengŭi hyoedaehan inshikkwa kachokgach'igwane yŏnghyang'ŭl mich'inŭn pyŏnin" [Consciousness of Filial Piety and Family Values among College Students], *Journal of the Korean Contents Association* 13 (2013), pp. 275–285; Ryu, "Han'guginŭi'; Shin, *Confucianism and Democratization*.

[74] Chong-sŏk Na, "Han'guk minjujuŭiwa yugyomunhwa" [Korean Democracy and Confucian Culture], in *Yuhagi onŭlŭi munchee tabŭl jul su innŭnga* [Can Confucianism Give an Answer for Today's Problems], eds. Chong-sŏk Na, Yŏng-to Park, and Kyŏng-ran Cho (Seoul: Hyean, 2014), pp. 242–270; Joel S. Fetzer and J. Christopher Soper, *Confucianism, Democratization, and Human Rights in Taiwan* (Lanham: Lexington Books, 2013); Chaibong Hahm, "The Ironies of Confucianism," *Journal of Democracy* 15 (2004), pp. 93–107; Geir Helgesen, *Democracy and Authority in Korea: The Cultural Dimension in Korean Politics* (Surrey: Curzon, 1998); Namhee Lee, *The Making of Minjung: Democracy and the Politics of Representation in South Korea* (Ithaca: Cornell University Press, 2007).

The key is that Confucianism in contemporary East Asia is "hardly visible on the surface and rarely manifests itself in any organization or institution. It survives only at the most basic level of the popular consciousness and in the routines of daily life."[75] I believe the following statement is generally true for East Asians who still adhere to Confucianism as their *habits of the heart*.[76]

Even those who identified themselves as Christians and adhered to Christian values and practices were very much inclined to Confucian values and practices as well, and when measured against the itemized scale, a substantial majority of Korean Christians were found in fact to be at least "marginal" members of Confucianism. ... This confirms the statement of a well-known Christian theologian, who said, "Our Christians are Confucians dressed in Christian robes."[77]

As a normative political theory, public reason Confucianism finds nothing regrettable about the reality of pluralism in East Asia in which Confucianism no longer enjoys the status of state ideology or doctrinal orthodoxy. In this regard, it is not analogous to religious or philosophical Confucianism; nor is it a comprehensive doctrine in any strong sense if we define comprehensive doctrine in terms of mutual incommensurability. Nevertheless, the Confucianism in public reason Confucianism holds substantively Confucian perfectionist values that give the East Asian people a Confucian public character. And this publicly intelligible Confucianism binds citizens horizontally as equal members of one political community, notwithstanding their internal differences and moral disagreements. Public reason Confucianism recognizes the East Asian people as *Confucian citizens* only in this sense. Since Confucianism here is a publicly intelligible ethical value, even though it is not tightly rooted in philosophical or religious Confucian doctrines, it is still a set of comprehensive ideas and values (in a weak and partial sense). Thus understood, public reason Confucianism is a type of comprehensive Confucian perfectionism.[78]

---

[75] Byung-ik Koh, "Confucianism in Contemporary Korea," in *Confucian Traditions in East Asian Modernity: Moral Education and Economic Culture in Japan and Four Mini-Dragons*, ed. Tu Wei-ming (Cambridge: Harvard University Press, 1996), pp. 191–201, p. 194.
[76] See Philip J. Ivanhoe and Sungmoon Kim (eds.), *Confucianism, A Habit of the Heart: Bellah, Civil Religion, and East Asia.* (Albany: State University of New York, forthcoming).
[77] Koh, "Confuicanism in Contemporary Korea," p. 199.
[78] Compare my position with Joseph Chan's (moderate) political Confucian perfectionism (Chan, *Confucian Perfectionism*, pp. 199–204).

P3: Public equality

Public reason Confucianism is qualitatively different from the traditional Confucianism practiced by East Asians in premodern periods and from the version some traditionalists in the region still cling to, a Confucianism that is heavily patriarchal, androcentric, and hierarchical.[79] Though public reason Confucianism has no ambition of transforming traditionalist Confucians into so-called "modern citizens," it is a modern normative political theory and a vision that treats every member of the political community as equal citizens.

This feature of public reason Confucianism is directly related to my qualified endorsement of state paternalism in the societal context of value pluralism in Chapter 1. Just briefly, in that chapter, I differentiated between two kinds of state paternalism – state paternalism aimed at protecting the physical well-being of citizens (e.g., preventing and treating drug addiction) and state value paternalism that aspires to harmonize different, often conflicting, moral interests of citizens. Though embracing the former kind of state paternalism with some caution, public reason Confucianism completely rejects state value paternalism and its pretense to have the transcendental eyes of a sage. Under the fact of value pluralism, every citizen is loaded with the burdens of judgment, which means that no one, including political elites, can claim to know one's moral interest better than he or she does. For instance, it is question-begging, nearly nonsensical, for a group of political elites to claim that a particular moral position in the abortion debate should be preferred because it serves the putative common good better. In the radical absence of an independent moral and epistemic standard to adjudicate moral disagreements among the citizens, each citizen demands to be seen and treated by others as rational and they all want their moral judgments to be respected, even when they are found objectionable to some. Therefore, public reason Confucianism derives the moral value of public equality from equal public standing of the people qua citizens under the societal condition of value pluralism.

The value of public equality can be vindicated from another angle. One of the distinctive features of Confucianism as a political tradition is that it never envisioned an alternative mode of political regime other than a one-

---

[79] Indigenous inhabitants in New Territories (新界) of Hong Kong and cultural villages in Andong area in South Korea are two best examples of the continued practice of traditional Confucianism in contemporary East Asia.

man monarchy. As I discussed elsewhere,[80] even Mencius, who had strong faith in moral equality in terms of the underlying goodness of human nature and a person's capacity for moral development, never considered the possibility of any other form of government.[81] In short, he was never a champion of political equality, not to mention democratic government; for him the only legitimate political relationship was that between the ruler and the ministers. Mencius argued that the monarch is given by Heaven a moral right to rule the people who vicariously reveal the will of Heaven. The ruler has immense moral responsibility to take care of the moral and material well-being of the people, but Mencius did not fail to note that it is only to Heaven that he is ultimately accountable because Heaven (or its delegates) alone can rightfully depose him from the throne.[82]

None of the contemporary East Asian societies has a one-man monarchy, on which traditional Confucian political theory and practice were predicated, and the complete abolition of it drives us to rethink the relationship between the ruler and the ruled, and more importantly, the relationships among ordinary people who are now citizens. In our "republican" age where there is no "son of Heaven" or other delegates of Heaven, the right to rule should ultimately go to the people whose dis/content with the incumbent ruler or government represents the will of Heaven, according to traditional Confucian political discourse.[83] That is, in our politically post-Heaven era, the most important political institution is *citizenship*, making the relationship between the ruler and the ruled of secondary importance and into that of (democratic) political accountability.

Under pluralistic societal conditions, citizenship understood as an equal share of political power can be exercised meaningfully only if each citizen's moral interest is equally respected. Equal share of political power and equal respect of moral interest together establish the moral value of public equality. As will be discussed in the following chapters, one of the

---

[80] See Kim, *Confucian Democracy*, pp. 191–196.
[81] More accurately, Mencius distinguished the Kingly Way (*wangdao* 王道) from the hegemonic rule (*badao* 霸道), which he basically equated with tyranny, but he never explored an alternative form of government to one-man monarchy even in this important normative distinction.
[82] Justin Tiwald, "A Right of Rebellion in the *Mengzi*?" *Dao* 7 (2008), pp. 269–282.
[83] What is interesting about Jiang Qing's political theory is that while acknowledging the republican condition of modern China, he still adheres to Heavenly political sanction as necessary and attempts to reinstate Confucian monarchy coached by a group of Confucian scholars.

central values integral to public reason Confucianism is gender equality because it tracks perhaps the most important feature of both public equality and common citizenship.

P4: Democratic pluralism

P3 establishes public equality as a value intrinsic to public reason Confucianism. It is important to note that although public reason Confucianism is qualitatively different from traditional Confucianism, which rejects, among others, the moral value of gender equality, it does not aim to transform traditional Confucians or those who belong to particular cultural or religious groups into what social scientists call "modern individuals."[84] Not only is public reason Confucianism compatible with a plurality of lifestyles in civil society but it further protects various freedoms – religious freedom, freedom of conscience, freedom of expression, and freedom of association, to name just a few – which are indispensable to the survival and flourishing of various groups and associations, by making them constitutional rights. In this regard, public reason Confucianism is starkly opposed to Jiang Qing's Confucian constitutionalism. Consider the following statement by Jiang:

> In Confucian understanding, the main purpose of sovereignty is to implement religious and moral values, using transcendent and sacred goodness to regulate sovereignty and guide it toward the good. Consequently, the fundamental purpose of Confucian constitutionalism is to regulate and educate the holders of supreme power in the state so that they will realize the transcendent values of China's Confucian culture. A state order in conformity with Confucian ideas encourages the political authorities to implement the goodness of the Way of heaven.[85]

As Joseph Chan rightly notes, Jiang's Confucian perfectionism is extreme.[86] Given the compulsory nature of the state, it is difficult to understand how Jiang's ideal Confucian regime can accommodate, let alone respect, values, ideas, and lifestyles that do not perfectly cohere with Confucianism, which he now wants to make the state religion. Public reason Confucianism has no desire to reinstate Confucianism as official

---

[84] Alex Inkeles, "Making Men Modern: On the Causes and Consequences of Individual Change in Six Developing Countries," *American Journal of Sociology* 75 (1969), pp. 208–225; Ernest Gellner, *Conditions of Liberty: Civil Society and Its Rivals* (New York: Penguin Books, 1996).
[85] Jiang, *Confucian Constitutional Order*, p. 52.
[86] Joseph Chan, "On Legitimacy of Confucian Constitutionalism," in Jiang, *Confucian Constitutional Order*, pp. 99–112.

state ideology. That said, public reason Confucianism also does not pretend to be neutral to all kinds of ideals, values, lifestyles. In fact, insomuch as public reason Confucianism is recognized by Confucian citizens as "Confucian," it is not completely severed from traditional Confucianism. It is for this reason that public reason Confucianism is a kind of comprehensive doctrine, if we understand the term somewhat loosely.

What differentiates public reason Confucianism from traditional Confucianism is its ambition to have, maintain, and reproduce one political community with a distinctive public culture that can accommodate different moral interests as far as possible within the constitutional limits set by Confucian public reason. Thus, public reason Confucianism aims to promote certain Confucian values such as filial piety and ritual propriety but it does not embrace other Confucian values cherished by traditionalist or religious Confucians as public values applicable to all members of the political community because such values are only relevant to a small number of self-claimed Confucians who still adhere to their traditional Confucian way of life. At the same time, under public reason Confucianism, traditional Confucians (for instance, members of the clan organizations in Korea) can continue their traditional way of life by resorting to their constitutional right to freedom of association.

Even if the conceptual distinction between public reason Confucianism, which is primarily concerned with the democratic citizens' public way of life, and traditional Confucianism, as practiced in East Asia in accordance with a certain doctrinal line, is accepted, a practical difficulty remains: what if a community of Confucian traditionalists persists in the kind of gender inequality that is part of their comprehensive doctrine? Is there a principled position that public reason Confucianism can take with regard to such a community? I turn to this issue in Chapter 4 by examining a recent Supreme Court decision in South Korea regarding clan membership between men (as sons) and women (as daughters). Leaving my detailed reasoning to that chapter, my brief answer to the question presented here is: public reason Confucianism would only attempt to regulate and rectify gender inequality that degrades women's public standing and rights but leaves the other inequalities, especially those voluntarily followed by women, to be resolved by members themselves. In any event, public reason Confucianism stipulates that what constitutes injury to women's "public" standing should be determined not by some putative universal liberal principle but in light of Confucian public reason.

P5: Confucian public reason

Confucian public reason refers to the reason of Confucian democratic citizens. It is what citizens in a Confucian democratic society share and appeal to when they are participating in public deliberation and making public judgments. It is a concept as well as a practice that is conceivable only if the idea of Confucian citizens as a self-governing people in a Confucian society is possible. As P1 and P2 stipulate, as a normative political theory public reason Confucianism is founded on the existence of self-governing Confucian citizens. One of the best ways to understand the distinctive characteristics of Confucian public reason is by comparing it to liberal public reason, which we have investigated extensively earlier.

First, in terms of content and character, Confucian public reason is clearly distinguished from liberal public reason. As we have seen, at the heart of liberal public reason, as far as the *idea* of public reason is concerned, is its complete detachment from any kind of perfectionist ends or comprehensive values. As purely political values, public reason is only formally concerned with certain rights, duties, or liberties. In contrast, Confucian public reason is grounded in substantive Confucian moral values such as filial piety, respect for elders (including ancestors), harmony within the family, and ritual propriety, and these values inform the contents of otherwise liberal political rights, duties, and liberties. For instance, in a Confucian democratic society where citizens generally cherish filial piety as one of the most important moral virtues, and thus the state is permitted (by its citizens) to promote it publicly, both the moral contents of core democratic rights and liberties such as freedom of expression and right to the pursuit of happiness and the public understanding of to what extent such rights and liberties can enjoy public protection are qualitatively different from those of a society where filial piety has no salient public value. Likewise, in a society where values like filial piety and ritual propriety are socially cherished and publicly promoted, the very conception of the state becomes radically different from that which we find in a liberal society – the state is deemed not so much as the outcome of (hypothetical) social contract but as kind of a family writ large in which citizens see (as well as feel) themselves *as* related through familial ties.

A more concrete case would be useful here. Freedom of expression is one of the essential liberal values and most East Asian societies hold it in their constitutions as an important civil right. There are a variety of reasons why freedom of expression is held sacred in Western liberal societies, constitutionally as well as socially, but one important reason has to do with the fact that it underlies both liberal individualism, concerned with *who I am* or personhood, and liberal pluralism, concerned with individual diversity and associational freedom.[87] However, in a society where "I" is understood in relational terms, family values and ritual propriety are publicly promoted, the society as a whole is deemed (or idealized) as a nationally extended family, and therefore social harmony and familial citizenship are valued, the value of freedom of expression is appreciated and exercised differently than it is in a liberal society. While liberal people embrace the "costs" accompanying their expressive liberty such as reputational injury and emotional distress[88] and make it a virtue to tolerate someone's free expression, though the expressed values may not be agreeable, Confucian people make every effort to avoid incurring even such mild harms to others, with whom they are indirectly and more distantly related, by constraining the way they exercise this freedom by means of ritual propriety and making the expression agreeable to communal norms and moral sentiments. The practical consequence of this difference is rather dramatic: whereas liberal people, by bearing certain costs of the freedom of expression and thus putting up with the "vicissitudes of pluralism,"[89] try to keep the state at bay from civil and private conflicts, Confucian people are more worried about uneasy social relationships than what liberals would consider "intervention" of the state, which they conceive of in terms of the image of the family. Thus understood, in a Confucian democratic society, freedom of expression is still valued as a citizen's constitutional right but its moral content and social scope is always balanced with Confucian mores, values, and moral sentiments. Confucian public reasoning involves this complex balancing process.[90]

---

[87] George Kateb, "The Value of Association," in *Freedom of Association*, ed. Amy Gutmann (Princeton: Princeton University Press, 1998), pp. 35–63; William A. Galston, *Liberal Pluralism: The Implications of Value Pluralism for Political Theory and Practice* (Cambridge: Cambridge University Press, 2002); Nancy L. Rosenblum, *Membership and Morals: The Personal Uses of Pluralism in America* (Princeton: Princeton University Press, 1998).
[88] Joshua Cohen, "Freedom of Expression," *Philosophy and Public Affairs* 22 (1993), pp. 207–263.
[89] Nancy L. Rosenblum, "The Democracy of Everyday Life," in *Liberalism without Illusions: Essays on Liberal Theory and the Political Vision of Judith N. Shklar*, ed. Bernard Yack (Chicago: University of Chicago Press, 1996), pp. 25–44, at p. 40.
[90] I elaborate on this point in greater detail in Kim, *Confucian Democracy*, chap. 10.

This, however, is not to say that grounded in certain perfectionist values, Confucian public reason is insulated from different, even contending, interpretations. Quite to the contrary, public reason Confucianism allows citizens to negotiate their comprehensive moral values with *Confucian* public reason, *then* with particular rights, duties, and liberties. As long as citizens are willing to do so, public reason Confucianism further allows them to contest the dominant understanding of public reason in the public space of civil society as well as in more formal public forums (such as parliament and the court) so that it can be more inclusive and accommodating without forfeiting its Confucian character.

Second, Confucian public reason is also different from its liberal counterpart in terms of structure. Unlike liberal public reason, which is in principle concerned solely with matters of constitutional essentials and basic structure, Confucian public reason is open to all kinds of public political debates among democratic citizens. I would even argue that the home of Confucian public reason is not so much the court and parliament but civil society, where Confucian citizens are struggling with various kinds of rights, duties, and liberties, that is, with what these political values mean to them both conceptually and practically, values with which they are culturally unfamiliar. For Confucian citizens (as well as their political representatives and other public officials including judges and justices), Confucian public reason mediates their habits of the heart – Confucian mores, moral sentiments, civilities, and practices – with rights and liberties, which are of Western provenance, thereby helping them exercise such rights and liberties *on their own terms*.

Finally, the defining characteristic of Confucian public reason is that it is constituted by familial moral sentiments. Recently, inspired by David Hume, Sharon Krause has challenged the rationalist understanding of public reason (of the kind advanced by Joshua Cohen) by claiming that "public reasons are constituted by the things we *all* care about – not by things that 'reason itself' tells us we *should* care about."[91] I argue that Confucian public reason has much in common with Humean public reason in that they are both nonrationalist: they are motivated not by the faculty of reason as such but by moral sentiment and they are equally concerned with what citizens care about with regard to collective self-government and the public good. What distinguishes Confucian public reason from its Humean counterpart is that it consists of sentiments and

---

[91] Sharon Krause, *Civil Passions: Moral Sentiment and Democratic Deliberation* (Princeton: Princeton University Press, 2008), p. 151.

emotions that are characteristically *familial*. When the state is envisioned as an extended family and values such as filial piety and ritual propriety are socially cherished and publicly promoted, public reason is deeply fused with or mainly composed of familial affectionate sentiments. Put differently, Confucian public reason is the reason of citizens who see themselves as members of "one family," which is now institutionally housed in a democratic civil society. And it is by sharing Confucian public reasons that citizens in a Confucian society continue to cherish the values of filial piety and ritual propriety, values/virtues inculcated first in (extended) family settings, especially through the interaction with parents and other senior members.

In a Confucian democratic society, therefore, public reason consists of concerns that citizens have in common, who, despite their awareness of the value of individual identity, individual rights, and value pluralism, nevertheless see themselves related *as* family members. On the other hand, Confucian democratic society is a society where citizens are committed to sustain their shared familial public norms and values. Then, it can be concluded that public promotion of some core Confucian values in a Confucian society is a natural corollary of the familial nature of Confucian public reasons.[92]

P6: Confucian legitimacy

It may be objected that the public promotion of certain Confucian values, which I admit cannot be perfectly severed from traditional Confucianism, may do injustice to those who do not share Confucianism as their cultural value. Given the increasing number of immigrants in East Asian societies (particularly from the South and South East Asian countries) and the resulting multiculturalization of those societies, this is a valid concern. In fact, one of the major differences between public reason Confucianism and public reason liberalism a la Rawls is that public reason Confucianism only embraces the external conception when it comes to the scope of public reason. That is, public reason Confucianism assumes that the fact of pluralism in East Asia is not a consequence of liberalism but a fact about the world East Asians find themselves in, to which political theory, liberal or Confucian, must accommodate itself. Therefore, public reason Confucianism stipulates that in a Confucian democratic society public

---

[92] For a fuller elaboration on the familial nature of Confucian public reason, see Kim, *Confucian Democracy*, chap. 5.

reason must be justifiable to those who are not Confucian in any strong moral or religious sense. At the same time, P3 and P4 clearly commit public reason Confucianism to the principle of nondiscrimination, especially regarding immigrants, on the basis of race, ethnicity, religion, or culture. As equal citizens they are entitled to enjoy the same set of political rights and are expected to fulfill duties that accompany their rights and liberties.

Does P6 contradict the core stipulations of P3 and P4? I think not. Public reason Confucianism is not a *liberal* political theory precisely because unlike (many) liberal theories,[93] it is not concerned with the boundary question. For instance, public reason Confucianism conceived of as a political theory for the self-governing Confucian people would not embrace the following statement – "democratic theory either rejects the unilateral right to close borders, or would permit such a right only derivatively and only if it has already been successfully and democratically justified to foreigners. This is because the demos of democratic theory is in principle unbounded, and the regime of boundary control must consequently be democratically justified to foreigners as well as to citizens."[94] Here "democratic theory" refers to liberal democratic theory and as long as we understand the boundary question as *internal* to liberal democratic theory, the statement has some force, for the internal conception in principle does not allow democratic citizens, insomuch as they are liberal, to draw the boundary unilaterally, that is, without a process of justification to foreigners. If we only embrace this liberal notion of democratic theory, then we may rightfully start to quibble about whether *current* democratic citizens have the right to control their borders as well as the right to national self-determination, and whether they have no prima facie right to integrate immigrants into the existing social, economic, and political order.

Public reason Confucianism as nonliberal democratic theory is not precommitted to liberalism's background cosmopolitan assumptions as some liberal political democratic theories are (especially when they are conceived of as pure philosophical arguments instead of rooted in the concrete political experiences of particular liberal societies). It understands

---

[93] For instance, see Joseph H. Carens, *The Ethics of Immigration* (New York: Oxford University Press, 2013); Arash Abizadeh, "Democratic Theory and Border Coercion: No Right to Unilaterally Control Your Own Borders," *Political Theory* 36 (2008), pp. 37–65.

[94] Abizadeh, "Democratic Theory and Border Coercion," p. 38.

national self-determination as one of the most important political rights of the Confucian people, especially in the face of the global hegemony of liberalism. Grounded in Confucian public reason, the reason of the self-governing Confucian democratic citizens, public reason Confucianism has no preconceived philosophical burden to prove or disprove that the Confucian demos owes justification to foreigners when it comes to its border policy and other domestic policies that may affect them.[95] Without embroiling itself with the boundary question, therefore, public reason Confucianism agrees with what Will Kymlicka says about immigrant multiculturalism – that is, what is at issue is not so much whether integration (including naturalization) as such is just but whether the societal integration of immigrants takes place *on fair terms* so that immigrant groups are able to equally participate within the mainstream (academic, economic, and political) institutions of the existing society.[96] Such fair terms include the right to basic freedoms, including freedom of association, based on which immigrant cultural groups can claim "polyethnic rights."[97]

Confucian public reason is the inevitable price for a fair integration of immigrants who have joined a new political community voluntarily, with full awareness that they are entering a Confucian society, a society that cherishes and publicly promotes certain Confucian values and in which citizens give justification to one another in light of Confucian public reason. As stipulated in P4 and P5, new citizens have the right to contest the currently dominant understanding of Confucian public reason first by negotiating it with their religious or nonreligious comprehensive doctrines and then by offering an alternative notion of public reason that is socially acceptable to other citizens. In no case, however, are the fair terms of social integration meant to embrace unreasonable pluralism that is likely to erode the society's Confucian public character and undermine the people's right to collective self-government based on it. Thus understood, the criterion by which to judge whether or not Confucian democratic citizens treat immigrants fairly is not so much whether they expect immigrant groups to appeal to Confucian public reason in public deliberation

---

[95] For a powerful refutation of liberal cosmopolitanism by a liberal democrat, see David Miller, "Why Immigration Controls Are Not Coercive: A Reply to Arash Abizadeh," *Political Theory* 38 (2010), pp. 111–120.

[96] Will Kymlicka, *Politics in the Vernacular: Nationalism, Multiculturalism, and Citizenship* (Oxford: Oxford University Press, 2001), pp. 162–171; also see Miller, *On Nationality*, pp. 126–130; Kim, *Confucian Democracy*, pp. 277–278.

[97] Kymlicka, *Multicultural Citizenship*, p. 31.

processes, but whether they respect the minority groups' right to basic freedoms (for instance, freedom of association) as equally as other cultural groups, especially Confucian groups and associations who may be under the wrong impression that they have a privileged connection with Confucian public reason.

CONCLUSION

Public reason Confucianism, which I present in this book as the most plausible mode of Confucian democratic perfectionism, mediates between comprehensive Confucian perfectionism and public reason, which is typically associated with political liberalism. In this chapter, I first constructed the idea of public reason perfectionism by closely examining John Rawls's political liberalism, in which he makes public reason, understood as a set of pure political values, an integral part of his political theory, with special interest in how the idea of public reason invites perfectionist reinterpretations of public reason liberalism, and then presented public reason Confucianism as a species of the genus public reason perfectionism that is most relevant in East Asia societies, the public culture of which is still characteristically Confucian.

Public reason Confucianism is not merely a philosophical theory, however, whose aim is to resolve the well-known tension between comprehensive perfectionism and the ideal of public reason in the Confucian societal context. Public reason Confucianism is a political theory that attempts to balance the concern with coerciveness of political power and collective self-determination of the citizens who want to build a robust democracy on Confucian soil. In this regard, P4 (democratic pluralism) and P6 (Confucian legitimacy) are of special significance because they are concerned with the inevitable price that a Confucian democratic people will have to pay in order to maintain and reproduce the collective way of life that they value in the face of the global hegemony of liberalism. But is the Confucian public way of life immutable as traditionalist Confucians often argue? How public reason Confucianism is differentiated meaningfully from traditional Confucianism is one of the most important questions in thinking about its political relevance in rapidly changing East Asian societies. I now turn to this question with special focus on the recent constitutional changes in South Korea.

PART II

CONSTITUTIONALISM

3

Public reason Confucian constitutionalism

Many Confucian political theorists single out family values such as caring for needy family members and filial piety as the defining characteristics of Confucianism and endorse their public promotion from a perfectionist perspective. For instance, Daniel Bell argues that the Confucian commitment that "the state should promote obligations to care for needy family members, including (especially) elderly parents[,] conflicts with certain versions of liberal democratic theory that prioritize individual autonomy such as liberal neutrality (a policy can't be justified by appealing to the superiority of one comprehensive comprehension of the good) and republicanism (citizens should seek the good in political life outside the family)."[1] No doubt, the value of care for needy family members is an important part of the Confucian way of life and its public promotion is consistent with core propositions of public reason Confucianism. Indeed, it is hard to imagine that a reasonable Confucian citizen, as stipulated in P1 and P5 in the previous chapter (i.e., one who may subscribe to a non-Confucian value system as a private individual), would denounce this particular value or protest against its public promotion, even if he or she may contest the specific perfectionist public policies employed by the state.[2]

---

[1] Daniel A. Bell, *Beyond Liberal Democracy: Political Thinking for an East Asian Context* (Princeton: Princeton University Press, 2006), p. 250. Also see Ruiping Fan, *Reconstructionist Confucianism: Rethinking Morality after the West* (Dordrecht: Springer, 2010); Joseph Chan, *Confucian Perfectionism: A Political Philosophy for Modern Times* (Princeton: Princeton University Press, 2014).

[2] Mainly focused on the authority of the state in promoting particular Confucian goods, however, many Confucian perfectionists rarely emphasize the importance of democratic contestation with regard to perfectionist public policies.

That said, the distinctively democratic character of public reason Confucianism allows its perfectionist ambition to be realized, not only by means of public policies made occasionally with a view to promoting some particular Confucian goods. Deeply concerned with the Confucian citizens' democratic self-government as well as collective self-determination (as a Confucian people), public reason Confucianism, precisely because of its democratic perfectionism, has far-reaching political implications for constitutionalism. When a democratic polity is publicly committed to a set of Confucian moral values, such as filial piety, respect for elders, ancestor worship, and harmony within the family, public policies are made not only to promote these values, though in balance with other moral values and within constitutional constraints, but, more fundamentally, to shape the polity's constitutional character implicitly yet profoundly, even if the constitution itself may not comprehensively be predicated on the philosophical doctrines of Confucianism.

In fact, it is crucial that in public reason Confucianism the democratic constitution, and the way it governs the citizenry's public life, has a Confucian public character without being comprehensively committed to philosophical or ethical Confucianism. If we understand the term "constitutionalism" in its oldest conception, as the citizenry's collective political way of life (i.e., *politeia*), public reason Confucianism enables a particular mode of constitutionalism, namely, *Confucian constitutionalism*. Confucian constitutionalism is not necessarily opposed to liberal constitutionalism as it is buttressed largely by democratic political institutions. However, its perfectionist commitment to Confucian values distinguishes it from liberal constitutional perfectionism (or public reason liberalism) of the kind, most notably, espoused by Stephen Macedo. As Macedo describes it, liberal constitutionalism in its proper sense is ineluctably perfectionist because liberal law exerts a significant educative influence on citizens. Liberal constitutional polity does not merely aim to protect the prepolitical, or inalienable, rights, possessed by individuals as libertarians claim. Rather, "[l]iberal law, properly understood, promotes a community of interpreters: a citizenry of self-critical reason-givers."[3] That is, liberal constitutionalism shapes private individuals into reasonable citizens and this shaping process a la Kant is possible[4] because

---

[3] Stephen Macedo, *Liberal Virtues: Citizenship, Virtue, and Community in Liberal Constitutionalism* (Oxford: Clarendon Press, 1990), p. 78.
[4] Immanuel Kant, *The Metaphysics of Morals*, ed. Mary Gregor (Cambridge: Cambridge University Press, 1996).

"[l]iberal law is composed not only of rules, but also of certain underlying aims and principles: ordered liberty, fairness, due process, reasonableness, and opposition to cruelty."[5] Such liberal aims and principles combine to generate the principles of liberal public morality and enable the practice of public justification based on the use of (liberal) public reason. The perfectionist aspect of liberal constitutionalism is best explained in the following statement by Macedo:

> The liberal public morality, as we will see, nurtures and draws upon the same capacities needed by persons to flourish in a pluralist liberal society. These traits of character, or liberal virtues, include a reflective, self-critical attitude, tolerance, openness to change, self-control, a willingness to engage in dialogue with others, and a willingness to revise and shape projects in order to respect the rights of others or in response to fresh insight into one's own character and ideals.[6]

The distinctive feature of liberal constitutional perfectionism is its ambition to achieve congruence between the principles of the constitution and the character of citizenship. Put differently, the perfectionist aim of liberal constitutionalism is to produce, sustain, and reproduce a liberal citizenship. And it is this very congruence thesis implied in liberal constitutionalism that some scholars find overbearing, particularly those who valorize moral pluralism as intrinsically valuable.[7] According to liberal pluralists, personal identity, which is naturally plural, does not have to be uniformly

---

[5] Macedo, *Liberal Virtues*, p. 84.
[6] Ibid., p. 129. Also see William A. Galston, *Liberal Purposes: Goods, Virtues, and Diversity in the Liberal State* (Cambridge: Cambridge University Press, 1991); Judith N. Shklar, *Ordinary Vices* (Cambridge: Belknap Press, 1984). While Macedo and Galston espouse what can be called positive liberal perfectionism, Shklar draws attention to the value of negative perfectionism in a liberal society. On the perfectionist elements in modern liberalism, see Peter Berkowitz, *Virtue and the Making of Modern Liberalism* (Princeton: Princeton University Press, 1999); Karen Zivi, "Cultivating Character: John Stuart Mill and the Subjects of Rights," *American Journal of Political Science* 50 (2006), pp. 49–61.
[7] See William A. Galston, *Liberal Pluralism: The Implications of Value Pluralism for Political Theory and Practice* (Cambridge: Cambridge University Press, 2002); George Crowder, *Liberalism and Value Pluralism* (New York: Continuum, 2002); John Gray, *Two Faces of Liberalism* (New York: The New Press, 2000); Nancy L. Rosenblum, *Membership and Morals: The Personal Uses of Pluralism in America* (Princeton: Princeton University Press, 1998). It should be noted that Galston's theoretical position straddles liberal perfectionism and liberal pluralism, and some scholars struggle with how to make sense of the apparent internal tension in Galston's liberal political theory. For instance, see James B. Murphy, "From Aristotle to Hobbes: William Galston on Civic Virtue," *Social Theory and Practice* 33 (2007), pp. 637–644. As an alternative to traditional liberal constitutionalism, Galston now advocates what he calls *pluralist constitutionalism*, a constitutional theory that best accommodates value pluralism. See his "Pluralist Constitutionalism," *Social Philosophy and Policy* 28 (2011), pp. 228–241.

molded by the moral principles of a liberal constitution, aimed at the formation of a *common* democratic citizenship. Likewise, it is argued, cultural or religious associations should be able to fully exercise their constitutional right to freedom of association and therefore their internal affairs should be neither dictated nor interfered by the public authority upholding constitutional principles, unless they pose a serious threat to the constitutional order. Pluralists assert that constitutional demand for congruence between self-identity and liberal personhood and between associational membership and democratic citizenship violates the very spirit of liberalism, particularly of the version the Reformation gave rise to.

Like liberal constitutionalism, Confucian constitutionalism attempts a certain congruence between constitutional principles and democratic citizenship, without which the constitutional integrity of the Confucian (in fact, *any*) democratic polity cannot be sustained over generations. What distinguishes Confucian constitutionalism from liberal constitutionalism is that unlike the latter, the former realizes the congruence only *indirectly*. While in liberal constitutionalism, constitutional principles, predicated on liberal values, directly produce a liberal democratic citizenship, in Confucian constitutionalism, as conceived from the perspective of public reason Confucianism (particularly P1 and P2),[8] constitutional principles (such as individual dignity and gender equality) produce a Confucian *and* democratic citizenship by balancing these otherwise liberal values with Confucian values and goods, to which the polity is publicly, if not direct constitutionally, committed. The institutional structure of the Confucian constitutional polity thus conceived would be similar to that of liberal constitutionalism, but its perfectionist constitutional aim is not so much to produce liberal rights-bearing individual-cum-citizens but to produce democratic citizens who cherish core Confucian values in a way that is harmonious with constitutional principles. In a Confucian constitutional democracy, the state's promotion of some Confucian

---

[8] Though there are considerable similarities between my vision of Confucian constitutionalism (justified from the perspective of public reason Confucianism) and Chaihark Hahm's notion of Confucian constitutionalism, my vision is clearly distinguished from Hahm's in that his is more concerned with constitutional continuity and stability than the democratic justification of constitutionalism. This difference will be discussed more explicitly and in philosophical terms in Chapter 6. For Hahm's notion of Confucian constitutionalism, see his "Constitutionalism, Confucian Civic Virtue, and Ritual Propriety," in *Confucianism for the Modern World*, eds. Daniel A. Bell and Chaibong Hahm (Cambridge: Cambridge University Press, 2003), pp. 31–53, and "Law, Culture, and the Politics of Confucianism," *Columbia Journal of Asian Law* 16 (2003), pp. 253–301.

values is politically justified because of the existence of such citizens, namely, *Confucian democratic citizens.*

In this chapter, I attempt to show how the core propositions of public reason Confucianism, introduced in the previous chapter, can together support Confucian constitutionalism of the type I have discussed so far, what I call *public reason Confucian constitutionalism.* Instead of making an argument in an abstract philosophical fashion, however, I illuminate what Confucian constitutionalism looks like in practice, justified from the standpoint of public reason Confucianism, by discussing a landmark court decision in postdemocratic South Korea, where the Constitutional Court declared unconstitutional the family-head system (*hojuje*), a core Confucian social and legal institution, thereby ending a fifty-year-long debate between traditionalist Confucians and political conservatives on the one side and liberal-feminists and political progressives on the other.

I pay special attention to this case for two reasons. First, the long and intense public debate surrounding the constitutionality of the family-head system was centered on precisely what it means to be a Korean citizen in contemporary Korea's culturally Confucian (in the legal and public sense) and politically democratic societal context. Should Koreans be treated equally regardless of sex? And should traditional public–legal institutions such as the family-head system be abolished if they contradict constitutional principles predicated on the values of individual dignity and gender equality? As a normative political theory concerned with Confucian citizens whose public culture is characteristically Confucian and yet who subscribe to diverse moral, philosophical, or religious doctrines, public reason Confucianism is motivated by a similar practical concern – how one can become a public citizen in a modern Confucian society, fully committed to intrinsic values of democracy, such as, among others, public equality, without forfeiting Confucian values.

Second, the Court's decision and its legal reasoning in this case represents remarkably well the course that public reason Confucianism should take. This is not to say that public reason Confucianism merely puts into philosophical terms what East Asian citizens, who have undergone democratic transition, already are doing. Nor is its primary aim to lend justification to various reform policies democratic East Asians have been pursuing, although I do not deny that public reason Confucianism is inspired in part by democratic East Asians' (especially Koreans') actual social, legal, and political practices. In fact, as will be shown, the Court's majority decision does not correspond perfectly with the normative position of public reason Confucianism. Rather, what I aim to show with this case is that public reason Confucianism is not a mere philosophical construct, completely deracinated from East Asians' actual social conditions and experiences; it provides a way to understand and explain current social, legal, and political practices in East Asia that are neither Western-style liberal democratic nor Confucian in the traditional sense while also offering a normative standard – what Kant calls a "regulative ideal" – that can be employed to justify, criticize, and emend such practices.

THE CASE: ABOLITION OF THE FAMILY-HEAD SYSTEM

Background

As a democratic political theory, public reason Confucianism stipulates that political authority or the exercise of political power be publicly justifiable to reasonable citizens. As a Confucian democratic political theory, public reason Confucianism is constrained by an additional stipulation – that Confucianism, insomuch as its core values are publicly promoted, be reasonable to *all* citizens who, though broadly saturated with Confucian mores and habits, subscribe to diverse moral, religious, or philosophical doctrines. Therefore, when conceived of in terms of public reason Confucianism (especially P4), Confucianism is clearly distinguished from religious Confucianism or Confucian ritualism predicated on (neo-)Confucian cosmology and metaphysics, to which some traditionalist Confucians in the region still adhere. Given the increasing pluralization of values in East Asian societies, these traditional types of Confucianism no longer hold public recognition as a legally binding social and political system. The Confucianism at issue here also cannot be identified with what contemporary Confucian philosophers reconstruct as modern Confucianism, which rarely engages with the Confucian social, legal, and political legacies that still characterize East Asian societies as "Confucian," the Confucianism with which ordinary citizens in the region are struggling daily. Rather, in public reason Confucianism, Confucianism is what citizens have in common as the resource for collective normative reasoning under democratic societal conditions. From the standpoint of practice, public reason Confucianism normatively requires Confucianism to be transformed into a particular version of itself, in order to be publicly reasonable and democracy-enhancing. Though neither public debate among Korean citizens (especially between traditionalist Confucians and liberal-feminists) nor the eventual Constitutional

Court's decision regarding the constitutionality of the family-head system explicitly recognized public reason Confucianism, the case provides an important insight into what public reason Confucianism might look like in a historically Confucian society that has democratized or is democratizing.

On February 3, 2005, the Constitutional Court in Korea held that Articles 778, 781(1), and 826(3) of the Civil Code were incompatible with the Constitution, ending a fifty-year-long dispute surrounding the constitutionality of the family-head (*hoju* 戶主) system.[9] Though the Korean Civil Code does not define the family-head system in clear legal terms, it had been widely acknowledged that the family-head system is a family institution inscribed in the Family Law, which is comprised of Books 4 and 5 of the Civil Code,[10] and that the articles in question constitute the core of the family-head system as a social practice as well as a legal reality. The articles in question read as follows:

Article 778: A person who has succeeded the family lineage or has set up a branch-family, or who has established a new family or has restored a family for any other reason, shall become the head of the family.

Article 781(1): A child shall assume its father's surname (*sŏng* 姓) and the [agnatic] origin of the surname (*pon* 本) and shall have the name entered in its father's family register.

Article 826(3): The wife shall have her name entered in her husband's family register [following part omitted].

When combined, the Court reasoned, these articles constitute a uniquely (Confucian) Korean family system whereby "a household (*ka* 家), a concept of collective, is formed around the family head at its core and passes down only through direct male descendants serving as successive house heads."[11] As the Court declared, "the house head system is a

---

[9] Unless noted otherwise, all transliterations of the Chinese characters in this chapter are based on their Korean pronunciations. When I transliterate the Chinese characters according to their original Chinese pronunciations, I add "c." before the transliterations.

[10] Hyunah Yang, "Vision of Postcolonial Feminist Jurisprudence in Korea: Seen from the 'Family-Head System' in Family Law," *Journal of Korean Law* 5 (2006), pp. 12–28, p. 12.

[11] 17-1 KCCR 1, 2001Hun-Ga9·10·11·12·13·14·15 and 2004 Hun-Ga5 (consolidated), February 3, 2005. Throughout this chapter, the English translation of the Court's decision is based, with additional English editing, on the version offered by the Court's homepage (http://search.ccourt.go.kr/ths/pr/ths_pr0101_P1.do). Among Korean scholars, it is highly controversial whether the family-head system, as practiced in post-1945 Korea, can be regarded as Koreans' traditional Confucian institution. While most traditionalist

statutory device to form a family with male lineage at the center and perpetuate it to successive generations. [Therefore] it is not a system that simply identifies the representative of the family called family head and complies the family register accordingly."[12] Then why is it that the "family" understood in this way was the source of a heated public debate, eventually being removed from the Civil Code? For many Koreans (especially for liberal feminists), this type of family, patriarchal (by making only a male adult the head of the family) as well as androcentric (by subjecting women, especially wives, to their husbands' patrilineal family upon marriage), granted public justification to legal and social discrimination against women.

The articles mandate that each individual be registered as a member of a family, which is led by a "head of the family (*hoju*)," typically the father. Though the second revision of the Korean family law in 1989 substantively diminished the power of the family-head, by eliminating his rights to decide the residence of his family members and to summon a

---

Confucians called Yurim 儒林 take for granted the historical continuity between the Confucian family system under the Chosŏn dynasty (1392–1910) and the current family-head system, Korean feminists such as Hyunah Yang forcefully argue that the family-head system in its contemporary form was heavily contaminated by the Japanese family (*Ie*) system during the colonial period (1910–1945). For Yang's argument, see her *Han'guk kajokbŏp ilkki: Chŏntong, shingminjisŏng, chendŏŭi kyoch'aroesŏ* [*Reading Korean Family Law: At the Crossroads of Tradition, Coloniality, and Gender*] (Seoul: Ch'angbi, 2011), pp. 99–176. An English excerpt can be found in Yang, "Vision of Postcolonial Feminist Jurisprudence," pp. 20–24. It is indeed true that the contemporary legal institutions of family head, succession of family headship, and family register, all based on the modern nuclear family, were established under Japanese colonialism. However, it is undeniable that not only was the colonial family system (especially the family-head system) modeled primarily after the traditional patriarchal and patrilineal Korean-Confucian family structure, including the family headship (which was not so much a legal concept but a ritual concept and practice, mainly to conduct ancestor worship following the patrilineal line) but the colonial elements that were directly at odds with traditional Korean family customs and practices were eliminated from the post-1945 Korean Civil Code. This is not to argue that the question of *coloniality* in the contemporary legal creation of the family-head system is negligible. My point is that it is one thing to note that Korean modernity is inexplicably intertwined with Japanese colonialism without much public awareness; it is another to acknowledge the traditional Confucian basis of patriarchal and patrilineal nature of the contemporary Korean family-head system. Even Yang does not deny this obvious historical continuity. See her *Han'guk kajokbŏp ilkki*, pp. 177–226. For excellent studies on the traditional Confucian Korean family system, see Martina Deuchler, *The Confucian Transformation of Korea: A Study of Society and Ideology* (Cambridge: Council on East Asian Studies, Harvard University Press, 1992); Mark A. Paterson, *Korean Adoption and Inheritance: Case Studies in the Creation of a Classic Confucian Society* (Ithaca: Cornell University Press, 1996).

[12] 17-1 KCCR1, p. 1.

family meeting,[13] no change was made with regard to the stipulation that family headship passes to the eldest son, irrespective of whether there are older sisters. Since the family is legally defined strictly by and for the patrilineal line, the former head's wife (i.e., the new head's mother) and even his mother (i.e., the new head's grandmother) are automatically excluded from the candidacy for the next headship. In cases where the former head's adult sons have already died, family headship as a legal title can succeed directly to the former head's eldest grandson, regardless of his age, bypassing all the senior women members in the family. Upon the father's death, younger sons who cannot succeed his headship automatically become members of their eldest brother's family until their marriage, upon which they can form new families and become their own family heads.

As already noted, women's place in the family-head system, morally justified with reference to Zhu Xi's *Family Rituals* (c. *Jiali* 家禮), the most authoritative classical source for the Confucian lineage system organized around the male descent line, is dramatically different from men's.[14] As long as there is any male offspring in her father's line, a daughter cannot become head of the family. The exceptional cases in which a daughter can assume family headship are when there is no living male offspring to succeed her father's headship[15] or where upon divorce (and before

---

[13] Erin Cho, "Caught in Confucius' Shadow: The Struggle for Women's Legal Equality in South Korea," *Columbia Journal of Asian Law* 12 (1998), pp. 125–189, at p. 166. Before the 2005 revision, the Korean Family Law has been revised twice – in 1977 and in 1989 – after its establishment in the Civil Code in 1958. For a detailed legal change in each revision, see Yang, *Han'guk kajokbŏp ilkki*, pp. 73–311 and "Gender Equality vs. 'Tradition' in Korean Family: Toward a Postcolonial Feminist Jurisprudence," *The Review of Korean Studies* 6 (2003), pp. 85–118. Also see Erin Cho's essay cited in this footnote.

[14] For the English translation of Zhu Xi's Family Rituals, see Patricia B. Ebrey, *Chu Hsi's Family Rituals: A Twelfth-Century Chinese Manual for the Performance of Cappings, Weddings, Funerals, and Ancestral Rites* (Princeton: Princeton University Press, 1991). On the dissemination and eventual social entrenchment of Zhu Xi's *Family Rituals* in Korea during the Chosŏn dynasty, see Hye-sun Yi (ed.), *Chosŏn chunggi yehaksasanggwa ilsangmunhwa: Chuja kagryerŭl chungshimŭro [Ritual Thoughts during the mid Chosŏn Period and the Culture of Everyday Lives: Focusing on Zhu Xi's Family Rituals]* (Seoul: Ehwa Womans University Press, 2008); Yŏng-chin Ko, *Chosŏn chunggi yehaksasangsa [A Historical Study of Ritual Thoughts in the mid Chosŏn Period]* (Seoul: Han'gilsa, 1995).

[15] Article 984 stipulates with respect to succession of the family headship: (1) a male person who is a lineal descendent of the person to be succeeded; (2) a female lineal descendant who is a member of the family of the person to be succeeded; (3) a wife of the inheritee; (4) a female lineal ascendant who is a member of the family of the person to be succeeded;

remarriage) she chooses to create a new household for herself. In principle, though, a divorced woman is supposed to revert back to her father's family registry (or her oldest brother's, if her father has passed away).[16] And if she remarries, she then automatically belongs to the family registry of her new husband.

In particular, the family-head system's fundamental bias against women puts a divorced woman's child in a challenging situation. When a child is born, he or she must take the surname (*sŏng*) and the ancestral seat of the surname (*pon*) and be registered on the father's family register. A series of legal and social issues occurs when the parents get divorced. Even if, as in many cases, the children are in their mother's custody, they must remain in their father's family registry and retain his surname. The situation does not get much better, even if the mother later marries another man. In fact, it gets worse. Consider Article 784 of the Korean Civil Code.

Article 784(1): If a wife has lineal descendants who are not her husband's blood relatives, she may, upon the consent of her husband, have their names entered in her husband's family register.

(2) If, in the cases mentioned in (1), the wife's lineal descendants are members of another family, their entry into her husband's register shall be subject to the consent of the head of such family.

A child can transfer to his or her stepfather's family registry only if his or her mother obtains two kinds of consent – one from the current family-head of the child (i.e., the child's biological father) and one from the mother's current husband, the child's future family-head.[17] The whole process of obtaining two consents alone can impose not only legal burden, but, perhaps more seriously, enormous mental distress on both the mother and the child. But most often, the child undergoes far more serious mental distress arising from identity crisis after being successfully transferred to the stepfather's family registry because he or she is still forced by law to keep the biological father's surname. Chaihark Hahm aptly summaries the troubling situation as the following:

---

and (5) a wife of a lineal ascendant who is a member of the family of the person to be succeeded.
[16] Chaihark Hahm, "Negotiating Confucian Civility through Constitutional Discourse," in *The Politics of Affective Relations: East Asian and Beyond*, eds. Chaihark Hahm and Daniel A. Bell (Lanham: Lexington Books, 2004), pp. 277–308, p. 301.
[17] My discussion of "two kinds of consent" here is greatly indebted to Yang, "Vision of Postcolonial Feminist Jurisprudence," p. 16.

Perhaps more serious, children from the mother's previous marriage often experience mental distress (e.g., constant teasing from their peers) due to the fact that their surname is different from their stepfather's. Even in cases where the stepfather is the only father they have ever known, and even if the stepfather loves them as his own children, the law is acting as a barrier to their efforts to form and behave as a normal household unit.[18]

The family-head system involves much more than what I have described thus far. Nonetheless, the description here captures the kernel of injustice implicated with the family-head system. In short, the family-head system is the social and legal institution that systematically discriminates against women, by institutionalizing and perpetuating their lower social status as mother, wife, or daughter vis-à-vis that of their male counterparts as father, husband, or son. On March 2, 2005, a month after the Constitutional Court had made the decision, the National Assembly of Korea passed revisions to the family law by scrapping virtually all patriarchal and patrilineal legacies of the traditional Confucian family sustained through the institutions of the family-head system. In the new family law, which became effective on January 1, 2008, the family registry system was replaced by an individual identification system, which automatically abolished the controversial family-head position.

The Court's decision

In a six–three vote, the Constitutional Court found that the articles under review were unconstitutional because they critically contradict the constitutional principles of human dignity and gender equality stipulated in Article 36(1) of the Constitution but issued a decision of "constitutional nonconformity" in order to avoid a vacuum in the legal order by temporarily enforcing the provisions under review until the Family Law is amended with a new population registry system not predicated on the family-head system.[19] The following is a summary of the Court's majority decision:

---

[18] Hahm, "Negotiating Confucian Civility," p. 301.
[19] The Korean Constitutional Court has adopted the German practice of rendering various categories of decision, and "constitutional nonconformity" (*hŏnpŏp pulhapch'i*; *Unvereinbar* in German) is one of the judgments between "constitutional" and "unconstitutional." This judgment is to "recognize the unconstitutionality of the law in question but let it stand until a given deadline for the legislature to enact a new legislation compatible with the Constitution." See Chaihark Hahm, "Conceptualizing Korean Constitutionalism: Foreign Transplant or Indigenous Tradition?" *Journal of Korean Law* 1 (2001), pp. 151–196, p. 154n8. Also see Tom Ginsburg, "Confucian Constitutionalism? The

(1) The Constitution is the supreme norm of the state. Therefore, even though the family system is distinctively an outcome of history and society, it cannot deviate from the superior force of the Constitution. In other words, if a law regulating the family system impairs actualizing the constitutional ideal and only strengthens the gap between the constitutional norm and reality, such a law must be amended.

(2) Our Constitution expressed its constitutional resolution to no longer tolerate the patriarchal and feudal order of marriage, [which] remains from our past society, by declaring equality of men and women in marriage as the basis of a constitutional marital order.[20] ... Meanwhile, "traditions" and "cultural heritage," respectively stated in the preamble and Article 9 of the Constitution, are concepts reflecting both their history and the times in which they were used. Thus, these concepts need to be defined according to their contemporary meanings considering the constitutional value order, the common values of mankind, justice, humanity, etc. Perceiving the meaning of these concepts in such a manner, we understand that a certain limit exists – that tradition and cultural heritage of the family system should not, at the very least, be contrary to the constitutional ideals of individual dignity and gender equality. Therefore, if a certain family system, remaining from the past, is contrary to the individual dignity and gender equality required by Article 36(1) of the Constitution, it cannot be justified on the basis of Article 9.

(3) The family-head system is discrimination based on stereotypes concerning gender roles. This system, without justifiable grounds, discriminates against women in determining the succession order of the family head, forming marital relations, and forming relations with children. Due to this system, many families are suffering inconvenience and pain in various ways since they cannot form a legal family relationship appropriate to family life in reality and the welfare of the family. Traditional ideology or public mores such as ancestor worship, respect for elders, and filial piety, and harmony in family can be passed down and developed through cultural and ethical aspects, but cannot justify the blatant gender discrimination of the family-head system.[21]

Emergence of Constitutional Review in Korea and Taiwan," *Law and Social Inquiry* 27 (2002), pp. 763–799, p. 780.

[20] Even though the Korean Constitution, from its establishment on July 17, 1948, proclaimed the general principle of gender equality, this principle had been rarely applied to the family law, governed largely by Confucian customs until its eighth revision on October 27, 1980. In this revision, the Constitution clearly declares the principles of individual dignity and gender equality specifically in the context of marriage and family life, thereby expressing its resolution to reform the Korean family structure in a way harmonious with (liberal) constitutional principles.

[21] Though the English translated summary of the decision by the Court renders the Korean-Chinese terms such as "경로" (kyŏngno 敬老; c. jinglao) and "효친" (hyoch'in 孝親; c. xiaoqin) as "respect for the aged" and "obedience to parents," I translate them in a way more faithful to their original Confucian meaning – as respect for elders and filial piety respectively. As a matter of fact, Confucianism never understands filial piety merely as "obedience to parents." On this point, see Sungmoon Kim, "The Virtue of Incivility:

(4) The family-head system one-sidedly prescribes and demands a certain family system deeply rooted in the ideal of maintaining and expanding a family centered on a male lineage regardless of the intention or welfare of the people concerned. It does not respect individual members of a family as individuals with dignity but rather treats them as a means to succeeding a family. Such attitude does not comply with Article 36(1) of the Constitution that demands respect for the right of autonomous decisions of individuals and families in deciding how to manage family life.

(5) The relationships within a family, these days, are ... becoming more democratic, where all members are respected equally as individuals with dignity regardless of gender. As society becomes more complex the structure of the family has become very diverse, including families with single mothers, remarried couples and their children from previous marriage, etc. Furthermore, due to the increased economic power of women and the rise of divorce, the rate of women fulfilling the role of a family-head is also increasing. ... [The family-head system] is no longer harmonious with the changing social environment and family relations. Therefore, there is no need for the family-head system to be retained.

TWO PERFECTIONIST COMMITMENTS: DIRECT AND INDIRECT

Seen from the standpoint of Korean constitutional jurisprudence, the family-head system case was, in essence, about how to adjudicate the apparent conflict between Article 9[22] and Article 36(1)[23] of the Constitution.[24] The Court's majority reasoning is that even though the family-head system is one of the nation's traditions (i.e., Confucianism), not all traditions deserve constitutional protection, and if a tradition is critically at odds with, or violates, core constitutional principles such as human dignity and gender equality, it cannot be maintained, even on the constitutional commitment to sustenance and enhancement of national

---

Confucian Communitarianism beyond Docility," *Philosophy and Social Criticism* 37 (2011), pp. 25–48, esp. pp. 38–40.

[22] Constitution Article 9: "The State shall strive to sustain and develop the cultural heritage and to enhance national culture."

[23] Constitution Article 36(1): "Marriage and family life shall be entered into and sustained on the basis of individual dignity and equality of the sexes, and the State shall do everything in its power to achieve that goal."

[24] Yang, *Han'guk kajokbŏp ilkki*, p. 336. As Marie Seong-Hak Kim rightly notes, this tension originates from certain ambiguity in the relationship between custom (however codified under the modern constitution) and statues in the Korean legal order. See her "In the Name of Custom, Culture, and the Constitution: Korean Customary Law in Flux," *Texas International Law Journal* 48:3 (2013), pp. 357–391.

tradition and/or cultural heritage.²⁵ Since the family-head system, as legally defined and socially practiced in contemporary Korea, critically violates the constitutional values of human dignity and gender equality "without justifiable grounds," it no longer deserves constitutional protection and thus ought to be abolished. The Court made its reasoning more socially relevant by paying due attention to modern Korea's drastically altered social conditions, marked by diverse forms of family and increasing divorce rates. Overall, the Court's conclusion was that the Confucian patriarchal and patrilineal family-head system not only does injustice to women but has become irrelevant in Korean society from a sociological viewpoint as well.

That being said, this case involves more than just how to clarify the relationship between two constitutional provisions that are in conflict or between two seemingly incommensurable sets of values – human dignity and gender equality, on the one hand, and the traditional culture of the Confucian family-head system, on the other. And this *more* is what makes this case highly relevant to public reason Confucianism as well as to Confucian constitutionalism, albeit with important caveats.

A close reading of the Court's majority decision reveals that what was at stake was not merely the conflict between two constitutional provisions or two values supported by the Constitution, but a tension between two kinds of perfectionist commitments implied in Korea's democratic constitution. First, the Court's reasoning and eventual decision clearly show that Korean constitutionalism aims to be a liberal constitutionalism, similar to the kind we have noted earlier with reference to Macedo's political theory, and this is hardly surprising given the fact that the modern Korean state (Republic of Korea) was self-consciously founded by its framers as a liberal democracy.²⁶ Faithful to the basic premise of liberal constitutionalism, the Court reasons that the Korean Constitution "expressed its constitutional resolution" to not tolerate any injustice

---

[25] The constitutional commitment to the promotion of cultural heritage can be justified on deeper moral grounds. Consider Bhutan's early implementation of Gross National Happiness (GNH) as a measure of national well-being. Bhutanese society, which is profoundly influenced by Buddhism, insists that beneficial development of human society requires material and spiritual development to complement and reinforce each other. The four pillars of GNH are the promotion of sustainable development, preservation and promotion of cultural values, conservation of the natural environment, and establishment of good governance. I am grateful to P. J. Ivanhoe for drawing my attention to this case.

[26] See, among others, Article 1(1), Article 10, Article 11(1), and Article 12(1) of the Korean Constitution.

associated with patriarchal or feudal elements of the traditional family within a freely entered marriage. Otherwise stated, the Korean Constitution is not just a legal parchment lacking substantive moral content, and thus neutral to competing moral values and value-claims. Quite to the contrary, it is ineluctably a moral document expressing its commitment to certain liberal values. The Constitution's liberal moral commitment, then, naturally also enables a nonneutral commitment on the part of the Korean democratic state to carrying out this perfectionist resolution by promoting core constitutional values such as human dignity and gender equality. Seen in this way, the statement in (5) that "the relationships within a family, these days, are ... becoming more democratic" is not merely a disinterested description of recent social changes. Rather, it is a normative statement, calling for an active engagement of the state in the task of reconstructing the family relationship from patriarchal to democratic. In short, one dimension of the Court's reasoning clearly vindicates the liberal constitutionalism's congruence thesis.[27]

The situation gets complicated once it is recognized that the Korean Constitution is committed simultaneously to nonliberal, characteristically Confucian, goods and values, arguably – at least in part but in an important way – affiliated with the family-head system, and encourages the Korean state to promote them publicly. Recall that Article 9 of the Korean Constitution stipulates that *the state shall strive to sustain and develop the cultural heritage and to enhance national culture.* This article does not clarify precisely what the Korean cultural heritage or national culture consists of. But it is evident that anything explicitly associated with "liberalism" or "democracy" is naturally excluded from the category of "cultural heritage and/or natural culture" because the Constitution's intention to hold this provision is to protect as well as enhance something that is difficult to protect or enhance under normal circumstances given the polity's constitutional commitment to liberal democratic principles and values and its ostensible neutralist posture, such perfectionist commitment notwithstanding.

Of course, there is no prima facie reason to assume that this *something* is exclusively Confucian. After all, various religious and cultural

---

[27] For a strong statement for democratic marriage and democratic justice in the marriage, see Ian Shapiro, *Democratic Justice* (New Haven: Yale University Press, 1999), pp. 110–142. One of the classical endorsements for congruence between liberal constitutionalism and conjugal relationship is found in Susan M. Okin, *Justice, Gender, and the Family* (New York: Basic Books, 1989).

traditions other than Confucianism – such as Buddhism, Daoism, Shamanism, and Tonghak 東學,[28] to name a few – also flourished, before Korea became heavily influenced by Western modernity. In fact, if by Korean cultural heritage or tradition the Constitution mainly means these non-Confucian religious or cultural traditions, there would be no politically meaningful "situation" necessitating what can be called the *circumstances* of Confucian constitutionalism, because these traditions can be more properly called cultural heritages, requiring certain public protection and support for their continued survival, and flourishing, as they have no enduring legal, public–cultural, or politico-institutional implications for the Korean constitutional polity. If that is the case, then, there would be just one perfectionist challenge, a typical liberal perfectionist question of whether or not it is appropriate for a liberal state to subsidize Buddhist or Daoist cultural organizations or cultural assets, tangible or intangible, in the name of enhancing the democratic citizenry's collective pride and common citizenship.[29]

In the present case, however, what was at issue was not a mere protection of or subsidy for a cultural heritage but what to do with a traditional institutional structure (namely, the Confucian family-structure undergirded on the family-head system) that is still integral to Korea's legal and social system and, more importantly, the Confucian values affiliated with it. In one sense, what the Court found difficult was not necessarily the decision to abolish the family-head system as such, given the obvious injustice that it had brought and was still bringing to women, an indisputable fact even for traditionalist Confucians. That is, if the family-head system (or the Confucian family structure in general) had been deemed by the Court merely as one cultural heritage, which has no eminent institutional and ethical implications for contemporary Korean people, its legality and social continuation could have been declared unconstitutional rather easily. The core of the difficulty confronting the

---

[28] Tonghak is an indigenous Korean religion founded by Ch'oe Che-u (1824–1864) in 1860. Ch'oe established Tonghak (literally Eastern Learning) as a Korean alternative to Western Learning (*sŏhak* 西學) by synthesizing Confucianism, Buddhism, and Daoism around the egalitarian religious motto of "Humans are none other than Heaven" (*in ne ch'ŏn* 人乃天).

[29] For a democratic case for such government subsidy, see Amy Gutmann, *Democratic Education* (Princeton: Princeton University Press, 1999), p. 260. In marked contrast, Rawls famously advocates liberal neutrality by claiming that "the principles of justice do not permit subsidizing universities and institutes, or opera and the theater, on the grounds that these institutions are intrinsically valuable, and that those who engage in them are to be supported even at some significant expense to others who do not receive compensating benefits" (John Rawls, *A Theory of Justice* [Cambridge: Belknap, 1971], p. 332).

Court rather consisted in the apparent dilemma of how to reform the traditional family system without abandoning the Confucian values underpinning it. This is why, to some radical feminists' dismay,[30] the Court came to the decision of constitutional nonconformity with an important caveat that Confucian values, such as ancestor worship, respect for elders, filial piety, and harmony in family, still cherished by Koreans in the form of public mores, would remain intact, even after the abolition of the family-head system.

From the Court's viewpoint, Article 9 had more far-ranging constitutional implications than Korean liberal feminists tend to believe. According to the Court's reasoning, Article 9 does not merely authorize the state to protect or enhance cultural heritage; more importantly, it enables the state to promote the values associated with them, especially those that have a lingering institutional influence over modern Korean society. Here arises an interesting question: what is the constitutional status of such values? Technically speaking, they are not constitutional values because the Korean Constitution is formally founded on liberal-democratic moral principles and values. In fact, the Court never declared the Confucian values in question as constitutional values. However, the fact that these values, often called cultural values, are publicly acknowledged and even promoted with reference to a key constitutional provision makes it possible to call them *quasi-constitutional values*, if we understand the term "constitutional" here not in a strictly legal sense but in a broader political sense that the constitution is the political community's supreme norm, which not only expresses the community's particular way of life publicly but also forms, sustains, and reproduces the public character of citizenship.[31] We may call this second type of

---

[30] See, for instance, Yang, *Han'guk kajokbŏp ilkki*, p. 339n34 where Yang questions whether the Confucian values acknowledged by the Court would be compatible with the (supreme) value of gender equality.

[31] On this broad political view of constitutionalism, see Rogers M. Smith, *Liberalism and American Constitutional Law* (Cambridge: Harvard University Press, 1985); Stephen L. Elkin, *Reconstructing the Commercial Republic: Constitutional Design after Madison* (Chicago: University of Chicago Press, 2006). Rejecting the conventional definition of constitutionalism in terms of a legal parchment, judicial review, representative democracy, the separation of powers, or even the rule of law, Chaihark Hahm argues that "constitutional norms need not always take the form of law, in the strict narrow sense of the word. Indeed, in most countries, constitutional norms comprise, in addition to judicially enforceable rules, a range of norms including political rules, precepts, conventions, and even tacit understandings about what is deemed proper in matters of government" ("Conceptualizing Korean Constitutionalism," p. 167).

constitutionalism *indirect constitutionalism*, in which certain cultural values, though not constitutional values in a strictly legal sense, attain public–constitutional significance.

Earlier, I distinguished Confucian constitutionalism, conceived from the perspective of public reason Confucianism, from liberal constitutionalism by stipulating that unlike the latter, the former realizes the congruence between constitutional principles and democratic citizenship indirectly. In other words, under Confucian constitutionalism constitutional principles consisting of, among others, human dignity and gender equality, commonly understood as liberal values, produce a Confucian yet democratic citizenship by negotiating formal constitutional principles and values with Confucian values and goods to which the polity is publicly, if not direct constitutionally, committed. What is noteworthy is that despite its formal subscription to liberal constitutionalism, the Court's practice of Korean constitutionalism turns out to track public reason Confucian constitutionalism remarkably well, with some critical caveats, which I will discuss shortly.

The Korean Constitution's indirect commitment to cultural, particularly Confucian, values renders them to be quasi-constitutional values and the Constitution's dual – direct and indirect or formal and tacit – commitments to liberal and Confucian values require that the latter accommodate the underlying moral principles of the former, to make them socially relevant and publicly meaningful. At the same time, these dual commitments make it difficult for the Korean Constitution to carry out its most supreme political mandate, namely, the perfectionist project of liberal democratic citizen-making of the kind championed by Western civic liberals who uphold the congruence between liberal constitutional principles and liberal citizenship.

That said, one thing that the Court failed to show was precisely how liberal constitutional values and the indirectly constitutional Confucian values are to be balanced, so that the two perfectionist commitments implied in Korean constitutionalism can be fulfilled harmoniously.[32] In a sense, though arguably, the Court's public recognition of and allegiance to such core Confucian values as filial piety, ancestor worship, respect for elders, and harmony in family, without an explication of how they can be sustained and further developed in the absence of their traditional

---

[32] Many Confucian political philosophers are persuaded that Confucian and (liberal) democratic values are mutually incommensurable. See, for instance, Chenyang Li, "Confucian Value and Democratic Value," *Journal of Value Inquiry* 31 (1997), pp. 183–193.

institutional underpinnings, most importantly the Confucian (-style) family system, reveals that Korean constitutionalism lacks a coherent normative standard that can weave together the Constitution's two perfectionist commitments in a publicly intelligible way and thereby produce a robust Korean citizenship. As it stands, Korean constitutionalism, enacted by the liberal-minded framers in 1948 under the U.S. military government (1945–1948), remains chronically vulnerable to an identity crisis: on the one hand it aspires to be liberal–democratic and on the other its sociocultural heart is still rooted in Confucian values, mores, habits, and moral sentiments.[33] In its majority decision, the Court could simply uphold human dignity and gender equality and declare the family-head system incompatible with what the Korean Constitution stands for, without mentioning Confucian values at all. The fact that they did mention such values shows that it is difficult to understand Korean constitutionalism in purely liberal terms.[34]

Public reason Confucian constitutionalism aims to provide a normative standard for historically Confucian East Asian countries whose legal systems and politics operate on a similar dual mode – liberal and Confucian. In addition to South Korea, public reason Confucian constitutionalism could be directly applied to other democratic or democratizing East Asian countries such as Japan, and particularly Taiwan, where citizens are still, albeit in varying degrees, saturated with Confucian mores and social habits and their liberal legal norms and democratic politics are deeply affected by Confucian values and practices.[35] Its applicability to

---

[33] Purely from a legal perspective, Marie Kim sums up the current Korean legal situation in the following way: "The insistence in recent jurisprudence on discovering and preserving true [largely Confucian] custom has caused unsettling influence on the relationship between custom and statues, with the consequence of obscuring the hierarchy of the sources of law. The courts' frequent resort to law-finding through custom and reason (*chori*) has tended to lead to a sort of jurisprudential quandary with looming uncertainty in adjudication" ("Korean Customary Law in Flux," p. 363).

[34] It should be noted therefore that though occasionally forcing the legislature to revise outdated provisions in family and succession laws, "justices [in the Korean Constitutional and Supreme Courts] were less willing to invalidate customs or law provisions that they viewed as the representation of the essence of Korean [Confucian] culture" (ibid., p. 373).

[35] Though there is virtually no study examining this sort of dual mode of East Asian constitutionalism, several studies show how in some East Asian countries formal political institutions, otherwise liberal-democratic, operate on Confucian discourse, rhetoric, and practices. See, for instance, L. H. M. Ling and Chih-yu Shih, "Confucianism with a Liberal Face: The Meaning of Democratic Politics in Postcolonial Taiwan," *Review of Politics* 60 (1998), pp. 55–82; Joel S. Fetzer and J. Christopher Soper, *Confucianism, Democratization, and Human Rights in Taiwan* (Lanham: Lexington Books, 2013); Chaibong Hahm, "The Confucian Political Discourse and the Politics of Reform in

communist East Asian countries such as China, Vietnam, and North Korea, however, is rather ambiguous: since Confucian constitutionalism is the constitutional expression of public reason Confucianism, which is fully committed to intrinsic values of democracy, it first normatively requires these countries to be democratized in their given Confucian cultural and societal contexts, and then subjects each country's dual – democratic and Confucian – constitutionalism to its normative standard, thereby facilitating a proper functioning of Confucian democracy. Chapter 6 elaborates the democratic aspiration of Confucian constitutionalism in depth by discussing how the premises and propositions of public reason Confucianism discussed in Chapter 2 require it (i.e., Confucian constitutionalism) to be a kind of democratic constitutionalism.[36] For now, let us continue our theoretical exploration of public reason Confucian constitutionalism with reference to the Korean case in hand.

PUBLIC REASON CONFUCIAN CONSTITUTIONALISM: A BETTER MODEL

As noted, what I call public reason Confucian constitutionalism is a particular mode of constitutionalism enabled by public reason Confucianism, with a view to making and reproducing *Confucian democratic citizens* as stipulated in P1 of Chapter 2. Now, if Confucian constitutionalism aims to provide a normative standard by which to weave the constitution's direct-liberal and indirect-Confucian perfectionist commitments in a publicly intelligible way, thus producing a robust Confucian democratic citizenship, how would the Korean Constitutional Court's majority decision be seen from the perspective of public reason Confucian constitutionalism?

Korea," *Korea Journal* 37 (1997), pp. 65–77; Geir Helgesen, *Democracy and Authority in Korea: The Cultural Dimension in Korean Politics* (Surrey: Curzon, 1998).

[36] For an idea of democratic constitutionalism that has strong resonance with public reason Confucianism, see Richard Bellamy, *Political Constitutionalism: A Republican Defense of the Constitutionality of Democracy* (Cambridge: Cambridge University Press, 2007). My view of the relationship between democracy and constitutionalism is significantly different not only from that of Confucian meritocratic perfectionists, who either reject or only partially accept democracy, but also from that of "Confucian constitutionalists," who recognize a significant value of democracy but advocate a sort of juristocracy by putting the court at the center of *constitutional democracy*. For this latter viewpoint, see Chaihark Hahm, "Beyond 'Law vs. Politics' in Constitutional Adjudication: Lessons from South Korea," *International Journal of Constitutional Law* 10:1 (2012), pp. 6–34.

Earlier, I noted that the Court's majority decision reveals Korean constitutionalism's chronic vulnerability to an identity crisis as it has failed thus far to develop a theoretical framework to weave its liberal and Confucian perfectionist commitments in a systemic way. As it stands, Korean constitutionalism produces neither a liberal democratic citizenship at a level satisfactory to most Korean liberals, West-educated or West-minded, let alone Western liberals, nor a Confucian democratic citizenship in a way publicly intelligible to ordinary Korean citizens, who are still soaked in Confucian mores, habits, moral sentiments, and practices, while embracing democratic institutions and liberal rights.[37] On top of the Court's lack of interest in creating a version of citizenship that is largely predicated on liberal democratic institutions and yet simultaneously embodies Koreans' cultural and historical connection with Confucian values, the Court also appears to subscribe to the simplistic but widely accepted view that human dignity and gender equality are exclusively liberal values, thus incompatible with traditional Confucian notions and practices of the family (*ka* 家; c. *jia*).

One may argue that in finding the family-head system incompatible with the Constitution, the Court only aimed to abolish this particular institution but never intended to deconstruct the (traditional) Korean family structure as such. However, neither traditionalist Confucians nor liberal feminists, the two social groups most actively involved in the public debate, understood the Court's decision this way. In fact, the abolition of the family-head system naturally entailed the scraping of the family-registry (*hojŏk* 戶籍) system from the Civil Code, which had bound an individual person to a family, and, accordingly, the Korean National Assembly's immediate task was to find an alternative registry system in its place. Not surprisingly, the public debate ensuing after the Court's decision revolved around precisely this question.[38]

However, the debate over a new population registry system was not merely a question of public administration. In the most profound sense, it

---

[37] For empirical evidence that Koreans are still saturated with Confucian values and practices, especially filial piety and other family values, see Mun-jo Bae and Se-jeong Park, "Taehaksengŭi hyoedaehan inshikkwa kachokgach'igwane yŏnghyang'ŭl mich'inŭn pyŏnin" [Consciousness of Filial Piety and Family Values among College Students], *Journal of the Korean Contents Association* 13 (2013), pp. 275–285; Tŏk-kyun Kim, "Yugyochŏk kachokjuŭi, haech'ein'ga pogwŏnin'ga" [Confucian Family Principles, Deconstruction or Restoration], *Yugyosasang munhwa yŏn'gu* [*The Journal of Confucian Thought and Culture*] 23 (2005), pp. 109–134.

[38] On this debate, see Yang, *Han'guk kajokbŏp ilkki*, pp. 504–520.

was about what constitutes the most basic unit of the Korean polity – family or individual?[39] And if the former, how can it be reconceived so that it can no longer buttress and be buttressed by the patriarchal, patrilineal, and androcentric elements characteristic of the traditional Confucian family? Seen in this way, the National Assembly's decision to replace the family-registry system with an individual identification system demonstrates the most radical aspect of liberalism in Korea, because by doing so it could finally "liberate" the Korean people, both men and women, from the traditional yoke of the Confucian family called *ka*.[40] That is, the Assembly's strong desire to weld the gap between liberal constitutional principles, to which the Korean constitutional polity is formally committed, and the Confucian family system, which, following the Court, it found undemocratic, drove it to opt for a relatively easy way out from the burden of finding a way to reconceive the Korean family in such a way as to make it just in light of constitutional principles without forfeiting traditional Confucian values. By making the individual the basic unit of Korean society and reconstructing the family (*ka*) into a social (largely contractual) institution centered around the individual (i.e., the *family* as the term is construed in the West), the Assembly imposed on the Korean citizenry the quintessential liberal ideals of the individual and the family.[41]

As a democratic political theory morally committed to public equality, public reason Confucianism agrees with the Court's reaffirmation of the Korean Constitution's resolution to uphold the values of human dignity and gender equality. Public reason Confucianism, too, finds the patriarchal, patrilineal, and androcentric structure of the Korean Confucian family heavily problematic, incompatible with its core premises and propositions. However, public reason Confucianism finds the Court's decision,

---

[39] From this perspective, Chaibong Hahm frames the dispute between traditionalist Confucians and liberal feminists surrounding the traditional Confucian family (*ka*) system in terms of "family versus the individual." See his "Family versus the Individual: The Politics of Marriage Laws in Korea," in *Confucianism for the Modern World*, pp. 334–359.

[40] It is important to note that in the Confucian-Korean context, *ka* refers not so much to a (nuclear) family as casually understood by Western liberals but to a special mode of the family institution with its unique worldview and philosophical underpinning. For an excellent discussion of the social and philosophical meaning of *ka*, especially in the Korean-Confucian context, see Chaibong Hahm, "Kaŭi inyŏmgwa ch'eche" [The Ideology and Institution of Ka 家], *Chŏntong'gwa hyŏndae* [*Tradition and Modernity*] 14 (2000), pp. 73–114.

[41] For my critical assessment of the new family law passed by the National Assembly, see Sungmoon Kim, "Family, Affection, and Confucian Civil Society: The Politico-Philosophical Implications of the New Family Law in Korea," *International Studies in Philosophy* 39 (2007), pp. 51–75.

especially with regard to Article 778, overbearing, and the National Assembly's subsequent enactment of the individual identification system replacing the family-registry system dismissive of Confucian values, by which Korean constitutionalism is indirectly bound. To be sure, Article 781(1) gives the patrilineal descent line a privileged public status and Article 826(3) publicly allows the elevated social status of men over women. As the Court rightly held, these and related clauses of the Korean Civil Code do not deserve constitutional protection.[42] But is the family-head system inherently unjust? In the Court's majority decision, what remained unclear was why Article 778, which establishes the family-head system and defines the basic structure of the Korean family (*ka*) system, is incompatible with constitutional principles of human dignity and gender equality. As noted, the Court's reasoning was that when *combined* with other, overtly discriminatory, clauses of the Korean family law, Article 778 is found unconstitutional. But considering its quasi-constitutional valorization of Confucian values, was this the best judgment of the Court?

The Court's reasoning is not unreasonable if we understand human dignity and gender equality purely in liberal terms a la John Stuart Mill, that they are moral values premised on the assumption of liberal autonomous personhood.[43] Furthermore, from the liberal perspective of autonomous personhood, the Korean Civil Code that defines a person (both man and woman) as a member of the *ka* or in terms of family relationality only reveals its feudal nature. Therefore, insomuch as the Korean Constitution is predicated on liberal moral principles and the liberal sense of justice, the very structure of *ka* as the basic unit of Korean society must be deconstructed into the Western-style "family" so that it (i.e., the family) can just be the first social institution of private individuals, all pursuing personal happiness, private interests, or individual autonomy. From this perspective, the Assembly's replacement of the family registry system with the individual identification system, thereby deconstructing the Korean-Confucian institution of *ka*, is reasonable, perhaps even desirable.

However, public reason Confucianism enables us to decouple the question regarding how to understand Korean personhood and conceive

---

[42] Some examples of such related clauses include Articles 782(1), 784(1) and (2), and 785. On how these clauses discriminate against women, see Yang, "Vision of Postcolonial Feminist Jurisprudence," pp. 16–17.

[43] J. S. Mill, *The Subjection of Women*, in *On Liberty and Other Writings*, ed. Stefan Collini (Cambridge: Cambridge University Press, 1989). Also see Nancy J. Hirschmann, "Mill, Political Economy, and Women's Work," *American Political Science Review* 102:2 (2008), pp. 199–213.

of the Korean family from the question regarding justice. From the standpoint of public reason Confucianism, the problem with the Court's majority decision is that it confounds these two different questions. That is, while attempting to address the latter question, the Court dismantled the *ka*, the social-cum-legal institution directly concerned with the character of Korean selfhood and the seedbed of Confucian values that are indirectly supported by the Korean Constitution, when it could have simply removed the discriminatory statutes from the Civil Code and reformed the Korean Confucian family structure in a way that is more just and compatible with constitutional principles. After all, Article 778 did not have to be removed because it gives no justification to discrimination against women. As Justice Kim Hyo-chong notes in his dissenting opinion, the article involves only three normative contents: (1) the Korean Constitution acknowledges the existence of a particular mode of the family called *ka*, (2) the Constitution regards each citizen simultaneously as a member of the family, and (3) in each family there should exist a family head selected by the means approved by law.[44] If the measure by which the family head is selected discriminates against women, it should be reformed, for instance, in a way that opens family headship to both men and women. This reform does not have to necessarily involve the abolition of the family-head system itself, and, more importantly, the deconstruction of the legal reality and social ideal that Korean citizens exist as members of the family, which is the *normative* expression of Korean selfhood. In this regard, public reason Confucianism finds the following dissenting statement by Justice Kim much more reasonable and more in agreement with ordinary Korean citizens' moral sentiment and social judgment.

Our Civil Code holds the family system (*kajedo* 家制度) in order to strengthen the legal basis of the family institution and to clarify legal relations among family and this system contributes to the formation and maintenance of the family institution which is guaranteed by the Constitution. Therefore, Article 778 of the Civil Code, which stipulates the existence of the family (*ka*) as a legal concept, does not necessarily violate any part of the Constitution, including Article 36(1). Moreover, the question of whether or not the fact that law forces individuals to be placed within the family violates human dignity requires a deep understanding of the

---

[44] Justice Kim also has a different interpretation of Article 36(1). According to him, the article mainly expresses the framers' conviction that family structure deserves constitutional protection and to this extent it should be acknowledged that the constitutional resolution has been made that the family system itself must be maintained even if it may conflict with individual rights (p. 34).

relationship between society and human beings. On the one hand, from the perspective that puts great emphasis on human reason and views individuals as abstract and separate entities, this kind of legal enforcement to associate individuals with others against their will would be seen negatively. On the other hand, from the perspective that holds that real living human beings are existentially structured to exist only in relation with other human beings, the reflection of the family relation, which is the most fundamental human relationship, onto [our] legal concept would be deemed to suit perfectly with human nature. Accordingly, given that the concept of human being and the [most proper] mode of human existence can be interpreted in different ways, it is difficult to conclude that the legislative action that places individuals within the constitutionally protected family (*ka*) system encroaches upon human dignity. Quite to the contrary, it could be concluded that our Constitution establishes that each person ought to build a firm foundation of social relationships through the family relationship and that family relation is the single most important [ethical] foundation of social solidarity and political unity.[45]

Clearly, Justice Kim's dissenting opinion, which finds only Articles 781(1) and 826(3) unconstitutional, supports the second perspective and this is the view and reasoning that public reason Confucianism endorses. Human dignity is not the exclusive moral property of liberalism and there is no reason to assume this supreme human value as underpinned by liberal assumptions of autonomous personhood.[46] Public reason Confucianism embraces the foundational Confucian convictions that human beings exist only in the intersections of complex relations and that individual personhood and social relationships are inextricably intertwined.[47] Though it is certainly an exaggeration to identify the Confucian self solely in terms of social roles, lacking the inner core of moral agency that performs such roles reflexively,[48] Confucianism, including public reason

---

[45] 17-1 KCCR1 (translation is mine).
[46] For a Confucian (especially Mencian-Confucian) argument for human dignity, see Irene T. Bloom, "Mengzian Arguments on Human Nature (*Ren Xing*)," in *Essays on the Moral Philosophy of Mengzi*, eds. Xiusheng Liu and Philip J. Ivanhoe (Indianapolis: Hackett, 2002), pp. 64–100.
[47] Chaibong Hahm, *T'algŭndaewa yugyo [Postmodernity and Confucianism]* (Seoul: Nanam, 1998); Chong-ŭn Yi, "Sŏguwa yugyomunhwaggwŏnesŏŭi kaein" [The Concept of Individual in Western and Confucian Cultures], *Chŏntong'gwa hyŏndae [Tradition and Modernity]* 9 (1999), pp. 201–225; Tu Wei-ming, *Confucian Thought: Selfhood as Creative Transformation* (Albany: State University of New York Press, 1985).
[48] This sort of argument has been advanced by so-called Confucian role-ethicists. See Roger T. Ames, *Confucian Role Ethics: A Vocabulary* (Honolulu: University of Hawaii Press, 2011); Henry Rosemont Jr., "Why Take Rights Seriously? A Confucian Critique," in *Human Rights and the World's Religions*, ed. Leroy Rouner (Notre Dame: University of Notre Dame Press, 1988), pp. 167–182; A. T. Nuyen, "Moral Obligation and Moral Motivation in Confucian Role-Based Ethics," *Dao* 8 (2009), pp. 1–11. My critical

Confucianism, understands the self as relational and the unencumbered self's personal autonomy as illusory. In his statement, Justice Kim does not cite Confucianism explicitly. However, it is undeniable that he is recapitulating the Confucian conception of the self that Koreans generally endorse and even embody themselves, through characteristically Confucian socialization and social practices.[49] For the Korean (and Confucian) people, family is the pivotal social institution that socializes them into Confucian mores, habits, moral sentiments, and ethical practices,[50] which broadly constitute the essence of Confucian public reason.

From the perspective of public reason Confucianism, therefore, family is not merely another democratic social institution to which liberal moral principles must be applied without qualification. Family relationships are the most fundamental human relationships and it is within the family that one learns the most basic ethical precepts, principles, and practices one needs to become a moral person. And it is by extending the familial relations that one can develop civilities and cultivate civic virtues, traits, and dispositions that enable him or her to care about the public good.[51] In public reason Confucianism, Confucian values and practices, such as filial piety, respect for elders, ancestor worship, and harmony within the family, may not be directly constitutional values, but they have significant (indirect) constitutional implications, allowing the state to promote them publicly. The constitutional deconstruction of the system of *ka* and the legislative replacement of family registry system with individual identification system signal the Court's official abandonment of the Confucian seedbeds of Korean civic virtues. What is ironic is that the Court still wanted to retain Confucian values and virtues affiliated with the ideal and institution of *ka* while it was actively deconstructing it.

---

philosophical engagement with this literature can be found in Sungmoon Kim, *Confucian Democracy in East Asia: Theory and Practice* (New York: Cambridge University Press, 2014), chap. 1.

[49] For social-psychological and philosophical-anthropological studies that show that the Korean social self is deeply relational or interdependent, see Sang-chin Choi, *Han'gugin shimnihak [The Psychology of the Korean People]* (Seoul: Chung Ang University Press, 2000), and C. Fred Alford, *Think No Evil: Korean Values in the Age of Globalization* (Ithaca: Cornell University Press, 1999), respectively.

[50] See Walter H. Slote and George A. DeVos (eds.), *Confucianism and the Family* (Albany: State University of New York Press, 1998).

[51] On how Confucian civilities can be extended from Confucian familial relationality, see Sungmoon Kim, "Beyond Liberal Civil Society: Confucian Familism and Relational Strangership," *Philosophy East and West* 60 (2010), pp. 476–498.

Still, a question might arise with regard to the family-head system. Even if it is accepted that the deconstruction of *ka* may not be a prudential action for the Korean Constitutional Court and National Assembly to take in light of public reason Confucianism, should it find the abolition of the family-head system equally unwise, perhaps even unreasonable? Indeed, there is no inherent philosophical connection between public reason Confucianism and the family-head system. And to the extent that it operates on social norms of gender inequality, the family-head system is incompatible with public reason Confucianism. However, public reason Confucianism's attitude toward the family-head system is much more nuanced than that shown by the Court's majority decision. Most significantly, public reason Confucianism places more weight on the ethical goal traditional Confucians (in this case neo-Confucians) aimed to achieve by instituting the family-head system than the negative effects of its patrilineal structure, although it would actively rectify such negativities including discrimination between men and women.[52] Zhu Xi (1130–1200), an authoritative compiler of Song neo-Confucianism, explains the ethical aims of the family-head system in the following way.

In order to control the minds of the people, unify one's kin, and enrich social customs so that people will not forget their origin, it is necessary to clarify genealogy, group members of the clan together, and institute a system of heads

---

[52] Many Korean liberal feminists claim that the patrilineal descent system of the Korean Confucian family itself discriminates against women not necessarily because it does active harm to the well-being of women, but mainly because the worldview it creates is deeply androcentric and phallocentric (Yang, *Han'guk kajokbŏp ilkki*, pp. 80–81). Though public reason Confucianism is compatible with certain types of feminism, including so-called *Confucian feminism*, it does not embrace a version of feminism that blames all traditional social and political institutions as phallocentric. From the perspective of public reason Confucianism, the patrilineal descent system is not itself the object of political or legal reform, as long as it does not encroach upon women's public status as equal citizens and constitutional rights. On various conceptions of Confucian feminism that in my view are largely compatible with public reason Confucianism, see Li-Hsiang L. Rosenlee, "A Feminist Appropriation of Confucianism," in *Confucianism in Context: Classic Philosophy and Contemporary Issues, East Asia and Beyond*, eds. Wonsuk Chang and Leah Kalmanson (Albany: State University of New York Press, 2010), pp. 175–190; Pauline Lee, "Li Zhi and John Stuart Mill: A Confucian Feminist Critique of Liberal Feminism," and Chenyang Li, "The Confucian Concept of *Jen* and the Feminist Ethics of Care: A Comparative Study," both in Chenyang Li (ed.), *The Sage and the Second Sex: Confucianism, Ethics, and Gender* (Chicago: Open Court, 2000), pp. 113–132 and 23–42, respectively; Sook-in Lee, "Transforming Gender Relations through Intimacy," *Korea Journal* 42 (2002), pp. 46–69; Han'guk yuhakhoe [Association for Confucian Studies] (ed.), *Yugyowa Peminisŭm [Confucianism and Feminism]* (Seould: Ch'ŏrakkwa hyŏnsilsa, 2001).

of descent. (This work should not be done year by year.) ... If the system of heads of descent were destroyed, people would not know their origin. The result would be that they would drift and wander in all directions. Very often there would still be relatives but they would not recognize them.[53]

According to Zhu Xi, without the family-head system it would be utterly difficult to keep track of the family's genealogy. And for him, tracking the family's genealogy is of pivotal ethical importance because without it people would "drift and wander in all directions," not knowing where they came from nor who they are. One's kin members then would be no different from strangers. From the perspective of Confucianism, however, what is worrisome is not so much that there is no ethical resource to come to terms with the otherness of the stranger as some scholars claim.[54] The worry lies first in the deracination of the person from his or her most basic social moorings as well as from the most important ethical foundation, and second in the estrangement among the family/kin (or *ka*) members, upon which their relationships ought to be regulated mainly through the system of justice. All the more problematic, estrangement among *ka* members makes it extremely difficult to sustain, let alone enrich, social customs, habits, mores, or moral sentiments underpinning and inculcating Confucian virtues such as filial piety, respect for elders, ancestor worship, and harmony within the family.

To repeat, it is not my intention to suggest that the family-head system is indispensable to public reason Confucianism or that *ka* is the best way to organize the family structure. My point is that as long as the family-head system is central to the organization of the *ka* institution by serving its moral purpose and to the extent that it is reformed so as to accommodate democratic constitutional principles, its abolition is not the central task of public reason Confucianism. What is central to public reason Confucianism is the *ka*, a complex ensemble of family institutions, familial relationships, and Confucian values, because it most saliently represents the type of human relationship and social values that Korean-Confucian citizens idealize and it is the institutional bastion of Confucian

---

[53] Wing-tsit Chan (trans.), *Reflections on Things at Hand: The Neo-Confucian Anthology Compiled by Chu Hsi and Lü Tsu-ch'ien* (New York: Columbia University Press, 1967), pp. 227–229.

[54] For instance, Jiwei Ci writes, "[T]hose who have absorbed the Confucian concept of human relations would be socially and ethically at sea if they were to enter into relations with strangers, where the conjunction of hierarchical-reciprocal relations and kinship ties simply does not exist" ("The Confucian Relational Concept of the Person and Its Modern Predicament," *Kenney Institute of Ethics Journal* 9 [1999], pp. 325–346, at p. 334).

virtues and values that they still cherish. Put differently, it is the social and legal institution that helps to maintain contemporary Korea as characteristically Confucian, culturally connecting modern Koreans with their ancestors, thereby contributing to their shared collective self-identity. What public reason Confucianism recommends then is not so much the deconstruction of the *ka* structure, by arbitrarily decoupling the institution of the *ka* from the ethical and social values it inculcates and buttresses, but its reconstruction into a *more* just social institution and legal entity that is compatible with democratic constitutional principles and sociopolitical institutions. As Justice Kim suggests, we can remake the *ka* so that it can support gender equality, by making family headship open to both men and women and removing gender-discriminatory elements from the Family Law. Thus understood, *ka*, when reformed properly, is the most crucial institutional basis of Confucian constitutionalism.[55]

From the standpoint of public reason Confucianism, then, the best way to make Korea (and other East Asian Confucian countries) a Confucian constitutional democracy is to reconceptualize the (direct) constitutional principles of human dignity and gender equality *from* the perspective of Confucian values to which it is publicly (i.e., indirect-constitutionally) committed, as much as adapt Confucian values, institutions, and practices to democratic constitutional principles. Since public reason Confucianism stipulates public reason as constituted by Confucian values, mores, and/or moral sentiments, the practical implication of this dual perfectionism is that the moral contents of human dignity and gender equality, otherwise liberal ideals, ought to be reconceived in light of Confucian public reason in various public forums including courts, congresses, and civil societies. A polity's perfectionist commitment to the values and institutions of the *ka* can directly contribute to its indirect Confucian constitutionalism.

CONCLUSION

In this chapter, I have illuminated the mode of constitutionalism (i.e., public reason Confucian constitutionalism) that public reason

---

[55] *Ka* can also be the basis of Confucian civil society if we understand "civil society" in Tocquevillian terms, that is, in terms of social intermediaries standing between the individual and the state. On this point, see Kim, "Family, Affection, and Confucian Civil Society." Compare my position with advocates of Confucian meritocracy, such as Jiang Qing, Daniel Bell, Joseph Chan, and Ruiping Fan, who make the nondemocratically selected upper house in the legislature the centerpiece of their own Confucian constitutionalist visions.

Confucianism gives rise to in the pluralist and democratic societal context by engaging with a landmark Constitutional Court case in postdemocratic Korea. What this Korean case reveals is that when a traditionally Confucian society is socially conditioned by social pluralism and constitutional democracy, it develops constitutional dualism because of its double perfectionist commitments to liberal constitutionalism on the one hand, to which the polity is formally committed, and to Confucian values and norms on the other, to which it is indirectly committed and which it promotes publicly. In Korea, the result of these double perfectionist commitments is chronic incoherence in the constitutional project of citizen-making: while formal liberal constitutionalism is constantly obstructed by indirect Confucian constitutionalism, Confucian constitutionalism is systematically prevented by the constitution's liberal commitment from producing a coherent public identity of Confucian democratic citizenship.

Public reason Confucian constitutionalism rectifies this institutional instability latent in Korean/East Asian constitutionalism by weaving two perfectionist commitments into a single constitutionalism, first by reformulating the internal duality of Korean/East Asian constitutionalism in terms of direct-liberal and indirect-Confucian constitutionalism and second by reconceiving the moral contents of direct-liberal constitutional principles in light of Confucian values and norms, the indirect constitutional values that make up the backbone of Confucian public reason. In this way, public reason Confucian constitutionalism aims to produce Confucian democratic citizens, as stipulated in Chapter 2 – citizens who, while subscribing to different comprehensive doctrines, deliberate on public problems with which they are commonly faced, with reference to Confucian public reason. Central to Confucian constitutionalism's citizen-making project is the innovative maintenance of the *ka* (c. *jia*) because it works as the seedbed of Confucian values, virtues, and norms.

That public reason Confucian constitutionalism formulates the relationship between liberal perfectionism and Confucian perfectionism in terms of direct and indirect constitutionalism should not be misunderstood as the former entertaining a political privilege vis-à-vis the latter. The direct and indirect distinction is not so much political but conceptual. This distinction reflects the East Asian reality that citizens in the region are not Confucian in the *fully* comprehensive moral sense and are deeply conditioned by the fact of pluralism, which they can come to terms with justly only under democratic political institutions and procedures. From the philosophical standpoint, this conceptual distinction corresponds with public reason Confucianism's commitment to the constitutive values of democracy as discussed in Chapter 1. In reality, though, it is Confucian values and norms that are more politically and culturally salient in the overall operation of public reason Confucian constitutionalism because they provide the moral content for otherwise "liberal" rights, values, and principles that define the polity's formal institutional structure.

4

Public equality and democratic pluralism

South Korea's dual constitutionalism reflects the reality in which many East Asians find themselves: while increasingly subscribing to diverse moral, philosophical, and religious doctrines, they still publicly cherish and are deeply saturated with Confucian values and social norms. In particular, in countries that have undergone (liberal) democratic transitions, such as South Korea and Taiwan, constitutional duality becomes even more salient because citizens there are under staggering institutional pressure to transform themselves into liberal citizens, as their constitutions have been reformed in a more liberal democratic way, even though they have no desire to forfeit their long-held Confucian values, such as, among others, filial piety, respect for elders, ancestor worship, ritual propriety, and social harmony (including harmony within the family). As discussed in the previous chapter, the central political goal of public reason Confucian constitutionalism is to produce a coherent public identity of Confucian *and* democratic citizens by weaving two perfectionist commitments – liberal and Confucian – into a single coherent constitutionalism.

Still, an important question about the Confucian nature of public reason Confucianism remains. Even if it may be granted, as revealed in the preceding chapter through critical assessment of the Korean family-head system case, that public reason Confucianism is significantly different from the traditional Confucianism that is patriarchal, patrilineal, and androcentric, the two are not completely unrelated. Since one of the core stipulations of public reason Confucianism is that it should be recognized as "Confucianism" to Confucian citizens who have long lived with traditional Confucianism with all its cons (as well as its pros), the question of how distinct public reason Confucianism is from traditional Confucianism requires further explanation.

As a first step, readers should keep in mind that while critically engaging with Joseph Chan's idea of moderate political Confucian perfectionism in Chapter 1, I argued that the only mode of contemporary normative Confucianism that is meaningful philosophically and socially is comprehensive Confucianism – a sort of comprehensive doctrine in the Rawlsian sense. Now, notice that distinguishing between the political conception of justice and moral doctrines, which are general and comprehensive views, Rawls writes about the latter as follows:

> A moral conception is general if it applies to a wide range of subjects, and in the limit to all subjects universally. It is comprehensive when it includes conceptions of what is of value in human life, and ideals of personal character, as well as ideals of friendship and of familial and associational relationships, and much else that is to inform our conduct, and in the limit to our life as a whole. A conception is fully comprehensive if it covers all recognized values and virtues within one rather precisely articulated system; whereas a conception is only partially comprehensive when it comprises a number of, but by no means all, nonpolitical values and virtues and is rather loosely articulated.[1]

Chan argues that his moderate political Confucian perfectionism is incompatible with comprehensive Confucianism because he understands comprehensive Confucianism in terms of a *fully* comprehensive doctrine. By "traditional(ist) Confucianism" I have meant thus far a Confucianism that is a fully comprehensive doctrine, particularly associated with a patriarchal, patrilineal, and androcentric Confucian worldview and way of life, and to the extent that public reason Confucianism is both conceptually and practically distinct from this type of Confucianism, it has a certain structural similarity with Chan's moderate perfectionism. The similarity does not go very far, however, because, as I have argued repeatedly, public reason Confucianism is nevertheless a form of comprehensive Confucianism, a Confucianism that is only *partially* comprehensive. The difference between Chan's moderate Confucianism and public reason Confucianism is that the latter, unlike the former, represents a comprehensive albeit evolving form of life, one that embraces and finds expression within constitutionally established constraints. Unlike Chan's moderate Confucian political perfectionism, public reason Confucianism is not merely concerned with certain items – traits, characters, or relationships – that are affirmed as Confucian (in light of classical Confucian

---

[1] John Rawls, *Political Liberalism* (New York: Columbia University Press, 1993), p. 13.

texts) but are clearly severed from a particular mode of the Confucian way of life. Rather, it is concerned with a Confucian way of life, but one affiliated with values socially adapted to democratic institutions as well as value pluralism. The partiality of the comprehensiveness of public reason Confucianism derives from such social conditioning to which (comprehensive) Confucianism has to adapt itself.

Keeping in mind this important distinction between traditional(ist) Confucianism as a fully comprehensive Confucianism and public reason Confucianism as a partially comprehensive Confucianism, in this chapter I continue to articulate the essential features of public reason Confucianism by engaging with another Korean legal case – the 2005 Korean Supreme Court case regarding membership within clan organizations (*chongjung* 宗中). In this case, the court ruled that women are entitled to formal membership with all accompanying rights of their paternal clan organization, overturning a 1958 decision that admitted only adult men as legitimate members. Contrary to the popular view that this case is a victory for gender equality and individual rights over archaic patriarchal Confucianism *tout court*, I argue that in this case, the Supreme Court offered itself as an institutional venue in which traditional Confucian values/practices and liberal rights/values could be negotiated with and accommodated to each other, thereby reshaping traditional Confucianism into a mode of Confucianism that is relevant in modern Korea, namely, public reason Confucianism.

By discussing this case from the perspective of public reason Confucianism, I aim to achieve several goals. First, I show how public reason Confucianism's partial comprehensiveness, which renders the Confucian way of life neither purely Western-style liberal nor traditional Confucian, can be (and is) produced, by examining and philosophically reconstructing cultural negotiations taking place between traditional Confucian values/practices and liberal rights/values under democratic constitutional conditions. Second, I articulate the crucial distinction between public reason Confucianism and traditional, fully comprehensive, Confucianism by discussing how public reason Confucianism protects the interests of those who persist in various forms of the traditional Confucian way of life (and other, non-Confucian and nonliberal, forms of associational life) as long as their ways of living within their respective associations and (extended) families do not seriously encroach upon the constitutional principles and values endorsed by public reason Confucianism. In public reason Confucianism (or, more accurately, public reason Confucian constitutionalism), various modes of traditional Confucian lifestyles preferred by fully comprehensive Confucians are given constitutional protection in terms of their right to freedom of association. Last, I show how public reason Confucianism's respect for the constitutional right to freedom of association enables the given polity to develop a two-layered social practice of equality. My central claim here is that public reason Confucianism's primary concern is with public equality, one's equal public standing as a citizen, and that it thus allows various sorts of moderate inequalities within freely formed cultural and/or religious associations including Confucian clan organizations.

Thus understood, while the previous chapter was focused mainly on P1 and P2, which were presented in Chapter 2 of this work (i.e., how these propositions of public reason Confucianism enable the circumstances of public reason Confucian constitutionalism), the present chapter extends the scope of public reason Confucian constitutionalism to questions of public equality and democratic pluralism, stipulated in P3 and P4, respectively. Like that of the previous chapter, the core argument of this chapter unfolds with special focus on gender equality, arguably the most important feature of public equality in a Confucian society.

THE DAUGHTERS' REBELLION: THE CASE

Background

In 1999, the clan organization of the Samaenggong Branch of the Lee Clan from the ancestral seat of Yong'in distributed among its members dividends resulting from a sale of the clan's land property.[2] According to its internal regulations predicated on traditional Confucian patrilineal clan law (c. *zongfa* 宗法), especially of the version strongly influenced by Zhu Xi's *Family Ritual* (c. *Jiali* 家禮), which admits only adult men as full members in the capacity of sons, the association gave adult male members 150 million won (approximately US$150,000) and male members under the age of 20, regarded as associate members, between 16.5 and 55 million won (approximately between US$15,000 and

---

[2] In Korea, a clan association consists of male descendants sharing the same surname, same ancestral seat, and (often but not necessarily) the same branch. In the present case, the clan association is composed of those whose surname is Lee, whose ancestral seat is Yong'in, and whose branch is Samaenggong. While the ancestral seat (*pon* 本 or *pon'gwan* 本貫) refers to the regional origin of the clan's founder, the branch (*p'a* 派) refers to a subgroup within the entire clan sharing the same ancestral seat and is often created by someone who either held a high governmental post or was hailed as a prominent Confucian scholar.

$50,000) each. Though not recognized as "formal" members in light of clan law, female members of the clan, namely unmarried daughters as well as daughters-in-law, who are responsible for, among other things, preparing the food for family rituals and clan activities, also each received 2.2 million won (approximately US$2,000) and 3.3 million won (approximately US$3,000) respectively, not in terms of dividends, which are only given to formal (and associate) members, but in terms of "inheritance."[3] In the course of distributing the clan's wealth, however, married daughters (i.e., the clan's daughters who had married members of another clan) were completely excluded based on the traditional patriarchal Confucian custom that regards daughters as "outsiders" upon marriage (in Korean words, *ch'ulgaoein* 出嫁外人).[4]

Infuriated, more than a hundred married daughters openly protested the clan council's decision and demanded their "due" share as members of the clan, pointing to the clan association's somewhat equivocal definition of membership as pertaining to "*any* descendant of the Samaenggong branch when one comes of age." In the face of unflagging protests from the married daughters, the clan council eventually offered each married daughter 2.2 million won (approximately US$2,000), also in terms of inheritance, hence not recognizing their formal membership. However, this decision fell far short of assuaging the protestors' anger and frustration, who soon found out that the clan's daughters-in-law had received more money than they did. As one of the participants in this protest expressed later, what frustrated them the most was not so much

---

[3] Originally, the clan council was going to distribute the dividends only to the formal members of the clan but upon vehement complaints from various "members" excluded from a share of the wealth, it eventually decided to give a certain amount of money to some female members including daughters-in-law.

[4] This Confucian norm was widely disseminated in Korean society after the *Family Ritual* by Zhu Xi (1130–1200), the authoritative complier of Cheng-Zhu Neo-Confucianism or the Learning of the Way (c. *Daoxue* 道學) during the Song dynasty, had become the orthodox guidelines regulating the yangban aristocratic families. Regarding the married women's inheritance rights during the Chosŏn period, Martina Deuchler writes, "The integration of women into their husbands' descent group as demanded by Confucian ideology is impressively illustrated by the daughters' gradual loss of inheritance rights.... [B]y the middle of the dynasty daughters who upon marriage left their natal family were deprived of their stake in their families' ancestral property and entered their husbands' home without the land and slaves they had brought in earlier.... Women thus lost the economic independence they had enjoyed at the beginning of the dynasty. This development was closely connected with the gradual acceptance of the rule of primogeniture that concentrated a descent group's ancestral land and slaves in the hands of its primary agnatic heir" (*The Confucian Transformation of Korea: A Study of Society and Ideology* [Cambridge: Council on East Asian Studies, Harvard University, 1992], p. 266).

the amount of money but the clan's patriarchal tradition that systematically discriminated against the married daughters simply because they were women (and admitted women's partial membership only in their capacity as the wives of the clan's sons).[5] Recognizing that verbal protests would not be sufficient to gain formal acceptance into the clan association as members, in 2000, some of these women brought the case to the district court, asking the court to adjudicate the legality of the clan's stipulations regarding membership. After losing in both district and appellate courts, five of the married daughters from Samaenggong, together with three of the married daughters from the Hyeryŏnggong branch of the Shim Clan from Ch'ŏngsong, who had suffered the same defeats in lower courts, appealed to the Supreme Court. After a long deliberation accompanied by a public hearing, the first of its kind in the history of Korean jurisprudence, the Court, attended by all thirteen justices, made a landmark decision in 2005 by ruling for the plaintiffs, thereby redefining the membership of clan organizations.[6]

The Court's decision

In Korea, cases advanced to the Supreme Court are usually assigned to sections (*pu* 部), each consisting of three justices, and most cases are adjudicated by one section. However, for cases that are likely to entail immense social consequences or to overturn previous decisions, all members of the Court participate in the deliberation and decision making. As noted, the full-member court participated in the present case, implying its significance in the Korean social context. The key message of the Court's ruling (i.e., the majority opinion) can be recapitulated as the following:

(1) The long-standing customary practice of clan associations admitting only adult men as members and denying women formal membership has become less legally certain among the members of our society.

(2) Above all, our entire legal order, in which the Constitution has the highest normative authority, not only ensures a family life based on individual dignity and gender equality, but it also does not tolerate

---

[5] *Han'gyŏre Shinmun* 7/21/2005.
[6] To avoid a disruption in legal order and continuity, however, the court noted that the decision was not retroactive, leaving unaffected male-only votes on clan leaders and clan property distribution made prior to this decision.

gender inequality in the exercise of rights and duties within the family. It has progressed by abolishing discrimination against women in all spheres of life, political, economic, social, and cultural, thereby realizing gender equality, and it will continue to make sure that the norm of gender equality is firmly maintained.

(3) Clan organizations (*chongjung*) are family clans, whose purpose is to maintain the tombs of common ancestors, carry out memorial ceremonies, and promote intimate relationships among their members, and they arose naturally by the efforts of descendants upon the demise of their common ancestor(s).

(4) The customary practice of clan organizations to admit, among the descendants of common ancestors, only adult men as members and to exclude women from formal membership, does not correspond with our entire legal order, which has significantly changed as explained earlier and thus lacks justification and reasonableness, because it endows and denies the opportunity to participate in clan activities, such as maintenance of the tombs of common ancestors and memorial ceremonies, solely on the basis of sex.

(5) Therefore, the customary practice of limiting formal membership in the clan exclusively to its male adults is no longer legally valid.[7]

CONFUCIANISM VERSUS LIBERALISM?

Mass media immediately framed the whole case in terms of a grand showdown between traditional Confucianism and progressive modernity, in the same way that they had presented a decision by the Constitutional Court a few months prior on the family-head system. Not surprisingly, progressives and liberal feminists on one side and traditionalist Confucians and conservatives on the other responded to the decision in diametrically different ways. For instance, Kwark Bae-hee, president of the Korea Legal Aid Center for Family Relations, said, "Along with the scrapping of the family-head system, this decision will become another cornerstone as our society truly moves toward gender equality." Nam Yun In-soon, the head of Korea Women's Associations United, hailed the

---

[7] Korean Supreme Court, judgment of July 21, 2005, 2002ta13850. For a discussion of this case in the English literature, see Marie S.-H. Kim, *Law and Custom in Korea: Comparative Legal History* (New York: Cambridge University Press, 2012), pp. 285–286, and "In the Name of Custom, Culture, and the Constitution: Korean Customary Law in Flux," *Texas International Law Journal* 48:3 (2013), pp. 357–391, at pp. 367–368.

decision by saying that it will greatly help eliminate discrimination between sons and daughters. In marked contrast, traditionalist Confucians (k. *yurim* 儒林) and conservatives were in an uproar, slamming the decision that in their view would not only bring irrevocable disorder to the traditional structure of the family, but, more fundamentally, destroy the very meaning of the (Confucian) family undergirded by different social roles and statuses according to gender. This point was most clearly pronounced by Lee Seung-gwan, the head of the Sungkyunkwan committee on Confucian ritual,[8] when he said, "Women can't participate in the family clan, a special organization inherited from our ancestors. If married women get to participate in the clan organizations of their maiden homes, does this mean [that] men have to assume responsibilities in their wives' family clans as well?"[9]

There is no denying that though not directly alluding to liberalism, the Court vindicated liberal moral principles championed by liberal feminists and progressives, and thus there was indeed good reason for Confucians and traditionalists to complain that the justices of the Court (particularly the seven justices upholding the decision) did not give full consideration to the legal status of customary practice in Korean society, which precedes the establishment of the (modern) constitution in 1948. However, it is worth noting that while the clan organizations' customary practice is largely at odds with contemporary Korea's constitutional commitment to individual dignity and gender equality, the Court never espoused substantively "liberal" notions of individual dignity and gender equality or abandoned core Confucian values such as filial piety, respect for elders, ancestor worship, and ritual propriety completely. Quite to the contrary, as clearly revealed in Justice Ko Hyŏn-chŏl's supplementary opinion to the majority opinion, the Court's true intention was rather to succeed and further develop the traditional clan system in a way compatible with Korea's constitutional norms and principles, such as individual dignity and gender equality, by allowing both men (as sons) and women (as daughters) to participate in the clan activities.

In this regard, the public hearing held two years before the decision was made is worthy of special attention because it helps us to better

---

[8] Sungkyunkwan 成均館 used to be the National Academy during the Chosŏn dynasty, and was and still is considered Korea's Confucian sanctuary.

[9] All direct and indirect quotations in this paragraph are adopted from the English edition of *Chosun Ilbo* (7/21/2005). Note that the Romanization of the Korean names here follows the Ministry of Education system promulgated in 2000. In other places in this chapter, I employ the McCune-Reischauer system.

understand what kind of reasoning was used when the Court later upheld equal membership within the clan organizations. During the hearing, Justice Yu Chi-tam asked the legal representative of the defendants (i.e., the clan organizations) whether, for example, it would be fair for the clan to prohibit formal membership to women simply because they are women, even though they are earnest filial daughters, while automatically admitting any adult man as a member regardless of his filial commitment to his ancestors. In addition, turning to the legal representative of the plaintiffs (the married daughters), Justice Cho Muje asked whether or not the plaintiffs had fulfilled their duties faithfully, the kinds of duties required of every clan member, such as payment of membership fees and participation in memorial ceremonies.

While the question Justice Yu raised to the defendants concerned the injustice of gender inequality perpetrated by the clan organizations in the name of customary practice, the reasoning behind it is undeniably Confucian.[10] If unpacked and reconstructed, Justice Yu's reasoning seems to consist of the following propositions:

(1) Clan organizations in Korea are Confucian institutions;
(2) As Confucian institutions, the operating moral principles of the clan organizations must be grounded in Confucian ethics;
(3) According to Confucian ethics, *ren* 仁 is the moral virtue par excellence and filial piety is thought to be the root of *ren*;[11] therefore,

---

[10] More reasons and arguments are easily found within traditional sources. For example, Confucian values such as benevolence (*ren* 仁) and harmony (*he* 和) might also play important roles in arguing for reform in the clan system and in order to realize the primary purpose of the clan system and preserve core Confucian values, such reform is needed. Such internal reasons are characteristic of Korean styles of argumentation and as long as they are conceived and advanced in ways consistent with the rights delineated in the constitution, they are the coin of public reason Confucianism. I am grateful to P. J. Ivanhoe for drawing my attention to this point.

[11] "The gentleman (*junzi* 君子) devotes his efforts to the roots, for once the roots are established, the Way will grow therefrom. Being good as a son and obedient as a young man is, perhaps, the root of a man's character" (*Analects* 1:2). The English translation is adopted from D. C. Lau (trans.), *The Analects* (New York: Penguin, 1979). On the fundamental importance of filial piety to *ren*, see Sin Yee Chan, "Filial Piety, Commiseration, and the Virtue of *Ren*," in *Filial Piety in Chinese Thought and History*, eds. Alan K. L. Chan and Sor-hoon Tan (London: RoutledgeCurzon, 2004), pp. 176–188; Chenyang Li, "Shifting Perspectives: Filial Morality Revisited," *Philosophy East and West* 47 (1997), pp. 211–232; Philip J. Ivanhoe, "Filial Piety as Virtue," in *Working Virtue: Virtue Ethics and Contemporary Moral Problems*, eds. Rebecca L. Walker and Philip J. Ivanhoe (Oxford: Oxford University Press, 2007), pp. 297–312.

(4) The quintessential criterion for Confucian clan membership must be the candidate's filial piety toward his or her ancestors, which would determine his or her overall commitment to the purposes for which the clan exists.[12]

According to this line of reasoning, which public reason Confucianism endorses, the injustice involved in this case has little (almost nothing) to do with the clans' failure to become a liberal voluntary association or to promote gender equality as the liberal critics claimed.[13] The true source of injustice is that the clan organizations have excluded female members from formal membership, violating their norm of filial piety, a virtue which must be possessed by both men and women according to Confucianism.[14] In other words, the injustice *depends on* the nature of the clan organization and particularly its essential aims and practices, and they are characteristically and unambiguously Confucian.

Of course, one caveat in making filial piety the sole criterion of clan membership is the practical difficulty of actually using it. Without an explanation by Justice Yu, it is difficult to know what he really had in mind when he raised the question about filial piety. After all, when the decision was made two years later, Justice Yu himself did not join the majority opinion. Rather, along with five other members, including Chief Justice Ch'oe Chong-yŏng, he formed a minority opinion in consideration of other equally (perhaps more) pressing legal problems that in his view were more directly relevant to clan membership than gender equality,

---

[12] I admit that only the last proposition is inferable directly from Justice Yu's question and the other propositions are my own reconstruction, which may not have been intended by the justice himself. However, there seems to be no better way to make sense of the reasoning that led to Justice Yu's question.
[13] For instance, see Whasook Lee, "Married Daughters Should Be Recognized as 'Jongjung' Members," *Munhwa Ilbo*, 12/17/2003 (English version).
[14] It is worth noting that during the late eighteenth and early nineteenth centuries, some Korean female Neo-Confucian scholars such as Im Yunjidang (1721–1793) and Kang Chŏngildang (1772–1832) advanced the idea of moral equality between men and women by revisiting classical Confucian texts such as the *Analects* of Confucius, the *Mencius*, and the *Doctrine of the Mean*. See Ŭn-sŏn Yi, *Irŏbŏrin ch'owŏrŭl ch'ajasŏ* [*In Search of Transcendence That Has Been Lost*] (Seoul: Mosinŭn saramdŭl, 2009), pp. 101–164; Youngmin Kim, "Neo-Confucianism as Free-Floating Resource: Im Yunjidang and Kang Chŏngildang as Two Female Neo-Confucian Philosophers in Late Chosŏn," in *Women and Confucianism in Chosŏn Korea*, eds. Youngmin Kim and Michael J. Pettid (Albany: State University of New York Press, 2011); Sungmoon Kim, "The Way to Become a Female Sage: Im Yunjidang's Confucian Feminism," *Journal of the History of Ideas* 75 (2014), pp. 396–416, and "From Wife to Moral Teacher: Kang Chŏngildang's Neo-Confucian Self-Cultivation," *Asian Philosophy* 24 (2014), pp. 28–47.

such as, among others, the (private) organization's constitutional right to freedom of association, though without disagreeing with one of the conclusions by the majority opinion that membership should be given to the plaintiffs. I will examine the Court's minority opinion shortly from the perspective of public reason Confucianism. In the present context in which the Court's reasoning behind its decision is being examined, however, questions such as what Justice Yu actually intended to ask or whether the justice changed his mind over two years of adjudication, assuming that his original reasoning was roughly along the lines of my reconstruction, are less important. What is important is what kind of reasoning was being employed during the lengthy processes of adjudication and decision making, and my point is that the question raised by Justice Yu and the moral reasoning implied in it enable us to question the popular view that the Court's eventual vindication of gender equality reflects its endorsement of Western-liberal notion of gender equality, because the same, ostensibly liberal, conclusion can also be supported by Confucian reasoning.

Yet there is another way to derive the same conclusion from Justice Yu's question, without being entangled in the caveat mentioned earlier. Irrespective of the justice's real intention, to make filial piety the sole criterion of clan membership is an unrealistic demand for the defendants to accept, not only because of the practical difficulty in measuring it, but also due to the *natural* origin of clan organizations. A more practical suggestion could be as follows: since the current practice admits only adult male descendants as legitimate members solely by virtue of family ties, regardless of their actual possession of filial piety, which in principle should be considered the most important criterion for membership, then, in fairness, family ties alone, not gender, should be employed as the criterion to determine whether or not one is eligible for formal membership.

At any rate, regardless of which criterion is employed (filial piety or family ties), the current practice is problematic in light of Confucianism, which is the basis upon which the clan operates. Although Justice Yu eventually joined the minority opinion, the question he raised makes this type of reasoning possible. In fact, the Court seems to have employed this line of reasoning when it said: "The customary practice of the clan organizations to admit, among the descendants of the same ancestors, only adult men as members, and to exclude women from formal membership ... lacks justification and reasonableness, because it endows or denies the opportunity to participate in clan activities such as maintenance of the tombs of common ancestors and memorial ceremonies solely on the basis of sex." Of course, from the Court's point of view, the standard against which its decision is "justified and reasonable" is liberal constitutionalism, to which the Korean polity is formally and directly committed, but given Korean constitutionalism's dual – direct and indirect – perfectionist commitments to liberalism and Confucianism as we have discussed in Chapter 3, the Court's decision is better justified and found more reasonable in light of public reason Confucian constitutionalism.

Unlike Justice Yu's case, Justice Cho's reasoning does not directly involve Confucianism (though it does involve public reason Confucianism, as will be discussed shortly) but it does not appeal to the liberal notions of individual dignity and gender equality either.[15] His question focuses on a member's duty, in return for which she can claim the affiliated right, in this case, to property. What is at stake, however, does not seem to merely rectify the asymmetry between duty (fulfilled) and right (not granted). The more important point has to do with what is implied in the justice's question, which is that at the heart of clan membership is a member's voluntary participation in various kinds of clan activities, mostly rites-related. Thus, the underlying reasoning is that only those who are participating in the rites are entitled to claim rights.[16] In response, Hwang Dŏk-nam, representing the plaintiffs, said that the plaintiffs indeed had rarely participated in memorial ceremonies for ancestors beyond their great-grandparents, but argued that the reason for the lack of participation had mainly to do with denial of their formal clan membership.[17]

In a sense, Justice Cho's question is full of irony because he is asking about duties where there are no recognized rights. In the absence of recognized membership, how can we think about "rights," to which only members are entitled? Wasn't the case precisely about recognizing daughters as formal members of the clan? Once again, available data do not tell

---

[15] Justice Cho retired in 2004, so he could not participate in the actual decision. However, this does not weaken the importance of his question because it cannot be doubted that the question, which was raised in a public hearing in the presence of all other members of the court, was part of the Court's reasoning process.

[16] For a philosophical study drawing on a similar reasoning, see D. W. Y. Kwok, "On the Rites and Rights of Being Human," in *Confucianism and Human Rights*, eds. Wm. Theodore de Bary and Tu Wei-ming (New York: Columbia University Press, 1998), pp. 83–93.

[17] *Ohmynews* 12/19/2003.

us exactly what the justice had in mind when he raised the question. His intention could be sheer fact-checking, to see if the plaintiffs had fulfilled their duties (both financial and, more importantly, ritual) as de facto members by virtue of family relations. However, strong emphasis on duty or exclusive focus on the asymmetry problem in adjudicating the question of membership does not so much solve the problem as generate another one, a problem more intractable; that is, what to do with male descendants who are negligent of their duties. Given that the duties at issue here cannot be thought of independently from filial piety, the virtue that generates duties on the part of the descendants, the whole conundrum associated with Justice Yu's question, is likely to be reintroduced.

In my view, the best way to make sense of Justice Cho's question while avoiding the filial piety–duty–right conundrum is to see it as a normative statement, again justified from the perspective of public reason Confucianism. The question then is seen in a fresh light as involving several propositions:

(1) Clan membership involves both rights and duties;
(2) Rights, including property rights, *ought* to depend upon the practice of rites (and other duties necessary for the sustenance of the clan);
(3) However, the plaintiffs have been systematically deprived of formal clan membership (and only as a member one can fulfill his or her rightful duties); therefore,
(4) Should the court decide for the plaintiffs, both sons and daughters ought to be equally obligated to fulfill their duties.

According to this reasoning (i.e., Confucian public reasoning), equal formal membership is granted according to one's birth right regardless of gender, but the real point is the way in which gender equality is realized within the clan structure. It is not by imposing the Western-liberal notion of gender equality on clan members but by virtue of equal participation in the rites and fulfillment of duties.

This line of reasoning is not incidentally compatible with the Court's decision. There is a good reason to suspect that the Court indeed purposely employed this very line of reasoning.[18] After all, the Court never alluded to, let alone imposed, any substantively liberal notion of gender

---

[18] The reasoning at issue is not a legal reasoning, strictly speaking. However, it is impossible to think of any sound legal reasoning that does not involve a complex set of moral propositions, beliefs, and reasoning, which I call Confucian public reasoning.

equality, nor did it uphold a mechanical equality between men and women on the grounds of a liberal political theory such as social contract theory, irrespective of differences in roles that they have traditionally played as sons and daughters. The Court never took issue with the clan law, by which clan organizations operate and which stipulates various sorts of gendered ritual roles and obligations that many liberals and feminists find patriarchal and androcentric.[19] Moreover, by recognizing clan organizations as naturally originated, the Court endorsed the popular Confucian (hence noncontractual) understanding of them as extended families. Again, what the Court ruled problematic was the clan organizations' customary practice to endow or deny solely on the basis of gender the *rightful* opportunity to participate in clan activities and fulfill duties affiliated with that right. The plaintiffs took the decision precisely in this way, when Hwang said, "The decision means that women have [now] been given their proper position in light of gender equality, but it also means that women must carry out their share of duties as clan members."[20]

Seen in this way, the popular view of the court decision as a victory of liberalism over Confucianism should be reconsidered. The gender equality and individual dignity that the Court seemingly vindicated were based on equal rights to formal clan membership between men and women as *sons and daughters*. From a purely legal perspective, the Court derived the right to equal formal membership solely from the candidate's family ties. A close reading of the decision, however, tells us that the Court's real intent was to point out the substantive meaning of membership rights, fully justifiable in light of the (Confucian) purpose for which the clan organizations exist. In upholding gender equality, the Court, instead of appealing to the abstract notion of rights or enlisting the authority of any particular liberal notion of rights, vindicated a right that is most apposite in the given context by enabling female members to actively participate in clan activities. In other words, the Court negotiated rights, the backbone of liberalism, with rites (and associated duties), thereby creating

---

[19] See, for instance, Hyunah Yang, "Unfinished Tasks for Korean Family Policy in the 1990s: Maternity Protection Policy and Abolition of the Family-Head System," *Korea Journal* 42:2 (2002), pp. 68–99.

[20] *Chosun Ilbo*, 7/21/2005 (English edition). This point of living up to the role-specific duty of filial piety has nothing really to do with liberal values. It is most easily understood as an application of the Confucian *zheng-ming* 正名 doctrine. For the *zheng-ming* doctrine, see *Analects* 12.11; 13.3.

Confucian rights that can undergird the moral ideals of individual dignity and gender equality, commonly known as liberal values.

By dialectically intertwining rites and rights and balancing between otherwise liberal constitutional principles and Confucian values (particularly filial piety, ancestor worship, and ritual propriety), the Court, in practice, reshaped a traditional, fully comprehensive Confucianism into public reason Confucianism, though it did not present its normative position in a philosophically systematic way. One of the practical merits of public reason Confucianism is its ability to make coherent sense of East Asians' legal, social, and political practices and offer simultaneously a normative standard, or a regulative ideal, by which such practices can be justified, evaluated, and criticized.

CLAN ORGANIZATIONS AS VOLUNTARY PRIVATE ASSOCIATIONS?

My claim that the Supreme Court's decision cannot be framed in terms of liberalism versus Confucianism or modernity versus tradition is in part vindicated by the fact that the decision was a very close call. Seven out of thirteen justices formed the majority, while the remaining six, including Justice Yu Chi-tam, whose views I discussed earlier, submitted a minority opinion, which the media largely sidelined, thus depriving the Korean public of the chance to make better sense of what was further at stake in this case.

The minority opinion raised a question about the majority opinion's conclusion. The key points of the minority opinion can be recapitulated as follows:

(1) In general, we agree that our patrilineal customary practice needs to be revisited and reevaluated. However, considering the fact that the progenitors of the clans are all male ancestors, the scope and limit of gender equality within clan organizations require a more careful approach.

(2) Admittedly, [Confucian-style] clan organizations are uniquely Korean traditional cultural assets and Article 9 of the Constitution require us to strive to succeed and develop them in ways harmonious with contemporary legal order.

(3) In principle, the most important obligation of the clan members is to continue the ritual ceremonies of worshiping their common ancestors and [properly conducting this task] requires several

Public equality and democratic pluralism 153

associated services to the clan including maintenance of family ancestral burial grounds and mountains ... which are not so much duties coerced by law but only moral or ethical obligations. Since there is no relevant case of legal infringement upon the members' rights, public law has no reason to interfere with the clans' [internal operations]. Likewise, from a legal point of view, the customary practice that an adult man automatically acquires clan membership regardless of his willingness is not problematic.

(4) While the majority opinion states that the customary law in question has become incompatible with our "entire" legal order, in reality it evaluates the customary law governing clan organizations solely from the standpoint of the gender equality principle. We do not agree with this mechanical application of the gender equality principle to the current case.

(5) Moreover, in adjudicating the question of clan membership from the standpoint of Korea's entire legal order – clans which are associations for ancestral worship and familial intimacy in terms of their functions, hence essentially private voluntary associations – the more pressing legal issue to consider than the principle of gender equality is how clan membership can be understood in light of freedom of association in Article 22–1 of the Constitution. ... Also, since there can be various attitudes toward sacrificial rites from the view that it is a long-established fine custom (*mipungyangsok* 美風良俗) to the extremely negative view that it is a superstition, the clan membership question should be considered in relation to freedom of conscience (Article 19) as well as freedom of religion (Article 20).

(6) As for membership in private voluntary associations, it cannot be that someone should be included as a member, artificially or coercively, irrespective of his or her voluntary consent.

(7) Since the problem of the customary law governing clan organizations is limited to the case that those adult women who explicitly expressed their willingness to join their clans have been denied formal membership ... and since an increasing number of women want to participate in clan activities, open [currently] for only formal members, corresponding with their increasing self-awareness of the right and desire for clear self-identity, unless there is a justified and rational reason to deny membership (for instance, no familial ties with the clan's progenitor), an adult woman can acquire membership by expressing her willingness to become a member.

(8) Seen in this way, the majority opinion's conclusion that descendants who share with their common ancestors the same surname (*sŏng* 姓) and ancestral seat (*pon* 本) are automatically entitled to formal clan membership once they come of age, regardless of sex, is problematic.

Roughly, the minority opinion has two parts: while the first part (1 through 4) is focused on the reasonableness of the clan organizations' customary practices, especially with regard to membership, the second part (5 through 8) is concerned mainly with an argument from the perspective of the constitutional right to freedom of association. Whether these two parts logically cohere with each other, however, is unclear. The first part finds the customary law (*kwansŭppŏp* 慣習法) governing clan organizations reasonable, because it does not violate anyone's rights, and clan organizations are also found worthy of public protection because they are an important part of the cultural heritage and/or national culture that Article 9 aims to protect.[21] Worth noting here is that clan organizations are understood as *natural* kin groups, as customary law defines them, and it is such customarily defined clan organizations whose internal operation the minority opinion finds largely reasonable. The second part of the opinion, however, redefines the clan organization, in a way making sense in modern legal terms, by calling it a *private voluntary association*. This redefinition of clan organizations is of crucial significance because it shifts the focus of jurisprudence from the question of "customary law versus modern constitutional law" to that of "a cultural group's autonomy vis-à-vis the constitution."

As we have seen earlier, the Court's majority opinion revolves around the first framework, the question of how to balance customary law, represented by the ongoing practices of the clans, understood as natural kin groups, and Korea's modern constitutional law. Navigating within this framework, the majority opinion implies that Koreans, as long as they are of aristocratic origin,[22] are all (potential) members of their

---

[21] Constitution Article 9: "The State shall strive to sustain and develop the cultural heritage and to enhance national culture."

[22] This provision, however, is almost negligible, because while at the beginning of the Chosŏn dynasty, the number of Confucian yangban aristocrats amounted to merely 1–3% of the total population, by the end of the nineteenth century, approximately 70% of the Korean people had become yangban. See Sangjun Kim, *Maengjaŭi ttam sŏngwangŭi p'i* [*Sweat of Mencius and Blood of the Sacred Kings*] (Seoul: Akanet, 2011), pp. 497–509. In contemporary Korea, most Koreans consider themselves as descendants of the yangban family and many families possess their family genealogies

respective clans, regardless of whether they actually participate in them or not. And it is in part for this reason that the mass media understood the Court's (majority) decision as dismantling one of the country's oldest customary laws and thus covered it extensively and with great enthusiasm as if it concerned the entire Korean population.[23] Certainly, the Court did not subscribe to the pre-formulated framework of "liberalism versus Confucianism" as noted earlier, but it was clearly aware that its decision in favor of the plaintiffs would make the entire Korean legal order more modern as well as progressive. The distinction between public reason Confucianism, which works through public reason Confucian constitutionalism, and traditional Confucianism, governed by customary law, too, is intelligible, when the same jurisprudential and analytical framework is employed.

In the second part, however, the dissenting justices are seemingly chastising the majority opinion's grand ambition to transform traditional Confucianism into a modern Confucianism, constitutionally predicated on liberal values and principles, even though they generally concur with the rationale that traditional Confucianism and its underlying institutions need to be properly reconstructed, as evidenced in statements 1 and especially 2. In the dissenting opinion's view, a critical mistake of the majority opinion was to misunderstand the nature of clan organizations within the contemporary Korean constitutional structure. Historically speaking, clan organizations might have originated naturally. However, under the current (liberal) constitutional structure we are not equipped with proper legal language and concepts to make meaningful legal sense of them, *unless* we consider them private voluntary associations by focusing on the members' shared practical goal of organizing ritual ceremonies for ancestor worship as well as promoting familial intimacy among themselves.[24]

Thus reformulated, then, the case at hand should not necessarily be about progressing the Korean constitutional order by reforming the customary law that putatively concerns *all* Korean citizens. Rather, the Court's task should be far more modest, namely, to adjudicate the

---

(*zupu* 族譜), which traditionally belonged exclusively to the yangban class. Of course, whether a particular Korean family is organized through clan organization is a different story.

[23] *Hangyŏrye Shinmun*, 7/21/2005.
[24] For a similar suggestion, see Chang-hyun Lee, "Chongjungŭi chayulkkwŏn'gwa kŭ han'gye" [Clan's Autonomy and Its Limit], *Kachokpŏpyŏn'gu* [*The Korean Journal of Family Law*] 24 (2010), pp. 75–110.

question of who is qualified to be a member in a private voluntary association called *chongjung* in light of Korea's modern constitution. Hence, a completely different reasoning is evident in the dissenting opinion:

(1) Clan organizations are private voluntary associations;
(2) As private voluntary associations, membership in clan organization is determined by the candidate's voluntary consent to become a member; therefore,
(3) It is a violation of the constitutional right to freedom of association that a person is forced to become a member of the clan organization.

According to this reasoning, the target of the Court's decision is not so much women as *citizens* but women as *members* of the particular clans. Eventually, the dissenting justices concluded that only those adult women who want to be formal members of the clan organization should be given membership rights.

From a liberal political standpoint, and if we agree, for argument's sake, that clan membership is a *private* associational membership, the difference between the majority and minority opinions regarding private membership vis-à-vis the liberal-democratic constitution seems to track remarkably well the difference between political liberalism (or public reason liberalism) and liberal pluralism in contemporary liberal political theory. Since I have elaborated on the basic tenets of both theoretical positions in Chapters 2 and 3, here let me briefly recapitulate the kernel of each position. Political liberalism, championed most notably by John Rawls and Stephen Macedo, understands the essential characteristic of modern liberal democratic society in terms of pluralism, that a liberal society consists of individuals and groups holding different moral, philosophical, or religious doctrines.[25] Given pervasive pluralism marked by different comprehensive doctrines and moral disagreement among individuals and groups, the most pressing political question in a liberal-constitutional democracy, according to political liberals, is how to maintain social stability and constitutional order in the face of pluralism. As is well known, the political-liberal solution to this problem relies on overlapping consensus among groups and individuals on the principles of justice (i.e., the political conception of justice) governing the

[25] Rawls, *Political Liberalism*; Stephen Macedo, *Diversity and Distrust: Civic Education in a Multicultural Democracy* (Cambridge: Harvard University Press, 2000).

constitutional essentials and society's basic structure, but not the background culture of civil society.[26] The practical implication is that political liberalism puts greater emphasis on overlapping consensus and the common liberal-democratic citizenship that it undergirds than diversity (and various associational memberships composing it) as such.[27] From the constitutional standpoint of political liberalism, public institutions (including the courts as well as schools) should play a more active role in forming and reproducing liberal-democratic citizenship applicable to all reasonable citizens who otherwise belong to different moral, religious, or cultural communities as private individuals.[28] In the previous chapter, liberal constitutionalism's active role in producing a liberal-democratic citizenship was made sense of in terms of liberal political perfectionism.

Liberal pluralists, however, find political liberalism's perfectionist constitutional ambition to form or mold a common democratic citizenship overbearing and object to the congruence between the broader society's liberal-democratic principles and the principles that govern the internal affairs of private associations. Their central argument is that, for the most part, associations in civil society should be left insulated from state interference and enjoy their self-governing rights derived from the constitutional right to freedom of association, unless they vitally harm other groups upholding different comprehensive doctrines, thereby destabilizing the overall constitutional order seriously.[29]

---

[26] Rawls, *Political Liberalism*, pp. 214–216; "The Idea of Public Reason Revisited," in *The Law of Peoples* (Cambridge: Harvard University Press, 1999), pp. 129–180, at pp. 133–134. Notwithstanding Rawls's argument about "the limit of public reason," many Rawls-inspired political liberals apply public reasoning and deliberation more broadly to various cases of moral disagreement in civil society. See, for instance, Amy Gutmann and Dennis Thompson, *Democracy and Disagreement: Why Moral Conflict Cannot be Avoided in Politics, and What Should Be Done About It* (Cambridge: Belknap, 1996); Amy Gutmann, *Identity in Democracy* (Princeton: Princeton University Press, 2003); Henry S. Richardson, *Democratic Autonomy: Public Reasoning about the Ends of Policy* (New York: Oxford University Press, 2002); Gerald F. Gaus, *Justificatory Liberalism: An Essay on Epistemology and Political Theory* (New York: Oxford University Press, 1996).

[27] Most clearly, Rawls writes, "Public reason is characteristic of a democratic people: it is the reason of its citizens, of those sharing the status of equal citizenship" (*Political Liberalism*, p. 213).

[28] As Eamonn Callan puts it, "A powerful constraint on the background culture of liberal politics is an inevitable consequence of the education that Rawlsian political liberalism entails" (*Creating Citizens: Political Education and Liberal Democracy* [Oxford: Oxford University Press, 1997], p. 36).

[29] See William A. Galston, *Liberal Pluralism: The implications of Value Pluralism for Political Theory* (Cambridge: Cambridge University Press, 2002); Nancy Rosenblum,

Returning to our case, the structural affinity between the Supreme Court's majority decision and political liberalism is not difficult to see. The Court's decision upholds the congruence thesis by claiming that the clan organizations' associational freedom should adapt to the constitutional principles of gender equality and individual dignity concerned with *all* Korean citizens. In this reasoning, clan organizations can exercise their constitutional right to freedom of association *as long as* the moral principles governing their internal affairs – particularly the way they define membership – are congruent with the principles of gender equality and individual dignity. Of course, there is an important caveat in drawing this implication from the majority opinion because, as I showed earlier, the Court achieved this seemingly "liberal" congruence by negotiating liberal rights with Confucian rites, rather than imposing substantively liberal notions of gender equality and individual dignity upon the clan organizations that operate mainly on Confucian laws and rituals. Thus, although the Court's majority decision tracks well the mode of political reasoning characteristic of political liberalism, its *liberal* dimension is significantly qualified by Confucian moral reasoning. Public reason Confucianism offers a new theoretical framework that is necessary for making sense of the substantive difference between the Court's majority decision and political liberalism, despite their structural affinity.

Whether the minority decision also tracks well liberal pluralism, however, is less clear, although apparently the dissenting justices' attention to freedom of association in determining membership in a free association strongly resonates with liberal pluralism. From the perspective of liberal pluralism, it is troubling, as much as the majority opinion's congruence thesis, that the minority opinion does not fully endorse the clan organizations' freedom of association and the right to self-government that follows. Why do the dissenting justices still conclude that the clan organizations should accept women (who want to be members) as members, when the defendants' core claim is that acceptance of women *critically* threatens their traditional Confucian way of life? Does the clans' right to self-government in accordance with their tradition, which precedes the establishment of the modern legal system, *seriously* or *vitally* threaten the constitutional order of the Korean polity? Correspondingly, what is the *compelling* reason for the state to intervene with internal affairs of the

---

Membership and Morals: The Personal Uses of Pluralism in America (Princeton: Princeton University Press, 1998); George Crowder, *Liberalism and Value Pluralism* (New York: Continuum, 2002).

clan organizations, which the minority opinion understands as private voluntary associations, given the very small number of Korean citizens who even belong to clan organizations in contemporary Korea? Put differently, if the minority opinion recognizes the clan organizations as private voluntary associations, why does it still force them to embrace, albeit partially, the liberal ideal of gender equality, when they actively reject a liberal way of life? Shouldn't Korea's liberal-democratic constitution protect this nonliberal way of life in the very name of liberty (i.e., freedom of association) as long as it does not vitally threaten the foundation of the constitutional order?

There is yet another problem. Even if it is granted, contrary to the majority opinion, that the clan organizations are private associations and thus it is problematic for the majority opinion to treat the clan organizations' internal way of life as if it concerned all Korean citizens, it is unclear why the minority opinion regards the clan organizations as purely voluntary associations. If the clan organizations were purely voluntary private associations, why did the dissenting justices not find the involuntary nature of (established) male membership equally problematic, while forcing the organizations to accept women on a voluntary basis? In this regard, the Court's decision was not entirely wrong when it defines the clan organizations as *natural* associations, of course, if by "natural" the court meant to stress the involuntary nature of membership, which applied to both men and women.

In the end, notwithstanding more attention to liberty through the invocation of freedom of association, the minority opinion also turned out to be not fully *liberal* in its intended sense (i.e., liberal pluralism), because it still upheld the moral principle of gender equality in clan membership by applying contractarian reasoning to clan organizations, which are in fact involuntary associations whose membership is formed by virtue of family ties.[30] Nor did it uphold the more substantively liberal meaning of freedom of association, namely the compelling moral and constitutional justification of the state to intervene in internal affairs of

---

[30] Michael Walzer says that "freedom requires nothing more than the possibility of breaking involuntary bonds and, furthermore, that the actual break is not always a good thing, and that we need not always make it easy. Many valuable memberships are not freely chosen; many binding obligations are not entirely the product of consent. We can think of our life together as a 'social construction' in which we, as individuals, have had a hand; we cannot plausibly think of it as something wholly made by ourselves" ("On Involuntary Association," in *Freedom of Association*, ed. Amy Gutmann [Princeton: Princeton University Press, 1998], pp. 64–74, at p. 64).

private associations, particularly involuntary associations formed by cultural and religious groups.[31]

DEMOCRATIC PLURALISM: THE CASE REVISITED

Examination of the Court's majority and minority opinions thus far boils down to one important conclusion: despite the Court's struggle to adjudicate the case from the perspective(s) of liberal constitutional jurisprudence, whether political liberalism or liberal pluralism, neither perspective can explain the mode of public reasoning underlying each opinion. Though the majority opinion has a striking structural affinity with political liberalism, it neither attempts to overcome Confucian customary law and its affiliated values such as filial piety, ancestor worship, and ritual propriety, on behalf of liberal principles of individual dignity and gender equality, nor does it aim to produce an unalloyed liberal conception of citizenship, notwithstanding the Court's formal commitment to liberal constitutionalism. What the majority justices attempted to do was to negotiate Confucian rites and moral values with liberal rights and principles, thereby generating a new mode of Korean citizenship that is compatible with Confucian democratic citizenship endorsed by public reason Confucianism.

More intriguing is the minority opinion. Though it draws on the constitutional right to freedom of association by redefining clan organizations as private voluntary associations in order to adjudicate the case more effectively from a liberal constitutional standpoint, it surprisingly finds the clan's involuntary nature of male membership reasonable. Moreover, it also allows consenting adult women to enjoy formal membership, thereby publicly encroaching upon the autonomy of the clan organizations, which it aims to respect and protect. Put differently, while the minority opinion proposes to view clan organizations as private voluntary associations, making the case relevant only to members, not only is it still, at least partially, attached to the customary understanding of the clan organization as a natural kin group, but, quite ironically, it imposes the ideal of gender equality on the clans. Then, in practice, the only difference between the majority and minority opinions lies in the way each realizes this ideal: while the former wants gender equality to be fully realized within the clan organizations mainly by virtue of family ties, the latter

---

[31] See William A. Galston, *The Practice of Liberal Pluralism* (Cambridge: Cambridge University Press, 2005).

wants it to be applied by making female descendants' voluntary consent a necessary condition for formal membership.

Where liberal theories fail or nearly fail in providing Koreans (and East Asians in general, for that matter) with a principled way to balance traditional Confucianism and liberal-democratic constitutionalism and thereby make coherent and evaluative sense of their legal, social, or political practices in the culturally Confucian and sociopolitically democratic context, public reason Confucianism stands quite strong. First of all, as noted already, public reason Confucianism is never embarrassed by the Korean Supreme Court's "failure" to produce a Western-style liberal citizenship in which Confucian values such as filial piety, ancestor worship, and ritual propriety have no place in public. While liberal constitutionalism, to which the Korean polity is formally committed, has great difficulty in making sense of the Court's struggle to negotiate Confucian values and rites with liberal constitutional principles, public reason Confucianism sees it as integral to its own constitutional theory and practice. From the perspective of public reason Confucianism, the Court's indirect perfectionist commitment to Confucian values requires it to find a way to balance them with liberal values. Central to this balancing or negotiating process is Confucian moral reasoning, which renders otherwise liberal values and principles – in the present case, one's right to private property, individual dignity, and gender equality – socially meaningful and publicly intelligible in light of Confucian habits, mores, and moral sentiments, with which contemporary East Asians are still saturated.

However, this does not imply that public reason Confucianism overlaps perfectly with the Court's majority decision. Public reason Confucianism parts company with the majority opinion by embracing the minority opinion's core stipulation about the nature of clan organizations – that they ought to be considered private voluntary associations, once they have been placed within the modern democratic constitutional structure.

Public reason Confucianism agrees with the majority opinion that *traditional* clan organizations are essentially natural kin groups, hence the object of customary law, concerning virtually *all* Korean citizens. Also from the perspective of public reason Confucianism, what is at stake in the present case is more than merely legal adjudication about clan membership; the case offers an important venue where traditional, fully comprehensive Confucianism can be revisited and recreated into modern democratic Confucianism (i.e., public reason Confucianism), which is only partially comprehensive as "Confucianism," through legal and social adaptations to a new liberal democratic social and constitutional condition.[32] Equal clan membership is (and should be) the consequence of such complex adaptive processes.

What the Court's majority opinion failed to address was how the complex adaptive processes through which traditional Confucianism is recreated into public reason Confucianism simultaneously require the customary definition of clan organizations as natural kin groups to adapt to a new liberal-democratic constitutional structure. The minority opinion is correct in this regard when it considers clan organizations as private voluntary associations, though it never articulates why this redefinition is normatively necessary.

Then, a question arises: how can both the majority and minority opinions be rendered coherent within public reason Confucianism? This question is important because it is also connected with a larger, more theoretically significant question about how public reason Confucianism is qualitatively distinguished from traditional Confucianism, the question with which this chapter began. Public reason Confucianism agrees with the majority opinion that the *chongjung* membership case is primarily about how to remake traditional Confucianism, generally under the jurisdiction of customary law and yet occasionally interfering with contemporary legal and social relationship, into a modern Confucianism compatible with core constitutional values and principles. Since clan membership concerns all Korean citizens, in the sense that it has far-reaching public implications for the collective identity of Korean citizens and the way they live, as attested by the Court's extraordinary seriousness and the media's strong interest in the case, what is at stake in the case was not so much private membership but *public equality*, apart from how we perceive clan organizations in light of the entire constitutional order.[33]

---

[32] In saying this, I do not mean that the Korean Supreme Court intended to create a new modern democratic Confucianism or that the present case alone represents the birth of public reason Confucianism. As discussed in Chapter 3, earlier in the same year (2005), the Korean Constitutional Court abolished the family-head system and it is through a series of legal and social reforms after democratization that Koreans could reform traditional Confucianism into its new mode, analogous to public reason Confucianism. Otherwise stated, regardless of the higher Courts' intentions, their jurisprudence regarding traditional Confucianism generally tracks the core stipulations of public reason Confucianism.

[33] My understanding of "what is public" or "the public" is indebted to John Dewey, who says, "[T]he line between private and public is to be drawn on the basis of the extent and scope of the consequences of acts which are so important as to need control, whether by inhibition or by promotion.... The public consists of all those who are affected by the

From the perspective of public reason Confucianism, the case problematizes Korean women's low public standing compared to that of men. If in a Confucian society such as Korea a woman's public standing is, in part, determined by her right to be a full member of her extended family, whose internal operations are organized and carried out by clan organization in accordance with the clan law, the question of whether or not the clan's adult women should be considered legitimate members cannot be subject solely to the clan council or the clan law, which would otherwise have the authority of deciding who to accept as a member. In the radically altered social context in which Koreans not only reject the patriarchal order of traditional Confucianism but even publicly promote the value of gender equality, equal clan membership becomes a quintessential political question. Since most clan organizations' current members are men, the decision of whether or not to accept the clans' adult women as full members cannot be reasonably entrusted to the clans themselves. It must be decided by all Koreans or their political or legal representatives in a public arena.

Earlier I wrote that the case must be seen as dealing with the question of public equality, "apart from how we perceive the clan organizations in light of the entire constitutional order." In saying this, I am suggesting, in agreement with the minority opinion, that clan organizations ought to be deemed private cultural associations in light of the contemporary legal and social order and this is how public reason Confucianism conceives of clan organizations. Whether they are voluntary or involuntary associations is not critical, however, because public reason Confucianism leaves how an association should be organized solely to the association itself, as long as the same membership policy is applied to men and women equally. The point is that clan organizations cannot be left in a legal limbo between Confucian customary law and the modern constitutional order. Public reason Confucianism normatively requires clan organizations to find a proper place – both legally and socially intelligible – within its constitutional framework (because public reason Confucianism is a comprehensive form of social and political life and not simply an unconnected assortment of values, norms, and practices taken from the tradition) and stipulates that they be considered private cultural associations, enjoying, regardless of whether they are voluntary or involuntary, associational autonomy by virtue of their constitutional right to freedom of association.

indirect consequences of transactions to such an extent that it is deemed necessary to have those consequences systematically cared for" (*The Public and Its Problems* [Athens: Swallow Press, 1954], pp. 15–16).

Conceived now as private cultural associations, clan organizations' internal operations should be, in principle, insulated from state intervention and they are under no legal, political, or moral obligation to align their associational norms, based on the clan law and rituals, with public norms including gender equality. That is, clan organizations can entertain their political autonomy to the extent that they, first, embrace equal membership policy, and, second, see themselves as private cultural associations, whose public standing is on par with that of other associations in civil society. As long as clan organizations meet these two conditions, required by public reason Confucianism, they are not obligated to comply with the public norm of gender equality "all the way down" by removing every sort of gendered ritual practice which defines their core cultural identity.[34]

In short, public reason Confucianism does not find problematic all gendered roles and ritual practices performed by male and female members of the clan organizations in the capacities of sons and daughters, each requiring public rectification, as long as they are conducted voluntarily and without injury to the female (or male) members' public standing as equal citizens. Deferential relationships and moderate inequalities between senior and junior members and between male and female members, characteristic within Confucian clan organizations and (extended) families, are compatible with public reason Confucianism, which is concerned mainly with the citizenry's public equality.[35] Thus understood, public reason Confucianism has no ambition to democratize all social relationships in civil society, nor does it desire to regulate the internal affairs of private associations, unless they are formed illegitimately and critically violate public norms.[36]

---

[34] In this way, we can avoid some scholars' concern that treating clan organizations as private voluntary associations and allowing them associational autonomy will only reinforce the ongoing practice of inequality in membership. See, for instance, Che-wan Kim, "Tanch'ebŏmniŭi chaejomyŏng: Chongjungchaesanŭi pŏpchŏk sŏngkkyŏk" [A Review of Incorporation and Non-Profit Fund Law in Korea], *The Korean Journal of Civil Law* 31 (2006), pp. 93–137.

[35] For similar arguments that the Confucian virtue of deference is compatible with a Confucian democratic life, see Aaron Stalnaker, "Confucianism, Democracy, and the Virtue of Deference," *Dao* 12 (2014), pp. 441–459; Stephen C. Angle, *Contemporary Confucian Political Philosophy: Toward Progressive Confucianism* (Cambridge: Polity, 2012), pp. 128–132. Some staunch liberals would object to this view. See for instance, Callan, *Creating Citizen*, pp. 152–157.

[36] For an insightful study on acceptable inequalities within a democratic polity, see Jane Mansbridge, "Acceptable Inequalities," *British Journal of Political Science* 7:3 (1977), pp. 321–336.

How does the discussion thus far illuminate our larger question about the distinction between traditional Confucianism and public reason Confucianism? Public reason Confucianism is a modern democratic perfectionist Confucianism recreated *from* traditional Confucianism and to this extent it is a partially comprehensive Confucianism. Yet public reason Confucianism does not quite supersede traditional Confucianism. While dialectically engaging traditional Confucianism with democratic and pluralist societal conditions, public reason Confucianism simultaneously houses various forms of traditional Confucianism within it by allowing their practitioners the constitutional right to freedom of association. By virtue of this right, traditional Confucians can form cultural associations, based on their own philosophical doctrines and ritual traditions, and continue their own traditional ways of life.

Therefore, though traditional Confucianism and public reason Confucianism are loosely connected, both as forms of comprehensive Confucianism, from an institutional point of view, their distinction is almost categorical: public reason Confucianism can house traditional Confucianism (and many other comprehensive doctrines) but it does not work the other way around. Traditional Confucianism has a legal and social place within public reason Confucianism only as a cultural association whose public standing is equal to that of other social associations in civil society. In sum, public reason Confucianism has a profound constitutional role to play in a Confucian democratic society, which traditional Confucianism would not be able to do without losing its distinctively Confucian perfectionist character.

CONCLUSION

This last part enables us to revisit Joseph Chan's notion of "moderate Confucian perfectionism" from a new perspective. As noted in Chapter 1, Chan's notion of moderate Confucian perfectionism is premised on two assumptions: first, comprehensive doctrines including comprehensive Confucianism are incompatible with value pluralism, which should be accommodated in modern politics, and second, only moderate perfectionism, a political perfectionism severed from comprehensive doctrines, can be a proper mode of perfectionism under pluralist societal conditions.[37] In this view, comprehensive Confucian perfectionism is "extreme" in the

---

[37] Joseph Chan, *Confucian Perfectionism: A Political Philosophy for Modern Times* (Princeton: Princeton University Press, 2014).

sense that when employed by the state, it is incompatible with the plurality of values in civil society. For this reason, Chan criticizes Jiang Qing's Confucian constitutionalism (or what Jiang calls "political Confucianism") in which Confucianism is elevated as a state religion.[38]

Public reason Confucianism demonstrates that comprehensive Confucianism does not necessarily lead to extreme perfectionism when promoted by the state, if it is only partially comprehensive, that is, when it embraces and finds expression within constitutionally established constraints. Moreover, while Chan's moderate Confucian perfectionism, concentrated on the reconstruction of classical Confucian philosophy into a modern political theory, does not articulate the way modern normative Confucianism can come to terms with traditional Confucianism in a principled way, public reason Confucianism offers a plausible way in which a traditional and fully comprehensive Confucianism can be institutionally housed within it by virtue of the constitutional right to freedom of association.

In this regard, a comparison between public reason Confucianism and Michael Oakeshott's political theory of civil association would be interesting because Oakeshott explores a mode of the constitutional polity that can best accommodate various kinds of purposive associations in civil society, operating on comprehensive doctrines. Oakeshott claims that the state ought to be a civil association, completely decoupled from any perfectionist ideas or comprehensive doctrines, because it is by nature a compulsory association in the sense that citizens cannot freely extricate themselves from it. If a state is connected with some perfectionist ends, thereby becoming a "purposive or enterprise association," an association that has substantive moral or political purposes, it inevitably becomes oppressive because the laws it makes promulgate instrumental rules, which regulate the activities of citizens pursuing their individual purposes.[39] In such a state, individuals and associations must acknowledge the state's common purpose as their own. Thus Oakeshott argues,

[J]ust as such a state [an enterprise association] cannot tolerate performances eccentric or indifferent to the pursuit of the purpose which constitutes the

---

[38] Joseph Chan, "On Legitimacy of Confucian Constitutionalism," in Jiang Qing, *A Confucian Constitutional Order: How China's Ancient Past Can Shape Its Political Future*, eds. Daniel A. Bell and Ruiping Fan and trans. Edmund Ryden (Princeton: Princeton University Press, 2012), pp. 99–112.

[39] But as Callan rightly notes, a connection between moral dissent and oppression requires explanation (*Creating Citizens*, p. 14).

association, so it cannot accommodate purposive associations whose purposes are eccentric or indifferent to its purpose. There can be an unregulated variety of self-chosen purposive associations only where a state is not itself a purposive association. What are called "minority" associations can exist only where a state is recognized in the terms of civil association; and there they require no authorization.[40]

Public reason Confucianism agrees that civil society should be filled with purposive associations with their own perfectionist ends. However, it does not agree with Oakeshott's maximalist pluralism when he states that there should be "unregulated variety of self-chosen purposive association" in civil society. Should a constitutional polity accommodate all kinds of self-chosen purposive associations, regardless of whether social or political ends such associations pursue are civil or uncivil, or reasonable or unreasonable?[41] For instance, should Koreans let clan organizations continue to deny membership to their daughters out of respect for their traditional Confucian purposes, despite the women's critically diminished public standing?

Putting aside Oakeshott's valorization of plurality for its own sake or his maximalist pluralism,[42] public reason Confucianism finds his core assumption problematic, which stipulates that for a polity to be civil, and thus able to accommodate value pluralism in civil society, it must be severed from any kind of substantive moral or political purpose, any kind of comprehensive doctrine, full or partial. Here we can see striking similarity, though unexpected, between Oakeshott, a liberal neutralist, and Chan, a Confucian perfectionist. But, again, this assumption is hardly sustainable because state perfectionism is compatible with a variety of *reasonable* types of pluralism, if the following two conditions are met: (1) if the state in question is a democratic state and (2) if the perfectionism in question is only partially comprehensive.

---

[40] Michael Oakeshott, *On Human Conduct* (Oxford: Clarendon, 1975), p. 316. Also see Paul Franco, *Michael Oakeshott: An Introduction* (New Haven: Yale University Press, 2004), p. 154.
[41] A similar question has been raised in Richard Boyd's "Michael Oakeshott on Civility, Civil Society and Civil Association," *Political Studies* 53 (2004), pp. 603–622.
[42] For a philosophical discussion on Oakeshott's maximalist pluralism, see Richard E. Flathman, "Idealism and Pluralism: Michael Oakeshott," in *Pluralism and Liberal Democracy* (Baltimore: Johns Hopkins University Press, 2005), pp. 109–161.

PART III

CIVIC VIRTUE

5

Between moral virtue and civic virtue

The previous chapter discussed the complex relationship between public reason Confucianism and traditional Confucianism with reference to Rawls's distinction between fully and partially comprehensive doctrines. My primary concern there was to show that Confucianism does not have to be completely severed from its moral comprehensiveness to be compatible with a modern democratic constitutional order, or to be *moderate*, by illuminating the important constitutional role public reason Confucianism can play as a partially comprehensive Confucianism vis-à-vis various forms of traditional, fully comprehensive Confucianism. In that chapter I also raised a broader political question: what is the proper way for a Confucian constitutional democracy to come to terms with the fact of pluralism in civil society? Or, what is the proper relationship between a multitude of moral and religious communities in civil society and the overarching democratic constitutional order of public reason Confucianism? My conclusion was that while upholding freedom of association as a core constitutional right, public reason Confucianism has an active political interest in ensuring that (nonsectarian) Confucian values as well as democratic-constitutional ideals endorsed by Confucian public reasoning are promoted within civil society. I captured this perfectionist interest in terms of democratic pluralism.

This chapter turns to the implications of public reason Confucianism's perfectionist interest in democratic pluralism for civic virtue. Whereas the key concern of the previous two chapters was the construction of public reason Confucianism as a democratic-constitutional normative idea and practice in East Asia's characteristically Confucian but increasingly pluralist societal context, the central question driving this chapter is the indispensability of character traits or virtues in citizens, or simply *civic virtues*, to the sustenance and further development of public reason Confucian constitutionalism, of which democratic pluralism is an integral component.

Within the overarching constitutional order, democratic pluralism refers to social (particularly associational) diversity that is moderated by democratic-constitutional public values and purposes. For instance, as discussed in Chapter 4, public reason Confucianism protects as well as constrains traditional Confucian clan organizations' associational autonomy. If unconstrained, traditional clans' associational autonomy can easily violate the democratic-constitutional norm of public equality, which public reason Confucianism embraces as one of its core normative propositions (P3), by granting formal membership only to male descendants, which results in additional discrimination against women with regard to their right qua daughters or daughters-in-law to participate in rites and fulfill duties affiliated with that right – an important *social* (hence public) right in a Confucian society.[1] Operating as a normative guideline of the Constitution, public reason Confucianism induces clan organizations to strive to reconcile their otherwise sectarian understandings of Confucian filial piety (*xiao* 孝), which are generally androcentric, with the democratic norm of gender equality, whose ethical value can also be endorsed from the perspective of the Confucian virtue of *ren* 仁.[2] Put differently, public reason Confucianism enables or normatively induces members of traditional Confucian clans to see and exercise the virtue of filial piety in nonsectarian ways compatible with public equality (including gender equality), when its exercise within or outside the clan environment has vital public implications. Of course this sort of normative inducement applies equally to other moral and religious communities that hold their own sectarian understandings of filial piety and its "authentic" social expressions.

What is important in the present context is that by subscribing to a particular and sectarian philosophical idea of filial piety (or any moral

---

[1] See Shaun O'Dwyer, "Democracy and Confucian Values," *Philosophy East and West* 53:1 (2003), pp. 39–63, at pp. 59–60; Stephen C. Angle, *Contemporary Confucian Political Philosophy: Toward Progressive Confucianism* (Cambridge: Polity, 2012), pp. 116–119. For an interesting philosophical discussion about filial daughters-in-law, see Sor-hoon Tan, "Filial Daughters-in-law: Questioning Confucian Filiality," in *Filial Piety in Chinese Thought and History*, eds. Alan K. L. Chan and Sor-hoon Tan (London: RoutledgeCurzon, 2004), pp. 226–240.

[2] Kelly J. Clark and Robing R. Wang, "A Confucian Defense of Gender Equity," *Journal of the American Academy of Religion* 72:2 (2004), pp. 395–422.

virtue), various moral, cultural, or religious associations in civil society define not only the idea of a good human being differently, but also what constitutes moral virtue, understood in terms of *human* excellence, virtues, or a set of traits that makes its possessor qua human being a good or moral person. When a certain virtue is understood as a human/moral virtue, a moral conflict surrounding its right philosophical meaning and its most authentic social practice (including whether to include women or not) becomes inevitable. In the case of moral conflicts of this sort, then, the traditional Confucian moral recommendation that a person be morally virtuous does not resolve the conflict. In fact, it is likely to exacerbate the moral conflict precisely because the cause of the conflict is rooted in one's earnest desire to be morally "virtuous" or "excellent" *as defined* by his or her own moral community, be it Confucian, Christian, Buddhist, or Muslim.

In contrast, civic virtues refer to a set of character traits, not of *members* belonging to particular moral communities with a sectarian, often idiosyncratic, philosophical understanding of what human excellence or moral virtue consists of, but of *citizens* concerned with survival, sustenance, and development of the polity's constitutional order and its public character. Civic virtues are a set of character traits and dispositions that motivate one, a private individual or a member of a particular moral community, to comply with what I called *normative inducement* earlier by redefining otherwise sectarian moral virtues from the broader perspective of an entire constitutional order. Thus understood, civic virtues are traits and/or dispositions that are urgently required in a pluralist society as bridging social capital.[3]

In this chapter, I argue that the survival and flourishing of the Confucian constitutional order, especially in pluralist East Asia, depends on certain civic virtues in the citizenry. In making this argument I revisit Joseph Chan's Confucian perfectionism, which valorizes human/moral virtue over civic virtue, and argue that Chan's perfectionist justification of virtue monism not only blurs the critical difference between perfectionist Confucianism and perfectionist republicanism, but is likely to undermine the theory's foundational premise that moderate perfectionism is decoupled from any kind of comprehensive moral doctrine by appealing to classical Confucianism in which human/moral virtue is not

---

[3] On the distinction between bonding and bridging social capital, see Robert D. Putnam, *Bowling Alone: The Collapse and Revival of American Community* (New York: Touchstone, 2000), pp. 22–24.

distinguished from civic/political virtue. After showing the potential tension between virtues pertaining to human beings and virtues pertaining to political agents in the overall monistic structure of classical Confucian virtue ethics-cum-politics, I argue that this tension, which presupposes the ethical connection between human/moral virtue and civic/political virtue, can be creatively reappropriated in the service of public reason Confucianism that makes a *practical, if not conceptual*, distinction between two kinds of virtues, corresponding to both the philosophical distinction between the traditional, fully comprehensive Confucianism and public reason Confucianism that is only partially comprehensive, on the one hand, and the institutional distinction between associational membership and Confucian democratic citizenship, on the other.

JOSEPH CHAN'S CONFUCIAN PERFECTIONISM REVISITED

One of the most salient features of Joseph Chan's Confucian perfectionism is that it presents the strong preference for moral/human virtue (and moral education) over civic virtue (and civic education) as one of its strengths in comparison with liberal democratic political theory.[4] Chan says,

> For Confucian masters, the teaching of precepts must be accompanied by the cultivation of character traits and the practice of rituals. This is a rather substantive kind of moral education that may be quite foreign to mainstream thinking in contemporary liberal democratic societies. For even though contemporary liberals are convinced of the necessity of education for democracy, they are generally skeptical of substantive programs of this nature, preferring to talk about *citizen* virtue rather than *human* virtue, about participation as a springboard of virtue, and about civic education rather than moral education ... wishing to steer clear of questions about personal morality and conceptions of the good person or the good life that might be regarded as controversial.[5]

Since a right to and the virtue of political participation will be discussed extensively in the next chapter, let me focus on Chan's general claim that human virtue should be preferred over citizen virtue. Chan chastises liberals for their skepticism toward the necessity of the Confucian-style cultivation of character traits, namely moral education, for a good social

---

[4] As will be discussed shortly, whether or not the conceptual distinction between moral virtue and civic virtue is feasible within the (traditional) Confucian ethical system is debatable.
[5] Joseph Chan, *Confucian Perfectionism: A Political Philosophy for Modern Times* (Princeton: Princeton University Press, 2014), pp. 95–96 (emphases in original).

and political (particularly democratic) order, and finds fault with the liberal tendency to "steer clear of questions about personal morality and conceptions of the good person or the good life that might be regarded as controversial." In order to make clear sense of Chan's chastisement of liberals, it is necessary to first examine how civic virtue is understood in liberal political theory.

As seen in previous chapters, in liberal political theory valorization of the common good and civic virtue is the hallmark of *civic liberalism* of which civic republicanism is an important part.[6] However, precisely because of the strong emphasis on the common good and civic virtue in civic liberalism, some liberals (especially liberal pluralists) find that civic liberalism verges on "civic totalism."[7] William Galston, for instance, describes the totalistic spirit latent in civic liberalism in the following way: "[c]ivic health and morality cannot be achieved without citizens' wholehearted devotion to the common good. Loyalties divided between the republic and other ties, whether to civil associations or to revealed religious truth, are bound to dilute civic spirit. And the liberal appeal to private life as against public life will only legitimate selfishness at the expense of the spirit of contribution and sacrifice without which the polity cannot endure."[8]

Chan would agree with Galston's criticism of the republican promotion of civic virtue but it is unlikely that he would accept Galston's pluralist alternative, at the center of which are the valorization of diversity (as opposed to autonomy and common citizenship) and the incongruence between regime-level principles and the association of civil society.[9] What drives the liberal pluralist objection to civic liberalism is a clearly political concern, that *in a liberal society*, the state (even a democratic state) cannot

---

[6] Leading contemporary civic republicans such as Michael Sandel, Cass Sunstein, and Philip Pettit are all devout liberal democrats who are only critical of certain brands of liberalism, particularly deontological liberalism that gives priority to the right over the good, and certain aspects of liberal theory and practice. They are all champions of public freedom and political liberty. See Michael J. Sandel, *Democracy's Discontent: America in Search of a Public Philosophy* (Cambridge: Belknap, 1996); Cass Sunstein, *Designing Democracy: What Constitutions Do* (New York: Oxford University Press, 2001); Philip Pettit, *On the People's Terms: A Republican Theory and Models of Democracy* (Cambridge: Cambridge University Press, 2012).
[7] I think, though, that this way of characterizing civic liberalism is not only unfair but also deeply misleading.
[8] William A. Galston, *The Practice of Liberal Pluralism* (Cambridge: Cambridge University Press, 2005), p. 24.
[9] See Chapter 4 for a more detailed discussion on the basic tenets of liberal pluralism.

wield a plenipotentiary power and paternalistic authority over individuals and associations.[10] Chan has different political reasons to object to civic liberalism (and, I suspect, *any* political theory that elevates civic virtue above moral virtue): civic liberals, republicans, and democrats generally uphold political participation as the foundation of citizenship and civic virtue, but participation, argues Chan, can lead to serious conflicts, especially when it takes an adversarial mode, generating polarization of positions, animosity, and resentment.[11] In other words, active political participation can do serious damage to civility.

Whether Chan's argument is valid or not is an empirical question and there is ample evidence to counter his judgment;[12] as Mark Warren powerfully argued, much hangs on how we conceptualize the self and how we construct our political institutions.[13] One problem with Chan's argument is that his *political* critique of the liberal democratic valorization of civic virtue depends almost exclusively on some negative effects of political participation, as if political participation exhausts the entire repertoire of civic virtues.[14] But can this worry about the side effects of political participation, though reasonable, pose a principled philosophical challenge to the moral and political importance of civic virtue and civic

---

[10] Of course, whether this objection is convincing in the context of liberal democracy is another matter.

[11] Chan, *Confucian Perfectionism*, p. 96.

[12] See for instance, Archon Fung and Erik O. Wright, *Deepening Democracy: Institutional Innovations in Empowered Participatory Governance* (London: Verso, 2003).

[13] Mark Warren, "Democratic Theory and Self-Transformation," *American Political Science Review* 86:1 (1992), pp. 8–23.

[14] It is worth noting that the liberal pluralist challenge is directly targeted at civic virtue and civic education. Nancy L. Rosenblum, another advocate of liberal pluralism, adds more reasons for being wary of the argument for civic virtue and citizenship to Galston's political concern. According to Rosenblum, the moral valence of associational life is indeterminate. She says, "voluntary associations are personally and politically evocative and changing [and] the vicissitudes of personal life affect what we take from membership. The significance of association depends on the experiences individuals bring to it, including the unique obstacles we each face in cultivating and exhibiting particular competences and dispositions" (*Membership and Morals: The Personal Uses of Pluralism in America* [Princeton: Princeton University Press, 1998], p. 8). In Rosenblum's view, primary importance of associational life lies in its important psychological benefits for members, and whether or not these benefits are congruent with the moral dispositions (i.e., civic virtues) liberal democracy requires is (and should be) a contingent matter. Here what counts is the *experience of pluralism* enabled by shifting involvements among various associations. The espousal of civic virtue and citizenship may critically impair the rich personal psychological experience of pluralism. A similar view can be found in George Kateb, *The Inner Ocean: Individualism and Democratic Culture* (Ithaca: Cornell University Press, 1992).

education? On what grounds can one say that the cultivation of virtues, such as patriotism, a sense of justice, a sense of common fate, moral criticism, self-restraint, tolerance, and of course active political participation, namely *civic virtues*, is not very effective in sustaining a viable democratic political order? That being said, Chan has additional stronger reasons to criticize the liberal preoccupation with civic virtue and civic education:

> First, these two [moral and civic] conceptions of education provide different forms of motivation and convey different messages. According to the moral conception, one should cultivate these virtues in order to be a good *person*. According to the civic conception, one should cultivate them in order to be a good *citizen*. ... [However, f]or many people, the desire to be (or to appear to be) a good person is stronger than the desire to be a good citizen. ... Second, as human virtues are relevant in many different social contexts besides the public arena, people not only have numerous opportunities to learn and practice them but also are expected to learn and practice them. ... Third, political republicans face "an assurance problem" that perfectionists do not. ... If civic virtues are tied only to citizenship, citizens may not see a reason to behave civilly and respectfully to others, especially if assurance from others is not forthcoming.[15]

We can call these reasons *the motivation reason, the opportunity reason*, and *the assurance reason*, respectively. Since I discuss the second and, especially, the third reasons extensively with special focus on political participation in Chapter 6, let me investigate for now whether the motivation reason supports Chan's core claim in favor of moral virtue.

Indeed, the motivation reason raises a reasonable question about how a person can be motivated to become a good citizen in the first place unless it is posited that the motivational force comes from moral/human virtues, character traits that one possesses as a human being. Moreover, it can be claimed, the polity's (or the Constitution's) dependence upon civic virtues would not be sufficiently firm if virtues in question are required only for instrumental reasons without any robust connection with genuine human excellence. What this claim takes issue with is a pluralist separation between moral virtue and civic virtue, which Paul Weithman, on whose argument Chan heavily draws, attributes to political republicans (who largely overlap with those I call civic liberals).[16]

---

[15] Chan, *Confucian Perfectionism*, pp. 97–98. It seems to me, though, that whether one has a stronger desire to be a good person or a good citizen depends on his or her conception of what it is to be a good person.

[16] Paul Weithman, "Political Republicanism and Perfectionist Republicanism," *Review of Politics* 66:2 (2004), pp. 285–312.

According to Weithman, contemporary republicans (democrats included) argue that "republican government depends upon citizens' possession of certain civic virtues [but] mindful of moral pluralism, they avoid basing their political theories on controversial premises about the human good.... Instead they claim only that these traits are derivatively valuable states of character, counting as virtues because they suit their possessors to take part in republican government."[17] Though not a political republican himself, the following statement by William Galston offers the strongest endorsement of the distinction between human and civic virtues with a view to value pluralism, thereby helping us better understand what aspects of political republicanism (or political liberalism in Galston's case) are so worrisome from Weithman's *perfectionist republican* standpoint.

> Human virtue is one thing, civic virtue another. Human virtue is desirable for its own sake, for all individuals. While modes of enactment may shift from culture to culture, its basic content does not vary among individuals, regardless of their time, place, or circumstances. By contrast, civic virtue is valued instrumentally, for its contribution to sustaining a political community. Because communities differ – in principle, purposes, institutions, and history – the substance of civic virtue varies from community to community.... Human and civic virtue, then, cannot be fully congruent. In all too many circumstances, the tension between them will be painfully manifest, and it will not be clear which is to be given priority.[18]

At the center of Galston's distinction between human and civic virtue is ineluctable incongruence between the two in a world of pluralism in which communities have different principles, purposes, and institutions. Weithman objects to this pluralist distinction, enabled by an instrumentalist or institutionalist approach to civic virtue, and advocates the monistic (in the Aristotelian sense) congruence between two kinds of virtues by comprehensively (in the Rawlsian sense) grounding civic virtues on human excellence.[19] Seen in this way, Weithman's major criticism of political republicanism turns out to be not so much a question of which should be given priority between human virtue and civic virtue, which assumes a practical distinction between the two, but a question of how civic virtue can be a virtue in a robustly moral sense that can firmly, not

---

[17] Ibid., p. 286.
[18] William A. Galston, "Pluralism and Civic Virtue," *Social Theory and Practice* 33:4 (2007), pp. 625–635, at p. 625.
[19] Thus, James B. Murphy criticizes Galston's pluralistic distinction between moral virtue and civic virtue from an Aristotelian standpoint. See his "From Aristotle to Hobbes: William Galston on Civic Virtue," *Social Theory and Practice* 33:4 (2007), pp. 637–644.

merely instrumentally, undergird political institutions and practices. The trouble is that Chan, while upholding a clear conceptual and practical distinction between human virtue and civic virtue like Galston, rejects Galston's pluralism in making such a distinction and instead agrees with Weithman's monistic and comprehensive understanding of virtue in which civic and moral virtues are congruent.

How does Chan (attempt to) resolve this seeming dilemma?[20] Or, more accurately, why does Chan not see a dilemma here? The reason is that he sees striking similarity between his Confucian perfectionism and Weithman's perfectionist republicanism. In fact, Chan almost likens the two. Consider the following statement.

> Confucianism is not a republican thought system, but it is a system of perfectionist ethics akin to perfectionist republicanism in its insistence on the cultivation of human virtues. The Confucian precepts discussed above define the way in which people, as moral persons, should behave. ... Confucius said the virtues of respectfulness, lenience, truthfulness, industry, and beneficence are what constitute *ren* – not *ren* as it is in imperfect reality, but as it can and should be in the ideal. These human virtues go hand in hand with the precepts above that aim to guide the actions of the gentleman in his interactions or work with others. Confucians today would join the perfectionist republicans in claiming that moral education is more effective than a political version of civic education in engendering the virtues necessary for a well-functioning democracy.[21]

The obvious problem with this statement is that perfectionist republicans (certainly Weithman) do not claim that moral education, distinct from civic education, not only conceptually but also practically, is more effective for a well-functioning democracy. Again, the gist of Weithman's perfectionist challenge to political republicanism lies in the belief that republican civic virtues can have firmer motivational incentives only when they are recognized, described, and practiced in terms of genuine human excellence.[22] The focus is not on moral virtue as opposed to civic virtue

---

[20] The reason why this dilemma is only seemingly so will be explained later. For now, suffice it to say that this "dilemma" can be effectively avoided by public reason Confucianism.
[21] Chan, *Confucian Perfectionism*, p. 97.
[22] Weithman says, "Political morality in a political republican regime will therefore be morality which stops with the invocation of political values. Education, exhortation, self-examination, and self-restraint will be quite different in a perfectionist republican regime. There public morality, public education, and political oratory could trade on the claims that helping to govern one's society is part of a well-lived life and that the temperance required for doing so is a human excellence." Political Republicanism and Perfectionist Republicanism, p. 305 Clearly, Weithman's interest is in redescribing civic virtues, concerned with public morality, public education, political oratory, and

(because of practical problems associated with its poor exercise), but on the moral underpinning of civic virtue. Weithman is a perfectionist but he is a perfectionist *republican* who fully embraces the paramount political value of civic virtue and a virtuous citizenry.[23]

This poses a salient challenge to Chan not only because his political theory is *Confucian* but also because his normative position is (moderate) *political* perfectionist.[24] Chan is clearly aware of this challenge when he says, "Liberals prefer the narrow notion of civic education to the robust notion of moral education because they wish to avoid controversies about what makes people good and what makes their lives better. By contrast, the perfectionist view on moral education seems to presuppose what John Rawls has called the 'comprehensive doctrines' of the good life, about which there is often deep disagreement among people in a pluralistic society."[25] Interestingly, Chan attempts to avoid the challenge of reconciling his political (Confucian) perfectionism with Weithman's comprehensive (republican) perfectionism by appealing to his idea of moderate (political) perfectionism.

> I believe it is possible to appeal to judgments about the good life without basing them on any comprehensive doctrine. ... Moderate perfectionism appeals to individual judgments about human goods and experiences in a piecemeal way and whenever they are relevant to a policy issue under question; it does not attempt to pursue a comprehensive doctrine of the good life through political action. ... The moderate way of conducting moral education, for example, is to promote specific human virtues that constitute the good life, without basing them on a comprehensive doctrine. It is, I believe, possible to understand and appreciate the value of such Confucian virtues as respect, reverence, trustworthiness, sincerity, and beneficence without accepting the whole philosophy of Confucianism.[26]

It may indeed be possible to "understand and appreciate the value of such Confucian virtues as respect, reverence ... without accepting the

---

temperance, rather than upholding a different category of virtues (i.e., moral virtues) such as respectfulness, lenience, truthfulness, industry, and beneficence, as Chan claims.
[23] In other words, Weithman's philosophical opponents are not so much critics of civic virtue such as liberal pluralists, with whom he has much to disagree politically, but neorepublican champions of civic virtue who dissociate civic virtue from human excellence. For recent revival of "neorepublicanism," generally focused on civic virtue as nondomination rather than the promotion of human excellences, see Philip Pettit, *Republicanism: A Theory of Freedom and Government* (Oxford: Oxford University Press, 1997); Maurizio Viroli, *Republicanism* (New York: Hill and Wang, 2002); Quentin Skinner, *Liberty before Liberalism* (Cambridge: Cambridge University Press, 1998).
[24] See Chapter 1 for my critical discussion of Chan's moderate political Confucian perfectionism.
[25] Chan, *Confucian Perfectionism*, p. 99. [26] Ibid., pp. 99–100.

whole philosophy of Confucianism."[27] However, as I noted in Chapter 1, it is far from clear how *human virtues*, such as respect, reverence, trustworthiness, and the like, can be called "Confucian" when they are detached from the comprehensive doctrine of Confucianism. Chan's core reasoning, it should be recalled, is that since comprehensive Confucianism is incompatible with value pluralism as well as modern democratic institutions, the only viable mode of normative Confucianism in modern East Asia is political Confucian perfectionism that is ethically *moderate* due to its ability to accommodate pluralism and democracy.

Now, it is difficult to understand how Chan can avoid a seeming dilemma. On the one hand, he needs to demonstrate that the human virtues he enumerates are important Confucian virtues; otherwise, it is difficult to distinguish his *Confucian* perfectionism from certain types of *liberal* perfectionism, equally focused on the state's nonneutral promotion of certain *human* goods. On the other hand, if Chan highlights Confucian moral characteristics of human virtues, which he gleans from Confucian classics,[28] the Confucianism in question is ineluctably a comprehensive Confucianism. The reason is intimately related to the very wholistic structure of Confucian virtue ethics, if we assume that Confucian virtue ethics is the virtue ethics of flourishing or character a la Aristotle.[29] Traditional Confucianism is a way of life and individual virtues are understood to be partly constitutive of that way of life. You cannot understand these virtues in isolation from one another any more than you can understand what a finger is without knowledge of the human body.

---

[27] One way to do so is to think of Confucianism as more like Humean virtue ethics (i.e., virtue ethics of sentiments) rather than Aristotelian virtue ethics (i.e., virtue ethics of flourishing). The salient difference between these is that the former does not rely on a wholistic conception of flourishing but instead appeals to how well a given set of dispositions functions in a particular context. However, Chan does not explore this line of argument and it is beyond my immediate concern here to investigate the perfectionist implications of virtue ethics of sentiments. For two possible different interpretations of Confucian virtue ethics, see Philip J. Ivanhoe, "Virtue Ethics and the Chinese Confucian Tradition," in *The Cambridge Companion to Virtue Ethics*, ed. Daniel C. Russell (Cambridge: Cambridge University Press, 2013), pp. 49–69.

[28] Particularly, Chan draws on *Analects* 13.19 and 17.6.

[29] And apparently this is how Chan understands Confucian virtue ethics. For an argument for similarity between Confucian and Aristotelian virtue ethics, see May Sim, *Remastering Morals with Aristotle and Confucius* (New York: Cambridge University Press, 2007); Jiyuan Yu, *The Ethics of Aristotle and Confucius: Mirrors of Virtue* (London: Routledge, 2007).

In my view, the root of this seeming dilemma lies in Chan's problematic understanding of comprehensive doctrine (in addition to a certain ambiguity in his understanding of Confucian virtue ethics): while Rawls attributes virtually *every* ethical doctrine to a comprehensive doctrine, including liberal perfectionism that promotes only a particular set of liberal moral values (pivoted around either autonomy [Raz or Kant] or freedom [Dworkin or Mill]), regardless of the doctrine's degree of moral comprehensivenss (full or partial), Chan understands the word "comprehensive" literally, that is, as encompassing every aspect of the life.[30] Put differently, Chan identifies comprehensive doctrine solely in terms of a *fully* comprehensive doctrine. In previous chapters, I have articulated how a perfectionist promotion of certain Confucian virtues can be possible in a democratic constitutional polity without accepting the whole philosophy of traditional, fully comprehensive, Confucianism by proposing public reason Confucianism as one particular mode of partial comprehensive Confucianism that is *moderate* in Chan's sense.

As noted earlier, Chan claims that even though Confucianism is not a republican system, it is a system of perfectionist ethics akin to perfectionist republicanism in its insistence on the cultivation of human virtues. However, it is dubious that perfectionist republicanism shares with Confucian perfectionism its strong emphasis on human virtue *over* civic virtue because such a sharp distinction and an exclusive focus on moral virtue go against the core tenets of republican political theory including perfectionist republicanism. If anything, their similarity consists in their monistic understanding of virtue – for Weithman's perfectionist republicanism, the ethical (especially motivational) continuum between human excellence and civic virtues or the grounding of civic virtues on human excellence, and for Chan's Confucian perfectionism, a valorization of moral virtues over civic virtues in all aspects of human affairs including political ones. But this structural similarity does not eliminate salient substantive differences between Confucian perfectionism, concentrated exclusively on moral virtue, and perfectionist republicanism, aimed to revitalize civic virtue through a firmer ethical foundation.

This last point brings us to another problem with Chan's perfectionist endorsement of moral virtue. It is unclear precisely how virtues such as respect, reverence, trustworthiness, sincerity, and beneficence – *human* virtues that make a person good qua human being, hence irrespective of

---

[30] Again, virtue ethics of sentiments is less susceptible to this problem because the comprehensive doctrine it generates is hardly life-encompassing.

the type and character of the political regime under which one lives – can effectively make a democratic polity function well. An example may be helpful here.

Admittedly, one of the pivotal democratic civic virtues, particularly in a pluralist societal context, is nondiscrimination.[31] It is important to note that in a pluralist democracy the vice of discrimination arises not necessarily because those who commit this vice are bad human beings, lacking human virtues. Even the most benevolent or sincere individuals can be susceptible to the vice of discrimination, when they find themselves in a situation in which they have to engage with those who are different from them in terms of religious or moral values. Precisely in what sense these discriminating individuals are bad as human beings is far from clear, however, once our concern about a viable democratic life is bracketed. For instance, Mencius, who was not a democrat, would not find *morally bad* a devout Confucian who morally vilifies non-Confucians who do not share the core principles of the Confucian Way.[32] As a devout Confucian comprehensively committed to the single right Way (*dao* 道), Mencius never regarded nondiscrimination as a human virtue.[33] He would find completely puzzling the very idea that nondiscrimination can be a human virtue, which enables one to become a (Confucian) sage, a perfect human being.

What is certain is that our protagonists are not good democratic citizens; what they lack is a moral disposition to tolerate cultural differences (or, more positively, appreciate cultural diversity) and to resolve resulting moral disagreement in ways that are reciprocally acceptable, however temporarily, both to them and to those they are engaging with. This sort of moral disposition or trait is civic in its character because it directly serves the inclusionary vision of democratic citizenship.[34] Its cultivation is primarily through education in democratic principles and

---

[31] See Amy Gutmann, *Identity in Democracy* (Princeton: Princeton University Press, 2003).
[32] See *Mencius* 7A26 where Mencius says, "Yangzi chose egoism. If by pulling out a single hair from his own body he could have benefited the entire world, he would not have done it. Mozi chose impartial care. If by rubbing his whole body smooth from head to heel he could have benefited the world, he would have done it. ... The reason I dislike holding to one point is that one steals from the Way, holding up one point while suppressing a hundred others." The English translation of the *Mengzi* 孟子 is adapted from *Mencius*, trans. Irene Bloom (New York: Columbia University Press, 2009).
[33] The same is true of devout (medieval) Christians such as Tomas Aquinas who appreciated the moral value of compassion (*misericordia*) but failed to develop this genuine *human* virtue into a democratic virtue of nondiscrimination.
[34] Iris M. Young, *Inclusion and Democracy* (Oxford: Oxford University Press, 2000).

practices that best represent the polity's constitutional purposes, namely civic education.[35] Which actions involve discrimination cannot be determined with reference to a certain universal ideal of the good that concerns every person qua human being; its content is always contextual, reflecting the polity's unique public character and moral commitment, and in most cases it is the Constitution, understood broadly, that defines what constitutes discrimination.

Chan's exclusive focus on human/moral virtues reflects his philosophical commitment to Confucianism in which the independent moral value of civic virtue is not recognized. However, not only does this commitment render his Confucian perfectionism a comprehensive philosophical doctrine, thereby undermining his overall philosophical foundation, but, more importantly, it takes our attention away from the paramount importance of civic virtue in a well-functioning Confucian constitutional democracy. Then the question is whether we can derive civic virtue from Confucianism, whose ethical system, as Chan rightly notes, is singularly predicated on moral virtues.

CONFUCIAN ETHICAL MONISM: TOWARD TEMPERED VIRTUE MONISM

Putting aside substantive differences in normative orientation between Chan's Confucian perfectionism and Weithman's perfectionist republicanism, there is indeed significant similarity between traditional Confucian virtue ethics-cum-politics and perfectionist republicanism. Recall that Weithman's problem with contemporary neorepublicans and civic/democratic liberals lies not in their emphasis on civic virtue but in their understanding of civic virtue as deracinated from human excellence. Neither classical nor neo-Confucians ever made a distinction, either conceptual or practical, between moral virtue and civic virtue; in fact, the ethical continuum between moral virtue and civic virtue is one of the defining characteristics of Confucian ethics and politics, even though Confucians never developed the concept of civic/citizen virtue. In a

---

[35] See Amy Gutmann, *Democratic Education* (Princeton: Princeton University Press, 1987); Sanford Levinson, *Constitutional Faith* (Princeton: Princeton University Press, 1988); Benjamin R. Barber, "Constitutional Faith," in *For Love of Country: Debating the Limits of Patriotism*, ed. Joshua Cohen (Boston: Beacon Books, 1996), pp. 30–37; Eamonn Callan, *Creating Citizens: Political Education and Liberal Democracy* (Oxford: Oxford University Press, 1997).

profound sense, the difference between Confucianism and republicanism with regard to the distinction between moral and civic virtue lies in differing conceptions of what a person is and what a good human life consists of. Consider the famous opening passage of the *Daxue* 大學 (Great Learning).

The Ancients who wished to clearly to exemplify illustrious virtue throughout the world would first set up good government in their states. Wishing to govern well their states, they would first regulate their families. Wishing to regulate their families, they would first cultivate their persons. Wishing to cultivate their persons, they would first rectify their minds. Wishing to rectify their minds, they would first seek sincerity in their thoughts. Wishing for sincerity in their thoughts, they would first extend their knowledge. The extension of knowledge lies in the investigation of things. For only when things are investigated is knowledge extended; only when knowledge is extended are thoughts sincere; only when thoughts are sincere are minds rectified; only when minds are rectified are our persons cultivated; only when our persons are cultivated are our families regulated; only when families are regulated are states well governed; and only when states are well governed is there peace in the world.[36]

Interestingly, the *Daxue* presents not only (what we now consider) epistemology, ethics, and politics but also human/moral virtue, required for self-development, and civic/political virtue, necessary for (both domestic and global) political governance, as constituting a seamless ethical whole. Among classical Confucians Mencius most directly echoed this remarkable ethical continuum between the public and private and between human/moral virtue and civic/political virtue, when he says that "[t]he world has its basis in the state; the state has its basis in the family, and the family has its basis in oneself."[37] In the same vein, Confucius refused to distinguish the public-political from the private-ethical by saying, quoting the *Shujing* 書經 (Book of Documents), "It is all in filial conduct (*xiao* 孝)! Just being filial to your parents and befriending your brothers is carrying out the work of government (*zheng* 政)."[38] The following statements by Confucius clearly demonstrate the Confucian faith in the inextricable intertwinement between (what Western scholars would call) statecraft and soulcraft.

---

[36] *Daxue* 1. The English translation is adapted by *Sources of Chinese Tradition*, vol. 1, eds. and trans. Wm. Theodore de Bary, Wing-tsit Chan, and Burton Watson (New York: Columbia University Press, 1960), p. 115.

[37] *Mencius* 4A5 (translation slightly modified).

[38] *Analects* 2.21. Unless noted otherwise, all English translations of the *Lunyu* 論語 in this chapter are adapted from Roger T. Ames and Henry Rosemont Jr., *The Analects of Confucius: A Philosophical Translation* (New York: Ballantine Books, 1998).

If proper (*zheng* 正) in their own conduct, what difficulty would they have in governing (*zheng* 政)? But if not able to be proper in their own conduct, how can they demand such conduct from others?[39]

[G]overning effectively (*zheng* 政) is doing what is proper (*zheng* 正). If you, sir, lead by doing what is proper, who would dare do otherwise?[40]

In both statements, Confucius does not clarify precisely what "being proper" (*zheng* 正) means, although it is obvious that by playing with two Chinese words that are graphically, phonetically, and semantically cognates he intends to stress the supreme importance of moral conduct *at a personal level* in effective governing. The content of "being proper" is given in *Analects* 2.3 when Confucius says, "Lead the people with administrative injunctions (*zheng* 政) and keep them orderly with penal law (*xing* 刑), and they will avoid punishments but will be without a sense of shame. Lead them with virtue (*de* 德) and keep them orderly through observing ritual propriety (*li* 禮) and they will develop a sense of shame, and moreover, will order themselves."[41]

According to Confucius, governing, otherwise a set of mere administrative injunctions undergirded by penal law, is made good by the ruler's moral virtue, at the core of which lies *ren* (often translated as benevolence), the Confucian moral virtue par excellence.[42] Though Confucius does not identify the virtue here in terms of *ren*, Xunzi, following Mencius as shall be discussed shortly, establishes an intrinsic connection between virtue, presented by Confucius as certain force or power, and *ren*.

In attempting to bring order to the myriad changes, to make use of the myriad things, to nurture the myriad people, and to control all under Heaven, nothing is as good for doing this as the goodness of the person who is *ren*. This is because his wisdom and deliberations are sufficient to order people, his generosity is sufficient to comfort them, and his virtuous reputation is sufficient to transform them. If you obtain him, then there will be order. If you lose him, then there will be chaos.... [The common people] truly admire his virtue. And so, when a person of *ren* serves as superior, then the common people will honor him like Shang Di

---

[39] *Analects* 13.13.   [40] *Analects* 12.17.
[41] Translation slightly modified. Also see *Analects* 2.1; 12.19.
[42] As Benjamin I. Schwartz aptly puts it, "[*Ren*] is an attainment of a human excellence which – where it exists – is a whole embracing of all the separate virtues" (*The World of Thought in Ancient China* [Cambridge: Belknap, 1985], p. 75). Also see Tu Wei-ming, *Humanity and Self-Cultivation* (Berkeley: Asian Humanities Press, 1979), pp. 7–10; Wing-tsit Chan, "The Evolution of the Chinese Concept *Jên*," *Philosophy East and West* 4:4 (1955), pp. 295–319.

[Lord-on-High], they will love him like their own parents, and they will happily march out to die for him.[43]

There is a plethora of discussion regarding what *ren* consists of and throughout the *Analects* Confucius himself is quite equivocal on this issue. Nevertheless, it is indisputable that he understood *ren* primarily as moral virtue or excellence attainable by *all human beings*, when he says, "To return to the observance of ritual propriety through overcoming the self constitutes *ren*.... [T]he practice of *ren* depends on oneself alone, and not on others."[44]

The discussion thus far shows that classical Confucians saw no qualitative difference between the virtue (*ren*) that would make a person moral qua human being and the virtue (*ren*) that would enable a ruler to become politically efficacious. Otherwise stated, classical Confucians subscribe to ethical monism with regard to virtue. Since classical Confucians neither recognized nor endorsed the political institution of citizenship, as they did not embrace the ideal of political equality, there is no way for us to know the Confucian attitude toward the virtue pertaining only to citizens, namely civic virtue.[45] That said, important contemporary implications to this effect can be drawn from our examination of the classical Confucian understanding of the relationship between moral virtue and political virtue (pertaining to mainly rulers and public officials): the embracing of republican citizenship in modern constitutional East Asia has made political virtue relevant to *all citizens* who have appropriated the sovereign

---

[43] *Xunzi* 10:5. The English translation of the *Xunzi* 荀子 is adapted from *Xunzi: The Complete Text*, trans. Eric L. Hutton (Princeton: Princeton University Press, 2014).

[44] *Analects* 12.1 The English translation here has been modified by *The Analects*, trans. D. C. Lau (New York: Penguin, 1979). However, whether or not Confucius would include women by "all human beings" is quite controversial. For more on this controversy, see Paul R. Goldin, "The View of Women in Early Confucianism," in *The Sage and the Second Sex: Confucianism, Ethics, and Gender*, ed. Chenyang Li (Chicago: Open Court, 2000), pp. 133–161, and Sandra A. Wawrytko, "Kongzi as Feminist: Confucian Self-Cultivation in a Contemporary Context," *Journal of Chinese Philosophy* 27:2 (2000), pp. 171–186.

[45] This is why Fred R. Dallmayr finds it imperative for East Asians to add a new relationship "between citizen and citizen in a shared public sphere and under common rule of law" to the so-called "five relationships" (*wulun* 五倫), cardinal human relationships cherished in the Confucian tradition. See his "Confucianism and the Public Sphere: Five Relationships Plus One?" in *The Politics of Affective Relations: East Asia and Beyond*, eds. Chaihark Hahm and Daniel A. Bell (Lanham: Lexington Books, 2004), pp. 41–59, at p. 54. Also see Edward Shils, "Reflections on Civil Society and Civility in the Chinese Intellectual Tradition," in *Confucian Traditions in East Asian Modernity: Moral Education and Economic Culture in Japan and Four Mini-Dragons*, ed. Tu Wei-ming (Cambridge: Harvard University Press, 1996), pp. 38–71.

political power, traditionally held by the Confucian monarch – in terms of civic virtue.[46] The contemporary East Asian challenge is how to make sense of and practice civic virtue in ways that track Confucianism's monistic approach to virtue without putting Confucian virtue monism at odds with East Asia's increasingly pluralist society. In the next section, I will show how public reason Confucianism can meet this challenge better than any other alternative, including Chan's political Confucian perfectionism. For now, let us continue to probe the nature of Confucian virtue monism.

What still remains unclear is how human/moral virtue can be extended to politics without transforming into something qualitatively different, specifically tailored for the public realm.[47] While Confucius and Xunzi are reticent on this, Mencius offers a compelling explanation about how such extension is possible. Mencius begins his virtue monism with the assumption, backed by empirical observations, that all human beings are born with moral sentiments, which incline them toward moral goodness. He then presents four types of moral sentiments as the "sprouts" (*duan* 端) of human virtue – the feeling of pity and compassion, the feeling of shame and aversion, the feeling of modesty and compliance, and the sense of right and wrong.[48] According to Mencius, every human being can cultivate his/her nascent moral sentiments through careful reflection on them and by taking joy in the moral actions that they engender. Continuous strengthening and cultivation of these moral sentiments, argues Mencius, will make a person become morally good, possibly even a sage.[49] Mencius then applies his developmental account of moral self-cultivation directly to politics, with special focus on the virtue of *ren* (and the feeling of pity and compassion). When King Xuan of Qi asked what one's virtue must be like in order to become a true king, Mencius replies as follows:

I have heard ... that while the king was seated in the upper part of the hall someone led an ox past the hall below [in the courtyard]. On seeing this, the king

---

[46] On republicanism in East Asia, see Jun-Hyeok Kwak and Leigh Jenco (eds.), *Republicanism in Northeast Asia* (London: Routledge, 2014).

[47] Not surprisingly, no classical Confucian admitted the case of "dirty hands," the resolution of which requires distinctively *political* virtue, even when they were confronted with a moral dilemma. See Sungmoon Kim, "Achieving the Way: Confucian Virtue Politics and the Problem of Dirty Hands," *Philosophy East and West* 66:1 (forthcoming).

[48] *Mencius* 2A6. According to Mencius, theses four moral feelings are the sprouts of moral virtues of *ren* 仁, *yi* 義, *li* 禮, and *zhi* 智, respectively.

[49] Mencius says, "When [virtue] is filled up within oneself, one may be called 'beautiful.' When it is filled up and brightly displayed, one may be called 'great.' When one is great and exercises a transforming influence, one may be called a 'sage'" (*Mencius* 7B25).

asked where the ox was going and was told that it was being taken to serve as a blood sacrifice in the consecration of a bell. The king said, "Spare it. I cannot bear its trembling, like one who, though blameless, is being led to the execution ground ... [But h]ow could [the consecration of the bell] be dispensed with? Substitute a sheep instead." ... With such a mind one has what it takes to become a true king.[50]

Elsewhere I discussed extensively Mencius's moral psychological reasoning on how the king's compassion toward an ox extends to his compassion to the people.[51] What is important in the present context is that in his analogical reasoning Mencius seems to believe that *only if* a ruler becomes a person of *ren* can he then become a true king. In this view, not only is political virtue motivated by and extended from moral virtue, but, furthermore, political virtue and moral virtue are perfectly congruent with each other. The underlying political message is surprisingly radical: in principle, *anyone* who is morally virtuous can become not only a sage but even a sage-king, as were the cases of Shun and Yu, former commoners to whom the throne was abdicated by incumbent (sage-) kings solely on the basis of their brilliant moral virtues.[52]

Does this imply that Mencius (or early Confucians, for that matter) failed to recognize the distinctive nature of the political, which is generally concerned with the Confucian polity's constitutional order? Or, given the perfect congruence between human virtue and political virtue, is Mencius claiming that a Confucian should only care about becoming a good person? Did classical Confucians dismiss the value of the virtues that directly contribute to a constitutional order and the reproduction of its public character?

Consider Yi Yin, the sagacious minister of King Tang (the founder of the Shang dynasty [1566–1046 BCE]), who took Tai Jia, King Tang's

---

[50] *Mencius* 1A7.
[51] Sungmoon Kim, *Confucian Democracy in East Asia: Theory and Practice* (New York: Cambridge University Press, 2014), pp. 142–144. Also see David B. Wong, "Reasons and Analogical Reasoning in Mengzi," and Philip J. Ivanhoe, "Confucian Self Cultivation and Mengzi's Notion of Extension," both in *Essays on the Moral Philosophy of Mengzi*, eds. Xiusheng Liu and Philip J. Ivanhoe (Indianapolis: Hackett, 2002), pp. 187–220 and 221–241, respectively.
[52] *Mencius* 5A5–6. However, a close reading of the *Mengzi* reveals that in the end Mencius embraced the legitimacy of hereditary succession of kingship, by paying attention to the nonideal reality of the Warring States period in which the theory of abdication could be (and was) easily manipulated by ambitious ministers for usurpation. See Yuri Pines, "Disputers of Abdication: Zhanguo Egalitarianism and the Sovereign's Power," *T'oung Pao* 91:4 (2005), pp. 243–300, at pp. 268–271.

grandson, into custody, and gave him the power back after three years of regent rule. In *Mencius* 7A31, Wan Zhang, Mencius's own student, asks Mencius whether or not Yi Yin's action constitutes usurpation. Famously, Mencius's answer is no. Mencius does not explicate why Yi Yin's seemingly problematic action is not morally wrong; he only points out that Yi Yin, a sage, had the right motive (*zhi* 志).[53] But what could be Yi Yin's motive when he temporarily deposed his king, thereby potentially (but not actually according to Mencius) violating the moral principles of *yi* (rightness) and *li* (ritual propriety), other than his desire to prevent Tai Jia from destroying Shang's constitutional order that his sagacious grandfather Tang had established? Here the question is whether or not we can understand the kind of virtue exercised by Yi Yin – what I call political virtue – purely in terms of human virtue, even if, as Mencian virtue ethics stipulates, the virtue in question could have been derived or developed from human virtue.[54] Is anyone who is morally good – respectful, benevolent, trustworthy, sincere, and so on – in his or her private interpersonal relationships capable of behaving like Yi Yin? Can any moral person have Yi Yin's motive in the politically relevant sense?[55]

Even more striking are Confucius's seemingly contradictory comments on Guan Zhong, the minister of Duke Huan of Qi, who helped Duke Huan to become the first Hegemon (*bazhe* 霸者) among the feudal lords during the Spring and Autumn period (770–476 BCE). While noting that Guan Zhong, who failed to understand the moral and political value and power of ritual propriety (*li*), "was lacking in capacity [to practice the Kingly Way],"[56] Confucius extols his *ren* solely with reference to his ability to protect the unity of the Zhou Kindgom.

---

[53] A fuller discussion of this case can be found in Kim, "Achieving the Way."

[54] On Mencius's developmentalist account of virtue ethics, see Philip J. Ivanhoe, *Confucian Moral Self Cultivation* (Indianapolis: Hackett, 2000), pp. 15–28; Bryan W. Van Norden, *Virtue Ethics and Consequentialism in Early Chinese Philosophy* (New York: Cambridge University Press, 2007), pp. 214–246.

[55] In *Xunzi* 8:1 and 8:8, Xunzi notes that Duke of Zhou, the younger brother of King Wu who with his father King Wen co-founded the Zhou dynasty (1044–256 BCE), acted as a screen for King Cheng, King Wu's son, and took charge of the registers of the Son of Heaven, and, in the same manner Mencius justifies Yi Yin's action, justifies Duke of Zhou's seemingly problematic action on the basis of his desire to protect the constitutional order of the newly founded dynasty. See Kim, "Achieving the Way."

[56] *Analects* 3.22. The Kingly Way (*wang dao* 王道) refers to a moral statecraft practiced by the (Confucian) sage-kings of Chinese antiquity and it is often contrasted to the Hegemonic Rule (*ba dao* 霸道), a mode of statecraft relying on force rather than virtue.

Consider the following conversations between Confucius (C) and his students Zilu (ZL) and Zigong (ZG).

ZL: When Duke Huan had his elder brother Prince Qiu killed, the tutor Shao Hu died with him, but Guan Zhong did not.[57] In this instance, did Guan Zhong fall short of *ren*?
C: Many times did Duke Huan assemble the various feudal lords, and it was always through Guan Zhong's influence rather than a resort to arms. Such was his *ren*, such was his *ren*.
ZG: Was it that Guan Zhong really was not a man of *ren*? When Duke Huan had his elder brother Prince Qiu killed, not only did Guan Zhong not die with him, he became the prime minister for Duke Huan!
C: When Guan Zhong served as prime minister for Duke Huan, he enabled the duke to become leader of the various feudal lords, uniting and bringing order to the empire. Even today the people still benefit from his largesse. If there were no Guan Zhong, we would likely be wearing our hair loose and folding our robes to the left [which is the custom of the Di barbarians]. Should we expect that he would have the earnestness of some country yokel, managing to strangle himself in an irrigation ditch with no one the wiser?[58]

In his responses, Confucius relies upon a more capacious conception of *ren*, which Mencius understands primarily in terms of *personal* moral virtue, and makes it *more* directly relevant to the political domain, thus understanding it a quintessential political virtue, indispensable in safeguarding the constitutional integrity of the Confucian polity, although it is controversial whether or not *ren* here is distinctively political.[59] When dealing with past sages' seemingly problematic political actions, later Confucians such as Mencius and Xunzi only note the potential tension between personal moral virtue, necessary in making a person morally good, and political virtue, required for a political agent deeply concerned with constitutional integrity. But neither admitted that this tension is a real moral tension as if moral and political virtues can be categorically differentiated and pitted against each other and thus never attempted to recast the monistic structure of virtue and the overall congruence between human virtue and political virtue in Confucian ethics.

---

[57] Duke Xiang of Qi had two sons, Prince Xiaobai (later Duke Huan) and Prince Qiu. After the assassination of Duke Xiang by one of his subjects, Prince Xiaobai and Prince Qiu (helped by Guan Zhong) fought in a bloody struggle for the throne, which ended with Prince Xiaobai's victory.
[58] *Analects* 14.16–17 (translation slightly modified).
[59] For an overtly "political" interpretation of *ren*, see Loubna El-Amine, *Classical Confucian Political Thought: A New Interpretation* (Princeton: Princeton University Press, 2015).

Our discussion thus far reveals two important aspects of Confucian virtue ethics-cum-politics. First, *other things being equal*, Confucianism subscribes to monistic virtue ethics in which human virtue is perfectly congruent with political virtue. Since political virtue is motivated by and extended from moral virtue, political virtue that is severed from human excellence is inconceivable and in principle there can be no substantive difference between the ruler's virtue and the virtue that ordinary people are expected to attain through moral self-cultivation. Although republicanism does not necessarily hold the second proposition, there is indeed notable similarity between Confucianism (especially Mencian Confucianism) and perfectionist republicanism with regard to the first proposition in that both ethico-political systems subscribe to virtue monism, according to which virtues required in the public realm are (to be) rooted in human excellence.

Again, it is unclear whether Chan's Confucian perfectionism simply reiterates this traditional Confucian virtue monism, in which there is no moral ground for civic/political virtue independent of human/moral virtue, or if it is indeed a qualitatively different version of Confucianism (i.e., moderate political Confucianism), decoupled from any sort of comprehensive Confucianism, including Confucian virtue monism, as Chan claims. As noted, the trouble is that Chan cannot have it both ways: if he grounds Confucian perfectionism on Confucian virtue monism, it cannot but become morally comprehensive. And if Confucian perfectionism is political in his intended sense that some items of virtues are selectively pulled from the comprehensive moral vision of the Confucian way of life in which they are otherwise nested with a view to creating moderate Confucian perfectionism, not only does its *Confucian* appeal to moral virtue and moral education (as opposed to civic virtue and civic education) become shaky, but, more importantly, its public intelligibility as *Confucianism* can be critically damaged, given that the selected virtues (respectfulness, trustworthiness, sincerity, etc.) are generic moral goods widely valued across cultural boundaries. Furthermore, as noted earlier, selective pulling of particular Confucian virtues critically violates the wholistic structure of Confucian virtue ethics, to which Chan seems to subscribe.

However, as revealed by some special cases such as Mencius's account of Yi Yin and Confucius's understanding of Guan Zhong (as well as Xunzi's explanation of the Duke of Zhou), despite its idealist account of virtue monism, Confucianism also pays close attention to the nonideal political situation in which political virtues, which are not wholly congruent with human virtues, are required for a political agent – hence my second point. Though classical Confucians generally believed in virtue monism, namely, overall congruence between virtue directly relevant to a political agent and ordinary moral virtue, they simultaneously acknowledged that in nonideal situations a tension could develop between *ren* as *more* politically relevant virtue and *ren* as personal moral virtue and that perhaps a political agent could possess as well as exercise the former kind of *ren* without being perfectly *ren* at a personal level. While Confucius does not tell us how Guan Zhong, lacking *ren* as a person, was capable of the political virtue of *ren*,[60] Mencius and Xunzi offer a more plausible account of how to understand the relationship between moral virtue and political virtue. For them, both are rooted in and extended from human excellence but political virtue has an additional, if not distinctive, moral character as it pertains, in practice, only to political agents (and not all human agents) with regard to protection and sustenance of the constitutional order. Let us call this revised version of Confucian virtue ethics that pays extra attention to the potential tension between more politically relevant virtues and ordinary moral virtues *tempered virtue monism*.

As a contemporary political theory, public reason Confucianism embraces the tempered virtue monism implied in the virtue-political theory of classical Confucianism and this embracement renders it a "comprehensive" moral doctrine that is only partially comprehensive. However, there are important differences between public reason Confucianism and traditional Confucian virtue monism. First, public reason Confucianism presupposes that contemporary East Asian societies are no longer one-man monarchies, on which Confucian virtue political monism was institutionally predicated, and are, to varying degrees, republics in which equal citizens possess political power collectively. This makes every citizen a political agent from the constitutional standpoint and the traditional Confucian discourse on political virtue relevant to all citizens. Second, public reason Confucianism acknowledges the fact of pluralism as an ineluctable societal condition of contemporary East Asian citizens to which its theory and practice should be adapted. This implies that public reason Confucianism allows room for civic virtue, distinct *practically*, *if not conceptually*, from moral virtue, which can bring citizens who are

---

[60] One explanation of the apparent tension in Confucius's accounts of Guan Zhong can be that Confucius might have deemed Guan Zhong as *ren* because his political actions manifested care for the people and for true culture, even though his personal virtue fell short of full virtue.

internally diverse as private individuals or members of associations into one political world under one constitution.

In the remainder of this chapter, I discuss how tempered Confucian virtue monism can be recast into public reason Confucianism in East Asia's republican and pluralist context.

PUBLIC REASON CONFUCIANISM AND CIVIC VIRTUE

In public reason Confucianism civic virtue is understood as political virtue, as conceived in traditional monistic Confucianism, extended to all citizens of the Confucian constitutional polity. If citizenship is not merely a matter of parchment but rather refers to a (or the) core political office of an increasingly democratic modern East Asian republican society, its essential political character is derived from its inherent connection with civic virtue as the virtue pertaining to a political agent called citizen. Since civic virtues are directly concerned with the survival of the constitutional order as well as sustenance and development of the citizenry's constitutional character, they can be properly called the citizens' virtues. They include virtues that impart to citizens their distinctive public identity. In particular, public reason Confucianism regards Confucian virtues such as filial piety, fraternal responsibility, respect for elders, harmony within the family, ancestor worship, and ritual propriety, among others, *as* civic virtues, and endorses their public, even constitutional, promotion.

From a conceptual standpoint, the Confucian civic virtues just enumerated (plus others) are hardly distinguishable from Confucian moral virtues. Once again, consider filial piety. In the *Analects*, filial piety (*xiao*) is defined as the foundation (*ben* 本) of *ren* and here *ren* mainly means a personal moral virtue.[61] But if filial piety is the quintessential human virtue in Confucianism that makes its possessor a good person (and by extension a good citizen and politician), it is imperative to understand what this virtue consists of or what it allows or prohibits in practice. When Confucius says that "[t]hose today who are filial are considered so because they are able to provide for their parents. But even dogs and horses are given that much care. If you do not respect [*jing* 敬] your parents, what is the difference?,"[62] he points out the proper spirit in conducting filial piety, but not what the virtue means practically. Mencius fills this lacuna by offering what constitutes the most serious violation of

---

[61] *Analects* 1.2.   [62] *Analects* 2.7.

filial piety (*bu xiao* 不孝): "There are three things that are unfilial, and the greatest of them is to have no [male] posterity."[63]

Mencius's statement is intelligible only in the context of the Zhou dynasty's clan ritual-cum-law (*zongfa* 宗法), which organized Zhou's political and social world in terms of ritually ordered patrilineal–familial relationships[64] and this was the civilization that Confucius emphatically called "this culture of ours" (*siwen* 斯文)[65] and followed wholeheartedly.[66] It is only against the backdrop of patrilineal family ritualism that a failure to produce a male heir who can succeed the paternal descent line and conduct ancestral worship can be considered the greatest violation of filial piety. And the failure in this supreme human virtue and responsibility implies moral imperfection, a fatal flaw in one's (and his wife's) human excellence.

In a monistic Confucian ethical society in which filial piety is cherished as the most fundamental human/moral virtue and is tightly associated with a particular mode of family/clan structure, there can hardly be a serious moral debate regarding who is morally good, and hardly any controversies arise when the state attempts to reward the good and punish the bad. In fact, traditional Confucian states in China and Korea rewarded filial sons, daughters, and daughters-in-law and punished the unfilial, based on the monistic moral standard (nested in the patrilineal structure of the family) of what constitutes filial piety, seeing no moral controversy with it. The traditional Confucian state even occasionally granted public posts to those with a reputation for filial piety. The point is that only in the monistic Confucian ethico-political community is filial piety (or any Confucian moral virtue) *believed* to be the essential component of merit that would qualify one to work for the public. Only in this sort of society can there be a perfect congruence between human/moral virtue and civic/political virtue.

---

[63] *Mencius* 4A26. According to Zhao Qi (108–201), an authoritative editor of the *Mengzi* during the Han dynasty, the other two violations of filial piety include acquiescing in a lack of rightness on the part of a parent and failing to provide for them in their old age. See p. 84n27 of Irene Bloom's translation of the *Mencius*.

[64] On Zhou's clan ritual-law system, see Xu Yang-jie, *Zhongguo jiazu zhidushi* [*A History of Chinese Family System*] (Beijing: Renmin chuban she, 1992); Kwang-chih Chang, *Art, Myth, and Ritual: The Path to Political Authority in Ancient China* (Cambridge: Harvard University Press, 1983), chap. 1; Sook-in Lee, *Tongasia kodaeŭi yŏsŏngsasang: yŏsŏngchuŭiro pon yugyo* [*Feminist Thought in Ancient East Asia: Confucianism Seen Through Feminism*] (Seoul: Yŏiyŏn, 2005), pp. 43–79.

[65] *Analects* 9.5.   [66] *Analects* 3.14.

Public reason Confucianism does not ground its theory and practice on controversial moral and philosophical assumptions about the essential feature of human nature, how human nature is related to human/moral virtue, and which virtues are directly or authentically connected with human excellence, although it affirms and maintains a loose ethical connection with traditional and tempered monistic Confucianism, as noted earlier.[67] A comparison with Mencian Confucianism, which is monistic and fully comprehensive, would be helpful here. Mencian Confucianism assumes that humans have natural moral inclinations toward goodness, and genuine human virtues include, among others, producing a male heir to succeed the paternal descent line. According to Mencian Confucianism, in principle, all human beings can attain moral perfection and all are equally capable of filial piety, the root of *ren*, but it is highly controversial whether *in practice* women are fully capable of filial piety as they are excluded from (full) participation in ritual expressions of filial piety, and more fundamentally, filial piety, otherwise a universal moral virtue, is inextricably intertwined with a particular (i.e., patrilineal and patriarchal) family/clan structure.[68]

The situation gets even more complicated and controversial when we introduce to our Mencian Confucianism discussion thus far the Confucian truism that ritual propriety (*li*), which presupposes someone's right to participate in a ritual-mediated social order, is the external expression of *ren*.[69] The problem is that what is ritually appropriate, which is a human virtue according to Mencius, is structurally dependent on what kind of ritual sets one is socially expected to practice, but ritual sets,

---

[67] As discussed in Chapters 3 and 4, what further enables this connection to be loose is the democratic constitutionalism that undergirds public reason Confucianism institutionally.

[68] This is not to say that Mencian Confucianism (or traditional Confucianism in general) cannot be given a new philosophical interpretation and further reconstructed in ways compatible with modern democracy or value pluralism. My point is precisely that such a reinterpretation or reconstruction is necessary in making Confucianism practically relevant in modern East Asia. For an interesting feminist rereading of Mencius's philosophical thought, see Joanne D. Birdwhistell, *Mencius and Masculinities: Dynamics of Power, Morality, and Maternal Thinking* (Albany: State University of New York Press, 2007).

[69] See Tu Wei-ming, "The Creative Tension between *Jen* and *Li*," *Philosophy East and West* 18 (1968), pp. 29–39; Chenyang Li, "*Li* as Cultural Grammar: On the Relation between *Li* and *Ren* in Confucius' *Analects*," *Philosophy East and West* 57 (2007), pp. 311–329. According to Karyn Lai, what Tu calls the creative tension between *li* and *ren* arises due to the Confucian emphasis of moral reflectivity in conducting *li*. See her "*Li* in the *Analects*: Training in the Moral Competence and the Question of Flexibility," *Philosophy East and West* 56 (2006), pp. 69–83.

encompassing the so-called "four rites" (*sili* 四禮),⁷⁰ vary community by community.⁷¹ Let us call this problem *ritual pluralism*. In Mencian Confucianism it is assumed that (1) one's capacity for ritual propriety is inherent in human nature, (2) ritual propriety is one of the cardinal human/moral virtues, and (3) ritual propriety expresses *ren*.⁷² Therefore, ritual pluralism naturally translates into *moral pluralism* with regard to how to most authentically express *ren*. In short, differing ritual expressions or practices of filial piety in various ritual communities are likely to undermine the monistic structure of *ren* and by implication what it takes, in practice, to become a good person in the moral universe.

Still, moral pluralism resulting from ritual pluralism may not be so hopelessly intractable, both morally and politically, if the larger political community is singularly committed to Confucian virtue political monism or Confucianism is embraced as the state ideology or religion.⁷³ For within the moral parameters of monistic Confucianism, moral pluralism arises mainly due to different interpretations of the same Confucian canon and/or development of different sets of rituals corresponding with such textual interpretations.⁷⁴ However, the fact that ritual-moral pluralism

---

⁷⁰ In the Confucian tradition, "four rites" refer to attainment of adulthood (*guanli* 冠禮), marriage (*hunli* 婚禮), mourning (*sangli* 喪禮), and ancestral worship (*jili* 祭禮).
⁷¹ This problem did not arise with classical Confucians because they all advanced their ritual theory in the context of "all under Heaven" (*tianxia* 天下) ruled by a universal sage-king.
⁷² Given that Mencius relies only on the moral feeling of compassion, the sprout of *ren*, as evidence of the innateness of all four moral virtues, it seems to be reasonable to assume that in Mencius's moral philosophy ritual propriety is internally connected, even coordinated, with *ren*.
⁷³ This is precisely what some recent strong Confucian perfectionists wish to achieve in China. See Jiang Qing, *Zhengzhi Ruxue: Dangdai Rujia de zhuanxiang, tezhi yu fazhan [Political Confucianism: Contemporary Confucianism's Challenge, Special Quality, and Development]* (Beijing: San lian shu dian, 2003); Kang Xiaoguang, *Renzheng: Zhongguo zhengzhi fazhan de disantiao daolu [Humane Government: A Third Road for the Development of Chinese Politics]* (Singapore: Global Publishing, 2005); Ruiping Fan, *Reconstructionist Confucianism: Rethinking Morality after the West* (Dordrecht: Springer, 2010).
⁷⁴ It is worth noting that during the Chosŏn dynasty (1392–1910) in Korea, especially since the sixteenth century, many neo-Confucian scholars published their own interpretations of Zhu Xi's *Family Rituals* (*Jiali* 家禮) and different regional, scholarly, or political sects or factions adopted different versions of family ritual theories, all with an aim for the most authentic practice of family rituals which in their views embody the truest meaning of filial piety as the root of *ren*. On plural interpretations of Zhu Xi's *Family Rituals* among Korean neo-Confucians, see Young-chin Ko, *Chosŏn chunggi yehaksasangsa [A Historical Study of Ritual Thoughts in the Mid Chosŏn Period]* (Seoul: Han'gilsa, 1995); Hye-sun Yi (ed.), *Chosŏn chunggi yehaksasanggwa ilsangmunhwa: Chuja kagryerŭl chungshimŭro [Ritual Thoughts during the mid Chosŏn Period and the Culture of Everyday Lives: Focusing on Zhu Xi's Family Rituals]* (Seoul: Ehwa Womans University Press, 2008).

may not be devastatingly divisive in a strongly perfectionist Confucian state does not mean that such a state would be necessarily tolerant of unorthodox interpretations of the Confucian canon,[75] nor does it justify a creation of the strongly perfectionist Confucian state as a way to come to terms with moral pluralism in contemporary East Asia.[76]

What drives moral pluralism in East Asia now is not so much different interpretations of the same canon but radical disagreement on the very source of moral authority. Thus, going back to our previous discussion, filial piety might be cherished as an important human/moral virtue by all (at least most) kinds of ethical communities, albeit in varying degrees, but for morally incommensurable reasons and with different sets of practices justified by such reasons. Under East Asia's present circumstance of moral pluralism (or, more accurately, value pluralism), a doctrinal and deeply comprehensive understanding of filial piety (and other human/moral virtues) might help a person as a member of a certain ethical community to become moral from the perspective of the given doctrine, however gendered, hierarchical, or undemocratic it may be, but it is dubious how filial piety thus understood can be embraced by all citizens.

Though public reason Confucianism understands civic virtue as extended from human/moral virtue, it clearly parts company with traditional monistic Confucianism of which Mencian Confucianism is a dominant branch. From a conceptual standpoint, Confucian virtues that are publicly affirmed and promoted in public reason Confucianism are hardly distinguishable from traditional Confucian moral virtues such as, among others, filial piety, respect for elders, and ritual propriety. However, the *public* significance of these virtues as *Confucian* virtues is acknowledged only if they are understood as civic virtues, virtues pertaining to all citizens. Their public-constitutional promotion is not necessarily due to a universal moral assumption that they are human virtues to be embraced

---

[75] It should be reminded that during the heyday of neo-Confucianism, the Korean Confucian state punished some unorthodox Confucian scholars by calling them "despoilers of the Way." See Martina Deuchler, "Despoilers of the Way – Insulters of the Sages: Controversies over the Classics in Seventeenth-Century Korea," in *Culture and the State in Late Chosŏn Korea*, eds. JaHyun K. Haboush and Martina Deuchler (Cambridge: Council on East Asian Studies, Harvard University, 1999), pp. 91–113. Also see Joseph Chan, "Confucian Attitudes toward Ethical Pluralism," in *Confucian Political Ethics*, ed. Daniel A. Bell (Princeton: Princeton University Press, 2008), pp. 113–138.

[76] In this regard, I strongly agree with Joseph Chan, "On Legitimacy of Confucian Constitutionalism," in Jiang Qing, *A Confucian Constitutional Order: How China's Ancient Past Can Shape Its Political Future*, eds. Daniel A. Bell and Ruiping Fan and trans. Edmund Ryden (Princeton: Princeton University Press, 2012), pp. 99–112.

by all, as was claimed by traditional Confucianism, but rather due to their largely instrumental (and perfectionist) role in sustaining and reproducing the Confucian public character of the polity, with ceaseless modifications and adjustments, under the modern circumstances of politics marked by value pluralism and moral disagreement.[77]

One may wonder how public reason Confucianism's instrumental understanding of civic virtue is distinguished from William Galston's pluralist distinction between human virtue and civic virtue, which also appreciates the value of the latter from an instrumental standpoint. The important difference between public reason Confucianism and liberal pluralism with regard to civic virtue is that while the latter is completely disinterested in – almost denies – any moral connection between human and civic virtue, the former acknowledges a connection between the two, though a loose one, and reconceives of virtues that are cherished as human virtues by various associations in civil society (including the Confucian ones) *as* civic virtues that directly contribute to a constitutional order, its public character, and common citizenship. Furthermore, they make citizens *good* in light of Confucian democratic ideals and constitutional purposes.

Seen in this way, public reason Confucianism follows a middle path between perfectionist republicanism as conceived by Paul Weithman and what Galston and company call "political realism" that severs political/civic virtue from human/moral virtue, on the assumption that "appropriate standards of [political] evaluation arise from within politics rather than from an external moral standpoint," emphasizing the internal requirement of political morality as well as the decisionist features of political agency.[78] Even though public reason Confucianism acknowledges the practical distinction between human/moral virtue and citizen/civic virtue, which our modern circumstances require, it does not go further to argue for the autonomy of the political and the idea of political virtue that is completely severed, normatively as well as psychologically,

---

[77] By "largely instrumental" I mean that Confucian civic virtues are not wholly instrumental. In fact, I am sanguine about the possibility that these virtues can be constitutive of a morally attractive, even admirable, form of political life.

[78] William A. Galston, "Realism in Political Theory," *European Journal of Political Theory* 9 (2010), pp. 385–411, at pp. 387–388; Mark Philip, "What Is To Be Done? Political Theory and Political Realism," *European Journal of Political Theory* 9 (2010), pp. 466–484. On "political realism," see also Bernard Williams, *In the Beginning Was the Deed* (Princeton: Princeton University Press, 2005); Raymond Geuss, *Philosophy and Real Politics* (Princeton: Princeton University Press, 2008).

from moral virtue. Philosophically speaking, therefore, public reason Confucianism navigates a difficult terrain between virtue monism and political realism and attempts to balance the two positions by imparting to civic virtue a distinctive public significance, which is morally justified from the perspective of the overall Confucian–democratic constitutional order embedded in value pluralism, while viewing it as extended from and in part motivated by moral virtue.

In the end, public reason Confucianism tracks the complex relationship between moral virtue and political virtue as being derived from fully comprehensive Confucianism. As I argued in Chapter 4, public reason Confucianism is a modern democratic perfectionist Confucianism recreated *from* traditional, fully comprehensive Confucianism, and this sociological connection, rendering the former publicly intelligible as a species of Confucianism, makes it partially comprehensive. The morally "partial" dimension of public reason Confucianism, attained through traditional Confucianism's adaptations to democratic constitutionalism and value pluralism, enables it to make a pluralist distinction between human/moral virtue and citizen/civic virtue. However, its "comprehensive" moral dimension induces it to philosophically reappropriate the monistic Confucian connection between human/moral virtue and citizen/civic virtue through the Confucian moral psychological mechanism of extension.

Therefore, the virtues – such as filial piety, respect for elders, harmony within the family, ancestor worship, and ritual propriety – might (in fact, quite likely will) be cherished by both Confucian associations in civil society and public reason Confucianism, though the institutional meanings of these virtues are radically different. Within Confucian associations the virtues are understood and promoted as universal human virtues and this moral universalism is circumscribed by the moral or religious doctrine each association holds, which defines the ideal of a good human being as well as the proper moral practices to be used in achieving such an ideal. An example might be helpful here. If we render the generic moral virtue of filial piety endorsed by traditional Confucian philosophy as X, the distinctive moral conceptions of filial piety cherished and practiced within particular Confucian moral communities in contemporary East Asian societies can be rendered as $X_1, X_2, X_3 \ldots X_n$, where X represents the virtue's full comprehensive moral character. From the standpoint of public reason Confucianism, however, each association's (fully) comprehensive conception of the good life and/or moral virtue means a particular social expression of a group value, which deserves constitutional protection based on the right to freedom of association.

Still, the "Confucian" virtues promoted by public reason Confucianism as civic virtues are comprehensively Confucian as they were once universal human virtues themselves in premodern Confucian East Asia (the legacy of which is still reflected in customary laws of contemporary East Asia, as we saw in Chapter 3) and are not conceptually distinguished from those virtues cherished in Confucian associations, but they are nonsectarian, nontraditionalist (i.e., nonpatriarchal, nonpatrilineal, and nonandrocentric), and generally germane to all citizens as bridging capital and a civically vitalizing energy for Confucian democratic citizenship. So, for example, filial piety as Confucian civic virtue is not conceptually distinct from either the generic X or its equally comprehensive particulars in various Confucian communities and associations within the society ($X_1, X_2, X_3 \ldots X_n$); generally applied to all citizens who are not traditionalist Confucians, it is only *practically* or *institutionally* differentiated from either version of the fully comprehensive conception of filial piety. Let us call this civic version of filial piety x in contradistinction to its fully comprehensive counterpart of X (and its pluralized variations), where the small x still tracks the concept of the generic X. Nonetheless, by virtue of its moral connection, however attenuated, with the fully comprehensive notion of filial piety (X), the civic filial piety (x) is still morally comprehensive, though only partially, and its partial character is reinforced by its ceaseless cultural negotiations with democratic principles of individual dignity and gender equality, as we have examined in Chapters 3 and 4.

Public reason Confucianism normatively induces members of various associations (including and especially Confucian associations) to reconceive and exercise otherwise sectarian moral virtues as civic virtues, and Confucian civic virtues in return strengthen the public identity of citizens as (modern democratic) Confucian citizens.

CONCLUSION

At this point, a question may arise regarding whether public reason Confucianism is meaningfully differentiated from Joseph Chan's Confucian perfectionism with regard to virtue from a practical standpoint. After all, it can be argued, public reason Confucianism only suggests that citizens in East Asia are to reconceive most traditional Confucian virtues *as* civic virtues and therefore does not introduce a whole new set of virtues as distinctively civic vis-à-vis conventional Confucian virtues. The argument may continue, though Chan does not remake Confucian human/moral virtues into citizen/civic virtues in his valorization of the former over the latter but rather wants to apply them consistently to all life spheres, along with traditional Confucian virtue monism, the practical results of his argument and mine would be the same: citizens of East Asia should exercise certain kinds of Confucian virtues in order to be a good person as well as a good citizen; as long as these virtues are conducive to Confucian citizenship, what practical difference does public reason Confucianism make?

It is true that the difference between public reason Confucianism and Chan's Confucian perfectionism with regard to virtue is primarily philosophical, but the practical-institutional implications of this philosophical difference are rather significant. My argument thus far can be recapitulated in this way: given the way public reason Confucianism is constructed against the backdrop of the democratic and pluralist context, as a partial comprehensive Confucianism distinct from traditional, ethically monistic, and fully comprehensive Confucianism, the practical distinction between human virtue and civic virtue follows from the institutional distinction between Confucian associational membership and Confucian democratic citizenship.

One may oppose that view, since Chan (and many other contemporary Confucian political theorists) does not share my philosophical perspective and instead upholds a different normative framework that does not recognize the constitutional significance of civic virtue and civic education; one may say that it would be pointless to critique Chan's monistic approach to virtue in favor of moral virtue. This critique would make sense if I questioned the virtue monism in Chan's Confucian perfectionism from the perspective of public reason Confucianism. The gist of my critique, however, lies in whether Confucian perfectionism's virtue monism can indeed come to grips with the pluralist reality of contemporary East Asia where citizens are not "Confucian" in a morally monistic sense. Chan attempts to avoid this difficulty by presenting seemingly universal virtues such as respectfulness, trustworthiness, beneficence, lenience, and sincerity as Confucian virtues, but, as I have argued in this chapter and in Chapter 1, such an attempt is likely to eclipse the distinctively Confucian characteristics in the political theory of Confucian perfectionism and make it a borderline liberal, or a certain ideal type of, perfectionism. More importantly, it appears to be limited in responding adequately to actual, Confucianism-related, social and political problems arising in East Asian societies. How to deal with Confucian associations operating on traditionalist Confucianism with an idiosyncratic and highly sectarian interpretation of core Confucian virtues such as filial piety is just one such problem.

My point is that the Confucian virtues or values that East Asians are struggling with in their personal as well as associational lives are not the ideas (or ideals) of filial piety, respect for elders, ritual propriety, or harmony within the family as such, but very specific kinds of virtues, often heavily gendered, strongly affiliated with a particular mode of the family institution. By distinguishing Confucian civic virtues, generally applicable to all Confucian citizens and fully compatible with public equality, from such sectarian Confucian virtues, moral virtues attached to specific gendered social roles, and attributing the latter to associational membership (including membership in clan and other traditionalist Confucian organizations) and the former to Confucian democratic citizenship, public reason Confucianism opens up a way to promote Confucian virtues publicly without doing injustice to the plurality of values in civil society.

A question still remains: even if the philosophical need to revamp Confucian virtue monism is granted, how would public reason Confucianism respond to Chan's and other Confucian perfectionists' deep skepticism toward civic virtues, most importantly political participation? I turn to this question in Chapter 6.

6

The right to political participation

In Chapter 2, we called the third proposition (P3) of public reason Confucianism the public equality proposition, which stipulates that *in a Confucian society, all citizens are equal to one another qua public citizens and together they exercise popular sovereignty*. In Chapters 3 and 4 we examined the practical implications of P3 in a Confucian constitutional democracy (i.e., a polity reconceived from the standpoint of public reason Confucianism) with special focus on gender equality. It should be clear by now that P3 is of pivotal importance in the overall theoretical structure of public reason Confucianism, rendering it a perfectionist yet robustly democratic political theory. Other theoretical stipulations, especially P4 (democratic pluralism), P5 (Confucian public reason), and P6 (Confucian legitimacy), are all philosophically dependent on P3. More specifically, P3 offers a foundational reason for moderating individual and associational diversity that might encroach upon citizens' equal public status, renders Confucian public reason not so much as the reason of the ruling elites but as that of the ordinary citizens, and encourages democratic citizens to forge the fair terms of integration for immigrants. The present chapter shifts our attention from P3's practical implications to its core postulates – namely political equality and popular sovereignty – and explores the proposition's philosophical implications for the right to political participation. My central argument is that the core postulates of P3 combine to justify the right to political participation, making this another crucial postulate of the proposition.

The incorporation of the interrelated postulates of political equality, popular sovereignty, and right to political participation in the public equality proposition is perhaps the most controversial aspect of public reason Confucianism, distinguishing it not only from traditional Confucian philosophy, arguably a complete stranger to democratic values,[1] but also from other recent Confucian political theories (mostly those advocating Confucian political meritocracy) that reject, either completely or partially, the universal right to political participation.[2] For instance, though not denying the value of political participation wholesale, Daniel Bell justifies political elitism in a Confucian society by saying,

> In East Asian societies with a Confucian heritage, where the good of the family has been regarded as the key to the good life for more than two millennia, the republican tradition is so far removed from people's self-understanding that it is a complete nonstarter. Most people have devoted their time and energy to family and other "local" obligations, with political decision making left to an educated, public-spirited elite. Elite politics does not rule out democratic participation by ordinary citizens, but democracy will take "minimal" forms, not much more demanding than visiting the voting booth every few years.[3]

As noted in the previous chapter, a more robust philosophical critique of popular political participation has been advanced by Joseph Chan, who rejects democratic values of political equality and popular sovereignty for reasons of motivation, opportunity, and assurance.[4] Overall, Chan's philosophical skepticism toward political participation is based on the opportunity reason, echoing Bell's argument for nonpolitical social participation:

---

[1] On this point, see Chenyang Li, "Confucian Value and Democratic Value," *Journal of Value Inquiry* 31 (1997), pp. 183–193; David Elstein, "Why Early Confucianism Cannot Generate Democracy," *Dao* 9 (2010), pp. 427–443; Eric L. Hutton, "Un-Democratic Values in Plato and Xunzi," in *Polishing the Chinese Mirror*, eds. Marthe Chandler and Ronnie Littlejohn (New York: Global Scholarly Publications, 2008), pp. 313–330. For an opposite view, see Sangjun Kim, *Yugyoŭi chŏngch'ijŏk muŭishik* [*The Political Subconsciousness of Confucianism*] (Seoul: Kŭlhangari, 2014); Jung In Kang, *Nŏmnadŭmŭi chŏngch'isasang* [*A Political Thought of Cultural Crossing*] (Seoul: Humanitasŭ, 2013), pp. 189–231.
[2] Important exceptions include Sor-hoon Tan, *Confucian Democracy: A Deweyan Reconstruction* (Albany: State University of New York Press, 2004) and Stephen C. Angle, *Contemporary Confucian Political Philosophy: Toward Progressive Confucianism* (Cambridge: Polity, 2012).
[3] Daniel A. Bell, *Beyond Liberal Democracy: Political Thinking for an East Asian Context* (Princeton: Princeton University Press, 2006), pp. 150–151. For a similar minimalist view of democracy, see Tongdong Bai, "A Mencian Version of Limited Democracy," *Res Publica* 14 (2008), pp. 19–34.
[4] Joseph Chan, *Confucian Perfectionism: A Political Philosophy for Modern Times* (Princeton: Princeton University Press, 2014), p. 85.

> Participation can take place in many social contexts, and it is not clear that participation in the political context is necessary for moral growth. What is important to our moral growth is that we participate in a common life and are given certain tasks and responsibilities in a social group and institution. ... In a modern society there are numerous social groups that present such opportunities, whether they exist in the context of families, the workplace, schools, religious organizations, civil society groups, or political parties. While these social groups, taken together, constitute a fertile soil for people's moral growth, there seems to be no particular group in which participation is indispensable, except perhaps, from the Confucian point of view, the family. For this reason, the participation argument in the context of a modern society does not seem to provide a strong justification for the necessity of political democracy.[5]

As this statement evidently suggests, Confucian meritocrats' distinction between social and political participation and strong preference for the former over the latter is not merely due to their philosophical commitment to Confucianism, in which "the political" entertains no ethical privilege over other social realms.[6] The fundamental reason for this preference is their insufficient sensitivity to the *circumstances of modern politics*, the key characteristics of which are value pluralism, moral disagreement, and the coerciveness of political power (and that of the state as an institutionally organized and concentrated political power).

One of my key underlying premises in this chapter is that the traditional Confucian conception of the political as merely one of many ethical realms is no longer tenable within a modern Confucian constitutional polity. In a preconstitutional age, there can hardly be an

---

[5] Joseph Chan, "'Self-Restriction' and the Confucian Case for Democracy," *Philosophy East and West* 64:3 (2014), pp. 785–795, at pp. 790–791. Note that Chan calls the following statement by Angle *the participation argument*: "[T]he situations in which one can actively participate in shaping public goals and endeavors are of great importance to one's moral development. ... [I]f a state were to make all the major decisions for its citizens, leaving them space for decisions only about personal matters, it would be infantilizing its citizens. That is, it would be denying them access to situations crucial for developing moral maturity. Genuine ethical development requires engaging with issues in all their complexity, because only by recognizing the many dimensions of each given situation can we see our way toward harmonious resolutions" (Angle, *Contemporary Confucian Political Philosophy*, p. 115).

[6] The reason for this is closely related to Confucianism's multilayered, heavily ethical, understanding of the public (*gong* 公). For an excellent study of the Confucian conception of the public, see Chun-chieh Huang, "East Asian Conceptions of the Public and Private Realms," in *Taking Confucian Ethics Seriously: Contemporary Theories and Applications*, eds. Kam-Por Yu, Julia Tao, and Philip J. Ivanhoe (Albany: State University of New York Press, 2010), pp. 73–97. Also see Seung-Hwan Lee, "The Concept of *Gong* in Traditional Korea and Its Modern Transformations," *Korea Journal* 43:4 (2003), pp. 137–163 (especially pp. 140–149).

intelligent idea of citizenship; there the political community exists primarily as a people sharing stories of their own peoplehood[7] or nation, an intergenerational community that has cultural inheritance.[8] Under the constitutional order, however, the people or nation is transformed into and constituted as citizens and the office of citizenship, with associated rights and accompanying duties and obligations, is constitutionally organized and promulgated, thereby giving rise to an important legal–political distinction between the private individual and the public citizen within a single person.[9] Given that traditional Confucianism made no such distinction and that contemporary Confucian political theorists largely embrace modern constitutional arrangements,[10] to seek philosophical justification in traditional Confucianism for the valorization of social participation over political participation in contemporary East Asia is likely to prove both implausible and anachronistic.

Citizens are both being constituted and constituting. In being constituted, citizens acquire their distinctive public identity and in Chapter 3 we discussed extensively this aspect (i.e., the perfectionist ambition) of public reason Confucian constitutionalism. Just as important, perhaps more so, is the constituting dimension of citizenship: it is citizens in whose name the constitution, the highest norm of the political community, is made and remade, and it is within the parameters of the constitutional principles that public policies are and ought to be designed, then implemented. Put differently, "the members of the population acting as citizens determine how things are set up and run."[11]

Of course, it is open for debate whether citizens' constituting power and control over the state with regard to both the order it imposes on its citizens and the overall direction along which it pushes public policies are to be exercised directly or vicariously through the representation mechanism. Equally debatable is whether or not citizens must actively participate

---

[7] See Rogers M. Smith, *Stores of Peoplehood: The Politics and Morals of Political Membership* (Cambridge: Cambridge University Press, 2003).
[8] For this particular understanding of nation, see Bernard Yack, *Nationalism and the Moral Psychology of Community* (Chicago: University of Chicago Press, 2012).
[9] Cf. Benjamin R. Barber, *Strong Democracy: Participatory Politics for a New Age*, 20th anniversary edition (Berkeley: University of California Press, 2003), p. xxvii.
[10] A notable exception is Jiang Qing's radical proposal for Confucian constitutionalism. See his *A Confucian Constitutional Order: How China's Ancient Past Can Shape Its Political Future*, eds. Daniel A. Bell and Ruiping Fan and trans. Edmund Ryden (Princeton: Princeton University Press, 2012).
[11] Philip Pettit, *On the People's Terms: A Republican Theory and Model of Democracy* (Cambridge: Cambridge University Press, 2012), p. 286.

in all public affairs at every possible moment as the Rousseauist republican ideal recommends.[12] Nonetheless, citizens' *right* to political participation in terms of democratic control and direction can neither be dispensed with nor compromised. This right could be supplemented, even enhanced, by participation in various social groups and organizations in civil society but it can never be replaced by opportunities for social participation and accompanying social capital, even when social capital thus accumulated can contribute to personal moral growth. We should not forget Tocqueville's reminder that civil society is quintessentially a *political* institution, indispensable to political liberty and public freedom by functioning as a bulwark and counterforce against the centralized power of government and the tyranny of the majority.[13] Moral growth disconnected from civic virtue and social participation decoupled from political participation are likely to incubate docility, the worst enemy of citizenship.[14]

In this chapter I argue that the right to political participation, the third postulate deriving from the public equality proposition, is an integral element of public reason Confucianism, in that without it, the constituting dimension of Confucian democratic citizenship can hardly be satisfied. The challenge, of course, is how to justify this right from a Confucian perspective while simultaneously satisfying P3's postulates of political equality and popular sovereignty.

In order to meet this challenge, I proceed in the following way. First, I reinterpret classical Confucianism, particularly Mencian Confucianism, which had the greatest influence on traditional Confucians' philosophical imagination, ethical thought, and political ideas, with special focus on moral equality and human dignity, and draw attention to the apparent

---

[12] Even strong democrats such as Benjamin Barber who are strongly influenced by the Rousseauist ideal of direct democracy do not advocate such a republican active citizenship. Barber, for one, argues that "[c]itizens are governors: self-governors, communal governors, masters of their own fate. They need not participate all of the time in all public affairs, but they should participate at least some of the time in at least some public affairs" (Barber, *Strong Democracy*, p. xxix).

[13] See Alexis de Tocqueville, *Democracy in America*, trans. Harvey C. Mansfield and Delba Winthrop (Chicago: University of Chicago Press, 2000), pp. 52, 181–182. Also see Sungmoon Kim, "On Korean Dual Civil Society: Thinking through Tocqueville and Confucius," *Contemporary Political Theory* 9:4 (2010), pp. 434–457.

[14] Sheri Berman's case study of the collapse of the Weimar Republic powerfully attests to the fact that high social participation generating a plethora of social capital in local communities is not enough in sustaining a democratic regime unless there is robust political participation in formal political institutions. See her "Civil Society and the Collapse of the Weimar Republic," *World Politics* 49 (1997), pp. 401–429.

tension between his expressed commitment to these moral values and his lingering adherence to political inequality embedded in the previous Zhou dynasty's aristocratic political ritualism. This textual reinterpretation is followed by a reconstruction of Mencian political thought, marked by an uneasy tension between moral equality and political inequality, in a way directly aligned with Mencius's moral and philosophical commitment to moral equality and human dignity. Here I argue that Mencius's conscious refutation of the exclusive connection between sagehood and kingship not only enables what can be called the *democratization* of the ideal of sagehood but, more importantly, the universal accessibility of public office to *any* virtuous person regardless of his social pedigree, engendering a new ideal of political equality. From this reconstructed Mencian idea of political equality understood in terms of *equal moral opportunity to become a public official*, I further derive and justify seminal Mencian Confucian ideas of popular sovereignty and the right to political participation. I then explore how interrelated values of popular sovereignty, political equality, and political participation justified *in Confucian terms* can give rise to a more robust moral right to political participation under the circumstances of modern politics marked by value pluralism and moral disagreement. I conclude this chapter by discussing how embracing the right to political participation as integral to its normative system renders public reason Confucianism distinctively different from Chan's moderate political Confucian perfectionism in particular and Confucian meritocratic perfectionism in general.

MORAL EQUALITY AND HUMAN DIGNITY: A MENCIAN CONFUCIAN PERSPECTIVE

Moral equality

When I outlined the six propositions of public reason Confucianism in Chapter 2, readers, especially those familiar with Confucian philosophy, may have questioned on what Confucian grounds I was presenting public equality as public reason Confucianism's foundational philosophical proposition. Even if public equality itself can be accepted as an important component of modern Confucian political theory aimed specifically at a self-governing Confucian people under the modern constitutional order, one may challenge how the posited postulates of political equality and popular sovereignty can be justified in light of Confucianism. Offering a satisfying answer to this question is additionally important because it can also lead us to find a way to derive the right to political participation from Confucianism. That is, only under the assumptions of political equality and popular sovereignty, which are core democratic ideals, can we begin to think about, let alone justify, the right to political participation for all citizens.[15] With this premise in mind, I now turn to Mencius, one of the originators of the Confucian philosophical tradition.

As is well known, Mencius begins his moral philosophy by grappling with what Confucius left ambiguous, that is, his controversial statement on human nature: "Human beings are close by nature [although] they can be different from one another through repeated practices."[16] The problem with this statement is that Confucius never explicates what "close" (*jin* 近) means: does it imply that human beings are by nature good, or bad, or good and bad, or morally neutral? Mencius attempts to resolve the ambiguity in Confucius's statement by claiming as well as demonstrating that human beings are by nature good (*xing shan* 性善). For him, however, the goodness of human nature does not mean moral perfection. As we saw in Chapter 5, the kernel of Mencius's *xing-shan* thesis consists of the belief that human beings are born with moral sensibilities, which incline them toward moral goodness, and that such inclinations are a critical part of human flourishing. According to him, humans are endowed with four "sprouts" (*duan* 端) of virtue, which he describes in terms of moral sentiments – the feeling of pity and compassion is the sprout of humanness (*ren* 仁), the feeling of shame and aversion is the sprout of rightness (*yi* 義), the feeling of modesty and compliance is the sprout of propriety (*li* 禮), and the sense of right and wrong is the sprout of wisdom (*zhi* 智).[17]

What is important in the present context is Mencius's claim that *all* human beings have these moral sprouts. Implicit in this claim is that *all* human beings, regardless of their social backgrounds, are equal, naturally as well as morally.[18] This does not mean that all human beings, simply because they have equal moral potential, will *become* morally good with no qualitative distinction. As Donald Munro has noted, Confucians, Mencius in particular, distinguish natural equality, equality in the sense that human beings are born equal (which encompasses Mencian moral

---

[15] On the other side of the same coin, it is because of their rejection or partial embracement of these core democratic ideals that advocates of Confucian meritocracy either reject or only partially allow the right to political participation.
[16] *Analects* 17.2 (my translation).   [17] *Mencius* 2A6.
[18] Irene Bloom, "Mencius and Human Rights," in *Confucianism and Human Rights*, eds. Wm. Theodore de Bary and Tu Wei-ming (New York: Columbia University Press, 1998), pp. 94–116, at pp. 101–102.

equality), from evaluative equality, which suggests that all human beings are of equal worth, thus deserving equal treatment.[19] One of Mencius's greatest insights is that natural or moral equality is perfectly compatible with evaluative inequality as similar moral potential can be developed to varying degrees. By using his trademark "agricultural" metaphor of moral self-cultivation, captured aptly by Philip Ivanhoe in terms of a *developmental model*,[20] Mencius gives a powerful statement on how moral equality and evaluative inequality can overlap.

> In years of abundance, most of the young people have the wherewithal to be good, while in years of adversity, most of them become violent. This is not a matter of a difference in the native capacities sent down by Heaven but rather of what overwhelms their minds. Now, let barley be sown and covered with earth; the ground being the same, and the time of planting also the same, it grows rapidly, and in due course of time, it all ripens. Though there may be differences in the yield, this is because the fertility of the soil, the nourishment of the rain and the dew, and the human effort invested are not the same.[21]

It is in this line of reasoning that some recent Confucian meritocrats claim that the gist of Mencian Confucianism (or early Confucianism in general) lies in political meritocracy, a rule by superior virtue and ability.[22] However, singularly concentrated on Mencius's acknowledgement of evaluative inequality, the meritocratic interpretation misses Mencius's central argument: although the quality of moral development depends greatly on the degree of effort a person has put in (as well as the environment and opportunities), evaluative inequalities among people do not disqualify the fundamental similarity among human beings. Put differently, what Mencius is concerned with is not so much to classify people into different political groups based on the level of their moral cultivation but to encourage all of them to make an effort at moral development.

That Mencius's focus is on moral effort, not so much on evaluative inequality, is even more evident in his famous analogy between Ox Mountain, which has become barren due to excessive logging and

---

[19] Donald J. Munro, *The Concept of Man in Early China* (Stanford: Stanford University Press, 1969), pp. 1–2.
[20] Philip J. Ivanhoe, *Confucian Moral Self Cultivation* (Indianapolis: Hackett, 2000), pp. 15–28.
[21] *Mencius* 6A7. Throughout this chapter, the English translation of the text of the *Mengzi* 孟子 is adapted from *Mencius*, trans. Irene Bloom and ed. Philip J. Ivanhoe (New York: Columbia University Press, 2009).
[22] See Chenyang Li, "Equality and Inequality in Confucianism," *Dao* 11 (2012), pp. 295–313; Bai, "A Mencian Version of Limited Democracy."

sheep-grazing, and the people who have failed to cultivate their innate good nature and, as a result, have gone astray. Mencius says,

> Seeing this barrenness, people suppose that the mountain was never wooded. But how could this be the nature of the mountain? So it is also with what is preserved in a human being: could it be that anyone should lack the mind of humanness and rightness? ... Thus, given nourishment, there is nothing that will not grow; lacking nourishment, there is nothing that will not be destroyed. Confucius said, "Hold on and you preserve it; let it go and you lose it. The time of its going out and coming in is not fixed, and there is no one who knows the place where it goes." In saying this, he was referring to the mind.[23]

Again, Mencius's point here is not to stress how immoral or uncultivated laypeople are and thus to politically differentiate them from moral elites who are qualified to rule, but rather to draw our attention to what *all* human beings are capable of given their similar human nature.

One may challenge Mencius's moral egalitarianism by pointing out that the claim that all human beings are capable of moral effort does not necessarily entail that all are *equally capable* of moral effort. The implicit reasoning underlying this challenge is that even if all human beings possess a similarly good nature, not only do people differ in their moral efforts, but, more tellingly, many of them fail to become morally good. If people differ in their effort-making abilities, how can Mencius's moral egalitarianism hold? As George Sher notes, however, the *possession* of an ability to exert effort is distinguished from the *exercise* of that ability and "[w]e cannot infer the conclusion that people differ in their effort-making abilities directly from the fact that they differ in their efforts."[24] Although Mencius does not offer a robust philosophical explanation on equal effort-making capacity, throughout the *Mencius* he seemingly believes that there is no significant difference among human beings in this basic human capacity. Consider the following statement by Mencius:

> What people are able to do without having learned it is an expression of original, good ability. What they know without having to think about it is an expression of original, good knowledge. There are no young children who do not know enough to love their parents, and there are none who, as they grow older, do not know enough to respect their older brothers. To be affectionate toward those close to one – this is humanness (*ren* 仁). To have respect for elders – this is rightness (*yi* 義). All that remains is to extend these to the entire world.[25]

[23] *Mencius* 6A8.
[24] George Sher, "Effort, Ability, and Personal Desert," *Philosophy and Public Affairs* 8:4 (1979), pp. 361–379, at p. 368.
[25] *Mencius* 7A15.

For Mencius what counts as "moral effort" is one's capability of cultivating the virtues, and surprisingly, he understands the kernel of these cardinal moral virtues as consisting of nothing more than one's ability "to be affectionate toward those close to one" and "to have respect for elders." Of human beings, Mencius asks, who is incapable of doing these things?[26] Who would possibly be unable to extend such fundamental human affection to others? Mencius's unswerving conviction that all human beings are equally capable of becoming virtuous, regardless of one's sociopolitical status or physical endowment, is most clearly revealed when he boldly claims that "[t]he sage and we are the same in kind."[27] Quoting Yan Yuan, Confucius's favorite disciple, Mencius proclaims the fundamental equality of human beings as this: "What kind of man was Shun? What kind of man am I? One who exerts effort will also be like [the sages]."[28]

Thus understood, Mencius's idea of human nature as inherently good in terms of the capacity of all human beings for moral development should not be understood *merely* as a philosophical account of human nature. In a more profound sense, it is unflinching faith in human perfectibility, an ability possessed by *all human beings* to become a sage, a perfect moral paragon.[29] This is how later Confucians, including Song-

---

[26] See *Mencius* 6B2 where Mencius says, "To walk slowly behind an older brother is called fraternal; to walk quickly ahead of an older brother is called unfraternal. Is there anyone who is unable to walk slowly? It is just that he does not do it. The Way of Yao and Shun was that of filial and fraternal duty, that is all. By wearing the clothes of Yao, speaking the words of Yao, and performing the actions of Yao, you become Yao.... The Way is like a great road. It is not difficult to know it."

[27] *Mencius* 6A7.   [28] *Mencius* 3A1.

[29] I admit that this statement, though widely accepted by Chinese philosophers and sinologists, is not uncontroversial. For instance, scholars who interpret (early) Confucian ethics in terms of the virtue ethics of flourishing a la Aristotle take different levels of moral achievement seriously and claim that for early Confucians, becoming a sage was not the goal that ordinary people *should* aim at. In this interpretation, while sages are likened to be "moral connoisseurs" who have a special taste of virtue and thus are able to *fully* realize it upon themselves, ordinary people are understood as lacking the capacity to become a sage, merely as those who are encouraged to become a decent and good person, a *junzi* 君子. One of the pieces of textual evidence that these scholars rely on in making this claim is that Mencius thought sages are extremely rare, appearing around one every five hundred years. The trouble is that this interpretation does not take the distinction between the sage, a moral ideal, and the sage-king, a political ideal, seriously. It is true that Mencius (and Confucius) thought that a rise of the sage-king is an extremely rare event but it is not entirely clear that he believed that ordinary people lack the capacity to become a sage. On the virtue-ethical interpretation of early Confucianism, see Eric L. Hutton, "Moral Connoisseurship in Mengzi," in *Essays on the Moral Philosophy of Mengzi*, eds. Xiusheng Liu and Philip J. Ivanhoe (Indianapolis: Hackett, 2002), pp. 163–186; "Han Feizi's Criticism of

Ming neo-Confucians, understood Mencius's *xing-shan* thesis,[30] and, more strikingly, it is on the basis of this Mencian faith in universal human perfectibility that some later Confucians, such as Li Zhi,[31] and some remarkable female neo-Confucians in Korea were able to espouse moral and spiritual equality between men and women.[32]

Prior to Confucius and especially Mencius, sagehood, the ultimate stage of moral perfection, had been exclusively tied with kingship, and virtue (*de* 德) had been considered a divine benefaction from the king (and some selective aristocrats) to the people, authorized by the Mandate of Heaven (*tianming* 天命) to rule as a mediator between Heaven and the people.[33] Inspired by Confucius, who made virtue accessible to all human beings,[34] Mencius further advanced Confucius's seminal moral egalitarianism by stipulating as well as demonstrating the innateness of virtues (albeit in an incipient form) within *every* single human being. In doing so, he enabled the people not only to directly access virtue but to attain sagehood.

Human dignity

Mencian innovation in the East Asian philosophical tradition does not end with his *xing-shan* thesis, the culmination of which is the accessibility of sagehood by *all human beings*. Certainly, for Mencius, sagehood is a moral *stage* to arrive at through relentless self-cultivation as attested in the following statement: "When [virtue] is filled up within oneself, one

---

Confucianism and its Implications for Virtue Ethics," *Journal of Moral Philosophy* 5 (2008), pp. 423–453.

[30] Wm. Theodore de Bary, *The Liberal Tradition in China* (New York: Columbia University Press, 1983).

[31] See Pauline C. Lee, *Li Zhi, Confucianism, and the Virtue of Desire* (Albany: State University of New York Press, 2012).

[32] See Sungmoon Kim, "The Way to Become a Female Sage: Im Yunjidang's Confucian Feminism," *Journal of the History of Ideas* 75:3 (2014), pp. 395–416; "From Wife to Moral Teacher: Kang Chŏngildang's Neo-Confucian Self-Cultivation," *Asian Philosophy* 24:1 (2014), pp. 28–47.

[33] Julia Ching, *Mysticism and Kingship in China: The Heart of Chinese Wisdom* (Cambridge: Cambridge University Press, 1997); Huaiyu Wang, "A Genealogical Study of *De*: Poetical Correspondence of Sky, Earth, and Humankind in the Early Chinese Virtuous Rule of Benefaction," *Philosophy East and West* 65:1 (2015), pp. 81–124.

[34] H. G. Creel, *Confucius and the Chinese Way* (New York: Harper & Row, 1949), pp. 75–99; Frederick W. Mote, *Intellectual Foundations of China* (New York: Alfred A. Knopf, 1971), pp. 39–40; Benjamin I. Schwartz, *The World of Thought in Ancient China* (Cambridge: Belknap, 1985), p. 76.

may be called 'beautiful.' When it is filled up and brightly displayed, one may be called 'great.' When one is great and exercises a transforming influence, one may be called a 'sage.'"[35] One way to make sense of Mencius's idea is that sagehood is the final stage of moral self-cultivation, attainable only by extraordinary people, and the state of being a gentleman (*junzi* 君子) is the moral stage that all human beings can reasonably aim to arrive at. As noted, there is no denying that Mencius acknowledged evaluative inequality. However, when Mencius reappropriated the pre-Confucian ideal of sagehood in a way accessible to all human beings, thereby making it a universal moral ideal, not only did he believe that *everyone* can become a sage by practicing moral self-cultivation (even if in the nonideal situation he, like Confucius, sought to produce *junzi*), but he also saw *everyone* as a dignified person, regardless of his or her level of moral development, a person who has fundamental moral worth. Consider the following statement:

If, among a person's desires, there were none greater than life, then why should he not do anything necessary in order to cling to life? If, among the things he detested, there were none greater than death, why should he not do what he had to in order to avoid danger? There is a means by which one may preserve life, and yet he does not employ it; there is a means by which one may avoid danger, and yet one does not adopt it. Thus there are things that we desire more than life and things that we detest more than death. It is not exemplary persons alone who have this mind; all human beings have it. It is only that the exemplary ones are able to avoid losing it; that is all.

Suppose there are a basketful of rice and a bowlful of soup. If I get them, I may remain alive; if I do not get them, I may well die. If they are offered contemptuously, a wayfarer will decline to accept them; if they are offered after having been trampled upon, a beggar will not demean himself by taking them. And yet when it comes to a stipend of ten thousand *zhong*, I accept them without regard for decorum and rightness. What do the ten thousand *zhong* add to me? ... What formerly I would not accept even at the risk of death, I now accept for the sake of beautiful houses. ... Could such things not have been declined as well? This is what is called "losing one's original mind."[36]

The most common interpretation of this passage draws attention to Mencius's emphasis of rightness (*yi*) over material advantages (even including life in a purely materialistic or hedonistic sense) from the perspective of his apparently moralistic extolment of virtues *ren* and *yi* over profit (*li* 利) as most clearly shown in his famous conversation with

---

[35] *Mencius* 7B25.   [36] *Mencius* 6A10.

King Hui of Liang in the opening lines of the *Mencius*.[37] It is arguable whether Mencius indeed pitted morality against material interest,[38] but his key point is that ordinary people often lose their righteous minds, which are still there, deep in their hearts, when they pursue material interests blindly.[39] As Irene Bloom observes, however, what is also found in this statement is Mencius's acknowledgment of the sense of dignity.[40] Though all human beings desire life and detest death, there are times they desire something other than life (i.e., rightness) and detest something more than death (i.e., something dishonorable). Even the most uncultivated people such as wayfarers and beggars hate being treated with disrespect or contempt, even if such might be the only way they can be fed. Implicit in the passage is Mencius's conviction that no one should be treated with disrespect due to his or her low sociopolitical or economic standing.

Understanding Mencius's virtue ethics as a moral justification for evaluative inequality and political meritocracy, some contemporary Confucian scholars argue that in Mencius's moral and political thought only those who are virtuous have moral dignity. In this view, dignity is a sort of entitlement attached to a person of virtuous character. However, Mencius's own view belies this interpretation because he does not necessarily associate human dignity with the achievement of high levels of virtue. For him, dignity is the moral entitlement of *everyone* qua human being, and it is rooted in the foundational idea that all human beings are able to become sages. Thus understood, to distinguish between sagehood and the ideal of sagehood is of crucial importance in making proper sense of Mencius's idea of human dignity: while in Mencius's virtue ethics sagehood is the final stage of moral self-cultivation, hence subject to evaluative inequality, in his overall moral and political philosophy the *ideal* of sagehood or human perfectibility entails a reconceptualization of the moral worth of human beings *as they are*, that is, all human beings are

---

[37] Mencius says, "Let the king speak only of humanness (*ren*) and rightness (*yi*). What need has he to speak of profit?" (*Mencius* 1A1).
[38] For a skeptical view on the conventional view, see Sungmoon Kim, "Politics and Interest in Early Confucianism," *Philosophy East and West* 64:2 (2014), pp. 425–448.
[39] Mencius also says, "[A]ll human beings have in themselves what is honorable (*gui* 貴). It is only that they do not think about it; that is all" (*Mencius* 6A17). Xunzi echoes Mencius by saying that "[h]umans have *qi* [vital force] and life and awareness, and moreover they have *yi*. And so they are the most precious (*gui* 貴) things under Heaven" (*Xunzi* 9.16a). The English translation of the *Xunzi* 荀子 is adapted from *Xunzi: The Complete Text*, trans. Eric L. Hutton (Princeton: Princeton University Press, 2014).
[40] Bloom, "Mencius and Human Rights," pp. 107–108.

capable of sagehood and as far as such fundamental moral capability is inherent in human nature, *all* are morally dignified. In short, for Mencius human dignity derives directly from (natural) moral equality.

The question of political equality

At this point a question may arise: why did Mencius not further advocate political equality, a core postulate of the public equality proposition? To many contemporary scholars, juxtaposition of moral equality and political inequality in Mencius's overall philosophical thought may look odd, because in liberal political theory equality among citizens (i.e., political equality) derives directly from the foundational normative conception of persons as free and equal (i.e., moral equality).[41] Why did Mencius not approach the question of political equality directly from his philosophical ideas of moral equality and human dignity? An important clue to answering this question can be gleaned from Mencius's lingering adherence to political ritualism established during the Zhou 周 dynasty (1044–256 BCE), at the center of which lies the universal monarch, the Zhou king.[42]

Mencius acknowledged that there are some fundamental goods to which all human beings are entitled, but he claimed that when the government fails to deliver such goods, the remedy ought to be sought according to procedures stipulated in the rites or rituals, and therefore only by aristocrats, the carriers of rituals, who were simultaneously regulated by them. Though Mencius was deeply concerned with the people's moral and material well-being and he believed in their moral entitlement to certain goods, he (following Zhou ritualism) did not

---

[41] See most notably Amy Gutmann, *Liberal Equality* (Cambridge: Cambridge University Press, 1983); Charles R. Beitz, *Political Equality* (Princeton: Princeton University Press, 1989); Joshua Cohen, "Is There a Human Right to Democracy?," in *The Egalitarian Conscience*, ed. Christine Sypnowich (Oxford: Oxford University Press, 2006), pp. 226–250. Among recent Confucian political theorists Ranjoo S. Herr attempts to derive the related notions of political equality, Confucian participatory politics, and collective self-determination from the Confucian idea of moral equality. See her "Confucian Democracy and Equality," *Asian Philosophy* 20:3 (2010), pp. 261–282.

[42] In this regard, Mencius faithfully followed Confucius whose most eminent concern was to restore the Zhou civilization that he admired the most among the three civilizations of Chinese antiquity by calling it "this culture of ours" (*siwen* 斯文). For Confucius's strong attachment to Zhou ritual-based civilization, see *Analects* 3.14; 7.5; 9.5. Also see Kung-chuan Hsiao, *A History of Chinese Political Thought, Vol. 1: From The Beginnings to the Sixth Century A.D.*, trans. Frederick W. Mote (Princeton: Princeton University Press, 1979), chap. 2.

promote active political agency among laypeople.[43] Discrepancy between universalist concern with the well-being of the entire political community and selective endorsement of active political agency in Mencius's political thought is best shown in his famous justification of tyrannicide, which many modern scholars have used to interpret Mencius as having advocated the people's *right* to rebellion.[44]

When King Xuan of Qi asks whether it is true that Tang (a sage-king who founded the Shang 商 dynasty [c. 1600–1100]) banished Jie (the last ruler of the Xia 夏 dynasty [c. 2205–1600]) and King Wu (a sage-king who co-founded the Zhou dynasty with his father, King Wen) assaulted *Zhou* (the last ruler of the Shang dynasty), Mencius responds, "One who offends against humaneness is called a brigand; one who offends against rightness is called an outlaw. Someone who is a brigand and an outlaw is called a mere fellow. I have heard of the punishment of a mere fellow *Zhou* but never of the slaying of a ruler."[45] Now consider the following statement by Mencius:

There are ministers who are from the royal line and ministers who are of other surnames.... If the ruler has great faults, they should remonstrate with him. If, after they have done so repeatedly, he does not listen, they should depose him.... [As for high ministers of a different surname] they should remonstrate with [the ruler]. If they do so repeatedly, and he does not listen, they should leave.[46]

Mencius's key argument is that even though the ruler has immense moral and political responsibility to protect the people's moral and material well-being, when he has failed in this fundamental moral duty and has become a tyrant, the (ritual-prescribed) *right* to depose him falls upon a selected group of aristocrats. Even in the passage quoted here, where Mencius appears to endorse the people's right to tyrannicide, the agent who is to actually carry it out is the tyrant's sagacious minister, not laypeople. In another place, Mencius calls the ministers who are entitled

---

[43] On this point, see Justin Tiwald, "A Right of Rebellion in the *Mengzi*?" *Dao* 7 (2008), pp. 269–282; Sungmoon Kim, "Confucian Constitutionalism: Mencius and Xunzi on Virtue, Ritual, and Royal Transmission," *The Review of Politics* 73:3 (2011), pp. 371–399.

[44] See, among others, Sumner B. Twiss, "A Constructive Framework for Discussing Confucianism and Human Rights" and Chung-ying Cheng, "Transforming Confucian Virtues into Human Rights: A Study of Human Agency and Potency in Confucian Ethics," both in de Bary and Tu, *Confucianism and Human Rights*, pp. 27–53 and pp. 142–153 respectively.

[45] *Mencius* 1B8. Note that Bloom, the translator, has italicized "Zhou" 紂 here in order to distinguish it from "Zhou" 周, the name of an ancient Chinese dynasty.

[46] *Mencius* 5B9.

to depose the incumbent king "Heaven's delegated officers" (*tianli* 天吏),[47] thus differentiating them from the laypeople who lack this important *political right*.

That said, Mencius's fundamental political premise that only (selected) aristocrats are permitted by Heaven to remedy the government's failure to deliver essential human goods should not be understood as representative of his philosophical claim. The inconsistency between Mencius's philosophical advocacy of moral equality and individual dignity and his subscription to political inequality only reveals that Mencius, like Confucius, had yet to clearly part company with the pre-Confucian political ritualism of feudal aristocracy embedded in Zhou civilization. My point here is that the political inequality that we occasionally encounter in the *Mencius* is not necessarily Mencius's most developed philosophical ideas. When approached independently from its foundational virtue-ethics,[48] Mencius's political theory can be easily mistaken as merely reiterating moral ideals and political practices prevalent during the Zhou period.

If conceived directly in light of Mencius's philosophical commitment to moral equality and human dignity, however, his political theory can be freshly revealing, though this would require a substantive reconstruction of it, given that Mencius was neither a democrat nor a self-conscious advocate of popular political right. But such reconstruction is necessary not only for exploring the political implications of Mencius's ideas of moral equality and human dignity, uninhibited by his cultural loyalty to Zhou ritualism, but, more importantly, for modernizing Confucianism in a way compatible with public equality, indispensable under the circumstances of modern politics marked by value pluralism and moral disagreement. I take up this reconstruction project in the next section.[49]

---

[47] *Mencius* 2B8.
[48] On Mencian (and more generally Confucian) virtue ethics, see Bryan W. Van Norden, *Virtue Ethics and Consequentialism in Early Chinese Philosophy* (Cambridge: Cambridge University Press, 2007); Philip J. Ivanhoe, "Virtue Ethics and the Chinese Confucian Tradition," in *The Cambridge Companion to Virtue Ethics*, ed. Daniel C. Russell (Cambridge: Cambridge University Press, 2013), pp. 49–69.
[49] Therefore, methodologically speaking, what follows is not so much textual interpretation, as commonly understood by intellectual historians, as philosophical reconstruction with a view to its democratic possibility. Of course, the underlying motivation for my philosophical reconstruction is not merely intellectual but, more importantly in the current context, political.

RECONSTRUCTING MENCIAN CONFUCIANISM

As we have seen earlier, even when Mencius gave moral justification for tyrannicide, he never allowed laypeople to depose or enthrone the ruler. That right, if we can call such a political privilege a right, was held exclusively by a small number of aristocrats. Put differently, democratic values such as political equality and popular sovereignty were not Mencius's (or early Confucians') guiding concern. Nevertheless, if we understand the notion of human rights as premised upon moral equality and human dignity,[50] it would not be far-fetched to say that Mencius indeed developed a seminal idea of political right in the Confucian context.

According to Justin Tiwald, possession of some territory is the visible qualification to become Heaven's delegated officer, that is, someone authorized to replace the incumbent ruler with a new ruler.[51] In practice, which is prescribed by Zhou ritualism, either a feudal lord or a minister at the court of the Zhou king, the suzerain ruler of all feudal lords in "all under Heaven" (*tianxia* 天下), is a possible candidate for this position. Laypeople might be able to engage in collective protest against the tyrant[52] but the right to replace him with a new ruler is exclusively held by Heaven's delegated officer(s), often consisting of ministers of noble families.[53] Given these realities, how can Mencius's allegiance to this old aristocratic ideal of political inequality be aligned with his fundamental faith in universal moral equality and human dignity?

Recall that Mencius upheld moral equality on the basis of good human nature and the equal capacity to become a sage, objecting to the older paradigm of hereditary privilege and natural/moral inequality among human beings. Furthermore, by claiming that sagehood is accessible to all human beings, he questioned the exclusive connection between sagehood and kingship, a paradigm Confucius still subscribed to, and decoupled the former from the latter.[54] The result was what can be called the *democratization* of the ideal of sagehood.

Now, Mencius's inclusionary ideal of sagehood has three important political implications. First, the ruler, who ascends the throne by hereditary right and thus is not necessarily virtuous, must strive for virtuous

---

[50] For a philosophical attempt to derive the idea of human rights from human dignity, see Ronald Dworkin, *Justice for Hedgehogs* (Cambridge: Belknap, 2011); George Kateb, *Human Dignity* (Cambridge: Belknap, 2011).
[51] Tiwald, "A Right of Rebellion," p. 276.   [52] *Mencius* 1A2.
[53] Kim, "Confucian Constitutionalism," pp. 384–385.   [54] See *Mencius* 3B9.

character to merit the title of "king," the original meaning of which is the office of the Son of Heaven (*tianzi* 天子). Mencius's famous notion of "rectification of the ruler" (*ge jun* 格君)[55] and his advocacy of the ministers' right to remonstrate with the ruler find justification in this stipulation. Second, officialdom is open in principle to *everyone* who is virtuous, regardless of his pedigree,[56] and the highest rank at which the most virtuous one can arrive is ministership. If the highest public post is given to the most virtuous person, irrespective of his social background,[57] neither the territory qualification nor the pedigree of the minister acting as Heaven's delegated officer is of crucial importance. After all, in his justification of Yi Yin's controversial action as we discussed in Chapter 5 (i.e., his assumption of the role of Heaven's delegated officer), Mencius's focus was not so much on Yi Yin's territory as on his moral virtue and character.

These two points lead to what is in my view the most important implication of Mencius's inclusionary ideal of sagehood – that people are not only morally equal in the sense that everyone can become a sage but also politically equal (except with the king) in the sense that everyone has the opportunity to become a public official. In short, in our philosophical reconstruction, Mencius's moral commitment to universal moral equality and human dignity offers resources that could critically undermine his allegiance to old aristocratic ritualism. The implication is that whether or not an individual is indeed able to become a public official is a secondary issue, which entirely depends on one's merit, virtue, or other qualities. What is important is that public affairs are no longer a matter of the Son of Heaven's vertical responsibility to Heaven, the moral source of the mandate to rule, nor are they exclusive concerns of a small number of aristocrats whose decision-making authority is predicated on traditional ritualism.

---

[55] *Mencius* 4A20.
[56] Confucianism can be called "meritocratic" precisely in this sense. See Yuri Pines, "Between Merit and Pedigree: Evolution of the Concept of 'Elevating the Worthy' in Pre-Imperial China," in *The East Asian Challenge for Democracy: Political Meritocracy in Comparative Perspective*, eds. Daniel A. Bell and Chenyang Li (New York: Cambridge University Press, 2013), pp. 161–202. Of course, an official's rank would be determined based on the level of his virtue.
[57] Mencius presents Shun, Fu Yue, Jia Ge, Guan Yiwu, Sunshu Ao, and Boli Xu as sagacious ministers whose original social backgrounds were quite low (*Mencius* 6B15). According the *Mencius*, they were handpicked by the reigning sage-kings and promoted to minister positions because of their brilliant virtues.

In this reconstruction, people who are politically equal and whose political equality is enabled by their fundamental moral equality are entitled to care about public affairs that affect their moral and material well-being, and furthermore can participate in decision-making processes, either formally as public officials selected through a certain screening mechanism (about which Mencius is completely silent) or informally by means of collective resistance and protest. This moral entitlement to register their concern with moral and material well-being in the process of public decision making and their discontent with the government, whose sole purpose is to serve the people's well-being,[58] gives rise to a *right* to political participation.

This is not to argue that the people in our reconstructed Mencian political theory can be identified as citizens as conceived, in the Western republican or democratic political theory, as those who govern themselves by actively participating in collective self-government. Even in this reconstruction, let alone Mencius's own political thought, "people" (*min* 民) is not a formidable political institution as "citizenship" is understood in Western political theory. At the same time, however, it is equally problematic to understand the Confucian people as amorphous masses or helpless victims, completely lacking any active political agency, at least in our reconstructed Mencian Confucianism. They might not be fully equipped with, nor entitled by any means to, the variety of civil and political rights we know of, but in our reconstruction they possess at minimum the right to political participation, the right of rights.[59] In this regard, the following statement by Xunzi, who despite all his disagreements with Mencius nevertheless shared Mencius's idea of benevolent government (*ren zheng* 仁政) as well as the justness of tyrannicide,[60] is most telling:

> When the common people feel at ease with the government, only then will the gentleman feel at ease in holding his position. There is a saying, "The lord is the boat. The common people are the water. The water can support the boat. The water can also overturn the boat."[61]

Like Mencius, Xunzi does not speak of the right to political participation. But he clearly shows that people, as conceived in Confucianism, are not

---

[58] *Mencius* 1A7; 1B5; 3A3; 7B1. Also see Chan, *Confucian Perfectionism*, pp. 29–32.
[59] Jeremy Waldron, *Law and Disagreement* (Oxford: Oxford University Press, 1999), chap. 11.
[60] See *Xunzi* 18.2.
[61] *Xunzi* 9.4. Also see Alan T. Wood, *Limits to Autocracy: From Sung Neo-Confucianism to a Doctrine of Political Rights* (Honolulu: University of Hawaii Press, 1995), p. 12.

like a "thermometer" that merely *indicates* Heaven's acceptance of or discontent with the government.[62] The analogy Xunzi actually employs is the water that can *overturn* the boat, namely, the ruler. In the same vein, Mencius says, "[The tyrants] Jie and *Zhou* lost the world because they lost the people, and they lost the people because they lost the hearts of the people."[63] In our philosophical reconstruction, this view is recast as indicating that people as a collectivity possess and can exercise active political agency, especially during a political crisis. Thus reconstructed, the seminal ideas of popular sovereignty, which consists of the belief that the ruler should not only be responsible for the people's well-being but also be *accountable* to them, and the right to political participation are accordingly justified by the people's active collective political agency. As will be discussed later, this seminal affirmation of popular sovereignty and the right to political participation offers the Confucian philosophical underpinning to the constituting dimension of Confucian democratic citizenship in public reason Confucianism.

Of course, the affirmation of the right to political participation in the Confucian context does not necessarily translate into an endorsement of the republican mode of active political participation, nor the permission of any layperson to participate in key public decision-making processes including constitutional decisions, such as whether to depose (or even kill) the tyrant or whom to select as the new ruler. And this is precisely the Mencian insight. A comparison with modern representative democracy might be helpful in making sense of this. Though many understand popular sovereignty and popular participation as one and the same, they are not, conceptually or practically. Popular sovereignty is the *principle* of democracy that declares that sovereign political power resides in the people (people as citizens, more accurately) rather than the king or aristocrats. As such, popular sovereignty represents the ideal of political equality. Popular participation, however, is a particular *mode* of realizing the democratic ideal of popular sovereignty. Like any form of democracy, representative democracy upholds the ideal of popular sovereignty, but it does not make popular participation its essential component, for many

---

[62] The thermometer analogy is occasionally invoked by some contemporary scholars based on *Shujing*'s 書經 following statement, which Mencius famously quotes in *Mencius* 5A5: "Heaven sees as my people see, Heaven hears as my people hear." But it should be reiterated that Mencius quotes this phrase in the context of royal transmission (i.e., which ones people like or hate among royal candidates), not with regard to people's political agency during a political crisis.

[63] *Mencius* 4A9.

theoretical as well as practical reasons. Under representative democracy, *all* citizens possess the right to political participation, but in most cases of public decision making, this right is exercised by only a small number of political representatives selected through popular vote or other means.

This is not to say that something resembling the idea of democratic representation is present in Mencius's political thought or even in our reconstructed Mencian Confucianism. All I am suggesting at this point is that in our reconstruction, even if the people may not be able to directly influence public affairs as an organized power (i.e., as citizens), the lack of this particular political agency does not justify the conclusion that they therefore lack the right to political participation, especially if we take seriously the distinction between the right to political participation, open to everyone, and the qualification to exercise this right regarding a specific public (especially constitutional) question. This brings us back to the right to tyrannicide. In our reconstruction, people have a collective right to tyrannicide but it is only the qualified few who can actually exercise this right in the name of the Mandate of Heaven and for the sake of the people's well-being. Though not employing concepts such as popular sovereignty or the right to political participation, the following statement by Wm. Theodore de Bary reinforces my argument thus far.

> Does this then, call for revolt? No, for Mencius the next move is to have the responsible members of the ruling house depose the errant ruler (5B9). Failing that, it is understandable that some other leader will overthrow him, punish his misuse of power and replace the defaulting dynasty. While recognizing that unchecked misrule may well provoke rebellion, Mencius recommends a process entirely consistent with his – and the general Confucian – view that violence is to be avoided at all reasonable costs. Revolt is only a last desperate recourse for an exasperated people, understandable but not to be commended. That violence often prevails, Mencius is well aware, but the point of his teachings is to replace the use of force with a well-considered civil process, and above all with due process (what is right, fitting and orderly in the circumstances). It is in this sense then – that the observance of human rights is dependent on civility and due process – that Mencius and the Confucians can be said to offer what Twiss calls informed moral resources in support of human rights.[64]

As de Bary rightly notes, the fact that a ruler has lost legitimacy and deserves to be removed does not and should not automatically call for revolt because it will only exacerbate the political crisis already present under the tyranny. Regicide by a people's revolt is to be avoided by all

---

[64] Wm. Theodore de Bary, "Introduction," in de Bary and Tu, *Confucianism and Human Rights*, pp. 1–26, at pp. 8–9.

reasonable means in a civil, constitutional regime because a violent popular response to a violent ruler only drives the political community into a constitutional debacle, even further jeopardizing the people's welfare. What is needed is a due process according to which the errant ruler can be removed and, if necessary, even killed. I would argue, though, that in this whole process, the people's right to political participation in terms of resistance and protest, is an integral element of "due process" and that this right is compatible with the qualified few taking action to resolve the ongoing political crisis. That being said, the practical imperative that violence must be avoided by any reasonable means should not be understood to imply that the people do not possess a right to rebellion. It is rather that this right should only be exercised as a last resort.[65]

It has been a long journey to justify P3's core postulates – political equality and popular sovereignty – and to establish the right to political participation as another postulate of the proposition *in Confucian terms*. I hope that the public equality proposition, public reason Confucianism's foundational normative proposition that enables it to be a robust democratic theory, is now given a comprehensive moral Confucian basis, although, should be realized, in the course of our reinterpretive and subsequent reconstructive process the Mencian Confucianism that directly undergirds the public equality proposition (and public reason Confucianism in general) has been importantly modified from Mencius's original political thought. Public reason Confucianism is partially comprehensive in this sense as well, in that it is not directly connected with Mencius's original Confucianism but with Mencian Confucianism that has been reconstructed with a view to the democratic values of political equality, popular sovereignty, and the right to political participation.

Our next task, then, is to investigate what a Confucian right to political participation ought to look like under the circumstances of modern democratic politics. This is also a question about what the right to

---

[65] We should not forget that even John Locke, commonly understood as the champion of the right to revolution, made this particular right (among other political rights) extremely difficult to be exercised in reality by the participants of the social contract. Thus Leo Strauss writes, "Locke opposes Hobbes by teaching that wherever 'the people' or 'the community,' that is, the majority, have placed the supreme power, they still retain 'a supreme power to remove or alter' the established government, that is, they still retain a right of revolution. But this power (which is normally dormant) does not qualify the subjection of the individual to the community or society. On the contrary, it is only fair to say that Hobbes stresses more strongly than does Locke the individual's right to resist society or the government whenever his self-preservation is endangered" (*Natural Right and History* [Chicago: University of Chicago Press, 1965], p. 232).

political participation would mean in a Confucian society, as stipulated in P1, where the people have been transformed into citizens who subscribe to diverse moral, religious, or philosophical values as private individuals.

PUBLIC REASON CONFUCIANISM AND POLITICAL PARTICIPATION

As established in the Introduction, public reason Confucianism has three sociological premises:[66] (1) a one-man monarchy that has undergirded the political institution of traditional Confucianism is completely obsolete in contemporary East Asia (the republican premise); (2) with the advent of the republican era, traditional Confucianism's political ritualism, which divided people into different social classes and prescribed a set of proper social conduct for each class,[67] has become equally obsolete, rendering everyone as equal as citizens (the political equality premise); (3) with the collapse of traditional Confucian monarchy and therewith the sage-king paradigm, there is no *Confucian* political ground on which political leaders, however selected, can justify the monistic value system and the lexical ordering of values, which subsequently enables people to subscribe to diverse values (the value pluralism premise).[68]

Since these sociological premises or conditions were brought about in East Asia largely by historical contingencies, independently of the internal evolution of Confucianism, public reason Confucianism takes them as crucial social conditions of the modern East Asian world under which Confucianism has to be adapted for it to be socially relevant to the people there, rather than something to be justified by Confucianism and to be rejected if inconsistent with traditional Confucian philosophy. Put differently, public reason Confucianism has no desire to radically reshape the

---

[66] By calling these premises "sociological premises," I distinguish them from public reason Confucianism's *normative* premises that I introduced in Chapter 2: (1) there is a valuable Confucian way of life that is distinct from (if not starkly opposed to) a liberal way of life and (2) it is permissible for a state to promote or discourage some activities, ideas, or ways of life on the grounds of key Confucian values such as filial piety, respect for elders, ancestor worship, ritual propriety, and social harmony.

[67] Of early Confucians, Xunzi's political theory shows this aspect of Confucianism most systematically.

[68] Of course, whether or not some particular contemporary East Asian societies such as China and Vietnam have found an alternative ideological resource (i.e., Marxist-Leninism) on which to continue to justify value monism and state value paternalism is a different question.

existing world from the ethical standpoint of Confucian philosophy. Its perfectionist aim is quite modest.

What is important is that when the three sociological premises are combined with Mencian Confucianism's philosophical commitments to moral equality and human dignity, they create a circumstance in which our reconstructed Mencian Confucianism can realize its full democratic potential. What prevented original Mencian Confucianism from being democratic was its subscription to the sage-king paradigm predicated on the Mandate of Heaven and its allegiance to political ritualism of the Zhou dynasty: the ideal of the sage-king and the idea of the Mandate of Heaven, which offered an ethico-religious and political underpinning to the institution of kingship in terms of the Son of Heaven, allowed no room for popular sovereignty and collective self-determination and Zhou ritualism militated against the idea of political equality and the popular right to political participation. In our reconstruction, what is still preventing Mencian Confucianism from developing into a full-fledged democratic political theory is the absence of the institution of citizenship, resulting in the radical separation between common people's right to political participation, pronounced most saliently *during a political crisis*, and the political privilege of the few selected (aristocrats) to actually carry out this right following (ritually prescribed) due process. As such, in our reconstructed Mencian Confucianism, the absence of the office of citizenship prevents the establishment of a robust philosophical connection between the people's right to political participation and democratic representation.

The sociological premises of public reason Confucianism inform us that the critical obstacles that once blocked the democratic realization of Mencian Confucianism have been removed in modern East Asia. With the advent of the republican age as well as the institutionalization of citizenship by means of the modern constitution, our reconstructed Mencian Confucianism is furnished with an outlet to express its philosophical commitment to moral equality and human dignity within the institutional structure that allows these principles to directly undergird political equality and popular sovereignty. Public reason Confucianism provides one such institutional outlet, in my view the most attractive, for full realization of the democratic possibility of Mencian Confucianism without being embroiled in its metaphysical assumptions.

At this point, it is worth noting that the postulates of political equality and popular sovereignty, which are also vindicated by the first and second sociological premises of public reason Confucianism, offer only a necessary but not sufficient condition for the right to political participation, as this right does not derive naturally from them. What makes the right to political participation integral to public reason Confucianism is the third sociological premise, namely the value pluralism premise. In order to make clear sense of this connection between the right to political participation and value pluralism in the context of public reason Confucianism, it is necessary to revisit *Mencius* 6A10 where Mencius draws attention to the importance of human dignity.

In the passage, Mencius's central claim was that human dignity can in no way be trumped by one's concern with material interest, however important it may be, even to his or her survival.[69] This is a rather surprising claim given Mencius's profound concern with the people's material well-being. For instance, Mencius famously says, "It is only a gentleman who will be able to have a constant mind despite being without a constant means of livelihood. The people, lacking a constant means of livelihood, will lack constant minds, and when they lack constant minds there is no dissoluteness, depravity, deviance, or excess to which they will not succumb."[70] The two passages, however, do not have to be read as conflicting with each other, because Mencius's point seems to be that even though material well-being above a certain threshold is a necessary condition for human dignity, human dignity itself cannot be reduced to the satisfaction of that threshold as such. This implies that if we can glean any notion of human rights from Confucianism, it must be based on the supreme moral value of human dignity. And in the context of Mencius's original political thought, other things being equal, it is material interest that enables a person to live a dignified life.

Under the circumstances of modern politics, which are characterized by value pluralism and moral disagreement, however, the value of human dignity cannot be satisfied merely by material well-being. When members of a political community generally subscribe to one comprehensive moral system (such as Confucianism), they are primarily, if not solely, interested in their material well-being because it is the basis for a flourishing human life. Even when they are interested in their moral well-being, their major concern is with moral self-development along the lines of moral precepts

---

[69] In this respect, I disagree with Daniel Bell, who claims that the right to subsistence has an overriding value vis-à-vis civil and political rights, because this ignores the foundational importance of human dignity, which cannot be approached purely in material terms. See Bell, *Beyond Liberal Democracy*, pp. 237–243.
[70] *Mencius* 1A7.

and ethical norms prescribed by the dominant moral system. In a society where people hold diverse moral, religious, and philosophical doctrines, people are interested not only in promoting their material well-being but also, often more intensely, in protecting and promoting their moral well-being. In other words, in a pluralist society people have both material and what Max Weber calls ideal interests. Consider the following passage by Weber.

> Not ideas, but material and ideal interests, directly govern men's conduct. Yet very frequently the "world images" that have been created by "ideas" have, like switchmen, determined the tracks along which action has been pushed by the dynamic of interest.[71]

Weber's key point is that while ideas offer the world images that condition general human conduct, it is material *and* ideal interests that actually push human agents to act in a specific way. At the core of Weber's idea is that human beings are not merely self-interested economic actors concerned solely with their material well-being, as posited by both Marxism and classical liberalism and later rational choice theory, but are also, perhaps more importantly, agents who have an active interest in leading their lives according to the (moral or religious) ideas or the world views that they hold dear. In this latter sense, human beings are also understood as *self-interested*, but the "interest" here refers not so much to material well-being but to moral well-being broadly construed (including religious well-being).[72]

Weber contrived the concept of ideal interest to make sense of social action that cannot be reduced to or is largely independent of mere material interest. In the present context, the concept of ideal interest can help us better understand why value pluralism is occasionally accompanied by moral disagreement. Value pluralism implies plurality of ideas or worldviews that generate the plural "tracks" along which people's ideal (and material) interests can be pushed. As the conventional image of "interest"

---

[71] Max Weber, *From Max Weber: Essays in Sociology*, eds. and trans. Hans H. Gerth and C. W. Mills (New York: Oxford University Press, 1958), p. 280.

[72] Not surprisingly, Weber discusses his sociological concepts in the Protestant context. In a sense, Weber's *The Protestant Ethic and the Spirit of Capitalism* can be reinterpreted as offering an explanation as to how in a particular religious context one's material interest was profoundly dependent upon his or her ideal interest. My interpretation of Weber's notion of "interest" is indebted to Sangjun Kim, "Yeŭi sahoehakchŏk haesŏgŭl wihan ironjŏk tansŏ: Makssŭ Paebŏŭi 'inyŏmjŏk ihae'" [A Theoretical Clue to a Sociological Interpretation of the Confucian Ritual: Max Weber's "Ideal Interests"], *Sahoewa yŏksa* [*Society and History*] 59 (2001), pp. 11–50.

denotes, ideal interests originating from different values or ideas are often incommensurable with one another, and in the absence of a transcendental moral standard, thus when every citizen is equally loaded with "burdens of judgment,"[73] such incommensurability, especially when dealing with public policies that affect all citizens, is highly prone to become a volatile source of moral conflict.

Though public reason Confucianism does not cherish plurality of values for diversity's sake, it takes both material and ideal interests of each citizen seriously because public reason Confucianism, following traditional Confucianism, is deeply concerned with the people's moral and material well-being. And public reason Confucianism considers protection of one's material and ideal interests to be vitally important in respecting his or her dignity.[74] I agree in principle with Joseph Chan when he says that "[h]uman rights does not depend on the notion that human beings are egoistic, totally unconcerned with the well-being of others. Human rights protect legitimate interests of individuals. We must distinguish between '*self*-interest' and '*selfish* interest.'"[75] The only caveat in Chan's statement is its lack of attention to the fact that interest can be both material and ideal.

Perhaps this lack of attention to ideal interest and its critical implication for human dignity is why Chan rejects the pivotal importance of the right to political participation in modern Confucianism, which, as Chan acknowledges, must be plausible in East Asia's pluralist society. But under the circumstances of modern politics in which there are no sages or holders of the Mandate of Heaven to authoritatively tell us what is the right "way" to live our private moral lives – *dao* 道 as traditional Confucians called it – it is absolutely necessary for us, as democratic citizens, to be epistemically charitable to one another, respecting others' moral interests (and moral opinions, both deriving from our moral values or ideas), even if we do not agree with them. Rawls calls this attitude that democratic citizens ought to show one another a *duty of civility*, which involves

---

[73] John Rawls, *Political Liberalism* (New York: Columbia University Press, 1993), p. 56.

[74] Therefore, public reason Confucianism's view of human right mediates between the dignity argument (a la Dworkin and Kateb) and the so-called interest argument. For the interest argument, see Joseph Raz, *The Morality of Freedom* (Oxford: Clarendon, 1986); Thomas Christiano, *The Constitution of Equality: Democratic Authority and Its Limits* (Oxford: Oxford University Press, 2008).

[75] Joseph Chan, "A Confucian Perspective on Human Rights for Contemporary China," in *The East Asian Challenge for Human Rights*, eds. Joanne R. Bauer and Daniel A. Bell (Cambridge: Cambridge University Press, 1999), pp. 212–237, at p. 219.

"a willingness to listen to others and a fairmindedness in deciding when accommodations to their views should reasonably be made."[76] The point that is often glossed over and that Rawls takes for granted is that this duty, agreed upon by many contemporary Confucian scholars including Chan,[77] presupposes a right to political participation.

If the three sociological premises on which public reason Confucianism is grounded are granted, the duty of civility has profound implications for the right to political participation. Given the coercive nature of political power, which is based on and justified by collective self-determination of free and equal citizens in a democratic society,[78] the requirement of civility can only be met if all citizens, with their own moral values and ideas, are entitled to rightfully participate in (1) the constitutional (re)making processes that would (re)define public identity of their common citizenship; (2) public policy-making processes that affect their political, economic, and social lives; and (3) criminal–judicial processes that determine their status as free citizens.

In a pluralist society, individuals have different understandings of what kind of Constitution they want to have (or what kind of citizens they want to become), what kinds of public policies the government should implement (especially with regard to those that directly involve ethical questions), and what kinds of criminal codes they want to establish. Since the state is coercive in the sense that public decisions (including constitutional ones), once made, are binding for all citizens, regardless of whether they personally agree with them or not, and they vitally affect citizens' material and moral interests, each citizen ought to have the right to make his or her political opinions and moral arguments heard by other citizens and public officials in public forums. Civility, central to which is the virtue of reciprocity, gains political significance because it prescribes reasonable modes of participation in such forums that citizens and public officials ought to take in order to make sure that they can deliberate public affairs on terms that everyone can endorse.[79] Deeply concerned with the

---

[76] Rawls, *Political Liberalism*, p. 217.   [77] Chan, *Confucian Perfectionism*, pp. 201–203.
[78] As Amy Gutmann and Dennis Thompson put it, "[b]ecause the results of democratic deliberations are mutually binding, citizens should aspire to a kind of political reasoning that is mutually justifiable" (*Democracy and Disagreement* [Cambridge: Belknap, 1996], p. 53).
[79] Otherwise stated, so-called deliberative democracy is another integral element of public reason Confucianism. For my idea on this connection, see Sungmoon Kim, *Confucian Democracy in East Asia: Theory and Practice* (New York: Cambridge University Press, 2014), chap. 4. On the importance of civility, especially the virtue of reciprocity, in

coerciveness of political power, public reason Confucianism embraces the right to political participation, of which the right to vote is only a subset, as the best institutional means by which to protect each citizen's material and moral interests.

Does this mean that Confucian democratic citizens must actively participate in every public affair at every moment as traditional republican active citizenship requires? Not necessarily, because the fact that one has a right to do something does not morally require him or her to actually exercise that right all the time. Nor must this right be directly exercised by all citizens for all public affairs as the Rousseauist ideal of participatory democracy recommends. Citizens have a right to participate in the (re)making of the constitution but this does not mean that all citizens should actually participate in every step of the process. The right to participate can be reasonably fulfilled, perhaps even more effectively, by delegating the task to a small subset of citizens (say, members of the legislature) who are better qualified for the task, if they are selected according to democratic procedures. Likewise, though citizens have a right to participate in public policy-making processes, they can either directly participate in them – by running for public offices, by organizing various sorts of deliberative forums in civil society, or, in exceptional cases, by taking to the streets – or delegate the decision-making tasks to their political representatives, again selected according to due democratic procedures. In other words, the right to political participation is fully consistent with democratic representation broadly defined, which involves not only the legislature but also the courts and other governmental offices.[80]

What is important is that in any event the very procedures that stipulate the mode of selection of political representatives and public officials in the various branches of government should always be controlled by the

---

democratic deliberation, see Gutmann and Thompson, *Democracy and Disagreement*. For a view that attributes deliberation in the public forum only to political elites, see Daniel A. Bell, "Democratic Deliberation: The Problem of Implementation," in *Deliberative Politics: Essays on Democracy and Disagreement*, ed. Stephen Macedo (Oxford: Oxford University Press, 1999), pp. 70–87.

[80] For this broad understanding of democratic representation, see Christopher L. Eisgruber, *Constitutional Self-Government* (Cambridge: Harvard University Press, 2001); Pierre Rosanvallon, *Democratic Legitimacy: Impartiality, Reflexivity, Proximity*, trans. Arthur Goldhammer (Princeton: Princeton University Press, 2011). Committed to this broad idea of democratic representation, public reason Confucianism rejects the conventional distinction between democracy and constitutionalism and maintains that constitutional protection of rights is an important way to secure democratic control over government.

citizens themselves and this is how public reason Confucianism understands rule *by* the people. Of course, in the event that popular control of democratic procedures that govern the representation mechanism is systematically thwarted by the governing elites, or the direction in which they push public policies is seriously at odds with democratic-constitutional norms and principles, the ultimate power to address such problems reverts back to the people and this is how public reason Confucianism understands rule *of* the people.

In original Mencian Confucianism only rule *for* the people was affirmed and in our reconstructed Mencian Confucianism a seminal idea of the rule *of* the people has been developed from our discussion of political equality and popular sovereignty. Now, in public reason Confucianism people not only are sovereign as democratic citizens but they should also control government effectively. From the perspective of public reason Confucianism, government works *for* the people only if it is the government of *and* by the people simultaneously, that is, only if government represents the people's collective self-determination and is effectively controlled by them. The right to political participation is a critical postulate of public reason Confucianism that enables the government to be for, of, and by the people.

CIVIC VIRTUE REAFFIRMED

Though public reason Confucianism does not uphold the Rousseauist ideal of active political participation and is rather committed to a complex vision of democratic representation, it recognizes political participation as an important civic virtue and encourages citizens to exercise it judiciously as a means for effective democratic control and direction of government. Of course, like other virtues, political participation, when exercised less judiciously, is always susceptible to some side effects but it is not clear how occasional side effects undermine the importance of political participation as such. In Chapter 5 and earlier in this chapter, we examined and refuted the motivation reason and the opportunity reason that Chan offers as practical reasons for giving priority to moral virtue over civic virtue, particularly political participation. Now, with the right to political participation as well as the virtue of it fully integrated into public reason Confucianism, I return to Chan's third reason for being skeptical of the virtue of political participation, namely the assurance reason. First let me quote Chan's statement on the "assurance problem."

Third, political republicans face "an assurance problem" that perfectionists do not.... Citizenship, like justice, is a conditional virtue or duty, in the sense that one is obliged to act in accordance with the requirements of citizenship only if one has some assurance that other citizens will do the same. If civic virtues are tied only to citizenship, citizens may not see a reason to behave civilly and respectfully to others, especially if assurance from others is not forthcoming. According to the perfectionist conception, however, people should not easily discard virtues or duties just because others are not virtuous – if they do so they would not only cease to be responsible citizens but become quite different persons.[81]

According to Chan, one's practice of citizenship is contingent upon whether or not others will equally fulfill the duties affiliated with citizenship. What drives Chan's argument is the following question: why be a good citizen if there is no assurance that others are equally good citizens? Recapitulated in this way, whether or not citizenship and associated civic virtues are indeed a conditional virtue or duty hangs critically on the way we answer this question. Chan's response is that if one is a moral person, one will naturally be a good citizen, even in the absence of the assurance of others' equal compliance with the requirements of citizenship. That is, in Chan's view, the requirements of citizenship can be fully fulfilled by relying solely on moral virtue.

However, what exactly do we mean by "if assurance from others is not forthcoming"? Two interpretations seem to be possible, depending on how we understand "citizenship" in Chan's statement. One way to make sense of the assurance problem is to see it as a free rider problem by identifying citizenship narrowly in terms of political participation. Then Chan's skepticism can be recast as an equally rational response to a rational free rider who benefits from the public good without shouldering his or her fair share. In a democracy, the public good can be attained only if people participate in the public decision making process, most commonly by voting.[82] However, participation incurs various costs, which a rational free rider is unwilling to pay, such as the time for and the transportation fees in commuting to the ballot box, possible accidents during the commute, a need to examine a candidate's policy proposals or a proposition by popular referendum, and so on. Chan's argument seems to be that participants who are systematically underpaid by (what ought to be) a cooperative social and political scheme have no obligation to pay

---

[81] Chan, *Confucian Perfectionism*, p. 98.
[82] Thus, Gutmann and Thompson assert that "[t]hose who benefit or wish to benefit from the political process have an obligation to participate in that process, and therefore to develop their capacities to do so" (*Democracy and Disagreement*, p. 303).

their share. The logical corollary of this reasoning is rather unreasonably demanding, that unless *everyone* is provided a fair share, neither the underpaid (i.e., virtuous democratic citizens) nor the overpaid (i.e., free riders) is bound to the scheme.[83]

What we glean from the assurance problem understood in this way, however, is the limitation, if not a complete inadequacy, of *the principle of fair play* to be an ethics of participation or as a principle of political obligation, not so much the disvalue of political participation or even its practical difficulty.[84] That is, the critique does not prove why political participation is less important or can be reasonably substituted by nonpolitical social participation. The assurance problem falls away if we do not subscribe (solely) to fair play as an ethics of political participation in the first place, which makes perfect sense only in an ideal situation in which political society is deemed by *all* citizens as the fair scheme of mutual cooperation, and adopt, or supplement to it with, a different moral argument for political participation – say, an *argument from coercion*, an *argument from moral disagreement* – or the combination of the two as I adopt in this work, following the lead of Rawls – or an *argument from complicity*.[85] Perhaps, more fundamentally, if we do not conceive of the people as rational, (materially) self-interested human beings (and the Confucians have strong reason not to do so, given that Confucian ethics is deeply relational), the assurance problem does not arise as a formidable rationale against the virtue of political participation.[86]

The assurance problem can be approached somewhat differently, however, if we understand citizenship more literally, especially with reference to its constitutional making. This question was pursued by early modern social contractarians, especially John Locke, and his answer was to (re)create citizenship. Locke's argument was that since there is no assurance of equal fidelity to natural law in the state of nature, even if human beings are all born to be moral and rational, the best way to avoid this assurance

---

[83] Eric Beerbohm, *In Our Name: The Ethics of Democracy* (Princeton: Princeton University Press, 2012), p. 57.
[84] On the principle of fair play, see George Klosko, *The Principle of Fairness and Obligation* (Lanham: Rowman and Littlefield, 1992); Richard Dagger, *Civic Virtues: Rights, Citizenship, and Republican Liberalism* (New York: Oxford University Press, 1997), pp. 55–56; A. John Simmons, *Justification and Legitimacy: Essays on Rights and Obligations* (New York: Cambridge University Press, 2001), pp. 1–42.
[85] On the argument from democratic complicity, see Beerbohm, *In Our Name*.
[86] For a convincing argument for compatibility between Confucian relational ethics and the virtue of political participation, see Sor-hoon Tan, *Confucian Democracy: A Deweyan Reconstruction* (Albany: State University of New York Press, 2004).

problem – what he called "inconvenience" – should be to create a civil or constitutional government and institutionalize citizenship. In other words, for Locke, citizenship was pursued as the very cure of the assurance problem. And for him, as well as for Hobbes, it was by means of civic virtues (which are intelligible only under civil government and with the institutionalization of citizenship) that citizenship could become robust.[87]

The fact that Locke did not consider cultivation of personal moral virtue to address the assurance problem but rather opted for an institutional solution is highly suggestive for us. Let me go over Locke's reasoning and its implication for the present discussion step by step. First, even if all individuals subscribe to one comprehensive doctrine, say the doctrine of natural law, the assurance problem still cannot be avoided because there are always outliers.[88] Second, one way to avoid the assurance problem altogether is to make every individual perfectly moral, but this is only something God can do, hence not a proper subject of political theory.[89] Third, though this is not Locke's most prominent concern,[90] if individuals hold diverse moral values and they pursue their moral interests in ways that are *good* in light of the specific moral doctrines they cherish, moral conflict is inevitable and the assurance problem becomes more intensified. In this case, encouraging people to be (more) moral does not ameliorate the situation; instead the situation is likely to get worse. Fourth, it is for this reason that common citizenship (and education in citizenship or civic education) is required in

---

[87] For an excellent study on the critical importance of civic virtue in the making of modern liberalism, see Peter Berkowitz, *Virtue and the Making of Modern Liberalism* (Princeton: Princeton University Press, 1999), especially chaps. 1 and 2.

[88] For how Locke's political theory, especially his idea of the state of nature, is nested in the natural law tradition, see John Dunn, *The Political Thought of John Locke: An Historical Account of the Argument of the* Two Treatise of Government (Cambridge: Cambridge University Press, 1969); Jeremy Waldron, *God, Locke, and Equality: Christian Foundations in Locke's Political Thought* (Cambridge: Cambridge University Press, 2002).

[89] For an insightful account of how Locke resolved the assurance or coordination problem through the function of legislation, see Jeremy Waldron, *The Dignity of Legislation* (Cambridge: Cambridge University Press, 1999), chap. 4.

[90] It should be noted, however, that even though Locke did not construct his political theory with a focus on value pluralism, as we can see in *A Letter Concerning Toleration*, he was deeply concerned with the perils of pluralism in the Christian societal context and it is precisely in this context that he paid extra attention to the importance of civic virtue (what he called civility). On this point, see Richard Boyd, *Uncivil Society: The Perils of Pluralism and the Making of Modern Liberalism* (Lanham: Lexington Books, 2004), chap. 2.

which a private individual, with his or her moral and material interests, is and ought to be transformed into a public citizen, concerned with the well-being of all members of the polity. Civil government can punish only *citizens*, not private individuals in the state of nature, who fail to abide by the "assurance game" that the law promulgates and the ideal of citizenship demands. The civil state is coercive precisely in this sense.

Chan reads citizenship in the complete opposite way, as if citizenship is the cause of the assurance problem, and his perfectionist solution for the problem is focused on making individual persons morally good without suggesting any role for democratic government, law (including criminal law), or other political institutions, at the heart of which lies common citizenship. Perhaps if all members of the polity become morally good, we might be able to attain a good or harmonious society without having a robust practice of citizenship or related civic virtues. But not only is this requirement impossibly demanding, a task only God can fulfill in Locke's political theory; it also presupposes the Confucian counterpart of Lockean natural law as the authoritative source of the comprehensive moral doctrine, the Way (*dao* 道), the presence of which *everyone* can recognize and the moral precepts of which they can endorse and follow. This might not be a problem for some Confucian perfectionists such as Jiang Qing but it surely poses a serious challenge for Chan, who proposes his Confucian perfectionism as moderate political perfectionism completely decoupled from comprehensive Confucianism.

That being said, the assurance problem in a pluralist society is not a mere inconvenience that can be overcome by instituting civil society (and citizenship) and erecting a civil government, as Locke suggests. Since under the circumstances of modern politics the deepest source of the assurance problem lies in the plurality of values that guide one's moral interest and push his or her social action, the difficulty of coordinating coherent public actions and decisions across differences is a perennial challenge for which there is no perfect answer. All democratic citizens can do is endeavor to address it as far and as reasonably as they can, and it is public reason that delineates the limits of both such an endeavor and the public decision resulting from it.

Therefore, public reason Confucianism stipulates that within the parameters of public reason, each citizen should be given the right to advance one's moral and material interest freely as well as equally and when free public deliberation has failed to produce a public decision that every citizen can reasonably endorse, each should still retain the right to vote for or against it. As such, public reason Confucianism incorporates the right to political participation as a necessary, but not sufficient, requirement for addressing the assurance problem in the context of value pluralism. From the perspective of public reason Confucianism, citizens can minimize the assurance problem by participating in various kinds of public forums where they can freely discuss not only the content of public policies, but also, more importantly, the very terms of their public interactions and ultimately the public character of their shared citizenship. While Chan's Confucian perfectionism directly appeals to Confucian moral monism as its perfectionist inspiration, the perfectionist character of public reason Confucianism lies in its public promotion of democratic citizenship that is both enabled and circumscribed by Confucian public reason.

CONCLUSION

Together with political equality and popular sovereignty, two other postulates of the public equality proposition (P3), the right to political participation most clearly distinguishes public reason Confucianism from recent Confucian political theories, including Joseph Chan's moderate political Confucian perfectionism. The main purpose of this chapter has been to justify popular right to political participation, which advocates of Confucian meritocratic perfectionism uniformly reject, with reference to both a new version of Mencian Confucianism reconstructed with full attention to original Mencian Confucianism's philosophical commitment to moral equality and human dignity and the circumstances of modern politics marked by value pluralism and moral disagreement. But why are the related ideas of political equality, popular sovereignty, and right to political participation so unattractive to the advocates of Confucian meritocratic perfectionism? Their common explanation is that none of these ideas was justified in early Confucianism.[91] But what about human rights, personal autonomy, (local) election, or independent judiciary? Do these values or institutions that Confucian meritocrats sometimes support have a clear Confucian basis?

---

[91] Many who argue for the need for a Confucian form of government today in East Asia do so on the grounds that one's form of political practice must engage native values. However, since many of the strongly hierarchical and elitist values of traditional Confucianism no longer have any play in contemporary East Asian societies (any more than gender discrimination or monarchy do), such appeals do not lend strong support to their conceptions of meritocracy.

Why are some non-Confucian values or institutions accommodated in modern Confucian political theory, but not values that are directly related to the moral power and political capacity of ordinary people? From the perspective of traditional Confucianism, which recognized one-man monarchy as the only legitimate form of government, recent Confucian meritocratic proposals that generally push for an undemocratically selected upper house in the legislature would be equally problematic because the very institution of the legislature has no Confucian basis. Except for a handful of radical reformists, traditional Confucians during China's imperial age, were they still alive, would rightfully consider the upper house to be un-Confucian, even anti-Confucian, as it undermines the legitimacy of one-man monarchy. Then how can we make sense of recent Confucian meritocrats' strong antipathy toward political equality, popular sovereignty, and political participation?

In his critical engagement with modern antipopulists, mostly strong advocates of judicial supremacy, the American legal historian Larry Kramer is faced with virtually the same problem. Kramer argues that modern antipopulism in American law and politics has nothing to do with logic, evidence, or history.[92] Rather, as he sees it, it is "a matter of sensibility." Kramer says,

> The modern Anti-Populist sensibility presumes that ordinary people are emotional, ignorant, fuzzy-headed, and simple-minded, in contrast to a thoughtful, informed, and clear-headed elite. Ordinary people tend to be foolish and irresponsible when it comes to politics: self-interested rather than public-spirited, arbitrary rather than principled, impulsive and close-minded rather than deliberate or logical. Ordinary people are like children, really. And being like children, ordinary

---

[92] The books most cited by advocates of Confucian meritocracy to empirically vindicate their antipopulism are Jason Brennan's *The Ethics of Voting* (Princeton: Princeton University Press, 2011) and Bryan Caplan's *The Myth of the Rational Voter: Why Democracies Choose Bad Policies* (Princeton: Princeton University Press, 2007). Though it is beyond the scope of this book to thoroughly investigate the empirical evidence these two books offer, I want to point out that there is a plethora of counterevidence that challenges the antipopulism thesis. For instance, see Mark E. Warren and Hilary Pearse (eds.), *Designing Deliberative Democracy: The British Columbia Citizens' Assembly* (Cambridge: Cambridge University Press, 2008); John S. Dryzek, *Foundations and Frontiers of Deliberative Governance* (Oxford: Oxford University Press, 2010); Hélène Landemore, *Democratic Reason: Politics, Collective Intelligence, and the Rule of the Many* (Princeton: Princeton University Press, 2013). For a philosophical argument that the democratic process produces epistemically superior decisions, see Joshua Cohen, "An Epistemic Conception of Democracy," *Ethics* 97 (1986), pp. 26–38; David M. Estlund, *Democratic Authority: A Philosophical Framework* (Princeton: Princeton University Press, 2008).

people are insecure and easily manipulated. The result is that ordinary politics, or perhaps we should say the politics that ordinary people make, "is not just low in quality, but dangerous as well."[93]

It seems that the prevailing antipathy among advocates of Confucian meritocratic perfectionism toward political equality, popular sovereignty, and political participation tracks the same "sensibility" that antipopulists hold in America, although the Confucian focus is not so much on the Supreme or Constitutional Court as on the upper house of the legislature. But if the choice one makes between Confucian democracy and Confucian meritocracy "turns largely on differing sensibilities about popular government and the political trustworthiness of ordinary citizens,"[94] it cannot be maintained that only Confucian political theories that are explicitly meritocratic and antipopulist are authentically Confucian. Nor can it be ascertained that Confucian democracy has no meritocratic component, for it embraces various forms of representation mechanisms not only in the legislature but also in other branches of government. The real difference between Confucian democracy and Confucian meritocracy (as conceived by its recent advocates) is whether the meritocratic apparatuses that each position embraces are fully responsive to popular democratic control, or more fundamentally, whether political power is truly wielded in the name of the people.

Confucian meritocracy upholds the government for the people at the expense of the government of and by the people. The Confucian democracy justified by public reason Confucianism establishes the government for, of, and by the people. From the standpoint of public reason Confucianism, there can be no government for the people if that government is not simultaneously of and by the people. Highly susceptible to (unjustified) state paternalism, such a government can hardly sustain its expressed commitment to the moral and material well-being of the people in the face of the many contingencies of political life.

---

[93] Larry D. Kramer, *The People Themselves: Popular Constitutionalism and Judicial Review* (New York: Oxford University Press, 2004), p. 242. The quote inside is from Richard D. Parker, *"Here, the People Rule": A Constitutional Populist Manifesto* (Cambridge: Harvard University Press, 1994), p. 58. In fact, Kramer is indebted to Parker for the idea that modern American antipopulism is a matter of sensibility. For similar advocacy of popular constitutionalism, see Mark Tushnet, *Taking the Constitution Away from the Courts* (Princeton: Princeton University Press, 1999); Richard Bellamy, *Political Constitutionalism: A Republican Defense of the Constitutionality of Democracy* (Cambridge: Cambridge University Press, 2007).

[94] Kramer, *The People Themselves*, p. 246.

Conclusion

Public reason Confucianism, which I explored in this book as a normative political theory of Confucian democratic perfectionism, mediates between (partial) comprehensive Confucian perfectionism and public reason, which is typically associated with political liberalism. In this book, I first defended my normative position of Confucian democratic perfectionism by critically engaging with recent proposals for Confucian meritocratic perfectionism. I then constructed the political theory of public reason Confucianism by revisiting John Rawls's political liberalism from the perspective of democratic perfectionism, thereby justifying the idea of public reason perfectionism, of which public reason Confucianism is one particular type, and examining public reason Confucianism's constitutional implications for public equality, democratic pluralism, civic virtue, and the right to political participation. I presented public reason Confucianism as a democratic political theory that is most relevant in East Asian societies, the public culture of which still largely remains Confucian.

In Part II I tried to illuminate the critical difference between traditional(ist) Confucianism and public reason Confucianism, which I understand as fully and partially comprehensive, respectively. However, despite their loose moral connection as forms of a way of life, one may be left with lingering questions – namely, how can public reason Confucianism nevertheless be properly called "Confucianism"? And what if the public moral consensus on which I draw heavily in theorizing public reason Confucianism were to change, leaning more toward Western liberalism? I conclude this book by responding to these important questions.

First, one may wonder whether public reason Confucianism is too diluted or deracinated a version of Confucianism to be recognizable to self-identified Confucians. This is an important question, which no contemporary Confucian political theorist can afford to ignore, and not surprisingly recent Confucian democratic theorists who attempt to reconcile Confucianism and democracy and other progressive social values appear to be struggling equally with this challenge. For instance, Joseph Chan defends the Confucian aspect of his modern Confucian perfectionism as the following:

> One may wonder to what extent a society can be called "Confucian" if the legislative and policy-making process is guided by moderate perfectionism. The answer is that the actual extent of Confucian influence in a society will and always should be determined by the continuous process of democratic discussion and policy making over time. Just as human society is always changing, so should Confucianism.[1]

As I noted in Chapter 1 (n31), it is not clear how this statement, which tallies with what I call public reason Confucianism's *continuity condition*, can be completely decoupled from comprehensive Confucianism understood in terms of a way of life, at the heart of which lies the *intelligibility condition*. That being said, if this important philosophical question can be bracketed, Chan's statement, focused on the evolving nature of Confucianism as a cultural and philosophical tradition, shifts our attention from whether this is real Confucianism to whether this is the kind of Confucianism *we* can accept and wish to develop further.

After all, we should not forget that classical Confucianism, largely concentrated on moral self-cultivation and virtue politics, evolved into political Confucianism during the imperial period with a strong emphasis on bureaucratic institutions (including the civil examination system) and absolute monarchy. Then, passing through Song and Ming periods, this political (and quite authoritarian) Confucianism was radically revamped by a group of neo-Confucians (especially Cheng-Zhu neo-Confucians) into the "Learning of the Way" (*daoxue* 道學), characterized by a mesmerizingly complex system of *li* 理-*qi* 氣 metaphysics and its seamless entwinement with *xin*心-*xing*性 moral psychology and ethics.[2] In each stage of self-transformation, the Confucianism in question was always the rich product of ceaseless cultural, philosophical, and legal–political

---

[1] Joseph Chan, *Confucian Perfectionism: A Political Philosophy for Modern Times* (Princeton: Princeton University Press, 2014), p. 204.

[2] For a succinct yet insightful account on the evolution of Confucianism throughout East Asian history, see Wm. Theodore de Bary, *East Asian Civilizations: A Dialogue in Five Stages* (Cambridge: Harvard University Press, 1988).

negotiations, first between classical Confucianism and Legalism and second between classical Confucianism and then-prevailing heavily metaphysical Chinese (Hua Yen) Buddhism and neo-Daoism, which later Confucian critics understood as nothing more than "Buddhism in Confucian disguise."[3] And yet, no one who is familiar with the East Asian Confucian tradition would say that political Confucianism or Cheng-Zhu neo-Confucianism is not real Confucianism because of its distance from classical Confucianism and its active engagement with non-Confucian traditions such as Legalism, Buddhism, or Daoism. Thus understood, the mere fact that public reason Confucianism is a philosophical, cultural, and legal–political product of dialectic negotiations between traditional(ist) Confucianism and liberal democracy does not necessarily invalidate it as a particular mode of Confucianism. Again, the more important question is whether this is the kind of Confucianism *we* can accept and wish to develop further.

But who are "we" who have this authority? If *we* are self-identified Confucians, as our hypothetical critic insists, the next question should be: for a political theory to be properly labeled "Confucian," in what sense must it be intelligible as such to self-identified Confucians? The problem with this question is that "self-identified Confucians" is a vague category that includes vastly different conceptions and lacks clear boundaries. Are we referring to (mainly West-educated) Confucian academics who want to make the Confucian ethical and/or philosophical system safe within modern society, traditionalist Confucian scholars (called *yurim* 儒林 in Korea) still rigorously persisting in the traditional Confucian way of life, Confucian classicists devoted to the exposition and (re)interpretation of Confucian classics and commentaries, or members of Confucian associations and clans? For instance, from the traditionalist Confucians' standpoint, the very attempt to modernize Confucianism – be it a philosophical system, ethical tradition, or a way of life – can be considered less authentically Confucian, even un-Confucian, because it compromises and

---

[3] For instance, the nineteenth-century Korean Confucian philosopher Chŏng Yagyong (1762–1836) poignantly criticized orthodox Cheng-Zhu neo-Confucianism for the strong Buddhist influence in it, which in his view made it hopelessly alienated from the "authentic" Confucianism that Confucius and Mencius had upheld. See Mark Setton, *Chŏng Yagyong: Korea's Challenge to Orthodox Neo-Confucianism* (Albany: State University of New York Press, 1997). It is important to note that Cheng-Zhu neo-Confucianism was similarly challenged by Confucian critics in China and Japan. See Philip J. Ivanhoe, "New Old Foundations for Confucian Ethical Philosophy: Itō Jinsai, Dai Zhen, and Jeong Yakyong," *Taiwan Journal of East Asian Studies* 11:1 (2014), pp. 77–133.

thereby corrupts Confucianism with non-Confucian values and principles, mostly liberal democratic ones.

This is not to say that public reason Confucianism would disregard how self-identified Confucians – however we understand them – evaluate its theoretical system and philosophical arguments. The point is that there can be a variety of Confucian political theories, and public reason Confucianism is a special kind of contemporary Confucian political theory whose primary addressees are *Confucian citizens*, as stipulated in P1 and P2, rather than self-identified Confucians, whose political significance in the region is quite negligible. The Confucian dimension of public reason Confucianism may seem controversial, as it does not derive its concepts and philosophical postulates directly from Confucianism, as several self-identified Confucians understand the tradition, but it is still importantly Confucian in the *normative* sense, in that it aims to promote Confucian values in ways compatible with East Asia's increasingly democratic and pluralist societal context.[4]

Seen in this way, public reason Confucianism is qualitatively different, both structurally and argumentatively, from other conservative or traditionalist political movements, such as the Christian nation movement in the United States, which also calls for "traditional family values." While the Christian nation movement is inspired by values and a way of living acceptable only to those who wholeheartedly subscribe to a fully moral comprehensive doctrine of Christianity, public reason Confucianism aims to build a robust democracy on Confucian soil, which still deeply forms the habits of the heart of most East Asian citizens, despite their subscriptions to various religious or moral doctrines. Also, as the Korean court cases referenced in this book indicate, public reason Confucianism advocates more progressive politics in East Asia in a way justifiable to East Asians' Confucian moral sentiments and public reasoning.[5]

Finally, can public reason Confucianism remain socially relevant even if the public moral consensus, on which it is premised, has become more Western liberal? Though public reason Confucianism is inspired by the

---

[4] We can raise essentially the same question to liberal theorists. How "liberal" is Rawls's political liberalism vis-à-vis Raz's liberal perfectionism, or Nozick's libertarianism, or Galston's liberal pluralism? And whose liberalism (Locke's, Mill's, or Tocqueville's) should be embraced as the standard against which to evaluate whether or not someone's liberalism is authentically liberal?

[5] In this regard, I support Stephen C. Angle's proposal for "progressive Confucianism." See his *Contemporary Confucian Political Philosophy: Toward Progressive Confucianism* (Cambridge: Polity, 2012).

empirical evidence that East Asians are still saturated with Confucian values (even those who have undergone liberal democratization for the past three decades), it does not build its normative theory merely on the evidence of the *current* public consensus. As a normative political theory, public reason Confucianism is predicated on the philosophical conviction that Confucian values such as filial piety, respect for elders, ancestor worship, ritual propriety, harmony within the family, and social harmony are objectively good and thus its primary political aim is to find a philosophically justifiable way to permit the state to promote such perfectionist values without violating the constitutive values of democracy such as popular sovereignty, political equality, and the right to political participation in a pluralist society. In this regard, public reason Confucianism can offer a distinctive (i.e., neither Western-liberal nor Confucian in the traditionalist sense) normative standard, or a regulative ideal, against which the current East Asian political practices are to be evaluated, and can also prevent the East Asian polities from becoming too Western. The claim that there is a strong empirical basis for constructing public reason Confucianism only makes the theory more socially relevant and politically urgent.

Bibliography

Abizadeh, Arash. 2008. "Democratic Theory and Border Coercion: No Right to Unilaterally Control Your Own Borders." *Political Theory* 36: 37–65.
Ackerly, Brooke A. 2005. "Is Liberalism the Only Way toward Democracy? Confucianism and Democracy." *Political Theory* 33: 547–576.
Alford, C. Fred. 1999. *Think No Evil: Korean Values in the Age of Globalization*. Ithaca: Cornell University Press.
Ames, Roger T. 2011. *Confucian Role Ethics: A Vocabulary*. Honolulu: University of Hawaii Press.
Ames, Roger T. and Henry Rosemont Jr. 1998. *The Analects of Confucius: A Philosophical Translation*. New York: Ballantine Books.
Angle, Stephen C. 2005. "Decent Democratic Centralism." *Political Theory* 33: 518–546.
  2009. *Sagehood: The Contemporary Significance of Neo-Confucian Philosophy*. New York: Oxford University Press.
  2012. *Contemporary Confucian Political Philosophy: Toward Progressive Confucianism*. Cambridge: Polity.
Bae, Mun-jo and Se-jeong Park. 2013. "Taehaksengŭi hyoedaehan inshikkwa kachokgach'igwane yŏnghyang'ŭl mich'inŭn pyŏnin" [Consciousness of Filial Piety and Family Values among College Students]. *Journal of the Korean Contents Association* 13: 275–285.
Bai, Tongdong. 2008. "A Mencian Version of Limited Democracy." *Res Publica* 14: 19–34.
  2009. *Jiubang Xinming: Gujin zhongxi canzhaoxia de gudian Rujia zhengzhizhexue [A New Mission of an Old State: The Contemporary and Comparative Relevance of Classical Confucian Political Philosophy]*. Beijing: Beijing daxue chubanshe.
  2012. *China: The Political Philosophy of the Middle Kingdom*. New York: Zed Book.
  2013. "A Confucian Version of Hybrid Regime: How Does It Work, and Why Is It Superior?" In *The East Asian Challenge for Democracy: Political*

Meritocracy in Comparative Perspective, edited by Daniel A. Bell and Chenyang Li. New York: Cambridge University Press, 55–87.
Barber, Benjamin R. 1996. "Constitutional Faith." In *For Love of Country: Debating the Limits of Patriotism*, edited by Joshua Cohen. Boston: Beacon Books, 30–37.
  1998. *A Place for Us: How to Make Society Civil and Democracy Strong.* New York: Hill and Wang.
  [1984] 2003. *Strong Democracy: Participatory Politics for a New Age.* Berkeley: University of California Press.
Barry, Brian. 1995. "John Rawls and the Search for Stability." *Ethics* 105: 874–915.
Beerbohm, Eric. 2012. *In Our Name: The Ethics of Democracy.* Princeton: Princeton University Press.
Beitz, Charles R. 1989. *Political Equality.* Princeton: Princeton University Press.
Bell, Daniel A. 1999. "Democratic Deliberation: The Problem of Implementation." In *Deliberative Politics: Essays on Democracy and Disagreement*, edited by Stephen Macedo. Oxford: Oxford University Press, 70–87.
  2000. *East Meets West: Human Rights and Democracy.* Princeton: Princeton University Press.
  2003. "Confucian Constraints on Property Rights." In *Confucianism for the Modern World*, edited by Daniel A. Bell and Chaibong Hahm. Cambridge: Cambridge University Press, 218–235.
  2006. *Beyond Liberal Democracy: Political Thinking for an East Asian Context.* Princeton: Princeton University Press.
  2013. "Introduction: The Theory, History, and Practice of Political Meritocracy." In *The East Asian Challenge for Democracy: Political Meritocracy in Comparative Perspective*, edited by Daniel A. Bell and Chenyang Li. New York: Cambridge University Press, 1–27.
  2015. *The China Model: Political Meritocracy and the Limits of Democracy.* Princeton: Princeton University Press.
Bellamy, Richard. 2007. *Political Constitutionalism: A Republican Defense of the Constitutionality of Democracy.* Cambridge: Cambridge University Press.
Berkowitz, Peter. 1999. *Virtue and the Making of Modern Liberalism.* Princeton: Princeton University Press.
Berman, Sheri. 1997. "Civil Society and the Collapse of the Weimar Republic." *World Politics* 49: 401–429.
Birdwhistell, Joanne D. 2007. *Mencius and Masculinities: Dynamics of Power, Morality, and Maternal Thinking.* Albany: State University of New York Press.
Blake, Michael. 2001. "Distributive Justice, State Coercion, and Autonomy." *Philosophy and Public Affairs* 30: 257–296.
Bloom, Irene. 1998. "Mencius and Human Rights." In *Confucianism and Human Rights*, edited by Wm. Theodore de Bary and Tu Wei-ming. New York: Columbia University Press, 94–116.
  2002. "Mengzian Arguments on Human Nature (*Ren Xing*)." In *Essays on the Moral Philosophy of Mengzi*, edited by Xiusheng Liu and Philip J. Ivanhoe. Indianapolis: Hackett, 64–100.

(trans.). 2009. *Mencius*, edited by Philip J. Ivanhoe. New York: Columbia University Press.
Boyd, Richard. 2004. "Michael Oakeshott on Civility, Civil Society and Civil Association." *Political Studies* 53: 603–622.
2004. *Uncivil Society: The Perils of Pluralism and the Making of Modern Liberalism*. Lanham: Lexington Books.
Brennan, Jason. 2011. *The Ethics of Voting*. Princeton: Princeton University Press.
Brettschneider, Corey. 2007. *Democratic Rights: The Substance of Self-Government*. Princeton: Princeton University Press.
Bui, Ngoc Son. 2013. "Beyond Judicial Review: The Proposal of the Constitutional Assembly." *Chinese Journal of Comparative Law* 2: 43–77.
Callan, Eamonn. 1997. *Creating Citizens: Political Education and Liberal Democracy*. Oxford: Oxford University Press.
Caney, Simon. 1995. "Anti-Perfectionism and Rawlsian Liberalism." *Political Studies* 42: 248–264.
Caplan, Bryan. 2007. *The Myth of the Rational Voter: Why Democracies Choose Bad Policies*. Princeton: Princeton University Press.
Carens, Joseph H. 2013. *The Ethics of Immigration*. New York: Oxford University Press.
Chan, Joseph. 1999. "A Confucian Perspective on Human Rights for Contemporary China." In *The East Asian Challenge for Human Rights*, edited by Joanne R. Bauer and Daniel A. Bell. Cambridge: Cambridge University Press, 212–237.
2000. "Legitimacy, Unanimity, and Perfectionism." *Philosophy and Public Affairs* 29: 5–42.
2003. "Giving Priority on the Worst Off: A Confucian Perspective on Social Welfare." In *Confucianism for the Modern World*, edited by Daniel A. Bell and Chaibong Hahm. Cambridge: Cambridge University Press, 236–253.
2007. "Democracy and Meritocracy: Toward a Confucian Perspective." *Journal of Chinese Philosophy* 34: 179–193.
2008. "Confucian Attitudes toward Ethical Pluralism." In *Confucian Political Ethics*, ed. Daniel A. Bell. Princeton: Princeton University Press, 113–138.
2008. "Is There a Confucian Perspective on Social Justice?" In *Western Political Thought in Dialogue with Asia*, edited by Takashi Shogimen and Cary J. Nederman. Lanham: Lexington Books, 261–277.
2012. "On the Legitimacy of Confucian Constitutionalism." In Jiang Qing, *A Confucian Constitutional Order: How China's Ancient Past Can Shape Its Political Future*, edited by Daniel A. Bell and Ruiping Fan, translated by Edmund Ryden. Princeton: Princeton University Press, 99–112.
2012. "Political Authority and Perfectionism: A Response to Quong." *Philosophy and Public Issues* 2: 31–41.
2013. "Political Meritocracy and Meritorious Rule: A Confucian Perspective." In *The East Asian Challenge for Democracy: Political Meritocracy in Comparative Perspective*, edited by Daniel A. Bell and Chenyang Li. New York: Cambridge University Press, 31–54.
2014. *Confucian Perfectionism: A Political Philosophy for Modern Times*. Princeton: Princeton University Press.

2014. "'Self-Restriction' and the Confucian Case for Democracy." *Philosophy East and West* 64: 785–795.
Chan, Sin Yee. 2004. "Filial Piety, Commiseration, and the Virtue of *Ren*." In *Filial Piety in Chinese Thought and History*, edited by Alan K. L. Chan and Sor-hoon Tan. London: RoutledgeCurzon, 176–188.
Chan, Wing-tsit. 1955. "The Evolution of the Chinese Concept *Jên*." *Philosophy East and West* 4: 295–319.
 (trans.). 1967. *Reflections on Things at Hand: The Neo-Confucian Anthology Compiled by Chu Hsi and Lü Tsu-ch'ien*. New York: Columbia University Press.
Chang, Kwang-chih. 1983. *Art, Myth, and Ritual: The Path to Political Authority in Ancient China*. Cambridge: Harvard University Press.
Chen, Albert H.Y. 2011. "Three Political Confucianism and Half a Century." In *The Renaissance of Confucianism in Contemporary China*, edited by Ruiping Fan. Dordrecht: Springer, 205–223.
Cheng, Chung-ying. 1998. "Transforming Confucian Virtues into Human Rights: A Study of Human Agency and Potency in Confucian Ethics." In *Confucianism and Human Rights*, edited by Wm. Theodore de Bary and Tu Wei-ming. New York: Columbia University Press, 142–153.
 2004. "A Theory of Confucian Selfhood: Self-Cultivation and Free Will in Confucian Philosophy." In *Confucian Ethics: A Comparative Study of Self, Autonomy, and Community*, edited by Kwong-loi Shun and David B. Wong. Cambridge: Cambridge University Press, 124–147.
Ching, Julia. 1997. *Mysticism and Kingship in China: The Heart of Chinese Wisdom*. Cambridge: Cambridge University Press.
Cho, Erin. 1998. "Caught in Confucius' Shadow: The Struggle for Women's Legal Equality in South Korea." *Columbia Journal of Asian Law* 12: 125–189.
Choi, Sang-chin. 2000. *Han'gugin shimnihak* [The Psychology of the Korean People]. Seoul: Chung Ang University Press.
Chow, Kai-Wing. 1996. *The Rise of Confucian Ritualism in Late Imperial China: Ethics, Classics, and Lineage Discourse*. Stanford: Stanford University Press.
Christiano, Thomas. 2004. "The Authority of Democracy." *Journal of Political Philosophy* 12: 266–290.
 2008. *The Constitution of Equality: Democratic Authority and Its Limits*. Oxford: Oxford University Press.
Ci, Jiwei. 1999. "The Confucian Relational Concept of the Person and Its Modern Predicament." *Kenney Institute of Ethics Journal* 9: 325–346.
Clark, Kelly J. and Robing R. Wang. 2004. "A Confucian Defense of Gender Equity." *Journal of the American Academy of Religion* 72: 395–422.
Cohen, Joshua. 1986. "An Epistemic Conception of Democracy." *Ethics* 97: 26–38.
 1993. "Freedom of Expression." *Philosophy and Public Affairs* 22: 207–263.
 2006. "Is There a Human Right to Democracy?" In *The Egalitarian Conscience*, edited by Christine Sypnowich. Oxford: Oxford University Press, 226–250.
 2009. *Philosophy, Politics, Democracy: Selected Essays*. Cambridge: Harvard University Press.

Colburn, Ben. 2010. *Autonomy and Liberalism*. New York: Routledge.
Collier, David and James E. Mahon, Jr. 1993. "Conceptual 'Stretching' Revisited: Adapting Categories in Comparative Analysis." *American Political Science Review* 87: 845–855.
Collier, David and Steven Levitsky. 1997. "Democracy with Adjectives: Conceptual Innovation in Comparative Research." *World Politics* 49: 430–451.
Creel, H. G. 1949. *Confucius and the Chinese Way*. New York: Harper & Row.
Crowder, George. 2002. *Liberalism and Value Pluralism*. New York: Continuum.
Dagger, Richard. 1997. *Civic Virtues: Rights, Citizenship, and Republican Liberalism*. New York: Oxford University Press.
Dahl, Robert A. 1971. *Polyarchy: Participation and Opposition*. New Haven: Yale University Press.
  1998. *On Democracy*. New Haven: Yale University Press.
Dallmayr, Fred R. 2004. "Confucianism and the Public Sphere: Five relationships Plus One?" In *The Politics of Affective Relations: East Asia and Beyond*, edited by Chaihark Hahm and Daniel A. Bell. Lanham: Lexington Books, 41–59.
  2009. "Exiting Liberal Democracy: Bell and Confucian Thought." *Philosophy East and West* 59: 524–530.
De Bary, Wm. Theodore. 1983. *The Liberal Tradition in China*. New York: Columbia University Press.
  1988. *East Asian Civilizations: A Dialogue in Five Stages*. Cambridge: Harvard University Press.
  1998. "Introduction." *Confucianism and Human Rights*, edited by Wm. Theodore de Bary and Tu Wei-ming. New York: Columbia University Press, 1–26.
De Bary, Wm. Theodore, Wing-tsit Chan, and Burton Watson (eds. and trans.). 1960. *Sources of Chinese Tradition*, vol. 1. New York: Columbia University Press.
De Tocqueville, Alexis. 2000. *Democracy in America*, translated by Harvey C. Mansfield and Delba Winthrop. Chicago: University of Chicago Press.
Deuchler, Martina. 1992. *The Confucian Transformation of Korea: A Study of Society and Ideology*. Cambridge: Council on East Asian Studies, Harvard University.
  1999. "Despoilers of the Way—Insulters of the Sages: Controversies over the Classics in Seventeenth-Century Korea." In *Culture and the State in Late Chosŏn Korea*, edited by JaHyun K. Haboush and Martina Deuchler. Cambridge: Council on East Asian Studies, Harvard University, 91–113.
Deudney, Daniel H. 1995. "The Philadelphian System: Sovereignty, Arms Control, and Balance of Power in the American States-Union, circa 1787–1861." *American Political Science Review* 49: 191–228.
Dewey, John. 1954. *The Public and Its Problems*. Athens: Swallow Press.
Diamond, Larry and Marc F. Plattner (eds.). 2001. *The Global Divergence of Democracies*. Baltimore: Johns Hopkins University Press.
Dryzek, John S. 2010. *Foundations and Frontiers of Deliberative Governance*. Oxford: Oxford University Press.
Dunn, John. 1969. *The Political Thought of John Locke: An Historical Account of the Argument of the Two Treatise of Government*. Cambridge: Cambridge University Press.

Dworkin, Ronald. 2011. *Justice for Hedgehogs*. Cambridge: Belknap.
Ebrey, Patricia B. 1991. *Chu Hsi's Family Rituals: A Twelfth-Century Chinese Manual for the Performance of Cappings, Weddings, Funerals, and Ancestral Rites*. Princeton: Princeton University Press.
Eisgruber, Christopher L. 2001. *Constitutional Self-Government*. Cambridge: Harvard University Press.
El-Amine, Loubna. 2015. *Classical Confucian Political Thought: A New Interpretation*. Princeton: Princeton University Press.
Elkin, Stephen L. 2006. *Reconstructing the Commercial Republic: Constitutional Design after Madison*. Chicago: University of Chicago Press.
Elstein, David. 2010. "Why Early Confucianism Cannot Generate Democracy." *Dao* 9: 427–443.
Estlund, David. 2008. *Democratic Authority: A Philosophical Framework*. Princeton: Princeton University Press.
Fan, Ruiping. 2010. *Reconstructionist Confucianism: Rethinking Morality after the West*. Dordrecht: Springer.
  2013. "Confucian Meritocracy for Contemporary China." In *The East Asian Challenge for Democracy: Political Meritocracy in Comparative Perspective*, edited by Daniel A. Bell and Chenyang Li. New York: Cambridge University Press, 88–115.
Fetzer, Joel S. and J. Christopher Soper. 2013. *Confucianism, Democratization, and Human Rights in Taiwan*. Lanham: Lexington Books.
Flathman, Richard E. 2005. "Idealism and Pluralism: Michael Oakeshott." In *Pluralism and Liberal Democracy*. Baltimore: Johns Hopkins University Press, 109–161.
Franco, Paul. 2004. *Michael Oakeshott: An Introduction*. New Haven: Yale University Press.
Fung, Archon and Erik O. Wright. 2003. *Deepening Democracy: Institutional Innovations in Empowered Participatory Governance*. London: Verso.
Galston, William A. 1991. *Liberal Purposes: Goods, Virtues, and Diversity in the Liberal State*. Cambridge: Cambridge University Press.
  2002. *Liberal Pluralism: The Implications of Value Pluralism for Political Theory and Practice*. Cambridge: Cambridge University Press.
  2005. *The Practice of Liberal Pluralism*. Cambridge: Cambridge University Press.
  2007. "Pluralism and Civic Virtue." *Social Theory and Practice* 33: 625–635.
  2010. "Realism in Political Theory." *European Journal of Political Theory* 9: 385–411.
  2011. "Pluralist Constitutionalism." *Social Philosophy and Policy* 28: 228–241.
Gaus, Gerald F. 1996. *Justificatory Liberalism: An Essay on Epistemology and Political Theory*. New York: Oxford University Press.
  2012. "Sectarianism Without Perfection? Quong's Political Liberalism." *Philosophy and Public Issues* 2: 7–15.
Gellner, Ernest. 1996. *Conditions of Liberty: Civil Society and Its Rivals*. New York: Penguin Books.
Geuss, Raymond. 2008. *Philosophy and Real Politics*. Princeton: Princeton University Press.

Ginsburg, Tom. 2002. "Confucian Constitutionalism? The Emergence of Constitutional Review in Korea and Taiwan." *Law and Social Inquiry* 27: 763–799.
Goldin, Paul R. 2000. "The View of Women in Early Confucianism." In *The Sage and the Second Sex: Confucianism, Ethics, and Gender*, edited by Chenyang Li. Chicago: Open Court, 133–161.
Gray, John. 2000. *Two Faces of Liberalism*. New York: The New Press.
Gutmann, Amy. 1983. *Liberal Equality*. Cambridge: Cambridge University Press.
  [1987] 1999. *Democratic Education*. Princeton: Princeton University Press.
  2003. *Identity in Democracy*. Princeton: Princeton University Press.
  2003. "Rawls on the Relationship between Liberalism and Democracy." In *The Cambridge Companion to Rawls*, edited by Samuel Freeman. Cambridge: Cambridge University Press, 168–199.
Gutmann, Amy and Dennis Thompson. 1996. *Democracy and Disagreement: Why Moral Conflict Cannot Be Avoided in Politics, and What Should Be Done about It*. Cambridge: Belknap Press.
Hahm, Chaibong. 1997. "The Confucian Political Discourse and the Politics of Reform in Korea." *Korea Journal* 34: 65–77.
  1998. *T'algŭndaewa yugyo* [*Postmodernity and Confucianism*]. Seoul: Nanam.
  2000. "Kaŭi inyŏmgwa ch'eche" [The Ideology and Institution of Ka 家]. *Chŏntong'gwa hyŏndae* [*Tradition and Modernity*] 14: 73–114.
  2003. "Family versus the Individual: The Politics of Marriage Laws in Korea." In *Confucianism for the Modern World*, edited by Daniel A. Bell and Chaibong Hahm. Cambridge: Cambridge University Press, 334–359.
  2004. "The Ironies of Confucianism." *Journal of Democracy* 15: 93–107.
Hahm, Chaihark. 2001. "Conceptualizing Korean Constitutionalism: Foreign Transplant or Indigenous Tradition?" *Journal of Korean Law* 1: 151–196.
  2003. "Constitutionalism, Confucian Civic Virtue, and Ritual Propriety." In *Confucianism for the Modern World*, edited by Daniel A. Bell and Chaibong Hahm. Cambridge: Cambridge University Press, 31–53.
  2003. "Law, Culture, and the Politics of Confucianism." *Columbia Journal of Asian Law* 16: 253–301.
  2004. "Negotiating Confucian Civility through Constitutional Discourse." In *The Politics of Affective Relations: East Asian and Beyond*, edited by Chaihark Hahm and Daniel A. Bell. Lanham: Lexington Books, 277–308.
  2012. "Beyond 'Law vs. Politics' in Constitutional Adjudication: Lessons from South Korea." *International Journal of Constitutional Law* 10: 6–34.
Hall, David L. and Roger T. Ames. 1999. *The Democracy of the Dead: Dewey, Confucius, and the Hope for Democracy in China*. Chicago: Open Court.
Hampshire, Stuart. 2000. *Justice Is Conflict*. Princeton: Princeton University Press.
Han, Sangjin and Kisu Eun. 1999. "Kaehyŏkchiyangjŏk chungsanch'ŭngŭi kach'igwanchiyang'gwa ch'amyŏjŏk shillyoesahoe kuch'uk" [The Value Orientation of the Progressive-Minded Middle Class and the Construction of a Participatory Fiduciary Society]. The Ministry of Education Research Report, South Korea.
Han'guk yuhakhoe [Association for Confucian Studies] (ed.). 2001. *Yugyowa Peminisŭm* [*Confucianism and Feminism*]. Seoul: Ch'ŏrakkwa hyŏnsilsa.

Helgesen, Geir. 1998. *Democracy and Authority in Korea: The Cultural Dimension in Korean Politics*. Surrey: Curzon.
Herr, Ranjoo S. 2010. "Confucian Democracy and Equality." *Asian Philosophy* 20: 261–282.
Hirschmann, Nancy J. 2008. "Mill, Political Economy, and Women's Work." *American Political Science Review* 102: 199–213.
Ho, Lusina. 2003. "Traditional Confucian Values and Western Legal Frameworks." In *Confucianism for the Modern World*, edited by Daniel A. Bell and Chaibong Hahm. Cambridge: Cambridge University Press, 288–311.
Hsiao, Kung-chuan. 1979. *A History of Chinese Political Thought, Vol. 1: From The Beginnings to the Sixth Century A.D.*, translated by Frederick W. Mote. Princeton: Princeton University Press.
Huang, Chun-chieh. 2010. "East Asian Conceptions of the Public and Private Realms." In *Taking Confucian Ethics Seriously: Contemporary Theories and Applications*, edited by Kam-Por Yu, Julia Tao, and Philip J. Ivanhoe. Albany: State University of New York Press, 73–97.
Hutton, Eric L. 2002. "Moral Connoisseurship in Mengzi." In *Essays on the Moral Philosophy of Mengzi*, edited by Xiusheng Liu and Philip J. Ivanhoe. Indianapolis: Hackett, 163–186.
  2006. "Character, Situationism, and Early Confucian Thought." *Philosophical Studies* 127: 37–58.
  2008. "Han Feizi's Criticism of Confucianism and Its Implications for Virtue Ethics." *Journal of Moral Philosophy* 5: 423–453.
  2008. "Un-Democratic Values in Plato and Xunzi." In *Polishing the Chinese Mirror*, edited by Marthe Chandler and Ronnie Littlejohn. New York: Global Scholarly Publications, 313–330.
  (trans.). 2014. *Xunzi: The Complete Text*. Princeton: Princeton University Press.
Inkeles, Alex. 1969. "Making Men Modern: On the Causes and Consequences of Individual Change in Six Developing Countries." *American Journal of Sociology* 75: 208–225.
Ivanhoe, Philip J. 2000. *Confucian Moral Self Cultivation*. Indianapolis: Hackett.
  2002. "Confucian Self Cultivation and Mengzi's Notion of Extension." In *Essays on the Moral Philosophy of Mengzi*, edited by Xiusheng Liu and Philip J. Ivanhoe. Indianapolis: Hackett, 221–241.
  2007. "Filial Piety as Virtue." In *Working Virtue: Virtue Ethics and Contemporary Moral Problems*, edited by Rebecca L. Walker and Philip J. Ivanhoe. Oxford: Oxford University Press, 297–312.
  2013. "Virtue Ethics and the Chinese Confucian Tradition." In *The Cambridge Companion to Virtue Ethics*, edited by Daniel C. Russell. Cambridge: Cambridge University Press, 49–69.
  2014. "New Old Foundations for Confucian Ethical Philosophy: Itō Jinsai, Dai Zhen, and Jeong Yakyong." *Taiwan Journal of East Asian Studies* 11: 77–133.
Ivanhoe, Philip J. and Sungmoon Kim (eds.). Forthcoming. *Confucianism, a Habit of the Heart: Bellah, Civil Religion, and East Asia*. Albany: State University of New York Press.

Jiang, Qing. 2003. *Zhengzhi Ruxue: Dangdai Rujia de zhuanxiang, tezhi yu fazhan* [Political Confucianism: Contemporary Confucianism's Challenge, Special Quality, and Development]. Beijing: San lian shu dian.
  2013. *A Confucian Constitutional Order: How China's Ancient Past Can Shape Its Political Future*, edited by Daniel A. Bell and Ruiping Fan, translated by Edmund Ryden. Princeton: Princeton University Press.
Kang, Jung In. 2013. *Nŏmnadŭmŭi chŏngch'isasang* [A Political Thought of Cultural Crossing]. Seoul: Humanitasŭ.
Kang, Xiaoguang. 2005. *Renzheng: Zhongguo zhengzhi fazhan de disantiao daolu* [Benevolent Government: A Third Road for the Development of Chinese Politics]. Singapore: Global Publishing.
Kant, Immanuel. 1996. *The Metaphysics of Morals*, edited by Mary Gregor. Cambridge: Cambridge University Press.
Kateb, George. 1992. *The Inner Ocean: Individualism and Democratic Culture*. Ithaca: Cornell University Press.
  1998. "The Value of Association." In *Freedom of Association*, edited by Amy Gutmann. Princeton: Princeton University Press, 35–63.
  2011. *Human Dignity*. Cambridge: Belknap.
Kim, Che-wan. 2006. "Tanch'ebŏmniŭi chaejomyŏng: Chongjungchaesanŭi pŏpchŏk sŏngkkyŏk" [A Review of Incorporation and Non-Profit Fund Law in Korea]. *The Korean Journal of Civil Law* 31: 93–137.
Kim, Marie S.H. 2012. *Law and Custom in Korea: Comparative Legal History*. New York: Cambridge University Press.
  2013. "In the Name of Custom, Culture, and the Constitution: Korean Customary Law in Flux." *Texas International Law Journal* 48: 357–391.
  2015. "Confucianism that Confounds: Constitutional Jurisprudence on Filial Piety in Korea." In *Confucianism, Law, and Democracy in Contemporary Korea*, edited by Sungmoon Kim. London: Rowman & Littlefield International, 57–80.
Kim, Sangjun. 2001. "Yeŭi sahoehakchŏk haesŏgŭl wihan ironjŏk tansŏ: Makssŭ Paebŏŭi 'inyŏmjŏk ihae'" [A Theoretical Clue to a Sociological Interpretation of the Confucian Ritual: Max Weber's "Ideal Interests"]. *Sahoewa yŏksa* [Society and History] 59: 11–50.
  2011. *Maengjaŭi ttam sŏngwangŭi p'i* [Sweat of Mencius and Blood of the Sacred Kings]. Seoul: Akanet.
  2014. *Yugyoŭi chŏngch'ijŏk muŭishik* [The Political Subconsciousness of Confucianism]. Seoul: Kŭlhangari.
Kim, Sungmoon. 2007. "Family, Affection, and Confucian Civil Society: The Politico-Philosophical Implications of the New Family Law in Korea." *International Studies in Philosophy* 39: 51–75.
  2009. "Confucianism in Contestation: The May Struggle of 1991 in South Korea and Its Lesson." *New Political Science* 31: 49–68.
  2010. "Beyond Liberal Civil Society: Confucian Familism and Relational Strangership." *Philosophy East and West* 60: 476–498.
  2010. "On Korean Dual Civil Society: Thinking through Tocqueville and Confucius." *Contemporary Political Theory* 9: 434–457.

2011. "Confucian Constitutionalism: Mencius and Xunzi on Virtue, Ritual, and Royal Transmission." *The Review of Politics* 73: 371–399.

2011. "The Virtue of Incivility: Confucian Communitarianism beyond Docility." *Philosophy and Social Criticism* 37: 25–48.

2014. *Confucian Democracy in East Asia: Theory and Practice*. New York: Cambridge University Press.

2014. "From Wife to Moral Teacher: Kang Chŏngildang's Neo-Confucian Self-Cultivation." *Asian Philosophy* 24: 28–47.

2014. "Politics and Interest in Early Confucianism." *Philosophy East and West* 64: 425–448.

2014. "The Way to Become a Female Sage: Im Yunjidang's Confucian Feminism." *Journal of the History of Ideas* 75: 396–416.

2015. "John Dewey and Confucian Democracy: Towards Common Citizenship." *Constellations* 22: 31–43.

2015. "Oakeshott and Confucian Constitutionalism." In *Michael Oakeshott's Cold War Liberalism*, edited by Terry Nardin. New York: Palgrave Macmillan, 133–150.

Forthcoming. "Achieving the Way: Confucian Virtue Politics and the Problem of Dirty Hands." *Philosophy East and West* 66.

Kim, Tŏk-kyun. 2005. "Yugyochŏk kachokjuŭi, haech'ein'ga pogwŏnin'ga" [Confucian Family Principles, Deconstruction or Restoration]. *Yugyosasang munhwa yŏn'gu [The Journal of Confucian Thought and Culture]* 23: 109–134.

Kim, Youngmin. "Neo-Confucianism as Free-Floating Resource: Im Yunjidang and Kang Chŏngildang as Two Female Neo-Confucian Philosophers in Late Chosŏn." In *Women and Confucianism in Chosŏn Korea*, edited by Youngmin Kim and Michael J. Pettid. Albany: State University of New York Press, 71–88.

Klosko, George. 1992. *The Principle of Fairness and Obligation*. Lanham: Rowman and Littlefield.

2000. *Democratic Procedures and Liberal Consensus*. Oxford: Oxford University Press.

Knight, Jack and James Johnson. 2011. *The Priority of Democracy: Political Consequences of Pragmatism*. Princeton: Princeton University Press.

Ko, Dorothy, Jahyun K. Haboush, and Joan R. Piggott (eds.). 2003. *Women and Confucian Cultures in Premodern China, Korea, and Japan*. Berkeley: University of California Press.

Ko, Yŏng-chin. 1995. *Chosŏn chunggi yehaksasangsa [A Historical Study of Ritual Thoughts in the Mid Chosŏn Period]*. Seoul: Han'gilsa.

Koh, Byung-ik. 1996. "Confucianism in Contemporary Korea." In *Confucian Traditions in East Asian Modernity: Moral Education and Economic Culture in Japan and Four Mini-Dragons*, edited by Tu Wei-ming. Cambridge: Harvard University Press, 191–201.

Korean Ministry of Culture, Sports, and Tourism. 2011. "Religions in Korea" [Han'gugŭi Chonggyo hyŏnhwang]. Publication number: 11-1371000-000391-01.

Kramer, Larry D. 2004. *The People Themselves: Popular Constitutionalism and Judicial Review*. New York: Oxford University Press.

Krause, Sharon. 2008. *Civil Passions: Moral Sentiment and Democratic Deliberation.* Princeton: Princeton University Press.

Kwak, Jun-Hyeok and Leigh Jenco (eds.). 2014. *Republicanism in Northeast Asia.* London: Routledge.

Kwok, D. W. Y. 1988. "On the Rites and Rights of Being Human." In *Confucianism and Human Rights*, edited by Wm. Theodore de Bary and Tu Weiming. New York: Columbia University Press, 83–93.

Kymlicka, Will. 1995. *Multicultural Citizenship.* Oxford: Oxford University Press.

2001. *Politics in the Vernacular: Nationalism, Multiculturalism, and Citizenship.* Oxford: Oxford University Press.

Lai, Karyn. 2006. "*Li* in the *Analects*: Training in the Moral Competence and the Question of Flexibility." *Philosophy East and West* 56: 69–83.

Landemore, Hélène. 2013. *Democratic Reason: Politics, Collective Intelligence, and the Rule of the Many.* Princeton: Princeton University Press.

Larmore, Charles. 2003. "Public Reason." In *The Cambridge Companion to Rawls*, edited by Samuel Freeman. Cambridge: Cambridge University Press, 368–393.

2008. *The Autonomy of Morality.* New York: Cambridge University Press.

Lau, D.C. (trans.). 1979. *The Analects.* New York: Penguin.

Lee, Chang-hyun. 2010. "Chongjungŭi chayulkkwŏn'gwa kŭ han'gye [Clan's Autonomy and Its Limit]." *Kachokpŏpyŏn'gu [The Korean Journal of Family Law]* 24: 75–110.

Lee, Namhee. 2007. *The Making of Minjung: Democracy and the Politics of Representation in South Korea.* Ithaca: Cornell University Press.

Lee, Pauline C. 2000. "Li Zhi and John Stuart Mill: A Confucian Feminist Critique of Liberal Feminism." In *The Sage and the Second Sex: Confucianism, Ethics, and Gender*, edited by Chenyang Li. Chicago: Open Court, 113–132.

2012. *Li Zhi, Confucianism, and the Virtue of Desire.* Albany: State University of New York Press.

Lee, Seung-Hwan. 2003. "The Concept of *Gong* in Traditional Korea and Its Modern Transformations." *Korea Journal* 43: 137–163.

Lee, Sook-in. 2002. "Transforming Gender Relations through Intimacy." *Korea Journal* 42: 46–69.

2005. *Tongasia kodaeŭi yŏsŏngsasang: yŏsŏngchuŭiro pon yugyo [Feminist Thought in Ancient East Asia: Confucianism Seen Through Feminism].* Seoul: Yŏiyŏn.

Lee, Whasook. 2003. "Married Daughters Should Be Recognized as 'Jongjung' Members." *Munhwa Ilbo*, December 17. Op-Ed.

Levinson, Sanford. 1988. *Constitutional Faith.* Princeton: Princeton University Press.

Li, Chenyang. 1997. "Confucian Value and Democratic Value." *Journal of Value Inquiry* 31: 183–193.

1997. "Shifting Perspectives: Filial Morality Revisited." *Philosophy East and West* 47: 211–232.

2000. "The Confucian Concept of *Jen* and the Feminist Ethics of Care: A Comparative Study." In *The Sage and the Second Sex: Confucianism, Ethics, and Gender*, edited by Chenyang Li. Chicago: Open Court, 23–42.

 2007. "*Li* as Cultural Grammar: On the Relation between *Li* and *Ren* in Confucius' *Analects*." *Philosophy East and West* 57: 311–329.
 2012. "Equality and Inequality in Confucianism." *Dao* 11: 295–313.
 2013. *The Confucian Philosophy of Harmony*. New York: Routledge.
Ling, L.H.M. and Chih-yu Shih. 1998. "Confucianism with a Liberal Face: The Meaning of Democratic Politics in Postcolonial Taiwan." *Review of Politics* 60: 55–82.
Linz, Juan J. and Alfred Stepan. 1996. *Problems of Democratic Transition and Consolidation: Southern Europe, South America, and Post-Communist Europe*. Baltimore: Johns Hopkins University Press.
Macedo, Stephen. 1990. *Liberal Virtues: Citizenship, Virtue, and Community in Liberal Constitutionalism*. Oxford: Oxford University Press.
 2000. *Diversity and Distrust: Civic Education in a Multicultural Democracy*. Cambridge: Harvard University Press.
 2013. "Meritocratic Democracy: Learning from the American Constitution." In *The East Asian Challenge for Democracy: Political Meritocracy in Comparative Perspective*, edited by Daniel A. Bell and Chenyang Li. New York: Cambridge University Press, 232–256.
Mang, Franz F. L. 2013. "Liberal Neutrality and Moderate Perfectionism." *Res Publica* 19: 297–315.
Mansbridge, Jane. 1977. "Acceptable Inequalities." *British Journal of Political Science* 7: 321–336.
 1997. "Taking Coercion Seriously." *Constellations* 3: 407–416.
 2003. "Rethinking Representation." *American Political Science Review* 97: 515–528.
 2009. "A 'Selection Model' of Political Representation." *Journal of Political Philosophy* 17: 369–398.
 2011. "Clarifying Political Representation." *American Political Science Review* 105: 621–630.
 2012. "On the Importance of Getting Things Done." *PS: Political Science and Politics* 45: 1–8.
 2012. "What is Political Science For?" *Perspectives on Politics* 12: 8–17.
Michelman, Frank L. 2003. "Rawls on Constitutionalism and Constitutional Law." In *The Cambridge Companion to Rawls*, edited by Samuel Freeman. Cambridge: Cambridge University Press, 394–425.
Mill, J.S. 1989. *The Subjection of Women*. In *On Liberty and Other Writings*, edited by Stefan Collini. Cambridge: Cambridge University Press.
Miller, David. 1995. *On Nationality*. Oxford: Oxford University Press.
 2010. "Why Immigration Controls Are Not Coercive: A Reply to Arash Abizadeh." *Political Theory* 38: 111–120.
Mills, Chris. 2012. "Can Liberal Perfectionism Generate Distinctive Distributive Principles?" *Philosophy and Public Issues* 2: 123–152.
Mote, Frederick W. 1971. *Intellectual Foundations of China*. New York: Alfred A. Knopf.
Mouffe, Chantal. 1993. *The Return of the Political*. London: Verso.
Mulhall, Stephen and Adam Swift. 2003. "Rawls and Communitarianism." In *The Cambridge Companion to Rawls*, edited by Samuel Freeman. Cambridge: Cambridge University Press, 460–487.

Munro, Donald J. 1969. *The Concept of Man in Early China*. Stanford: Stanford University Press.
Murphy, James B. 2007. "From Aristotle to Hobbes: William Galston on Civic Virtue." *Social Theory and Practice* 33: 637–644.
Na, Chong-sŏk. 2014. "Han'guk minjujuŭiwa yugyomunhwa" [Korean Democracy and Confucian Culture]. In *Yuhagi onŭlŭi munchee tabŭl jul su innŭnga [Can Confucianism Give an Answer for Today's Problems]*, edited by Chong-sŏk Na, Yŏng-to Park, and Kyŏng-ran Cho. Seoul: Hyean, 242–270.
Neville, Robert C. 2000. *Boston Confucianism: Portable Tradition in the Late-Modern World*. Albany: State University of New York Press.
Nuyen, A. T. 2009. "Moral Obligation and Moral Motivation in Confucian Role-Based Ethics." *Dao* 8: 1–11.
Oakeshott, Michael. 1975. *On Human Conduct*. Oxford: Clarendon.
   1996. *The Politics of Faith and the Politics of Scepticism*, edited by Timothy Fuller. New Haven: Yale University Press.
O'Dwyer, Shaun. 2003. "Democracy and Confucian Values." *Philosophy East and West* 53: 39–63.
Okin, Susan M. 1989. *Justice, Gender, and the Family*. New York: Basic Books.
Parker, Richard D. 1994. *"Here, the People Rule": A Constitutional Populist Manifesto*. Cambridge: Harvard University Press.
Paterson, Mark A. 1996. *Korean Adoption and Inheritance: Case Studies in the Creation of a Classic Confucian Society*. Ithaca: Cornell University Press.
Peerenboom, Randall. 1998. "Confucian Harmony and Freedom of Thought: The Right to Think Versus Right Thinking." In *Confucianism and Human Rights*, edited by Wm. Theodore de Bary and Tu Wei-ming. New York: Columbia University Press, 234–260.
Pettit, Philip. 1997. *Republicanism: A Theory of Freedom and Government*. Oxford: Oxford University Press.
   2012. *On the People's Terms: A Republican Theory and Model of Democracy*. Cambridge: Cambridge University Press.
   2013. "Meritocratic Representation." In *The East Asian Challenge for Democracy: Political Meritocracy in Comparative Perspective*, edited by Daniel A. Bell and Chenyang Li. New York: Cambridge University Press, 138–157.
Philip, Mark. 2010. "What Is To Be Done? Political Theory and Political Realism." *European Journal of Political Theory* 9: 466–484.
Pines, Yuri. 2005. "Disputers of Abdication: Zhanguo Egalitarianism and the Sovereign's Power." *T'oung Pao* 91: 243–300.
   2013. "Between Merit and Pedigree: Evolution of the Conception of 'Elevating of the Worthy' in Pre-imperial China." In *The East Asian Challenge for Democracy: Political Meritocracy in Comparative Perspective*, edited by Daniel A. Bell and Chenyang Li. New York: Cambridge University Press, 161–202.
Putnam, Robert D. 2000. *Bowling Alone: The Collapse and Revival of American Community*. New York: Touchstone.
Quong, Jonathan. 2011. *Liberalism without Perfection*. Oxford: Oxford University Press.
   2012. "*Liberalism without Perfection*: Replies to Gaus, Colburn, Chan, and Bocchiola." *Philosophy and Public Issues* 2: 51–79.

Rawls, John. 1971. *A Theory of Justice*. Cambridge: Belknap.
  1993. *Political Liberalism*. New York: Columbia University Press.
  1993. "Reply to Habermas." In *Political Liberalism*. New York: Columbia University Press, 372–434.
  1999. "The Idea of Public Reason Revisited." In *The Law of Peoples*. Cambridge: Harvard University Press, 129–180.
  1999. *The Law of Peoples*. Cambridge: Harvard University Press.
Raz, Joseph. 1986. *The Morality of Freedom*. Oxford: Clarendon.
  1990. "Introduction." In *Authority*, edited by Joseph Raz. Oxford: Basil Blackwell, 1–19.
Richardson, Henry S. 2002. *Democratic Autonomy: Public Reasoning about the Ends of Policy*. New York: Oxford University Press.
Ridge, Michael. 1998. "Hobbesian Public Reason." *Ethics* 108: 538–568.
Rosanvallon, Pierre. 2011. *Democratic Legitimacy: Impartiality, Reflexivity, Proximity*, translated by Arthur Goldhammer. Princeton: Princeton University Press.
Rosemont, Henry, Jr. 1988. "Why Take Rights Seriously? A Confucian Critique." In *Human Rights and the World's Religions*, edited by Leroy Rouner. Notre Dame: University of Notre Dame Press, 167–182.
  1991. "Rights-Bearing Individuals and Role-Bearing Persons." In *Rules, Rituals, and Responsibility*, edited by Mary I. Bockover. Chicago: Open Court, 71–101.
Rosenblum, Nancy L. 1996. "The Democracy of Everyday Life." In *Liberalism without Illusions: Essays on Liberal Theory and the Political Vision of Judith N. Shklar*, edited by Bernard Yack. Chicago: University of Chicago Press, 25–44.
  1998. *Membership and Morals: The Personal Uses of Pluralism in America*. Princeton: Princeton University Press.
Rosenlee, Li-Hsiang L. 2010. "A Feminist Appropriation of Confucianism." In *Confucianism in Context: Classic Philosophy and Contemporary Issues, East Asia and Beyond*, edited by Wonsuk Chang and Leah Kalmanson. Albany: State University of New York Press, 175–190.
Ryu, Su-yeong. 2007. "Han'guginŭi yugyojŏk kach'ich'ŭkchŏngmunhang kaebal yŏn'gu" [Item Development for Korean Confucian Values]. *Korean Journal of Management* 15: 171–205.
Sandel, Michael J. 1996. *Democracy's Discontent: America in Search of a Public Philosophy*. Cambridge: Belknap.
Sartori, Giovanni. 1970. "Conceptual Misformation in Comparative Politics." *American Political Science Review* 64: 1033–1053.
Scanlon, T. M. 2003. "Rawls on Justification." In *The Cambridge Companion to Rawls*, edited by Samuel Freeman. Cambridge: Cambridge University Press, 139–167.
Schwartz, Benjamin I. 1985. *The World of Thought in Ancient China*. Cambridge: Belknap.
Setton, Mark. 1997. *Chŏng Yagyong: Korea's Challenge to Orthodox Neo-Confucianism*. Albany: State University of New York Press.
Shapiro, Ian. 1999. *Democratic Justice*. New Haven: Yale University Press.

Sher, George. 1979. "Effort, Ability, and Personal Desert." *Philosophy and Public Affairs* 8: 361–379.
  1997. *Beyond Neutrality: Perfectionism and Politics*. Cambridge: Cambridge University Press.
Shils, Edward. 1996. "Reflections on Civil Society and Civility in the Chinese Intellectual Tradition." In *Confucian Traditions in East Asian Modernity: Moral Education and Economic Culture in Japan and Four Mini-Dragons*, edited by Tu Wei-ming. Cambridge: Harvard University Press, 38–71.
  1997. *The Virtue of Civility: Selected Essays on Liberalism, Tradition, and Civil Society*, edited by Steven Grosby. Indianapolis: Liberty Fund.
Shin, Doh Chull. 2012. *Confucianism and Democratization in East Asia*. New York: Cambridge University Press.
Shklar, Judith N. 1984. *Ordinary Vices*. Cambridge: Belknap Press.
Sim, May. 2007. *Remastering Morals with Aristotle and Confucius*. New York: Cambridge University Press.
Simmons, A. John. 2001. *Justification and Legitimacy: Essays on Rights and Obligations*. New York: Cambridge University Press.
Skerrett, K. Roberts. 2005. "Political Liberalism and the Idea of Public Reason: A Response to Jeffrey Stout's *Democracy and Tradition*." *Social Theory and Practice* 31: 173–190.
Skinner, Quentin. 1998. *Liberty before Liberalism*. Cambridge: Cambridge University Press.
Slote, Walter H. and George A. DeVos (eds.). 1998. *Confucianism and the Family*. Albany: State University of New York Press.
Smith, Rogers M. 1985. *Liberalism and American Constitutional Law*. Cambridge: Harvard University Press.
  2003. *Stores of Peoplehood: The Politics and Morals of Political Membership*. Cambridge: Cambridge University Press.
Stalnaker, Aaron. 2014. "Confucianism, Democracy, and the Virtue of Deference." *Dao* 12: 441–459.
Stout, Jeffrey. 2004. *Democracy and Tradition*. Princeton: Princeton University Press.
Strauss, Leo. 1965. *Natural Right and History*. Chicago: University of Chicago Press.
Sun, Anna. 2013. *Confucianism as a World Religion: Contested Histories and Contemporary Realities*. Princeton: Princeton University Press.
Sunstein, Cass. 2001. *Designing Democracy: What Constitutions Do*. New York: Oxford University Press.
Tamir, Yael. 1993. *Liberal Nationalism*. Princeton: Princeton University Press.
Tan, Sor-hoon. 2004. *Confucian Democracy: A Deweyan Reconstruction*. Albany: State University of New York Press.
  2004. "Filial Daughters-in-law: Questioning Confucian Filiality." In *Filial Piety in Chinese Thought and History*, edited by Alan K. L. Chan and Sor-hoon Tan. London: RoutledgeCurzon, 226–240.
  2009. "Beyond Elitism: A Community Ideal for a Modern East Asia." *Philosophy East and West* 59: 537–553.
Tiwald, Justin. 2008. "A Right of Rebellion in the *Mengzi*?" *Dao* 7: 269–282.

Tu, Wei-ming. 1968. "The Creative Tension between *Jen* and *Li*." *Philosophy East and West* 18: 29–39.
  1979. *Humanity and Self-Cultivation*. Berkeley: Asian Humanities Press.
  1991. "The Search for Roots in Industrial East Asia: The Case of the Confucian Revival." In *Fundamentalisms Observed*, edited by Martin E. Marty and R. Scott Appleby. Chicago: University of Chicago Press, 740–781.
  1995. *Confucian Thought: Selfhood as Creative Transformation*. Albany: State University of New York Press.
Tushnet, Mark. 1999. *Taking the Constitution Away from the Courts*. Princeton: Princeton University Press.
Twiss, Sumner B. 1998. "A Constructive Framework for Discussing Confucianism and Human Rights." In *Confucianism and Human Rights*, edited by Wm. Theodore de Bary and Tu Wei-ming. New York: Columbia University Press, 27–53.
Van Norden, Bryan W. 2007. *Virtue Ethics and Consequentialism in Early Chinese Philosophy*. New York: Cambridge University Press.
Viroli, Maurizio. 2002. *Republicanism*. New York: Hill and Wang.
Waldron, Jeremy. 1999. *The Dignity of Legislation*. Cambridge: Cambridge University Press.
  1999. *Law and Disagreement*. Cambridge: Cambridge University Press.
  2002. *God, Locke, and Equality: Christian Foundations in Locke's Political Thought*. Cambridge: Cambridge University Press.
Wall, Steven. 1998. *Liberalism, Perfectionism and Restraint*. Cambridge: Cambridge University Press.
  2006. "Democracy, Authority, and Publicity." *Journal of Political Philosophy* 14: 85–100.
  2012. "Perfectionism in Moral and Political Philosophy." In *The Stanford Encyclopedia of Philosophy*, edited by Edward N. Zalta, http://plato.stanford.edu/archives/win2012/entries/perfectionism-moral.
Walzer, Michael. 1998. "On Involuntary Association." In *Freedom of Association*, edited by Amy Gutmann. Princeton: Princeton University Press, 64–74.
Wang, Huaiyu. 2015. "A Genealogical Study of *De*: Poetical Correspondence of Sky, Earth, and Humankind in the Early Chinese Virtuous Rule of Benefaction." *Philosophy East and West* 65: 81–124.
Warren, Mark E. 1992. "Democratic Theory and Self-Transformation." *American Political Science Review* 86: 8–23.
Warren, Mark E. and Hilary Pearse (eds.). 2008. *Designing Deliberative Democracy: The British Columbia Citizens' Assembly*. Cambridge: Cambridge University Press.
Warren, Mark E. and Jane Mansbridge, et al. 2013. "Deliberative Negotiation," In *Negotiating Agreement in Politics*, edited by Jane Mansbridge and Cathie J. Martin. Washington, DC: American Political Science Association, 86–120.
Wawrytko, Sandra A. 2000. "Kongzi as Feminist: Confucian Self-Cultivation in a Contemporary Context." *Journal of Chinese Philosophy* 27: 171–186.
Weber, Max. 1958. *From Max Weber: Essays in Sociology*, edited and translated by Hans H. Gerth and C. W. Mills. New York: Oxford University Press.

Weithman, Paul. 2004. "Political Republicanism and Perfectionist Republicanism." *Review of Politics* 66: 285–312.

Wenman, Mark. 2013. *Agonistic Democracy: Constituent Power in the Era of Globalisation.* New York: Cambridge University Press.

Williams, Bernard. 2005. *In the Beginning was the Deed.* Princeton: Princeton University Press.

Wolterstorff, Nicholas. 2012. *Understanding Liberal Democracy: Essays in Political Philosophy.* Oxford: Oxford University Press.

Wong, David B. 2002. "Reasons and Analogical Reasoning in Mengzi." In *Essays on the Moral Philosophy of Mengzi*, edited by Xiusheng Liu and Philip J. Ivanhoe. Indianapolis: Hackett, 187–220.

  2004. "Rights and Community in Confucianism." In *Confucian Ethics: A Comparative Study of Self, Autonomy, and Community*, edited by Kwong-loi Shun and David B. Wong. Cambridge: Cambridge University Press, 31–48.

Wood, Alan T. 1995. *Limits to Autocracy: From Sung Neo-Confucianism to a Doctrine of Political Rights.* Honolulu: University of Hawaii Press.

Xu, Yang-jie. 1992. *Zhongguo jiazu zhidushi* [A History of Chinese Family System]. Beijing: Renmin chuban she.

Yack, Bernard. 2012. *Nationalism and the Moral Psychology of Community.* Chicago: University of Chicago Press.

Yang, Fenggang. 1999. *Chinese Christians in America: Conversion, Assimilation, and Adhesive Identities.* University Park: The Pennsylvania State University Press.

Yang, Hyunah. 2002. "Unfinished Tasks for Korean Family Policy in the 1990s: Maternity Protection Policy and Abolition of the Family-Head System." *Korea Journal* 42: 68–99.

  2003. "Gender Equality vs. 'Tradition' in Korean Family: Toward a Postcolonial Feminist Jurisprudence." *The Review of Korean Studies* 6: 85–118.

  2006. "Vision of Postcolonial Feminist Jurisprudence in Korea: Seen from the 'Family-Head System' in Family Law." *Journal of Korean Law* 5: 12–28.

  2011. *Han'guk kajokbŏp ilkki: Chŏntong, shingminjisŏng, chendŏŭi kyoch'ar-oesŏ* [Reading Korean Family Law: At the Crossroads of Tradition, Coloniality, and Gender]. Seoul: Ch'angbi.

Yi, Chong-ŭn. 1999. "Sŏguwa yugyomunhwaggwŏnesŏŭi kaein" [The Concept of Individual in Western and Confucian Cultures]. *Chŏntong'gwa hyŏndae* [Tradition and Modernity] 9: 201–225.

Yi, Hyesun (ed.). 2008. *Chosŏn chunggi yehaksasanggwa ilsangmunhwa: Chuja kagryerŭl chungshimŭro* [Ritual Thoughts during the mid Chosŏn Period and the Culture of Everyday Lives: Focusing on Zhu Xi's Family Rituals]. Seoul: Ehwa Womans University Press.

Yi, Ŭn-sŏn. 2007. *Irŏbŏrin ch'owŏrŭl ch'ajasŏ* [In Search of Transcendence That Has Been Lost]. Seoul: Mosinŭn saramdŭl.

Young, Iris M. 2000. *Inclusion and Democracy.* Oxford: Oxford University Press.

Yu, Jiyuan. 2007. *The Ethics of Confucius and Aristotle: Mirrors of Virtue.* London: Routledge.

Zivi, Karen. 2006. "Cultivating Character: John Stuart Mill and the Subjects of Rights." *American Journal of Political Science* 50: 49–61.

Index

agency goods, 43–44
   Chan on, 77
all under Heaven (*tianxia*), 197, 220
Ames, Roger T., 3, 37, 61–62
   on political meritocracy, 3–4
Analects (Confucius), 186–187, 194–195
ancestral seat (*pon*), 113, 154
Angle, Stephen, 43, 206, 244
antiperfectionism, 75
Aquinas, 36–37, 183
aristocracy, 11
Aristotelian ethics, 181
   Confucian ethics and, 37
Aristotle, 10, 36–37, 213–214
associational life, 176
assurance problem, 233–238
assurance reason, 177
asymmetry thesis, 76
   objections to, 76–77
   perfectionism and, 76–77
authoritarianism, 89
authority, 20, 63–64
   Raz on, 21–22
aversion, 188

badao (hegemonic rule), 95
Bai, Tongdong, 5, 9, 56–57
   on Confucian ethics, 42–43
Barber, Benjamin, 17
   on citizenship, 208
Bell, Daniel, 56–57, 60, 135, 204–205, 228
   bicameral legislature of, 5
   on China, 2

   on democracy, 4–5
   on economic performance, 6
   exam-model of, 5
   on political meritocracy, 2
   on state, 107
ben (foundation), 194–195
benevolence (*ren*), 35, 146, 172
   Confucian ethics in, 146–147
   Confucius on, 186–187, 191
   differences in, 187–188
   filial piety and, 194–195
   ritual propriety and, 196–197
   Schwartz on, 186–187
benevolent government (*renzheng*),
   6, 222–223
Berman, Sheri, 208
bicameral legislature, 5
bicameralism, 60
Bloom, Irene, 216
boundary theory, 102
Brennan, Jason, 239–240
Buddhism, 120–122

Callan, Eamonn, 54, 157
Caplan, Bryan, 239–240
Chan, Joseph, 5–6, 9, 20, 26–27, 36, 43–44,
   47, 56, 66, 135, 238–239, 241–242
   on agency goods, 77
   on citizenship, 234, 237
   on civic education, 177
   on civic virtue, 175–176, 179
   on civility, 46, 48, 50–51
civility consideration, 51

265

Chan, Joseph (cont.)
  on coercion, 22
  on comprehensive Confucianism, 53
  on comprehensive doctrine, 52, 182
  Confucian perfectionism of, 174–184, 201–202
  Confucianism of, 46
  on democracy, 58–59
  dyadic framework, 54
  on extreme perfectionism, 52–53
  on family, 51
  on filial piety, 51
  on good life, 43–44, 46–47, 77, 180
  on Grand Union, 90–93
  on human rights, 230
  on Jiang Qing, 53, 96–97, 165–166
  on justification condition, 50
  Li and, 57
  moderate perfectionism of, 12–13, 44–45, 139
  moderate political Confucian perfectionism of, 43–52
  on moral education, 180
  on moral virtue, 182–183
  participation argument of, 206
  on paternalism, 63
  on perfectionism, 38
  on political participation, 205–206
  on political perfectionism, 43
  on prudential goods, 77
  Raz and, 48–49
  on reciprocity condition, 50
  on republicanism, 179, 182
  on rituals, 174
  on second chamber, 62
  on service conception, 61–63
  virtue monism of, 29–30, 173
  on ways of life, 77
China
  Bell on, 2
  democracy in, 2
  economy of, 2
  political meritocracy in, 2
Cho, Muje, 146, 149–150
Ch'oe, Chong-yŏng, 147–148
Chŏng, Yagyong, 243
chongjung. *See* clan organizations
Chosŏn dynasty, 142, 154–155, 197
Chosun Ilbo, 145–146, 151
Christianity, 183
  habit of heart and, 93

Christiano, Thomas, 11–12
  on public equality requirement, 65, 87
ch'ulgaoein (outsiders), 141–142
circumstances of politics, 13
citizenship, 18, 95, 222
  Barber on, 208
  Chan on, 234, 237
  Confucian, 67, 88, 90–91, 110–111
  Confucian democratic, 110, 126
  constitutions and, 206–207
  Locke on, 235–236
  in Mencian Confucianism, 227
  pluralism and, 95–96
  political liberalism and, 83–84
  in public reason Confucianism, 207
  Rawls on, 83–84
civic education, 179
  Chan on, 177
civic liberalism, 175
civic virtue, 187–188
  Chan on, 175–176, 179
  civic liberalism and, 175
  definition, 171–173
  Galston on, 178, 199
  Mencius on, 185
  moral virtue and, 171–174
  public reason Confucianism and, 194–201
  reaffirmation of, 233–238
  Weithman on, 178–179, 184–185
civil association
  Oakeshott on, 166–167
  public reason Confucianism and, 166–167
Civil War, 81
civility
  Chan on, 46, 48, 50–51
  conceptions of, 54–55
  Confucianism and, 47
  consideration, 51
  duty of, 50, 72–73, 230–231
  political participation and, 175–176
  Rawls on, 50, 230–231
  Wall on, 50–51
clan organizations (*chongjung*), 140, 144, 146–147
  filial piety and, 147–148
  gender inequality and, 160–161
  public equality and, 162
  public reason Confucianism and, 161–162
  rituals and, 152–153

state intervention in, 158–159
as voluntary private associations, 152–161, 164
coercion, 235
 Chan on, 22
 Pettit on, 21–22
 political power and, 21–22
Cohen, Joshua, 100–101
coloniality, 113
common bond, 48–49
common good, 48–49
common ground, 48–49
common sense, 82–83
comparative philosophy, 47
compassion, 188
 Mencius on, 197
complex instrumentalist monism, 11–12
complicity, 235
comprehensive antiperfectionism, 39
comprehensive Confucian antiperfectionism, 39–40
comprehensive Confucian perfectionism, 26–27, 39
 Fan on, 42
comprehensive Confucianism, 139
 Chan on, 53
 public reason Confucianism and, 140
comprehensive doctrine, 97, 236–237
 Chan on, 52, 182
 full, 16, 29
 partial, 16, 29
 public reason and, 81
 public reason liberalism and, 86
 Rawls on, 43, 52–53, 80, 171
comprehensive liberalism, 37
 political liberal perfectionism and, 47
 political liberalism and, 90
comprehensive perfectionism, 39
 public reason and, 20
conceptual stretching
 Confucian democracy, 9
 innovation and, 7
 Sartori on, 7
conceptual traveling, 7–8
Confu-China, 9
Confucian aristocracy, 9
Confucian citizens, 67, 88, 90–91, 110–111
Confucian constitutionalism, 9, 124
 Jiang Qing on, 53
Confucian democracy, 1, 3–4, 70, 90, 240
 conceptual stretching, 9

as conceptual traveling, 7–8
defense of, 5–6
liberal democracy contrasted with, 8
normative theory of, 9
renaming, 9
requirements of, 7–8
Confucian democratic citizens, 110, 126
Confucian democratic perfectionism, 4, 27–28, 35–36
 comprehensiveness of, 16
 conditions of, 14–17
 definition of, 18
 ethics in, 15
 normative premises of, 23, 67–68
 politics in, 15
 role of state in, 14
Confucian ethics, 3
 Aristotelian ethics and, 37
 benevolence in, 146–147
 Confucian politics and, 2–3, 41
 Jiang Qing on, 42–43
 Tongdong Bai on, 42–43
 virtue ethics and, 36–37
Confucian legitimacy, 101–104
Confucian meritocracy, 135, 240
 perfectionism and, 2–3
 stipulations of, 41, 55–56
Confucian meritocratic perfectionism, 3
 democracy and, 4–5
 difficulties, 4–14
 on government, 60
 paternalism and, 64
Confucian monarchy, 5–6, 23–24
Confucian perfectionism, 1–4, 9
 of Chan, 174–184, 201–202
 definition, 37
 of Fan, 53
 state and, 107
 value paternalism and, 65
Confucian rights, 151–152
Confucian self, 129–132
Confucian society
 constitution in, 88
 public reason Confucianism and, 88
Confucianism. *See also* public reason Confucianism; traditional Confucianism
 as aesthetic ideal, 3
 of Chan, 46
 civility and, 47
 history of, 25, 242–243

Confucianism (cont.)
  Jiang Qing on, 53
  liberalism and, 144–152
  Mencian, 220–233
  moderate, 140–167
  moderate perfectionism and, 45–46
  normative, 36–42
  public reason Confucianism and, 202
  virtue ethics and, 181
Confucius, 187
  on benevolence, 186–187, 191
  on filial piety, 194–195
  on Guan Zhong, 193
  Mencius on, 210
  on *zheng*, 185–186
congruence thesis, 158
consensus, 83
consent, 153
constitution, 28
  citizenship and, 206–207
  in Confucian society, 88
  cultural heritage and, 120
  Jiang Qing on, 96
  South Korea, 117, 119–126
constitutionalism, 28–29
  Confucian, 9, 53, 124
  democratic, 126
  dual mode of, 125–126
  liberal, 108–109, 160–161
  pluralist, 109
  public reason Confucian, 107–112, 126–137, 140–141
content considerations, 50–51
continuity condition, 15, 242
criminal code, 14–15
cultural values, 19
customary law (*kwansŭppŏp*), 154

Dallmayr, Fred R., 187
dao (the Way), 37
Daoism, 121–122
daughter's rebellion, 141–143
  court decision in, 143–144
Daxue (Great Learning), 185
de Bary, Theodore, 224–225
democracy, 1, 9, 87. *See also* Confucian democracy
  accountability, 59–60
  alternative conceptual forms of, 7
  authoritarianism and, 89
  Bell on, 4–5
  Chan on, 58–59
  in China, 2
  Confucian democracy contrasted with, 8
  Confucian meritocratic perfectionism and, 4–5
  definition of, 18
  deliberative, 231–232
  Deweyan Confucian, 3–4
  dualistic account of authority in, 11
  elections in, 7–8
  instrumentalist view of, 59, 66
  liberalism and, 77–78
  marriage and, 121
  minimal, 6–7
  minimum requirements for, 7–8
  perfectionism and, 2–3, 58
  political meritocracy and, 1–2, 5
  postulates of, 9
  public reason Confucianism and, 104
  representative, 11, 21
  Sartori on, 7
  in South Korea, 89
  value of, 55–56
democratic constitutionalism, 126
democratic perfectionism, 17–19
  cultural values in, 19
  definition of, 18
  Gutmann on, 17–19
  Sher on, 18
democratic pluralism, 172
  public equality, 138–141
  public reason Confucianism and, 96–97
democratic representation, 6–7
democratic theory, 102
deontological liberalism, 175
deontology, 47
despoilers of the Way, 198
Deuchler, Martina, 142
Deudney, Daniel, 10
Dewey, John, 162–164
Deweyan Confucian democracy, 3–4
dezhi (virtue politics), 37
direct perfectionist commitment, 119–126
dirty hands, 188
diversity
  justice and, 156–157
  Macedo on, 73–74
duan (sprouts), 188, 210
duty of civility, 50, 72–73, 230–231
Dworkin, Ronald, 48

elections, 9, 57
  in democracy, 7–8
elitism, 3, 13, 71, 204–205
  perfectionism and, 12–13
ethical liberalism, 48, 75
ethical monism, 184–194
ethics. *See also* Aristotelian ethics;
    Confucian ethics; virtue ethics
  in Confucian democratic
    perfectionism, 15
  perfectionism and, 37
  role, 37
exam-model, 5
extreme perfectionism, 44–45, 52–55
  Chan on, 52–53
  Shils on, 52

fair play, 235
family, 100–101, 127
  Chan on, 51
  Fan on, 42
  public reason Confucianism and,
    132–133
Family Rituals (Zhu Xi), 115–116,
    141–142, 197
family-head system (*hojuje*)
  abolition of, 112–119
  children in, 116–117
  court decision, 117–119
  demands of, 119
  discrimination in, 118
  gender inequality and, 118
  justifications of, 119–120
  in South Korea, 111
  women in, 115–116
  Zhu Xi on, 133
family-registry system (*hojŏk*), 127–128
Fan, Ruiping, 5, 9, 42, 53, 135
  on comprehensive Confucian
    perfectionism, 42
  Confucian perfectionism of, 53
  on family, 42
  on filial piety, 42
  on ritual, 42
feminism, 113, 123, 128
  traditional Confucianism and, 144–145
filial piety (*xiao*), 14–15, 35, 50–51, 92, 97,
    148, 151, 172
  benevolence and, 194–195
  Chan on, 51
  clan organizations and, 147–148

Confucius on, 194–195
Fan on, 42
public expression of, 70
traditional Confucianism and, 195
foundation (*ben*), 194–195
freedom of association, 159–160
freedom of expression, 98–99
friendship, 47
full comprehensive doctrine, 16
  Rawls and, 29

Galston, William A., 109, 244
  on civic liberalism, 175
  on civic virtue, 178, 198–199
  on liberalism, 39
  Murphy on, 178
  on political liberalism, 85
  on Rawls, 41, 85
Gaus, Gerald, 85
gender inequality, 25, 97, 119–120, 140,
    150–151, 158
  clan organizations and, 160–161
  family-head system and, 118
  public reason Confucianism and, 97,
    164
general participation principle, 56–57
  Li on, 57–58
gentleman (*junzi*), 146, 214–215
good life, 61, 76
  Chan on, 43–44, 46–47, 77, 180
  moderate perfectionism and, 44
  in public reason perfectionism, 87
  Rawls on, 180
Grand Union, 90–93
Great Learning (*Daxue*), 185
Guan Zhong, 190–193
  Confucius on, 193
gui (honorable), 216
Gutmann, Amy, 234
  on democratic perfectionism, 17–19
gyroscopic representation, 59

Habermas, Jürgen, 74, 90
habit of heart, 67
  Christianity and, 93
  pluralism and, 90–93
Hahm, Chaibong, 90
  on household system, 128
Hahm, Chaihark, 110, 116–117, 123
Hall, David L., 3, 61–62
  on political meritocracy, 3–4

harmony (*he*), 146
  Li on, 62–63
he. *See* harmony
head of family (*hoju*), 114
Heaven, 95
hegemonic rule (*badao*), 95
Hobbes, Thomas, 80–81
hojŏk (family-registry system), 127–128
hoju (head of family), 114
hojuje. *See* family-head system
Hong Kong, 94
honorable (*gui*), 216
households (*ka*), 113, 117–131
  Chaibong Hahm on, 128
  civil society and, 135
  definition, 128
Huan (Duke), 190–191
human dignity, 228
  Mencius on, 214–217
human nature, teleological views of, 37
human rights, 230
Hume, David, 100–101
Hyeryŏnggong, 142–143

ideal interests, 229
Im, Yunjidang, 147
inclusive view, 81
indigenous inhabitants, 94
indirect perfectionist commitment, 119–126
individual identification system, 116–117
inequality, 56
inheritance, women and, 141–143
intelligibility condition, 242
Ivanhoe, P. J., 120, 146, 211

Jiang, Qing, 5, 9, 55, 60, 135
  Chan on, 53, 96–97, 165–166
  on Confucian constitutionalism, 53
  on Confucian ethics, 42–43
  on Confucianism, 53
  constitutionalism of, 96
  on monarchy, 95
junzi (gentleman), 146, 214–215
justice, 76
  consensus on, 82
  disagreements about, 80
  diversity and, 156–157
  moderate perfectionism and, 44
  Rawls on, 49, 78–79
justification condition, 49–50
  Chan on, 50

ka. *See* households
Kang, Chŏngildang, 147
Kang, Xiaoguang, 6
Kant, Immanuel, 111–112
Kantian deontology, 47
Kateb, George, 89
Kim, Hyo-Chong, 129–130
Kim, Marie, 125
King, Martin Luther, Jr., 81
Kingly Way (*wangdao*), 95
kings, 214
  Mencius on, 188–189, 220–221
Ko, Hyŏn-chŏl, 145
Korea Legal Aid Center for Family
  Relations, 144
Kramer, Larry, 239–240
Krause, Sharon, 100–101
kwansŭppŏp (customary law), 154
Kwark, Bae-hee, 144
Kymlicka, Will, 69
  on multiculturalism, 103

Larmore, Charles, 74
The Law of Peoples (Rawls), 85–86
Learning of the Way (*Daoxue*), 142, 242–243
Lee, Seung-gwan, 144–145
li. *See* rituals
Li, Chenyang, 5, 55–56
  Chan and, 57
  on Confucianism, 57
  on general participation principle, 57–58
  on harmony, 62–63
liberal constitutionalism, 160
  Macedo on, 108–109
  traditional Confucianism and, 161
liberal cosmopolitanism, 102
liberal democratization, 89
liberal fundamentalism, 53–54
liberal perfectionism, 12–13, 20, 70
liberal pluralism, 157–159
liberal political theory, 38–39
liberalism, 3, 39–40, 244. *See also* political
  liberalism
  civic, 175
  comprehensive, 37, 47, 90
  Confucianism and, 144–152
  democracy and, 77–78
  deontological, 175
  ethical, 48, 75
  Galston on, 39
  normative, 39

perfectionist critique of, 77–78
political power and, 72–73
public reason and, 72–78
public reason liberalism, 82–87
of Rawls, 41
traditional Confucianism and, 161
Locke, John, 225, 236–237
on citizenship, 235–236
on pluralism, 236
love, 47

Macedo, Stephen, 109, 156
on diversity, 73–74
on liberal constitutionalism, 108–109
Mandate of Heaven (*tianming*), 214, 227
Mansbridge, Jane, 58–59
marriage, democracy and, 121
maximalist pluralism, 167
Mencian Confucianism
citizenship in, 227
political participation and, 226–233
reconstructing, 220–226
Mencius, 30–31, 183, 208–209, 213, 216
on compassion, 197
on Confucius, 210
developmental model of, 211
on human dignity, 214–217
on kings, 188–189, 220–221
on moral and civic virtues, 185
on moral equality, 209–214
on Ox Mountain, 211–212
on political equality, 95, 217–219
on tyranny, 95
virtue ethics of, 190, 216–217
virtue monism of, 188–189
Yi Yin and, 189–190
Michelman, Frank, 73–74
Mill, J. S., 37, 129
minimal democracy, 6–7
mixed regimes
definition, 10
purposes of, 11
in United States, 10
moderate Confucianism, 140–167
moderate perfectionism, 52–55, 78
of Chan, 12–13, 44–45, 139
Confucianism and, 45–46
constitutive elements of, 44
good life and, 44
justice and, 44

moderate political Confucian perfectionism
caveats of, 47–48
of Chan, 43–52
monarchy, 95
Jiang Qing on, 95
Montesquieu, 10
moral conception, 139
moral disagreement, 61–62, 235
moral education, 179
Chan on, 180
moral equality, 209–214
moral pluralism, 196–198
moral virtue, 189–190, 236–237
Chan on, 182–183
civic virtue and, 171–174
definition, 172–173
Mencius on, 185
morality, 3, 63
public equality proposition and, 25
public reason Confucianism and, 200
Weithman on, 179–180
motivation reason, 177
Mozi, 183
Mulhall, Stephen, 83–84
multiculturalism, 103
Munro, Donald, 210–211
Murphy, James B., on Galston, 178

Nam Yun, In-soon, 144–145
negarchy, 10
negative perfectionism, 109
negative values, 238
neorepublicanism, 180
noncoercive perfectionism, 22
nondiscrimination, 183
normal justification thesis (NJT), 20–21
normative Confucianism
conceptual space of, 39–40
mapping, 36–42
types of, 39

Oakeshott, Michael, 53
on civil association, 166–167
maximalist pluralism of, 167
one person one vote (OPOV), 5–6, 9
opportunity reason, 177
outsiders (*ch'ulgaoein*), 141–142
Ox Mountain, 211–212

partial comprehensive doctrine, 16
  Rawls and, 29
participation argument, 206
paternalism, 21, 63–64
  Chan on, 63
  Confucian meritocratic perfectionism, 64
  public reason Confucianism and, 94
  state, 94
  state value, 94
patriarchy, 140
  public reason Confucianism and, 128–129
  traditional Confucianism and, 163
patrilineal clan law (*zongfa*), 141–142, 152, 195
perfectionism. *See also specific perfectionisms*
  agents of, 55–56
  asymmetry thesis and, 76–77
  Chan on, 38
  Confucian meritocracy and, 2–3
  definition, 36–37
  democracy and, 2–3, 58
  dilemma, 3–4
  elitism and, 12–13
  liberalism critiqued by, 77–78
  political meritocracy and, 4
  political theory and, 48
  public reason and, 72–78, 81
  public reason Confucianism and, 100
  of Rawls, 49
  virtue ethics and, 36–37
  Wall on, 11–12, 38
perfectionist political theory, 41–42
personal autonomy, 48
personhood, self-identity and, 110
Pettit, Philip, 175
  on coercion, 21–22
pity, 188
pluralism, 13, 23–24, 27–28, 56
  citizenship and, 95–96
  democratic, 96–97, 138–141, 172
  in East Asia, 61–62, 101–104
  experience of, 176
  habit of heart and, 90–93
  liberal, 157–159
  Locke on, 236
  maximalist, 167
  moral, 196–198
  political liberalism and, 156
  public reason and, 82
  public reason perfectionism and, 78–82

Rawls on, 49, 85–86
reasonable, 49–50, 167
ritual, 196–197
state and, 231–232
value, 48, 71, 91–92, 229–230, 237–238
vicissitudes of, 99
Waldron on, 49
pluralist constitutionalism, 109
plurality path, 78
political antiperfectionism, 39
political Confucian antiperfectionism, 39–41
political Confucian perfectionism, 39–41
political equality, 9, 204–205, 222
  Mencius on, 95, 217–219
  popular sovereignty and, 227–228
political liberal perfectionism, 47
political liberalism, 38–39
  citizenship and, 83–84
  comprehensive liberalism and, 90
  external conception of, 84
  Galston on, 85
  internal conception of, 84–85
  pluralism and, 156
  public reason and, 83
  Quong on, 84
  of Rawls, 82–83
Political Liberalism (Rawls), 16, 80–81, 85–86
political meritocracy, 9
  Bell on, 2
  in China, 2
  definition of, 2
  democracy and, 1–2, 5
  Hall and Ames on, 3–4
  perfectionism and, 4
  representative democracy compared to, 11
political participation, 6, 9, 223–224
  Chan on, 205–206
  civility and, 175–176
  Mencian Confucianism and, 226–233
  public reason Confucianism and, 226–233
  right to, 204
political perfectionism, 70
  Chan on, 43
political power
  coercion and, 21–22
  liberalism and, 72–73
  public reason and, 21–22
  Rawls on, 72–73
  restraint and, 80–81
  state and, 75

Index

political realism, 199–200
political theory
  liberal, 38–39
  perfectionism and, 48
  perfectionist, 41–42
pon (ancestral seat), 113, 154
popular election, 6
popular sovereignty, 6, 9, 204–205, 223–224
  political equality and, 227–228
positive liberal perfectionism, 109
private voluntary associations, 152–161, 164
prudential goods, 43–44
  Chan on, 77
public equality, 163
  clan organizations and, 162
  democratic pluralism, 138–141
  intrinsic value of, 65
  public reason Confucianism and, 94–96
public equality proposition, 30–31
  morality and, 25
  public reason Confucianism and, 24
  stipulations of, 24
public equality requirement, 65, 87
public reason, 156–157
  competing interpretations of, 80–81
  comprehensive doctrine and, 81
  comprehensive perfectionism and, 20
  inclusive view of, 81
  liberalism and, 72–78
  perfectionism and, 72–78, 81
  in pluralist society, 82
  political liberalism and, 83
  political power and, 21–22
  Rawls on, 73–75, 79–80, 86
  Wall on, 73–74
public reason Confucian constitutionalism, 107–112, 126–137, 140–141
public reason Confucianism, 4, 19–26, 28–29, 69–72, 98–101, 104, 162, 225, 241, 244
  citizens in, 207
  civic virtue and, 194–201
  civil association and, 166–167
  clan organizations and, 161–162
  comprehensive Confucianism and, 140
  Confucian legitimacy and, 101–104
  Confucian society and, 88
  Confucian virtues and, 202
  democracy and, 104
  democratic pluralism and, 96–97
  family and, 132–133
  gender inequality and, 97, 164
  moderate Confucianism and, 140–167
  morality and, 200
  normative premises of, 87–88
  paternalism and, 94
  patriarchy and, 128–129
  perfectionism and, 100
  political participation and, 226–233
  public equality and, 93–96
  public equality proposition and, 24
  relevance of, 244–245
  sociological premises of, 23–24
  stipulations of, 138–139
  tempered virtue monism and, 193–194
  traditional Confucianism and, 140, 162, 165
  way of life and, 88–90
public reason liberalism
  comprehensive doctrine and, 86
  public reason perfectionism and, 82–87
public reason perfectionism, 19–20
  good life in, 87
  pluralism and, 78–82
  public reason liberalism and, 82–87
public sphere, 162–164

Qiu (Prince), 191
qualification principle, 57
quasi-constitutional values, 123
Quong, Jonathan, 20–21, 47, 73–74
  on liberal political theory, 38–39
  on political liberalism, 84

Rawls, John, 3, 15–16, 44, 48–49, 61–62, 66, 71, 74, 76, 83–84, 90, 156–157, 241
  antiperfectionism of, 75
  on citizenship, 83–84
  on civility, 50, 230–231
  comprehensive doctrine, 43, 52–53, 80, 171
  on disagreements, 79–80
  full comprehensive doctrine, 29
  Galston on, 41, 85
  on good life, 180
  on inclusive view, 81
  on justice, 49, 78–79
  liberalism of, 41
  partial comprehensive doctrine, 29

Rawls, John (cont.)
  perfectionism of, 49
  on pluralism, 49, 85–86
  on plurality path, 78
  political liberalism of, 82–83
  on political power, 72–73
  on public reason, 73–75, 79–80, 86
  on reasonable pluralism, 49–50
  on reasonableness, 84
  on self-discipline, 74
  on stability, 82
  Wall on, 51
  on wide view, 81
Raz, Joseph, 20–21, 37, 48, 53–54, 81, 244
  on authority, 21–22
  Chan and, 48–49
reasonable pluralism, 167
  Rawls on, 49–50
reasonableness, 83, 85
  Rawls on, 84
rebellion, 217–218, 224–225
reciprocity condition, 49–50
  Chan on, 50
regulative ideals, 111–112
ren. See benevolence
renzheng. See benevolent government
representative democracy, 21
  political meritocracy compared to, 11
republicanism
  Chan on, 179, 182
  Weithman on, 178–180
restraint, political power and, 80–81
rightness (yi), 189–190, 212, 215–216
ritual pluralism, 196–197
rituals (li), 25, 97, 189–190, 196–197
  benevolence and, 196–197
  Chan on, 174
  clan organizations and, 152–153
  Fan on, 42
  public expression of, 70
role ethics, 37
Rosemont, Henry, Jr., 37
Rosenblum, Nancy L., 176
Rousseau, Jean-Jacques, 21, 207–208, 232

sacrificial rites, 153
sagehood, 61, 208–209, 214–215, 221–222
Samaenggong, 142–143

Sandel, Michael, 175
Sartori, Giovanni
  on conceptual stretching, 7
  on democracy, 7
Schumpeter, Joseph, 6–7
Schwartz, Benjamin I., 186–187
second chamber, 60, 62
sectarianism, 85
self-determination, 21, 67, 69–71, 81, 87, 102–104, 108, 217, 227, 231, 233
self-discipline, 74
self-identity, 90
  personhood and, 110
service conception, 61–63
Shamanism, 121–122
shame, 188
Shang dynasty, 189–190, 218–219
shared reason, 48–49
Sher, George, 47, 67, 212
  on democratic perfectionism, 18
Shils, Edward, 46
  on extreme perfectionism, 52
Shklar, Judith N., 109
Smith, Rogers M., 123
societal culture, 69
sociological premises, 226–227
Song dynasty, 142
soulcraft, 185–186
South Korea, 23
  Civil Code in, 113, 116, 129–131
  Constitution Articles, 119–126
  constitutional nonconformity, 117
  criminal code in, 14–15
  family-head system in, 111
  liberal democracy in, 89
  traditional Confucianism in, 127
  United States and, 125
  value systems in, 91–92
  women in, 163
sprouts (duan), 188, 210
stability, 82
state
  Bell on, 107
  clan organizations intervened by, 158–159
  in Confucian democratic perfectionism, 14
  Confucian perfectionism and, 107
  paternalism, 94
  pluralism and, 231–232

political power and, 75
value paternalism, 94
statecraft, 185–186
Strauss, Leo, 225
Sungkyunkwan committee, 144–145
Sungmoon Kim, 128
Sunstein, Cass, 175
Swift, Adam, 83–84

Taiwan, 23, 92
Tan, Sor-hoon, 4
Tang (King), 189–190, 218–219
tempered virtue monism, 184–194
  public reason Confucianism and, 193–194
thermometer analogy, 223
Thompson, Dennis, 234
tianming (Mandate of Heaven), 214, 227
tianxia (all under Heaven), 197, 220
Tiwald, Justin, 220
Tocqueville, Alexis de, 135, 208
Tonghak, 121–122
traditional Confucianism, 29, 68, 111
  feminism and, 144–145
  filial piety and, 195
  in Korea, 127
  liberal constitutionalism and, 161
  liberalism and, 161
  patriarchy and, 163
  public reason Confucianism and, 140, 162, 165
  transforming, 155
tricameralism, 5
tyrannicide, 218–219, 222–225
tyranny
  of the many, 11
  Mencius on, 95

United States
  mixed regimes in, 10
  South Korea and, 125

value paternalism, 63–64
value pluralism, 3–4, 13, 24, 27, 31, 36–37, 46, 48, 53–56, 58, 61–66, 70–71, 77, 80, 91–92, 94, 101, 109, 140, 165, 167, 178, 181, 196, 198–200, 206, 209, 219, 226, 228–230, 236–238

vicissitudes of pluralism, 99
virtue ethics, 47, 192, 213–214
  Confucian ethics and, 36–37
  Confucianism and, 181
  of Mencius, 190, 216–217
  perfectionism and, 36–37
virtue monism, 192, 202–203
  of Chan, 29–30, 173
  of Mencius, 188–189
  tempered, 184–194
virtue politics (*dezhi*), 37
virtues, 42, 202. *See also* civic virtue; moral virtue

Waldron, Jeremy, 13, 62
  on pluralism, 49
Wall, Stephen, 53–54
  on civility, 50–51
  on perfectionism, 11–12, 38
  on public reason, 73–74
  on Rawls, 51
Walzer, Michael, 159
Wan Zhang, 189–190
wangdao (Kingly Way), 95
Warren, Mark, 176
the Way (*dao*), 37
ways of life
  Chan on, 77
  public reason Confucianism and, 88–90
Weber, Max, 229
Weithman, Paul, 177
  on civic virtue, 178–179, 184–185
  on morality, 179–180
  on republicanism, 178–180
Western culture, 19–20
wide view, 81
Wisconsin v. Yoder, 17
women
  in family-head system, 115–116
  inheritance and, 141–143
  in South Korea, 163
Wong, David, 56
Wu (King), 218–219

Xiang (Duke), 191
xiao. See filial piety
Xiaobai (Prince), 191
xing-shan thesis, 214–217
Xunzi, 186–187, 190, 192–193, 216, 222–223

Yan Yuan, 213
Yang, Hyunah, 113
Yangzi, 183
yi (rightness), 189–190, 212, 215–216
Yi Yin, 189–190, 192–193
Yu, Chi-tam, 146–149, 152
Yurim, 113, 243

Zhao Qi, 195
Zhou dynasty, 195, 208–209, 217–218, 220, 227
Zhu Xi, 115–116, 141–142, 197
  on family-head system, 133
zongfa (patrilineal clan law), 141–142, 152, 195

CPSIA information can be obtained at www.ICGtesting.com
Printed in the USA
LVOW11*1802270416

485605LV00005B/39/P